PALOUSE COUNTRY
A Land and Its People

Oral History Edition

*Afternoon Storms**

Looking Northeast from Steptoe Butte

i

For Mildred Repp, Jim Leonard, Louise Braun, Ray Smith, Dan Birdsell, and Mr. Yenney;

teachers who encouraged the exploration of local surroundings.

Text by *Richard Scheuerman* • Photography by *John Clement*

Foreword by *Alexander McGregor*

BEADED SERRATE DIAMOND, ALALUMTI KAMIAKIN

Palouse Country: A Land and Its People was published with support from
The Students Book Corporation, Pullman, Washington,
The McGregor Company, Colfax, Washington,
Schweitzer Engineering, Pullman, Washington.

ISBN 0-9637310-2-5 (Soft Cover)
ISBN 0-9637310-1-7 (Hard Cover)

Printed and bound in the United States by
Color Press, Walla Walla, Washington

TABLE OF CONTENTS

Acknowledgements vi

Foreword ix

Introduction 1

Chapter I. The Regional Setting and Native Peoples 17
    Oral History: Mary Jim; Parker, Washington 52

Chapter II. The Pathfinders and Exiles 55
    Oral History: Andrew George; Lewiston, Idaho 79

Chapter III. The Americans and Canadians 81
    Oral History: Anna Person; Palouse, Washington 120

Chapter IV. The Irish and British 123
    Oral History: Leonard Devlin; Dusty, Washington 133

Chapter V. The Chinese and Japanese 135
    Oral History: Owen Eng; Colfax, Washington 154

Chapter VI. The Empire Germans and Swiss 155
    Oral History: Bertha Engelland Williams; Tekoa, Washington 170

Chapter VII. The Norwegians and Swedes 173
    Oral History: Arthur Bjerke; Deary, Idaho 190

Chapter VIII. The Volga and Black Sea Germans 193
    Oral History: Conrad Schmick; Colfax, Washington 201

Conclusion 203

Bibliography 216

Index of Names and Places 221

LIST OF COLOR PLATES

Afternoon Storms*	i	Cashup Flats Storm	128
Leonard's Barn Sunrise*	vii	Red Barn	131
Isolation's Hope*	xi	Rolling Palouse Summer*	136
Golden Harvest*	xii	Rolling Palouse Winter*	138
Morning Reds	6	Evening Light Moscow Mountain	142
Abandoned	11	Manning Bridge Winter*	145
Verdant Thumbprint	15	Palouse Country Barn/Winter-Summer*	147
Spring Velvet	16	Shades of Green	149
Morning Mist*	18	Palouse Pastels*	152
White Bluffs, Columbia River	19	Needs Paint	156
Eomoshtoss (Steptoe Butte)	21	Rolling Palouse Fall	160
Palouse River Canyon*	24-25	Genesee Luthern	161
Snake River Canyon	33	Palouse Rainbow	172
In the Shadow of Steptoe	54	Morning Squall*	174
Lewiston Grade Vista*	61	Paradise Ridge Blizzard	178
Boone's Farm Spring*	65	Golden Mist	182
Divine Protection*	69	Palouse Pastoral*	185
Freeze Church Summer*	69	Cautious Looks	189
Baled and Ready	84	Evening Glow Palouse River*	192
Fall Patterns	87	Palouse Evening Storm*	195
Rosalia Railroad Bridge*	88	Quilted Hills*	204
Little Kamiak Butte Sunset*	93	Kamiak Butte Spring*	207
Summer Patterns	95	Weathered and Worn	215
Palouse River Sunset*	101		
Palouse Canola*	107		
Palouse Country Barn Canola*	112		
Retired to Reuse	115		
Hoodo Mountains Vista	121		
Spring Twilight*	122		
Palouse Perspective	125		

*Custom color prints available at John Clement Gallery (509-735-7699) or *www.johnclementgallery.com*

ACKNOWLEDGEMENTS

This book is the result of efforts by individuals throughout the Palouse Country to better understand, celebrate, and perpetuate a special heritage. These people live in the numerous small towns and cities that are nestled in the region's distinctive rolling hills where the values of living close to the land and neighborliness outweigh the economic challenges of rural life. Palouse area communities evidence a vibrancy and pride in such annual community events as Tekoa's Slippery Gulch Days, Pullman's National Lentil Festival, the Coeur d'Alene Tribal Memorial Warriors Horse Ride from Plummer to Rosalia, and the St. John Fair and Horse Show; active church fellowships, and support for local school sports teams, FFA programs, and marching bands. The "university cities" of Pullman, Moscow, and Cheney offer cultural and educational opportunities not often accessible to a rural populace and provide repositories for research by those interested in a deeper awareness of our legacy and responsibility as residents of the Palouse. Volunteers work throughout the year to perpetuate the region's cultural and natural heritage through the Palouse Empire Threshing Bee Association, Palouse Folklore Society, Palouse-Clearwater Environmental Institute, county fairs, and quilting circles.

I am deeply indebted to individuals in many of these places and organizations for sharing their stories and expertise. Our communities' immigrant elders and family historians are especially thanked for their contributions to this work. Persons whose memories particularly enriched this study include Conrad Schmick, Vern Hilty, Owen Eng, Bill and Polly McNeilly, and Ray and Evelyn Reich, Colfax; Bertha Williams and Jacob Adler, Tekoa; Julia Blank, Rosalia; B.E. Lockhart, Swede Gentry, and Charlie Jenkins, St. John; Louis and Joyce Gaiser, Winona; Oscar Slind, Kendrick; Leonard Jones, Dusty; Rosa and Louisa Stueckle, Lacrosse; Marlo Ochs and Anna Weitz, Endicott; and Dick Parrish, Benge. Valued information on Palouse area Indian history was shared in an atmosphere of warmest hospitality by the families of Mary Jim and Carrie Jim Schuster, Toppenish; Andrew George, Wapato; Emily Peone and Arthur Kamiakin, Nespelem; Joe Thompson, Mission; and Carol Bull and Jim Speer, Lapwai.

Historians whose works have greatly benefited my research include Donald Meinig, Syracuse, New York; Glen Adams, Fairfield; Alexander McGregor, Sue Armitage, Birgitta Ingemanson, and David Stratton, Pullman; Keith Peterson, Moscow; Father Thomas Connolly, S. J.; Nona Hengen, Spangle; Lorraine White, St. John; Vince Evans, Ritzville; Walter Gary, Walla Walla; Jack Nisbett, Bob and Shelia Clark, Stan Roth, and Jerry Peltier, Spokane. Jerry is a Northwest Americana bibliophile and author who operated Clarke's Old Bookstore in Spokane for many years and who was instrumental in organizing the Spokane Westerners Corral and the Eastern Washington Historical Society. When I became interested enough in Northwest history to begin acquiring books on the subject myself, I was directed to Clarke's with the warning not to be disappointed if many of the standard works were no longer in print. Unable to find a copy of Andrew Splawn's *Ka-mi-akin* amid stacks of books that rivaled most libraries I had known, I introduced myself to Jerry and told him of my quest. With eyes brightening behind rimless glasses, he excused himself to go downstairs and returned several minutes later bearing the precious volume as if a treasured vintage from the cellar. This was the first of many helpful sources to which Jerry would direct me as he has for countless others.

The idea of a Palouse area cultural history was conceived by Dixie Ehrenreich at the University of Idaho who procured support through the National Endowment for the Humanities for me to conduct research on the subject. Additional support was forthcoming through the Washington Centennial Commission due to the efforts of co-chairs Ralph Munro and Jean Gardner and project director Sid White at The Evergreen State College. I also gratefully acknowledge the helpfulness of Mary Reed and Michelle Farrah of the Latah County Historical Society and Ed Garretson and Fred Bohm of the Whitman County Historical Society for allowing me access to these groups' oral history collections. Useful materials were also made available through Jay Rea and Charles Mutchler of Eastern Washington University's Kennedy Library; Laila Miletic-Vejzovic, Trevor Bond, Larry Stark, Patsy Tate, Bob Smawley, and Chris Parrish at Washington State University's Holland Library and Alumni Center; Terry

Leonard's Barn Sunrise＊   *East of Pullman, Washington*

Abraham and Charles Webbert at the University of Idaho Library; Ed Nelson and Doug Olson at the Eastern Washington State Historical Society, Spokane. I also thank Kristie Kirkpatrick, Cindy Wigen, Peggy Bryan, and Neva Jean DeYoung of the Whitman County Library in Colfax.

The priceless images and maps drawn by Gustavus Sohon in the 1850s provide the first comprehensive visual documentation of the Palouse Country. Sohon, born in Tilsit, Prussia in 1825, immigrated to the United States in 1842 and eventually enlisted in the U. S. Army. In the 1850s, he was assigned to supply food and equipment to the reconnaissance crews of Isaac Stevens's monumental Northern Transcontinental Railway survey. Stevens, a man with wide-ranging interests, abilities, and ambitions, recognized Sohon's creative talents and had him transferred under his direct command. In addition to new responsibilities as cartographer and occasional interpreter, Sohon skill-fully drew intriguing images of the Inland Northwest from 1852 to 1863 and sketched the major leaders of the Columbia Plateau tribes at the Walla Walla Treaty Council of 1855 including the Yakima-Palouse Chief Kamiakin and Looking Glass of the Nez Perces. Sohon also accompanied the army during Colonel George Wright's campaign against the Indians in the Palouse and Spokane areas in 1858. He drew many dramatic scenes during the conflict including the "Battle of Four Lakes," and "Horse Slaughter Camp," and later mapped substan-tially the entire course of the Palouse River and Palouse North Fork. Many of his drawings were later rendered in watercolors, including Palouse Falls, and some as oil paintings.

The voluminous 1860 Senate report on the transcontinental sur-veys contains a number of Sohon lithographs including the first image ever made of the Palouse Hills, titled "Source of the Peluse," which Sohon drew from the eastern slopes of Kamiak Butte in the late 1850s. A tragic fire in the 1890s at the New York printing firm that printed the color lithographs destroyed these plates before additional copies could be made of the limited edition congressional report. Sohon's "Map of Reconnaissance from the Mouth of Paloos River to South Fork of St. Joseph River, via Tathuna Hills is in the National Archives (Record Group 77) while one titled "G. Sohon's Explorations in 1859" showing the Mullan Road route along the eastern Palouse in the Library of Congress's Sohon Collection. I am grateful to the W.S.U. Archives, Washington State Historical Society Archives in Tacoma, and the Library of Congress to reproduce selections from Sohon's work for this book. Panoramic lithographs of pioneer Palouse com-munities and farms are from Elwood Evans's *History of the Pacific Northwest: Oregon and Washington* (1889).

The historical photographs included in this work are from the R.

Raymond Hutchison Collection in the Manuscripts, Archives, and Special Collections branch of WSU's Holland Library. This remarkable assembly of 200,000 images documents the visual history of the Palouse Country recorded throughout the lifetime of pioneer photographer R. R. Hutchison (1887-1967) who established studios in Endicott, LaCrosse, and Pullman, Washington, and Moscow, Idaho. Hutchison's commercial interests were secondary to his passion for documenting the heritage and scenic beauty of the Palouse during the years of its transition from the homestead to modern eras. While just a boy on the family farm near Endicott, he carried his first Brownie on recreational trips to the Palouse River and into the fields surrounding his home to photograph men, women, and children working throughout the farm year—plowing, discing, harvesting grain, butchering hogs, thinning apples, canning fruit, and countless other ordinary tasks that Hutchison understood to be significant in the life of farm families.

With growing expertise and newer equipment, he expanded his interests to portraiture and the enormous wide-framed pictures of Palouse Country threshing outfits, family reunions, church conferences, and other special events identified by the small white lettered epigraph "Photo by Hutchison" for which he became so well-known. In the 1920s he founded the Inland Empire Professional Photographers Association and became the unofficial photographer of university events and personalities at both WSU and UI where his cameras captured hundreds of sporting events, construction projects, and celebrity visits. Individuals with rare and fragile pictures taken throughout the Palouse in the 1800s would often turn to Hutchison for copies and restoration work and he would retain negatives for his own files. Some of these scenes are included in this book. Given the length of his career in one area, the quality and prodigious output of his work that was safeguarded for decades, R. R. Hutchison bequeathed to the people of the Palouse one of the finest regional photographic collections in existence.

Clifford Trafzer, Bruce Holbert, and Eric Sorenson took time to read portions of the manuscript and to make suggestions for which I was most appreciative. Julie Lust, Kristen Larson, and Katie Clement prepared the final manuscript for publication and demonstrated considerable patience with me throughout the editing process. I also thank Gail Larson, Gary Schmauder, Palmer Wagner; as well as Lafe Bissell and Don Dyck of Color Press in Walla Walla. I acknowledge my parents, Don and Mary Scheuerman, for their abiding encouragement and my wife, Lois, and our children for their support of this special endeavor.

Richard Scheuerman
Endicott, Washington

HARVESTING NEAR COLFAX, WASHINGTON; c. 1890

FOREWORD

The Palouse Country has long been known as one of the most productive farming districts in the world. Here, in an unusual land of striking contrasts, immigrants three and four generations ago "broke" a mountain-girdled prairie of smooth, steep hills that resembled a rough sea at the height of a storm, converting it with their "footburner" walking plows into an interior ocean of waving grain. Located largely in Whitman and southern Spokane Counties of Washington and Latah County, Idaho, the land has long been studied for its remarkable productivity and for the unusual challenges it has presented to crop production—the hillsides tilled at angles of thirty degrees or more that have required adaptation of technology and cropping practices to harness its slopes and protect its soils. Geologists have written of the traumatic forces that shaped the land—the massive lava flows that inundated all but the highest peaks of earlier times, including Steptoe and Kamiak buttes, with the thickest outpourings of basalt known anywhere, the windborn soils that piled up in huge dunes to create an intricate terrain, the floodwaters of a glacial lake that ravaged nearby lands to the west and north creating boundaries for the Palouse graphically described by pioneers as "scabrock" or scablands."

Much remains to be learned about the families who came to lay claim to this unusual land. Historical geographer Donald W. Meinig twenty five years ago wrote his classic regional study of the exploration, organization, and settlement of the interior Northwest (*The Great Columbia Plain: A Historical Geography, 1805-1910*). Some of us who have written about the region have studied the changes farmers and ranchers made adjusting their practices to the demands of the land. In recent years a few writers have begun studying the fertile field of the ethnic origins of settlers on the land, including the native Palouse Indians (*Renegade Tribe; The Palouse Indians and the Invasion of the Inland Northwest*) and the Russian German pioneers (*The Volga Germans; Pioneers of the Pacific Northwest*) examined by Richard Scheuerman and Clifford Trafzer.

Palouse Country: A Land and Its People represents an important contribution toward a fuller understanding of the pioneer families who came in search of better opportunities in a new land. Devastated by diseases and warfare before the arrival of large groups of immigrants, the native Palouse Indians had "maintained an intimate relationship with the land and ranged extensively through a complex seasonal round planned to utilize the region's natural bounty." Richard Scheuerman presents a panoramic view of those who followed: the American and Canadian-born settlers and, more particularly, the foreign immigrants who contributed much to the transformation of the land into one of the world's most productive agricultural regions. A great grandson of one of the immigrant families, Scheuerman shares his love of the land, a thorough knowledge of conditions in the distant lands from which many Palouse immigrants came, and an appreciation for the diverse peoples who came to settle on the rolling prairie. John Clement, whose skillful and talented photography of the dryland Northwest has provided a sense of the region's dramatic nature, provides vivid visual perspective of the land of opportunity where immigrants came to put down their roots.

Though living conditions were primitive in the early years and farm tools makeshift at best (such as the crude harrows cut of thorn bushes and tied to long poles designed by German families of Spokane County), those who came from across the oceans were quick to recognize the opportunities of the new land. As Scheuerman tells us: "While the pioneering experiences of our first-generation relatives living throughout the regions were as varied as the languages they spoke, a common theme framed the stories they told us children: The Palouse was a Promised Land for which we chosen ones living here should be profoundly grateful."

Though the ranks of a few immigrant groups grew smaller over time — particularly the Chinese who built rail lines connecting the Palouse with distant markets only to face hostility and harassment— a large share of the foreign born immigrants stayed in the region. Representing almost twenty percent of the local population in 1880 and but ten percent in 1920, the immigrants from across the oceans more often remained than did many of their American-born neighbors, their heirs accounted for almost forty percent of the "Centennial Farms" honored in Whitman County in 1989. Many settled in districts or communities where they had a strong influence— the Onecho Swiss Mennonites: the Colton and Uniontown Catholic Germans; the Volga Germans of Endicott; the Norwegians of the Genesee Valley; the Selbu Lutheran Norwegians of Lacrosse; the Irish of Union Flat, Oakesdale and Genesee; the Swedes of Latah County; the Germans of southern Spokane County; the Black Sea Germans of Dusty, and others. The town of Potlatch alone once had distinctive Greek, Italian, Japanese, and Scandanavian neighborhoods. I am personally aware of the descendants of over 60 families mentioned by Scheuerman who still have their roots in the Palouse.

Scheuerman skillfully weaves the stories of these families and immigrant groups together with the overall fabric of the pioneering process, describing their search for available farmground, methods of land acquisition, development of towns, and changes in farming practices as settlers advanced from hand broadcasting of seed and subsistence crops toward commercial production in their new homeland. Most had been of middle or lower class background with little chance to inherit farmland and had come during times of economic adversity. Some had followed gold strikes into the mountains surrounding the plateau, had traversed the land packing supplies to the mines or had helped build early rail lines onto the land, many had failed to find a land of promise in earlier stops in the Midwest or elsewhere. Swedish immigrants Nils and Andrew Nelson, for example, had experienced a crop failure at the desolate confluence of the Columbia and Snake Rivers, whereupon "we buried our boots and machinery in a sand pit, saddled our horses. . . and started for greener pastures," eventually to settle in Latah County. Immigrants came on horseback, by wagon train, steamboat or rail, or on foot.

The process of settlement was largely completed around World War I; by then the Palouse had become the most densely settled rural area in the Inland Northwest and was already "producing more wheat per acre than any other place its size in the world." While the enclaves of foreign born immigrants became amalgamated in time with the broader population, a rich history of distinctive cultural ties is still reflected in the communities, churches, and social activities of the Palouse. Richard Scheuerman has told the story of the diverse groups who came to the Palouse in an interesting and articulate way. John Clement has enriched the account with photographs of a land as varied as the people who came to claim it. This account of the Palouse and its people will be a welcome addition to our understanding of the history of the Inland Northwest.

Alexander C. McGregor
Pullman, Washingtons

*Isolation's Hope**   *South of Kahlotus, Washington*

*Golden Harvest**

INTRODUCTION

"Many of the most lively, intimate expressions of spirit spring from the joyous, continuous contact of human beings with a particular locality. If life can be made secure in each community and if the rewards of the different communities are distributed justly, there will flower... not only those who attain joy in daily, productive work well done; but also those who paint and sing and tell stories with the flavor peculiar to their own valley, well-loved hill, or broad prairie."

—Henry Wallace

Stretching across the heartland of the Inland Pacific Northwest is a mystical expanse called the Palouse Country which was transformed between 1860 and 1920 from open prairie into one of the nation's premier dryland farming and ranching districts. Although the region's name has become synonymous with the steeply rolling hills in its center, the greater Palouse is a tousled tapestry of contrasts with valleys, hills, and mountains woven together by the twisted course of the Palouse River and its tributaries. My father's fields were located on some of the highest terrain near the Palouse River between the communities of Endicott and St. John, Washington near the geographic center of the Palouse. Our house stood in the shadow of a steep hill capped with a towering yellow pine growing in the protected northern arc of a "sodpatch," or slope too steep to farm that remained in wheatgrass. A favorite boyhood hiking route led across this hilltop to the wild beauty of the river bluffs a mile north. From the hill I could see Kamiak and Steptoe buttes standing advance guard for the forested Clearwater Mountains on the eastern horizon. Surrounded by undulations of hills and waving grain, a person depends on fence lines of rusty barbed wire to provide north-south orientation while the river's flow tends westward. The hills decline in that direction toward the channeled scablands where massive elongated islands of fertile soil lay like capsized hulls in a mottled sea of basaltic detritus.

Some of my most memorable jaunts through the Palouse were in the company of my uncle, Ray Reich of Colfax, whose hearty disposition, wit, and size earned him friends throughout the region and visibility in most any crowd. Most comfortable in a bolo tie or on horseback, Ray led the famed "Gentlemen on Horseback" after the passing of its founder, Chuck Glover, and never missed its annual ride from the time of the group's inception in 1948 to his death in 1993. After a lifetime in the Palouse, extensive work with area agricultural cooperatives, and horse rides throughout the region, Ray probably knew the rural Palouse and its people as well as about anyone. I envied his grasp of Palouse geography and history which was characteristically demonstrated on a springtime pick-up excursion in 1993 to locate the route of the historic Colville Road in eastern Adams County.

As teacher and principal at Endicott-St. John Middle School, I was planning to take the eighth grade class and kindergartners by wagons for a few miles along a trail devoid of cars, fences, and any form of electronic entertainment. I remembered that Ray had once mentioned something to me about the old trail and when I asked if he could give me some specifics, he volunteered to show me its location. Traveling in the company of rancher Louie Gaiser, who uses draft horses to this day during haying season and for other farm work, Ray pointed out remnants of the Texas and Mullan trails as we passed points along the road west of Winona where they intersected the highway. I recognized one rutted stretch he identified as the Mullan route as the dirt road I had used to haul grain for Pat Kleweno during harvest season when I was in high school. Louie then conferred upon me the honor of being a Mullan Trail teamster and offered me any of his Percherons on my "next run to Ft. Walla Walla." I had no doubt he could manage the haul but recalled having enough trouble navigating Pat's International Loadstar truck the short distance needed to get out of his field using that route.

We finally left the highway several miles north of Benge to follow a dirt trail until it deteriorated into two faint ruts which appeared to drift endlessly southward. Satisfied that we had established the trail's location, I suggested turning back but Ray would hear nothing of it. He loved the spring scenery and wanted to show us the entire course down to another highway we could take back home so I settled back between the two men to hear a litany of tales about Ray and Louie's earlier ranching experiences. Louie, I learned, was among the charter members of the Palouse Empire Appaloosa Horse Club, an organization that helped launch one of the nation's largest breed registries headquartered in Moscow. As the stories and green Chevy rolled on, the trace we had been following gradually faded away entirely and, seeing no sign of life for miles in any direction, even Louie began to have doubts about our scout's memory. Still, Ray was undeterred. "I know where I'm at," he reassured us, "I just don't know exactly where I'm at." I decided this was an appropriate moment to ask Ray if it was true that he had once ridden his blaze-faced sorrel Topper through the front door of the tavern in St. John and out the back. Louie chuckled imaging the image, or perhaps the memory while Ray glanced furtively out the side window. "Folks can't believe everything they hear, though I do have some special memories of the Rialto," he grinned before turning the conversation to deep-furrow seed drills and Hamley saddles.

After another half-hour of bumps that were starting to damage my hat and approaching the edge of the Palouse universe, we came to a knoll and spotted a solitary figure far to the south. Louie volunteered that it might be Captain Mullan himself since no one else apparently had been this way for at least a century. On closer inspection we saw a man in overalls feeding some Herefords and apart from wondering how we had come to that point, Dick Coon was glad to see an old acquaintance in Uncle Ray. Dick confirmed that we had indeed been following the old trail all the time, and I never questioned Ray's bearings again. Three weeks later the air above that prairie was punctuated with the shouts of sixty kids from our school and tiny Benge rolling along in five wagons with my two mentors serving as drivers. Other volunteers included teacher Arden Johnson of Colfax who insisted we also partake only of pioneer fare while on the trail—hardtack, sardines, dill pickles, and warm water. Not even the Johnson family's Fonk's Variety Store, famed for carrying supplies of every sort, stocked hardtack so we settled for soda crackers.

Standing next to Ray for most of the stretch was ninety-year-old Dick Parrish who had lived his entire life in the vicinity. He shared some boyhood memories with the students which included witnessing the last teamsters and mules hauling freight on the Mullan Trail. He

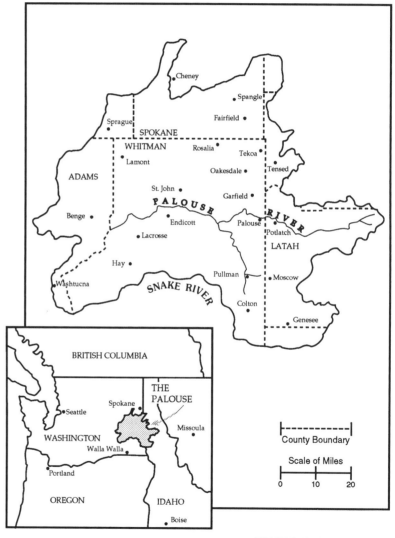

THE PALOUSE COUNTRY TODAY

also shared how in "earlier days six yokes of oxen were needed to pull one large freight wagon" for the two-week journey from Walla Walla to Ft. Colville. The contributions of people like Ray Reich, Louie Gaiser, and Dick Parrish to the quality of life for persons of all ages and to the research of historians and other scholars have been significant. Theirs is the spirit of Henry Wallace's "joyous contact" between persons and locality that has enriched historical perspectives and engendered preservation efforts in a land as fragile as it is beautiful.

My maternal grandparents, Edward and Emily (Sunwold) Johns, had settled in "the upper country" and farmed in the Waverly, Fairfield, and Chester areas of southeastern Spokane County. Grandfather Johns had come West as a young bachelor from Missouri in a futile search for gold and silver at famed Cripple Creek, Colorado but found better opportunity in selling meat and other provisions to the miners and he steadily moved further westward. Grandma's people were from the Hallingdal Valley in Norway. Her father, Andrew Sunwold, came to America in the 1870s long before he brought his family. The *America-briefe* he frequently sent home described the Northwest's boundless landscapes and his work supplying wood for steamboats at Ft. Benton, Montana. The fort was the eastern terminus for the legendary Mullan Road, the primary immigrant route to Washington Territory before the advent of railroad travel, which linked the upper Missouri River with Ft. Walla Walla. This was the path he was to follow. In later years his hopes for land of his own were fulfilled when he and his two sons established farms in the vicinity of Fairfield.

On the Palouse River about a mile west of our farm, near a rickety swinging footbridge, several clapboard houses remained clustered together at a remote place known locally as the "Palouse Colony." Our grandfather made sure we knew that this was the first home for our people in the Pacific Northwest. My great-grandfather, Henry B. Scheuerman, was among the region's *Russland-deutschen*, or Germans from Russia. They were people of the soil who for generations had sown their grain and gathered harvests in a progression that led from the Hessian countryside and Volga steppe to the Palouse prairies. H.B. and his family had arrived in 1891 and lived with earlier colonists on this fertile bottomland

until arrangements could be made to acquire land nearby.

Some of our favorite family photographs depict the everyday scenes of their life in the Palouse Hills. One shows Great-Grandma Sunwold feeding her agitated flock of Plymouth Rocks; another casts Uncle Art in a sea of stiff club wheat on his farm near Waverly. While the pioneering experiences of our first-generation relatives living throughout the region were as varied as the languages they spoke, a common theme framed the stories they told us children: The Palouse was a Promised Land and we should be grateful for our blessings here and work hard to ensure an equally secure future for our families. Having eeked out a hardscrabble existence in the Colorado Rockies, on stony Norwegian slopes, inclement Swedish coastlines, and in politically unstable Russia; they seemed in a position to know.

My grandfather, Karl Scheuerman, knew his land intimately. He and my father taught us to distinguish the swales, saddles, and other unique topographic features and soil conditions of the Palouse meaningful to a farmer. As with farm families throughout the Palouse, many features on the landscape hold a special significance. We learned such names and locations as the *Huvaluck* (Hessian dialect for "Oathole"—a notoriously steep horseshoe basin), "Barley Hill," and

GERTRUDE SUNWOLD, FAIRFIELD, c. 1905

"Three-Finger Draw." Grandpa would recount the experiences of the first Russian German immigrants to the region who had labored for years to turn the tawny, knee-high bunchgrass and plant the Turkey Red wheat that their Mennonite countrymen had brought from Russia. Grandpa knew of their exploits first-hand and understood that other groups had shared in these pioneering experiences. He also was aware that the area's native population had succumbed to the pressures of European-American immigration and he spoke wistfully of the days his father traded flour and fruit on the river for the Indians' salmon.

Faith, Family, and Farm

Our tiny half-section farm clung precariously to economic vitality by the thrift and uncanny ability of my father to keep second-hand machinery running indefinitely with sufficient supplies of bailing wire, canvas, and "Rock-Hard"—a gritty gray goop that turned to stone moments out of the can and guaranteed to plug up any hole in sheet metal. Like his talent for picking up a guitar, mandolin, or most any other stringed instrument to play while singing plaintive country tunes, this mechanical aptitude was not passed down to my generation. Grandpa Scheuerman was also a musician-farmer who loved to visit the ranch long after his retirement, especially during August's sweltering hot "thrashing weather," as he called it, a desire entirely lost on an adolescent bondservant. We would sit in a black Ford grain truck that Dad would insist be polished before harvest, perched for view as he reaped some of the finest crops around with a growling mechanical dinosaur of speckled red skin that slowly ate its way through rolling seas of wheat. The high yields produced year after year reflected an agrarian sense in both men that had been passed down over centuries from the viridian fields of Hesse and Volga steppes to the Palouse Country.

Grandpa was a citadel of understanding and I greatly enjoyed his presence. Though deeply informed of the struggles his German ancestors had endured in Russia and on the plains of frontier Kansas, he did not allow the siren sounds of memory to romanticize our people's history. He encouraged me to ask questions, to listen and read for fuller understandings. While David's Psalms and the Proverbs of Solomon were his favorite readings, a couple winter terms of country schooling in the Palouse had introduced him to Tennyson and Wordsworth whose lines he could quote but only upon request. I thought it peculiar that various corners of our household were inhabited by objects foreign to the contemporary culture as regularly seen on our black and white Capehart television. Hanging on a bearing beam downstairs was a monstrous greatcoat of bear fur called the *Belz* (Hessian for "pelt") that Grandpa said had come from the Old Country and that he had often worn while herding a team of horses or driving tractor in bitter weather.

From Grandpa Scheuerman I learned that folks in our area had come from places all over the world and country. While Dad's people hailed from Russia and the Ukraine, Mom's were from Norway and Sweden, the Wakefields, Brookfields, and Mansfields were of English extraction; the Bachmanns, Shermans, and Kackmans had German roots; and the Cutlers, Dollarhides, and Smith-Rockwells qualified to be frontier Americans since they had been here when the Indians roamed through the Palouse digging roots along Rebel Flat and Union Flat creeks. Other pioneer families, were more transient but still left melancholy evidence of their passage. Once while hunting only a mile from our farm, I happened upon a dreary lilac bush far past bloom and strangely out of place on an eastern slope sodpatch far from any house. On closer inspection I spotted a small squared post, tapered at the top, and still bearing a few flecks of white paint. When I reported the oddity to my grandfather, he told me that an immigrant family who had once lived near there lost a

KARL & MARY SCHEUERMAN (LEFT) AND PHILLIP & SOPHIE LITZENBERGER FAMILIES, ENDICOTT, c.1920

child when a boiling cauldron of water fell upon him. The boy died from severe burns and was buried in an anonymous grave in the near-by hillside. Grandpa never missed putting a flower on Floyd Duchow's grave every Memorial Day. The boy, son of a short-term preacher and his wife, died in Endicott the day after his thirteenth birthday sometime back in the 1940s.

My grandfather also told me about venerable Phillip Ochs, a kindly ancient man I slightly knew from a respectful distance who had to be the closest thing the Palouse Country ever had to Little Big Man's Jack Crabb. Nearly a century old when I was a boy, Phillip was raised on the Kansas frontier and after coming to the vicinity in the early 1880s unwittingly fell in as a young teen with the area's Wild Bunch and found himself rustling Indian ponies along the lower Snake River. According to Grandpa, not one to fabricate stories, he barely escaped their buckshot and arrows. But Phillip was arrested with several gang members by a Lewiston marshal who surmised the boy's circumstances and allowed him to return home on his pledge to keep better company. Phillip took his vow seriously and settled down to raise horses and wheat, became a stalwart member of the local church, and never lost a steeled resolve to abide by the law and confront anyone who might not. He packed a six-gun for years, and rendered helpless brutish gunfighters at least three times—on the road near Mockonema, on the streets of Colfax, and with the vigilante posse that helped bring the notorious Bill Masterson Gang to justice in 1892. Every time I saw him outside, the old fellow wore his signature circle-brimmed tan cowboy hat. Just about the time I worked up enough nerve to personally inquire about his legendary exploits, Phillip passed away. I was fifteen and quietly mourned the loss of a spirit uncommonly gentle and stalwart. I made my own vow to resist timidity and make forthright and timely inquiry regarding matters I considered of some significance.

Each year of our life on the farm, our parents, Donovan and Mary Scheuerman, made caring for the large garden behind our house a family affair. We grew dozens of cabbages for late summer slicing bee using the *Hoofel* and a fifteen gallon crock to make sauerkraut, cucumbers and dill for pickles, and parsnips and carrots for Sunday pot roast feasts. Recurrent attempts to grow melons met with only marginal success. Butternut and Indian squash added colorful orange, green, and yellow splashes to the area and we kept neighbors and relatives supplied with all the zucchini they could ever desire with the fruit of just two plants. We picked red raspberries and strawberries for preserves and fresh eating from blossoming bushes that attracted hordes of viceroy butterflies, and carefully tended patches of perennial rhubarb although I wished the adjacent asparagus would somehow perish forever. Dad was extremely particular about the amount and method of watering each vegetable. Carrots had to be sprayed with a mist while the cucumbers were slowly drip irrigated with small canals resembling an exhaust manifold that reached the entire spread. Grandpa taught us that Good Friday was always the day to plant spuds and so we did. Usually we set out a row of freshly cut Netta Gem and Red Pontiac seed potatoes at least a hundred yards long into a plow furrow that Dad filled with the old Caterpillar D-6's next rumbling pass pulling two sections of moldboard plows. These would eventually be dug on a long afternoon of moil in late September when the vines had fully shriveled and dirt clods were perfect for throwing at siblings.

We kept a small alfalfa pasture behind the garden near the house for the livestock which included cattle, sheep, and a few pigs. I always marveled how ewes so skittish they blanched at our glance would sit as if in addled bliss while complete strangers stripped and bloodied them each March when shearing their fleeces. A small orchard planted by my great-grandparents lay beyond our alfalfa where we gathered green Transparents, Golden Delicious, and other apples each fall as well as apricots and Bartlett pears. Wood pruned from the trees each spring was stored to use for smoking up to a thousand pounds of pork sausage, *Wurst*, that we stuffed each December. An overgrown pie cherry tree provided camouflage for the skeleton of an ancient McCormick reaper that we pretended was a Sherman tank when we crawled down into its lever-laden interior while two severely weathered header-box wagons with their characteristic Picasso-like asymmetrical frames rested nearby. We had an old Hutchison harvest photograph in the house mounted on heavy gray cardboard showing Grandpa Scheuerman standing on a derrick table next to one of the oddly shaped wagons. He used the most peculiar vocabulary when

Morning Reds   *West of Spokane, Washington*

describing harvesting operations like those depicted in the scene. As if speaking in tongues, he told about hoedowns, sack jigs, roustabouts, band cutters, bindle stiffs, and water bucks whose roles I sought to understand.

Our nearest neighbors, the Jimmy and Maxine Smick family, ran a larger cattle herd in alternating years on one of their fields bordering our place. I was never more impressed with countryside friendliness than the day after a rare nighttime southwester fiercely blew across the Palouse. The wind picked up a heavy overturned sheet metal watering trough, at least ten feet in diameter, and blasted it directly across the field where the Smick cattle were pastured. The calamitous roar of bovine Armageddon apparently resounded across the hills because the following morning most members of the trough-shocked herd were wandering aimlessly along the road for a mile between our place and the Palouse River. Broken wire was everywhere in sight but Jimmy just laughed at the thought of what must have happened. We all set about to mend fences and round up those animals that survived judgment and were approved for return to the Smicks' heavenly acres.

Jimmy Smick also taught the junior high Sunday School class at Trinity Lutheran where most of our relatives attended although, like most towns in the Palouse Country, other denominations were represented. Endicott also had the oldest German Congregational Church in the region, a gleaming white testimony to pioneer faith; a beautiful Seventh-Day Adventist Church of brick and stone, and a memory of Methodists meeting somewhere. Jimmy had a son, Monty, my age with whom I often engaged in debates that I generally wound up losing though I do still contend that the Yanks played better ball than Milwaukee in the 60s. His father had a penchant for bringing contemporary issues to the forefront from verses studied in the Old and New Testaments. He spoke about stewardship in terms of more than the collection plate, but about caring for the land with which God had blessed us. Jim interpreted the reference in Genesis 1 about mankind having "dominion over all the earth" to mean we were stewards of the land, and that soil conservation was a moral issue. At that age I was more interested in how Mantle, Ford, and Maris were playing but the thought that the direction in which I drove the tractor might be considered sinful practice bothered me a bit.

Jimmy also spoke about the evils of atheistic communism and how many of our German relatives who had not left Russia for America were now suffering for their faith in faraway Siberia. Tens of thousands had been expelled from their homes along the Volga at the beginning of World War II and disappeared into oblivion. I had heard bits and pieces of our people's saga and of missing relatives during somber conversations between Grandpa Scheuerman and his older brother who bore a given name unique in my limited experience— Yost. I deduced a connection with timeworn letters addressed to the family years bearing postmarks and blue and green stamps dated from the turn of the century with what I determined to be typeface in Russian and Spanish as well as English. I once happened upon a cache of them in an attic steamer trunk. The letters had traveled to the Palouse from Rio de Janeiro, someplace in Canada named Bashaw, and Russia. The Cyrillic was wholly unintelligible to me as were the letters' contents. While the style of the script varied with the author, all were in an archaic German dialect just as incomprehensible to my parents except for an occasional family name.

I clearly remember when I first asked my grandfather about who had written the letters. His cheerful visage grew wistful but he proceeded forthrightly to tell me that their origin was rooted in our people's response generations earlier to a royal promise. A woman he identified as *"die Kaiserin Katarina"* had invited our German ancestors to leave their strife-ridden central European homeland in the 1760s and undertake a perilous year-long journey to the wilds of Russia's lower Volga frontier. In return they would be given free land and exemption from taxes and military service "forever." Enroute to the steppes they arrived at the port near St. Petersburg where, according to family tradition, the mysterious woman of regal bearing sought their company to hear her native language spoken. She encouraged them in their quest and a year later those who survived the trek founded a village they named Yagodnaya Polyana, or "Berry Meadow."

Some weeks later I mentioned Grandpa's fanciful story to the oldest person in our family, his eldest sister whom we called *Diela Vess*, Russian-born and nearing the century mark. "Yes, it happened as your grandfather says," she replied in heavily accented English. "And sometimes I think this is why my name is Katherine," she smiled. A brief investigation into the date and place revealed that the only "Katarina" who could have extended such a welcome was the tsarina of Russia herself, Catherine the Great, also a native of Germany. I learned in later years that she did frequent the docks at Oranienbaum to greet the weary Hessian arrivals at the very time others from that principality were being sent as mercenaries to fight with the British against American independence.

To young Americanized ears like mine, the nicknames borne by many elders in our area sounded peculiar, but was so accepted by young and old alike that even closest relatives sometimes did not know the given names of their aunts and uncles, let alone others of more distant kinship, until their funerals. "Hey Mary," I remember my dad announcing to Mom one morning while he read an obituary in the *Colfax Gazette*. "Knooga's name was really Henry." The word meant "boney" in Hessian dialect, fitting for his slim build and enormous hands. The subset of first and last names just in our small town was so limited that we had several Henry Kromms, Mary Repps, Adam Morasches, and many others of shared designation. The solution to distinguishing individuals in conversation came to the Palouse from the Old Country where identical formal names abounded in the village. A system of nicknaming as practical as it was bizarre emerged in the Old Country and endured with those who came to Endicott, St. John, Colfax, Farmington, and elsewhere in the Palouse and Ritzville-Odessa area.

First, depending on which half of Berry Meadow the ancestral home was located, one could either be Kalmooka, derived from the villagers' name for the Buddhist Kalmyk tribe, the southsiders; or *Totten*, from their word for Mongol Tartars, or those living to the north. Grandpa said we were *Kalmooka* so I assumed for a while we had been Lutheran Buddhists. Of course there were many such Scheuermans on the Volga and in the Palouse so each family clan, though descended from a single couple in the 1760s, had a second appellation—in our case *Watchka*, *Yusta*, or *Kosak* Scheuermans. Nobody even in our grandparents' time knew for certain the origin of these antiquated referents but they served the purpose well and their sound gave clues to some enigmatic former incident of comedy, lineament, or family tendency. We were *Kalmooka Yustas*, not one of those Cossacks.

Finally, virtually everyone had a personal moniker that could have arisen from a variety of circumstance and characteristics. In Endicott, Colfax, or St. John where many of our older relatives lived, streetside summons were rendered without diffidence to persons called *Schwartza* (Black) *Pete* and *Rud* (Red) *Marie*, *Huhnkil Hannas* (Chicken John) and *Krommageeglel* (Crooked Rooster). There was *Katya Yhugher* (George's Katie, one of two hex casters in town whose houses we scrupulously avoided) and *Kedda* (Katherine, from a nervous boyfriend who once stuttered in her presence), *Arbuza* (Watermelon) *Adam* and *Moslanga* (Sunflower) *Alex*, and in our family, *Badelya* (Small Bottle) and *Rahmbadya* (Cream Chin). My grandfather was distinguished simply by others invoking his father's German name, thus Karl Johann Scheuerman was more fully known to Palouse Country German Russians as that *Kalmooka Yusta Heinrich Karl*. The method sounded so reasonable yet along with *Hexeri* curses and incantations incredibly anachronistic in our 1960s realm of rock music and war protests.

Grandpa also informed me that our junior choir director at church, Clara Litzenberger, had special knowledge of our heritage. She was in her sixties at the time and still had the mettle and patience to meet every Wednesday afternoon during the school year with a passel of young people who struggled to remain silent between tunes in spite of Trinity Lutheran Church's awe-inspiring vaulted interior. The edifice is remarkable and features an Old World color scheme worthy of Catherine's Winter Palace—immense turquoise arches with lavender and Prussian blue trim embellished with lustrous gilded filigree stenciling. Wheat sheaves emerge in deep relief on wooden panels beneath a west wall of windows; Biblical images and verses are carved in massive lintels along the parish house. Virtually all furnishings including the pews, high altar, and molded exterior of one of the region's largest pipe organs were built of solid birch and alder smoothly lacquered to a gleaming sheen. But the church building, Grandpa emphasized to me, was not built as any testament to the pioneers' relative prosperity here in the new Canaan. Rather, everything in the grandiose design from the plaster shields of the Twelve Apostles to the massive wooden cross seemingly suspended in air before a massive purple dossal curtain stretching to the ceiling was to focus parishioners' attention upon divine majesty. "That is why," he informed me in German, "we chose the first words of Psalm 115, for the verse of dedication: "Not unto us, O Lord, Not unto us; but unto thy name give glory, for thy mercy, and for thy truth's sake.'"

I knew "Clara Litz" to be a relative by some distant connection yet close enough to occasionally join the extended family dinners held every Sunday after church at my grandfather's home in Endicott. With families of five grown sons and daughters spread across the Palouse Country from LaCrosse to Sunset, Grandpa supervised feasts that routinely drew no fewer than two dozen not including frequent guests. Almost invariably the fare included roast beef, mashed potatoes with gravy and sauerkraut, and a mixture of cooked carrots, onions, and parsnips. This was always followed by fruit pies unless someone's birthday, confirmation, wedding, or basketball championship also warranted cake. The identical meal was served in the same way at many homes in town that very hour with the only appreciable difference being the aperitif. Some old timers preferred a cruel concoction of fortified port and Jack Daniels to tamer Riesling. Once after dinner when Clara was present, I sacrificed listening to my older cousins debate the upcoming week's sporting prospects and asked her what she knew about our ancestral past. She had read all about Queen Catherine II and added that our people had been used as a buffer against the Mongol tribes who recurrently threatened the peace on Russia's southern borderlands. With images of Genghis Khan now entering the picture, more exotic images of past family adventures on both sides of the globe filled my boyhood brain.

In middle age, Grandpa Scheuerman had served as board chairman of School District No. 95, housed on a neighbor's farm until consolidation with the school in town put the building up for sale. He acquired the substantial structure and somehow relocated it to our place where it entered into a new era of service as a shop and chicken house. One of my least pleasant chores on the farm was to clean the eggs we gathered from the birds enrolled in what we always called "the schoolhouse" and be sure they were fed with grain stored in what had been the building's kitchen. My father's sister, Aunt Evelyn Reich, once pointed to a half-dozen tin cups suspended on a post in the schoolhouse. "We all took turns washing those for Miss Vera Longwell," she said, who had arrived from Kansas in 1920 to teach my aunts, uncles, and others in the vicinity who were then of school age.

Reminiscing today at three-quarter century's distance, Aunt Evelyn noted methods that shaped their lessons: pairings in which older pupils often assisted the younger, studying the classics and original historical documents, and periodic public presentations of written, dramatic, and musical works. Tales of Robin Hood and Sherwood Forest occasioned trips to an anonymous grove of willow and hawthorn down the road where botany easily became a topic of inquiry. *Saturday Evening Post* reviews of the Boston Symphony's 1920 premier of "The Pleasure Dome of Kublai Khan" led naturally to stories of Marco Polo, the poetry of Coleridge ("In Xanadu did Kublai Khan...."), and news of Babe Ruth's trade that year from Boston to the Yankees for $125,000. That remarkable sum, in turn, offered grist for a lesson in mathematics. Decades before terms like interdisciplinary studies, high expectations, and cross-age grouping entered the pedagogical lexicon of best practices, Miss Longwell and teachers like her in other country schools offered enriching educational experiences. A faded family photograph shows Miss Longwell surrounded by a sea of faces, children and

ARTHUR SUNWOLD, WAVERLY, c. 1950

parents, at a schoolhouse gathering in late spring of 1920 for a festive afternoon of picnicking, declamations, and group performance.

By the time I had grown to the age of the older children in the picture, I was aware that former residents of our immediate vicinity, friends of my father, were making their mark in the world. Union Flat's General John Kinney had been the only Marine officer in World War II to successfully escape from a Japanese prisoner-of-war camp—a feat he attributed in part to a history and geography lesson he had remembered from school in Endicott about the U.S.-Canadian border battle slogan "Fifty-four, Forty or Fight." Carl Litzenberger, one-time barnstormer with Amelia Earhart whose pilot's license bore Oroville Wright's signature, served as the Army Air Corps' Chief Pilot Trainer in Georgia during World War II. Dr. Margaret Henry, daughter of the town's physician and sister to three other doctors, was the nation's first A.O.A. board-certified woman ophthalmologist, while Rev. Dr. Carl Mau was serving in Geneva, Switzerland as head of the world's largest Protestant body, the Lutheran World Federation.

Our mother's brother, Uncle Willis Johns, who had spent so much of his youth in the Waverly-Fairfield area, directed the most comprehensive multi-state mapping project of the Northern Rockies ever undertaken by the U. S. Geological Survey. Despite his aversion to appearances at any formal event in favor of weeks in the wild, our lanky 6'6" uncle was honored for his efforts with induction into the Explorers Club where he shared the rarified air of fellowship with such luminaries as Sir Edmund Hillary and Neil Armstrong. The family had to find out about it from the newspapers and when I inquired about the benefits of membership, he deadpanned, "I can always get a free steak dinner when I'm in New York," the organization's international headquarters.

But our uncle was far more interested in showing us how the Palouse Hills were formed, where the Nez Perces and Palouses fought at the Battle of the Big Hole, the route of Lewis and Clark over the Lolo Trail, and the saber-toothed tiger skull he found carefully placed upon a rock shelf deep inside an obscure mountain cave. While his colleagues retired to such comforts as regular golfing at Spokane's Indian Canyon and Qualchan courses, Willis flew off to Israel to observe first-hand excavations at Jerusalem and Tell Lachish.

Something of a religious skeptic, he was nevertheless impressed with the recent discovery of the Tell Amarna tablets at Ebla which confirmed the existence of the Hittite Empire, hitherto mentioned in ancient manuscripts only in the Old Testament book of Judges. This news justified a trip to Turkey where our uncle investigated the new discoveries there with a team of university archaeologists. From the shape of the Palouse Hills to pottery shards in Jerusalem, Willis's curiosity knew few bounds.

Rural Schooling and Community Continuity

Interests nurtured in area youth by innate curiosity and encouraged by family members were extended by remarkable faculties of Palouse area schoolteachers. In our case, Mrs. (Mildred) Repp had fascinating bulletin boards in her fourth grade classroom featuring the major Indian cultures throughout North America. The word "Nez Perce" and "Spokane" were the only names on the map close to where we lived but she said Indians had once hunted and dug roots along Rebel Creek Flat. She read to us fantastic legends of the Northwest's First Nations featuring Blue Jay, Abalone Man, and other Animal People. During our sixth grade year Mr. (Jim) Leonard, a native of Palouse, read classical literature to us and when we first heard about Ulysses and Penelope I wondered what the journey across the Atlantic must have been like for my Grandmother Scheuerman, whom I only knew briefly before her death in 1961. She had come from Berry Meadow in 1898 as a small child with her parents aboard the *S. S. Hungarie* but something tragic and mysterious had happened to her mother. Throughout Grandma's lifetime she sought without success to learn if her mother had been buried at sea or somewhere near New York City where they had landed.

Grade school principal and eighth grade teacher Mr. Yenny, born and raised in Kooskia, was the most formidable figure we ever encountered at school. To us he was a man without a first name. We struggled to correctly diagram sentences and artistically render penmanship push-pulls, but what an incredible room. The place was more museum than desk space with rocks and mineral displays from the Hoodoos and the most intriguing exhibit of conifers from the eastern Palouse forests. Each specimen was precisely cut to the same dimen-

Abandoned   *North of Pullman, Washington*

sions with the bark remaining on the sides (he was also the junior high shop teacher), and stood about two feet high with a forty-five degree slice on the top revealing the ring structure and an inner chamber behind plastic showcasing seedlings, cones, and needles. A man of substantial girth who seemed forever to look sixty, Mr. Yenny was a strict disciplinarian who brooked no misbehavior or untucked shirts. He was also the giant in any crisis. When President Kennedy was assassinated in 1963 and I was in sixth grade, Mr. Yenny convened the entire student body in the multipurpose room and said with calm resolution, "Our president has fallen earlier this day. His death touches us all but America remains strong." I seem to recall that we were dismissed from school early and I joined my cousins in front of the television set at Grandpa Scheuerman's to watch the historic events of that November week unfold. There was sadness among us but no panic; mostly because Mr. Yenny had said everything was under control.

In high school, Mr. (Ray) Smith took us on outings in physical science class to archaeological digs on the Snake and Palouse rivers. These excavations were supervised by Dr. Roald Fryxell of W.S.U., co-discoverer of Marmes Man in 1965 with Dr. Richard Daughtery, and Dr. Roderick Sprague from U. of I. whose crew found an original Lewis and Clark Peace Medallion while relocating Indian burials at the ancient village of Palus to higher ground to salvage them from flooding. He also drove us across the basin to study the peculiar terrain of the Channeled Scablands and see the fossilized mold of the Blue Lake Rhino. Our high school FFA advisor, Mr. (Dan) Birdsell, from the St. John area, and introduced us to soil chemistry, crop and livestock judging—impossible for me to master, public speaking, and parliamentary procedure. He taught to the incessant background strains of Eddy Arnold's "Cattle Call" and other country music he defined as hits. Mr. Birdsell also served as our junior varsity basketball coach and once enabled us to salvage some dignity by keeping his alma mater from scoring 100 on us. (They managed 98.)

Author-educator Garrett Keizer writes about the F.F.A. in *Nowhere Else But Here*, his eloquent memoir about a scholarly city kid who reluctantly takes a job at a rural New England high school. Much to his wonder, F.F.A. came to impress him as the single-most important influence for shaping democratic values in young people and instilling an appreciation for Western civilization. The organization's memorized meeting ritual is steeped in references to Demeter, virtue, and ideals taken from the classical world to be put into contemporary practice. Mr. Birdsell imparted these understandings through example, humor, and endless hours of volunteered time helping students before and after school.

The spirit of the day and of unfettered young adult inquiry in any era arrived in the person of Mrs. (Louise) Braun on the first day of our senior year in the fall of 1968. She came clad in black leotards and matching leather jacket and we soon found her to be as demanding as she was iconoclastic and brilliant. At first glance that opening week, nothing traditional appeared on the horizon for our classroom experience except the plaster bas-relief of a Revolutionary War scene mounted high on the wall behind the teacher's desk. Under her tutelage, we deeply delved into English literature but were not assigned the customary required outside reading lists for writing and reporting. The fresh air of academic freedom rushed between her third-story room and the library across the hall. We could choose Ray Bradbury or Zane Grey, *Successful Farming Magazine* or *The Brothers Karamazov*. The important message was to read, and we grew to love her and the tales she brought about growing up in tiny Viola on the eastern edge of the Palouse Hills.

Virtually everyone from our classes went on to some form of higher education, usually at Washington State in Pullman, Eastern Washington University at Cheney, Moscow's University of Idaho, or to community college in Spokane. Most of us moved on feeling that our paths would likely lead beyond the Palouse Hills but that those who chose to return to the farm or a community business or set up house would also find success. Of the sixty graduates from my brother Don's Class of 1967, mine two years later, and my future wife Lois Morasch's in '72, one-third of them eventually returned to live in places from Spokane to Lewiston. "To strive, to seek, to find, but not to yield." Tennyson's words of dynamic challenge were the motto for my brother's graduation. I recalled Grandpa reciting those very lines to me long before this class ever entered high school.

Palouse country community ceremonials reflected a familiarity that bred less discontent than dependability and continuity. Under the abiding ministry of Trinity's Pastor Fred Schnaible, for example, my wife and I were baptized as infants, confirmed in adolescence, and married as young adults. Dr. John Hardy delivered both of us and our first-born daughter, Mary Katherine two decades later. Timeless Mr. Yenny, who had welcomed us to kindergarten and taught us in eighth grade, never missed a graduation. Local bank president Cliff Workman, who had helped many of us open our first bank accounts as children, presented scholarships when we received our diplomas. Most of these individuals and others like them retired in the community to join the ranks of elders who continued for years to volunteer in a variety of ways to benefit area youth. Throughout this period of our upbringing in the Palouse, most of my generation experienced what we thought was a sort of rural dullness. Holocaust survivor Ellie Wiesel terms such circumstances a "blessed ordinariness" that should never be taken for granted and instills a sense of solidarity and personal responsibility to family, community, and society at large.

Glimpsing the Palouse Primeval

A few weeks after my high school graduation, Grandpa Scheuerman expressed an interest in visiting relatives who lived in Brewster, Washington. Since we were caught up with summer field-work, I offered to drive him over for the weekend and I noticed on the map that our destination was only a few miles from the Colville Indian Reservation. I remembered Grandpa's tales about his parents bartering garden produce for the Indians' salmon at the immigrant Palouse Colony and had long wondered about the experiences of the region's First Peoples. Not far from our farm was the bridge over the Palouse River near the place known to old timers as "Kamiakin's Crossing" and a stream near the foot of Rock Lake still bore the name "Kamiacun Creek" on area maps. Somewhere I had read that Kamiak Butte had the same Native American namesake. Reflecting on this unusual word and Grandpa's boyhood memories of area Native Americans, I ventured to request a minor detour while on our way to Brewster. Highway 155 ran about fifteen miles north from Grand Coulee to the Colville Tribal Agency Headquarters in Nespelem. With Grandpa's permission, we were soon headed across the reservation. My investigative credentials consisted of curiosity about a name

attached to several Palouse Country landmarks.

I approached the public affairs office simply to ask if anyone bearing the name Kamiakin might live in the area and be willing to speak with me about the family's Palouse history. Though I read some initial skepticism in the eyes of the woman who fielded my query, Annie George, she then smiled and said an elder of the family, Arthur Tomeo Kamiakin, lived not far from the agency and might be inclined to speak with me. I carefully wrote down directions to his home, thanked Mrs. George for her trust, and rejoined Grandpa for the drive to "Art Tomeo's." We passed near a cemetery in which a massive white stone rose several feet above all others. I turned and parked the blue Ford Fairlane on a grassy trail next to the graveyard and we walked the short distance to a marble obelisk that I recognized from a school history text as Chief Joseph's headstone. A bust of the famed leader was carved into one side of the memorial. A few feet away we saw stones bearing the names Alalumti Kamiakin, Tomeo Kamiakin, and other members of that distinguished family. On almost every grave was a collection of reliquaries significant to donors who had paid tribute to loved ones— feather clusters, silver coins, dried flowers, and small brass bells that eerily sang in the wind.

Grandpa called my attention to a polished red granite marker on the other side of Joseph's grave. Engraved into the stone were the name and dates "Tom Poween 1852-1940" above a scene depicting an Indian fisher on a riverbank with the words, "Born at Almota on the Snake River." We seemed to be in the midst of exiled Palouses' final resting place, here in this place of sage and dust, so different from their original homes in the hills and on the mighty Snake. We returned to the car and continued on our journey back in time down a gravel road to a dirt lane that our map indicated would lead to the Arthur Kamiakin residence. Abandoned cars lay randomly near the road beyond town like slain bison carcasses White buffalo hunters once left to rot by the thousands on the Great Plains. Soon a white mobile home with yellow trim appeared ahead as had been indicated and I parked near the front door. After knocking several times a kindly fellow appearing to be about my grandfather's age with long gray-black braids opened the door. He quickly stepped outside and pulled the door shut behind him as if to prevent anyone inside from seeing him converse with me.

I introduced myself and Grandpa, identifying us as natives of the Palouse Country. Arthur Tomeo's eyes immediately brightened and he almost shouted, "Have you ever heard of place called Rock Lake?" "Yes," I replied, "we have been there many times." "Well that's my home country!" he said pridefully. "My father and uncles, Tomeo, Skolumkee, and Tesh Palouse; they were all raised there with my grandfather. *He was Chief Kamiakin.* Not far from the lake is Steptoe Butte—our "power mountain!" My mother's people were the Poweens from Almota and Penawawa." The word "Palouse Country" seemed to release a torrent of memory from the old man. While we both remained on the stoop I clumsily jotted down as best I could his many recollections of trips back to his grandfather's and great-grandfather's burial sites in the Palouse, information on family connections, and the story of how Kamiakin's wives brought their families to the reservation. Through the eyes of Arthur Tomeo Kamiakin and other friendships forged through his acquaintance, like Emily Peone and Mary Jim, I came to glimpse the Palouse primeval—a vast labyrinth of whorls and swirls as if a deific signature thumbprint.

Palouse Country pioneer doctor and poet John W. Lockhart expressed in the florid verse of "The Palouse and Progress" (1906) the tenor of the region's halcyon days as if poised for an period of unprecedented change:

On Steptoe's famous heights old Progress stood,
And viewed, with practiced eye, the broad domain
With the range of vision. The great Palouse,
With her rugged hills and hoary mountains,
With their mighty forests and liquid hands,
Of azure hue, winding their tortuous
And devious ways among the bunchgrass
Hills, to the great ocean of the West,
To swell her fair bosom, that she may bear
A nation's commerce, and proclaim her worth
Among the crowns of ancient heritage.
To eastward the high rolling prairies,
Buttressed with the everlasting dolomite,
Upheaved and seamed and creviced by the strong,

Covered layer upon layer, fathoms deep,
With the disintegration and decay
Of ages, awaiting the grand processional
Of inventive genius to fructify
The fertile soil, and there produced in rich
And rare abundance, rivaling in grand
Profusion the luxuriant storehouse
Of Egypt, harvests of cereal food
To feed the great Eternal purpose.

Height upon height they rise, in undulations,
Vast as the troubled sea when wind and storm
Hold high carnival and would feign uproll
The angry waves to lash their fury out
In that bright firmament of peace....

Verdant Thumbprint   *South of Farmington, Washington*

Spring Velvet

South of Potlatch, Idaho

Chapter I:

THE REGIONAL SETTING AND NATIVE PEOPLES

"There was a strong spirit in the river there; those that saw him became medicine men. It made a powerful song, 'Shaa..., Shaa....'

—Mary Jim, 1979

The Palouse region covers that part of Eastern Washington and Northern Idaho in the Palouse River basin as well as adjacent lands characterized by a rolling terrain of fertile loessal soils. This area covers approximately 4,000 square miles and lies largely in Washington's Whitman and Spokane counties, the eastern third of Adams County, and in Idaho's Latah County. Nearly seventy percent of the land is arable, composed of deep deposits of rich but fragile topsoil which cover immense layers of brown-black basalt. This bedrock shield is up to 10,000 feet thick resulting from successive lava flows through fissures across the Columbia Plateau during the late Miocene Epoch between six and seventeen million years ago when the area of today's Palouse Country, before the Cascade uplift, received as much as fifty inches of annual rainfall to host a mixed forest of conifers, maples, water tupelo, and oak similar to America's southeastern bald cypress swamps of today. The Palouse is bounded by the Snake and Clearwater rivers on the south and Idaho's imposing Bitterroot and Clearwater Mountains to the east. The evergreen forests of these eastern uplands extend across the northern half of Spokane County along a line roughly corresponding to the deepest penetration of the great Pleistocene glaciers to form the region's northern limit.

The Cheney-Palouse lobe of the Channeled Scablands comprises the region's western boundary which extends from the timber line near Tyler, Washington south to the mouth of the Palouse River. Annual rainfall increases from an average of fourteen inches in the western Palouse prairies to eighteen inches in the central Palouse Hills and up to twenty-two inches in the foothills of the eastern mountains. This pattern corresponds to a rise in elevation from 1,200 feet in the southwest corner of the Palouse prairie to the fringe of the Clearwater Palouse Range at 2,800 feet, almost exactly one inch of precipitation for every hundred feet of elevation. Variations in soil fertility developed over the ages due to increasing rainfall eastward led to climax vegetation associated with the Palouse's three climatic and life zones: Upper Sonoran in the western Palouse, Arid Transition across the central Palouse Hills, and Canadian in the eastern mountain uplands (H. St. John, 1937).

Looming above the panoramic Palouse near the heart of the region stands a promontory revered by the native peoples known today as Steptoe Butte. To the Palouse Indians it was *Eomoshtoss*, a sacred high place of spirit quests and the abode of mythical Bull Elk. An honored figure in tribal folklore, this creature was said to have found sanctuary during the time of the Animal People in the cleft of the butte's eastern face. Its majestic antlers stretched toward the summit and remain visible today. To the area's first European-American explorers, who dubbed it "Pyramid Peak" for resembling Egypt's great monument to Cheops, the butte served like a mariner's landmark, a strange island in an oceanic maelstrom of earthen waves cresting with wind-pulsed native wheatgrasses and fescues. Before the sextant and plow demarcated and denuded these fertile swells, they were seasonally transformed from soft springtime viridian hues with sun-tolerant wildflowered splashes of bluebells, flaming Indian paintbrush, and bright yellow arrowleaf balsamroot into summer and fall's muted green-brown pastels mixed in the bunchgrass billows. The butte continues to serve as a landmark Palouse portal to Native Americans today. On several occasions while in the company of Nez Perces returning to Lapwai from the Colville Reservation or with Coeur d'Alenes headed east from Warm Springs, I have heard elders say, "When I see Steptoe Butte, I know that I am home."

With its top at 3,612 feet often shrouded in purling clouds, Steptoe Butte is the highest and most ancient formation in the Palouse Hills. Its ascendance preceded the plateau lava flows by eons and is

*Morning Mist**   *South of Potlatch, Idaho*

composed of billion-year-old sandpaper orange quartzite related geo-
logically to the eastern upland shore of Precambrian metamorphic
strata twenty miles beyond in the foothills of northwestern Idaho's
rugged cordillera. I still look with awe at a chip of the butte given to
me as a paperweight. Formations similar to Steptoe Butte create an
inland atoll within this restless sea of grains and grasses which it is the
most western in a chain of prominents that includes Stratton, Granite,
and Kamiak buttes and Moscow and Tekoa mountains. A timeless
sentinel cloaked in beige and ochred beauty, Steptoe Butte's vista provides evidence of the surrounding terrain's geologic origins and a
point to view the twisted course of a river that unites its varied landscapes.

The Eastern Palouse Uplands

The Palouse River headwaters are born in the clear stony brooks
of Idaho's Hoodoo and Clearwater mountains and fed by tributaries
emerging from the Thatuna Range located between the river's north
and south forks. These eastern uplands are composed of the western
buttes' parent belt quartzites and argillites that rose with the Rocky
Mountains when the Cascade Range had not yet emerged above the
Pacific waters. In the formative processes of this early Mesozoic Age
of explosive Rocky Mountain stratovolcanoes, hot magmatic fluids
under great pressure penetrated this younger earth's crust and brought

certain metals in gaseous state nearer the surface to form soluble compounds like gold chloride and aluminum-iron silicate. In places where
water penetrated to great depth these compounds dissolved, mixed
with the magma, and were forced through fissures with other solubles
like silicon dioxide, or quartz, to create veins containing precious metals and alamandine garnet crystals. Where this petrographic drama
transpired under ancient weathered surfaces as in the Hoodoos, these
deposits were worn by water until soft yellow flakes, larger nuggets,
and violet-red gemstones fell out into streams which usually held these
heavy particles near their sources. As in other high places along the
Pacific Slope, indications of this placer gold in North Idaho resulted in
nineteenth century regional rushes as prospectors flocked to the
rumored Eldorados. Dodecahedron-faced garnets and rainbow-colored
"harlequin" opals have also been sought in the eastern Palouse as the
region's only semi-precious jewelry stones.

The eastern Palouse hosts a complex forest habitat that began several miles east of Steptoe Butte where scattered ponderosa pine grows
among the ubiquitous native grasses along the Palouse River with willow browse and brambles of wild rose and flowering shrubs. The
spotted timber gradually becomes a mixed forest as the moister climate eastward brings forth stands of Western larch, or tamarack—a
deciduous conifer, and Douglas fir. Pines were dominant on the
southern exposures. Thickets of black mountain huckleberry, service-

berry, and buckbrush flourish in sunlit meadows where their leaves and mountain bunchgrass have fed creatures of horn and hoof for centuries. Witness to a thousand years of whitened furies and springtime chinooks were stands of giant red cedar on Kamiak Butte and Moscow Mountain. The tallest trees in these ancient forests rose to heights of 250 feet and some remain in threatened huddles as the oldest living things in the region.

The nation's largest white pine forest mixed with larch, Engelmann spruce, and other conifers commences at about 3,000 feet and covers the upper elevations of the Clearwater Mountains with old growth several hundred years old and often over two hundred feet high. These areas provide summer habitat to several songbird species including yellow warblers and red-brested nuthatches as well as the smaller ruby-crowned kinglets, pine siskins, and black-capped chickadees. Beneath their flight patterns grow delicate orchid-like pink lady slippers and yellowbells that favor the canopy shade. Pioneer Palouse residents hunted these sylvan uplands for wild game and exploited the region's forests as sources of lumber and fuel unavailable on the bunchgrass prairies.

The Palouse Hills

When the undulant verdue of the central Palouse emerges from winter's chill, the snowdrifts viewed from Steptoe Butte highlight a barchan pattern of hills aligned northwest by southeast with recurrent concave headwalls of northeast-facing exposure. These features indicate hills of loess, or wind-blown silt, deposited by ancient winds from the Pasco Basin into gigantic earthen dunes connected by twisting benches, amphitheatres, and saddles. The fine-grained sediments far to the southwest had accumulated under prehistoric Lake Lewis after its appearance during the late Pliocene nearly a million years ago. These waters stretched across the lower Columbia Basin until the early Pleistocene when changes in weather and surface uplift reduced the lake to massive piles of dessicated silt. During the evaporation process microscopic crystals of silicon dioxide bonded together into distillate amber and gray-brown nodules to form some of the continents most spectacular chalcedony and banded agates.

The Lake Lewis deposits are strikingly evident in the cream-colored cemented sandstones and chalky siltstones of the Ringold Formation some 1,000 feet in depth which form the White Bluffs along the Columbia River north of Pasco. The lower elevations of Steptoe Butte and its metamorphic neighbors as well as the Palouse's irregular basaltic overlay became inundated with these displaced particles along with periodic dustings from Cascade volcanic ashfalls. Wafted gusts of primordial winds patiently formed the textured tiers of the region's fertile hills and sculpted a curving labrynth of swales, ridges, and slopes unique to the Palouse. The occasional dust storms

White Bluffs, Columbia River   *North of Pasco, Washington*

that today reduce the late summer sun to a gossamer balloon invariably blow from the same direction as these ancestral currents and give some indication of the suffocating swirls that visited the region for ages. Further evidence of this peculiar earthen displacement is found in the size of particulate grains in the Palouse Hills that range from the heavy, course sands of the Juniper Dunes Wilderness Area southwest of Kahlotus to the fine yellow subsoil silts of the eastern Palouse (A. Busacca, 1991).

Large prehistoric mammals lumbered throughout the hills seeking seasonal forage along grassy bottomlands during the later Pleistocene. Camel, giant sloth, antelope, mastodon, bison, and bighorn sheep which have been excavated at a dozen sites along the western tier of the Palouse Hills from Washtucna to Rosalia and many are displayed at W.S.U.'s Conner Museum of Natural History. Images of the bison and sheep appear in the red and yellow pictographs and chipped petroglyphs at Buffalo Eddy near Lewiston which are believed to be hundreds of years old. A fascinating array of four mammoth skeletons, a human skull, spearpoint, and other artifacts were unearthed a short distance south of Latah in 1876 by Henry Coplan and his five sons from which was assembled the largest skeleton of the species ever found in North America. Standing thirteen feet high at the shoulder and with fossilized ivory tusks curving ten feet in length, the popular attraction was shown at circuses throughout the West until being eventually acquired by Chicago's Field Museum where it serves today as one of its most popular exhibits (J. Nisbet, 2001).

The protected northeast crescents of the hills are shielded from the prevailing southwesterlies and lie silently in shadow throughout most winter days limiting evaporation and allowing deep drifts to form which often remain into spring. This phenomenon reoccurred over millenia penetrating the headwall soils with greater moister to foster banks of prodigious prairie and accumulations of enriching humus. Variations in biotic growth created a palette of topsoil browns across each hill's fertile patina with the three microenvironments including a steeper leeward sidehill and draw of black earth and greatest fertility, an exposed ridge of intermediate chestnut soil, and the more gentle but drier and

lighter southwest-facing slope. As precipitation increases across the central Palouse, three principal topsoil types of increasing fertility similarly characterize the hills from east to west known progressively as the Walla Walla, Athena, and Palouse associations.

Blue bunch wheatgrass, blue bunchgrass, ryegrass, and other mixed prairie perennials predominated on the legendary rolling Palouse Hills which provided luxurious forage for deer, bison, antelope, and in recent times, the Indians' vast horse herds that had descended from Spanish stock brought to New Mexico and New Spain in the 16th century. Several of these native grassland species are being reintroduced to the Palouse through the 1985 Conservation Reserve Program that has idled vast tracts of western Palouse farmland that was once in production. The Palouse Indians referred to the wild graminae species simply as *wasku*, or forage grass. In early summer the prairie base was a tufted universe of slender stalks, emerging petioles, and curling leaves inhabited by herbivorous nations of crickets, beetles, and grasshoppers. Equipped with tiny serrated sickle

PALOUSE COUNTRY MAMMOTH SKELETON

Eomoshtoss (Steptoe Butte)   *North of Colfax, Washington*

jaws, these species were integral to the grassland's ecological renewal by their ingestion of vegetative growth and its deposition into forms essential to plant nutrition.

Biblical numbers of wraithlike mayflies, midges, and damselflies still appear with the first warm days of spring to feed neotropical creatures of larger wing that nest in the Palouse during seasonal migrations including shimmering calliope and Rufus hummingbirds. Birds of prey like the prairie falcon and sparrow hawk that reside in the Palouse throughout the year were also capture dragonflies, moths, and other large insects flying against lucent summer skies. Under ground the patient labor of earthworms, one nearly footlong extinct species (*D. ameriicanas:* Magascolecidae) being unique to the Palouse, work diligently in the fibrous darkness to transform soil minerals into organics also usable by prairie flora. Their infinite twisting tunnels together with the penetrations of decaying roots kept the ground open to aeration and percolation (D. Bezdicek, 2003; C. Schroeder, 1958).

Five large tribes of the grass family (Poaceae) representing at least eighty-give native species once blanketed the Palouse in a rippling expanse of prodigious fecundity. These varieties were described by pioneer botantists Charles Piper and R. Kent Beattie who assembled a comprehensive taxonomy of grasses that formed the woof and weft of the Palouse Country patina and described them in *Flora of the Palouse Region* (1901). These five principal native grass groupings below are distinguished by the number and arrangement of the miniscule spikelet flowers during inflorescence.

Panicae: Spikelets with one perfect flower or neutral and perfect flowers which fall with the seed—previously widespread on the sandy banks of the Snake River (e.g., *Panicum barbipulvinatum*).

Phalarideae: Spikelets with one perfect flower which does not fall with the seed—typically occurring in wet places, and often in shallow water as with reed canary grass.

Agrostideae: Spikelets with a staminate or neutral flower in addition to the perfect one—found in both dry and moist places including *Calamagrostis rubescens*, the most abundant grass in the eastern Palouse pine forests.

Aveneae: Spikelets with a perfect and an imperfect flower which do not fall with the seed—including the once abundant annual

Deschampsia calycina and introduced members of the oats family.

Festuceae: Spikelets with two or more perfect flowers on a longer modified leaf (bract)—the widespread *bromus* (which later included foreign cheatgrass), *poa*, and *fescue* genera.

Chlorideae: Spikelets which do not fall with the seed and are crowded in two rows—coarse perennial grasses relatively rare in the Palouse.

Hordeae: Spikelets with two or more perfect flowers which do not fall with the seed and are arranged in opposite rows—including the Palouse Country's famed six native wheatgrass (*Agropyron*) and five ryegrass (*Elymus*) species.

In addition, some forty varieties of grass-like sedges, rushes, and reeds grew primarily in wetland areas. The sedge known as wool grass, however, preferred the drier areas of the western Palouse and would become a notorious pioneer plow-breaker. At least nine species of nutritious Lomatium were found along the Snake and Palouse river bluffs and on talus slopes. These plants intermixed with Poaceae members to create a complex Palouse prairie ecology of perennial, seed-producing, herbaceous mixtures. Several species had adapted to unique Palouse environmental niches of soil moisture, alkalinity, chemistry, and climate. The flame-colored blossoms of sphaerostigma are only found in the vicinity of Sprague Lake while rare orange-flowered balsam and purple Jacob's Ladder grow along Rock Lake. A unique pale green rush (*J. confusus*) exists along the forest perimeter near present Spangle and a potentilla of yellow petals is restricted to moist meadows along central Rebel Flat Creek. White-flowered dogbane appears among tufted goldenrod only in the Albion lowlands. The Pullman area hosts the Palouse's only growth of leafy, white-flowered *Piperia elegans* and spiky-podded entanglings of the tall grass *Calamagrosis macouniana*.

The microenvironments of several regional geographic features also weave unique patterns of uncommon species into the region's botanical tapestry. The lower slopes of Steptoe Butte hosts a densely tufted fescue (*F. hallii*) and reed meadow grass in the surrounding lowlands. Multicolored beard-tongue and pink-petaled Claytonia are fleshy herbs found only to the south on the slopes of Kamiak Butte. The pine-covered ridges of the Thatuna Hills north of Moscow shelter the delicate blue-blossomed bellflower amid one of the region's few stands of the bromegrass *B. eximius*. Clusters of scraggly hackberry grow on the basalt bluffs along the lower Palouse and Snake rivers while serviceberry bushes are found on the grassland bluffs east of Central Ferry. Copses of cinnamon-colored almond willow are located in the same areas where gentle springtime whirlwinds bring drowsy carousels of catkin and cattail cotton. A sea green sedge (*C. aristatus*) is found only at Almota and a densely tufted wheatgrass (*A. flexuosum*) and head-high ryegrass (*E. leckenbyi*) favored the sandy bars and lower hillsides near Wawawai.

Generations of wildlife browsing across slopes that were especially steep combined with the effect of annual frost heaves to create horizontal terracettes upon the hills. These natural stairsteps of mellow loam combined with the thick bunchgrass cover and rootlets to sponge up precipitation and deter any erosion. The waters of the Palouse River were clear throughout the year and while salmon were not found above Palouse Falls, trout, whitefish, and freshwater clams were plentiful in the upper river and its tributaries. Turtles were common along the water and, along with the mythical trickster Coyote, were often featured in tribal folktales to explain the origin of the natural world. According to Indian elders, the Palouse Hills were formed by *Spilya* (Coyote), who "outsmarted himself" in an attempt to be more clever than the other Animal People with whom he once shared the land. He scooped the earth into the distinctive pattern of undulating hills in a vain attempt to defeat Turtle and his brothers in a race from the Snake River to Spokane country. The story offered more than entertainment and explanation for it taught Indian youth the futility of deception and the value of persistence.

The serpentine Palouse River swims through the heart of the hills

PALOUSE FALLS, 1859 (STEVENS REPORT)

along a shallow western course beneath the base of Steptoe Butte, fed by quiet grassy streams that bore sibilant designations in the languages of the native peoples: *Mocallisah* (North Palouse Fork), *Ingossamen* (Pine Creek), *Oraytayous* (Rock Creek), and *Cherana* (Cow Creek). These verdant bottomlands have hosted a more diverse flora with isolated pines and clumps of willow, black hawthorne, and cottonwood brightened by the seasonal blossoms of golden currant bushes and tangled honeysuckle vines with rows of fiery tubular flowers. An imminence of redolent meadow wildflower blooms appear throughout spring and summer with bluebells, wild hyacinth, buttercups, purple iris, and yellow asters while sugar bowl clematis grows among riverbank conifers on southern exposures. The fuzzy purple heads of lupine were gathered by area Indians as grave decorations.

Low trees along Palouse streambeds provide habitat for the spherical twig and mudded mansions of magpies draped in their distinctive feathered robes of white and iridescent black, ever anxious to investigate and noisily render opinions in any riparian dispute. The magpie is the only bird with a greater length from beak to tail feather than its wingspan. Red-winged blackbirds also inhabit stream bank willows and arrive to nest several weeks earlier than their more aggressive yellow-headed cousins who attempt similar songs of guttural prattle. Each spring and summer clouds of delicate, white flowered ocean spray hang along the river and streambanks, held aloft on green stems that harden into brittle tracery each fall. (The present riverine stands of poison hemlock are Europeon invaders.) The sweet scent of pink roses emerges from thickets with scarlet wands of osier dogwood along creeksides. Mourning doves, mallards, and mergansers are common along the riverine brambles while badgers lumber along trails to their hillside burrows. Bobcats and coyotes prey upon pocket gophers, mice, ground squirrels, and other rodents that dwell in the adjacent rocky bluffs and surrounding hills. Birds, animals,

*Palouse River Canyon**

24

South of Washtucna, Washington

and valley flora draw life daily from the river which can often be traced for miles from Steptoe's heights at dawn by tissues of fog rising from the waters to meet the spectral sun.

The Channeled Scablands

Appearing abruptly twenty miles west of Steptoe Butte is an alien landscape with evidence of unimaginable cataclysm.The same panorama that evokes Dantesque visions of wrath from some travelers has been extensively studied by NASA scientists investigating similar Martian features. The Cheney-Palouse channel of the scablands represents the western boundary of the Palouse region. But the term "scablands" is an unkind name obscuring the area's zephyred melodies and mysteries. The land is alive with biological diversity in spite of past gargantuan assaults. The terrain was formed after the failure of massive ice dams near the mouth of the Clark Fork River in northern Idaho that had created massive glacial Lake Missoula some 15,000 years ago. The lake grew to cover 3,000 square miles across western Montana and contained approximately six hundred cubic miles of water—larger than the volume of Lake Erie. When pressure and melting due to a warming trend caused the ice dam to break, the lake surged into an explosive flood, termed a "joekulhaup," moving with a volume larger than in any similar event indicated on the planet. The lake may have filled and drained dozens of times over the last eight hundred millenia recurrently sending forth walls of water thundering southwest toward the lower Columbia and Pacific Ocean.

Unable to contain such volume in the Columbia's ancient canyon course, the onslaught tore across the soft rolling grasslands, which were violently "scabbed" or cut to bedrock, and formed three major drainages across the Columbia Plateau. The easternmost is the Cheney-Palouse lobe which contains massive boulders lying as ancient monuments carried from the Rockies, etched and shattered by mutilative force. These erratics are commonplace above the shallow soil and glacial outwash on the vast prairies and mesas from Cheney to Kahlotus. As the unimpeded waves sought declivities for escape, a peripheral branch of the eastern flow engorged what was likely an insequent streambed to form a torrential trench carving Hole-in-the-Ground's grandiose pavillioned walls, Rock Lake's incredible depth,

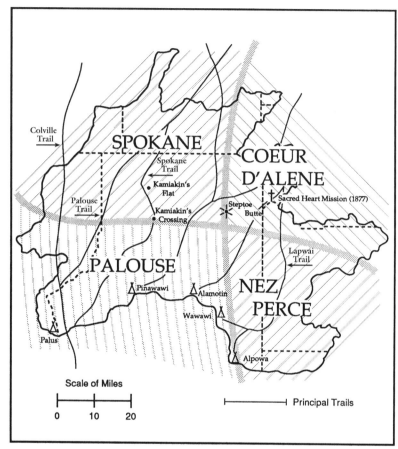

PALOUSE AREA TRIBAL GROUPINGS, c. 1850

and churned out the Rock Creek and lower Palouse River canyons. The ancestral Palouse River ran through Washtucna and Esquatzel coulees into the Columbia River at present Pasco until its course was diverted southward at Little Palouse Falls during the floods (J. Allen, M. Burns, and S. Sargent, 1986).

To the native tribes Rock Lake was known as "Never Freezing Water" in which were confined the remains of a great reptilian monster that had terrorized both humans and animals long ago. In response to the people's prayers for deliverance from the pestilence,

26

the Great Spirit slew the creature with a huge stone knife which then was used to tear the ground open for a grave. The dismembered creature was cast to the bottom and the chasm filled with water. Although tranquility to the region was restored, Indian legend held that the monster's tail did not die and periodically thrashed to the surface in menacing fury. For this reason Rock Lake was rarely fished by Indians who deemed it a fearful place and their stories of its creation may explain why pioneer travelers through the Palouse referred to it as "Specter Lake."

The same epochal forces that eroded the region's western loessal veneer and upper streambed strata penetrated at greater depth to fashion the lower Palouse River Canyon. Stretching from the confluence of the Palouse with the Snake River to Palouse Falls, the canyon stretches for five miles through a corporeal world of stair-stepped igneous solidity. Sparsely covered by clumps of scabland sagebrush, large-leaved forbs, scarlet Indian paintbrush, and bursts of ryegrass and bunchgrass, this Upper Sonoran zone of shrub steppe is home to coyotes and jackrabbits, marmots, rattlesnakes, and burrowing owls. Geese, canvasbacks, redhead ducks, and other migratory fowl find refuge on the many small lakes and in the sheltered river canyons of the western Palouse. These domains reveal austere clues to the mysteries of the land's creation in the lichen-painted sides of successive lava flows that lie in oppressive stacks.

Tens of thousands of years may have elapsed between these fissured Miocene outpourings giving rise to diverse prehistoric flora and fauna that was entombed beneath the flows. The average lava eruption resulted in a basaltic layer fifty to one hundred feet thick and the several flows dramatically evident along the lower Palouse River constitute but a cap upon related formations nearly two miles thick. Each flow erupted through lengthy fissures from which the hot vicious swells oozed for dozens of miles or more. As the molten rock cooled inward from both surfaces, the bottom tier often formed basaltic colonnades of jointed columns which supported an upper entablature of downward radiating fans and irregular shapes. The exposed crowns of each level are porous, highly weathered, and overlook rocky talus slopes below Palouse Falls that cascade beyond the fractured cliffs toward the distant canyon floor (W. Johns, 1983).

Located five miles above the river's mouth, Palouse Falls is a deafening cataract throughout the spring that pours down nearly two hundred feet into a spectacle of rainbowed spume. The falls pour over a basaltic layer some 15.5 million years old that divides the lower Grande Rhonde Flows from the Wanapam and subsequent flows that substantially ended abruptly some fourteen million years ago. The Palouse Indians knew the lower river as a favored fishing area and had several seasonal camps amid the quiet copses of Osage orange and hackberry. The tribe's namesake, which was later given to the vast domain over which they ranged and knew intimately, was their principal village of *Palus* located on the right bank of the river at its confluence with the Snake. The site was at the historic crossroads where the ancient east-west river route from the Columbia to Nez Perce country met the main north-south Indian trail leading from the Walla Walla Valley to the land of the Spokanes. The word Palus, meaning "Standing Rock," referred to a basaltic monolith central to Palouse Indian cosmology located a short distance upstream.

According to their ancient lore, in the time of the Animal People four Giant Brothers armed with spears attacked Beaver who peacefully resided near his lodge at present Hole-in-the-Ground. A terrific fight ensued during which Beaver clawed and chewed out the Rock Lake channel, one of the deepest lakes in the region with areas reaching

"STANDING ROCK" (RIGHT) IN THE SNAKE RIVER NEAR LYONS FERRY, c. 1900 (MASC, WSU LIBRARIES)

down 325 feet. Beaver tore his way toward the Snake River and where he beat his tail along this route small falls were formed along the lower Palouse River. He was struck again at *Aput Aput* (Falling Water) where in his pain Beaver cut the castellated formations and sheer cliffs that formed Palouse Falls. The massive creature finally fell from his wounds where the rivers met and his heart was turned to stone. The Palouse people were said to have sprung from this part of Beaver and Indian youth were taught to affirm courage as the tribe's most noble trait (E. Clark, 1953).

Marmes Man and Walsákwit

In anticipation of lower canyon flooding to be caused by the completion of Lower Monumental Dam in 1965, WSU archaeologists led by Richard Daughtery, Roald Fryxell, and Carl Gustafson began excavations in the summer of 1962 at the mouth of a cavernous rockshelter on property along the Palouse River owned by Roland and Joanne Marmes (mar´-mus). Located near the west bank of the river approximately a mile from its confluence with the Snake, the scientists were encouraged by their initial findings of artifacts and prehistoric animal remains at what became known as the Marmes Rockshelter. By 1965 they had penetrated beneath the thick ash layer from the massive eruption of Mt. Mazama that formed Oregon's Crater Lake some 6,700 years ago. In the summer of 1965 the first remains of "Marmes Man" were found at a depth of fourteen feet near the bones of an Arctic fox, pine marten, and other species associated with a significantly colder climate. Several weeks later two more individuals and artifacts were discovered including a delicately fashioned whalebone needle and coastal olivella necklace shells dating back ten millennia. The bones were determined to be from the burials of two young adults and a child about seven years old and were the oldest human remains ever recovered in the Western Hemisphere.

In the words of American Archaeological Society president Hannah Worthington, the Marmes Rockshelter constituted America's foremost "calendar of the centuries," but soon fell victim to the backwaters of the dam. Another discovery of major anthropological significance was made in July, 1996 southwest of the Palouse periphery near the confluence of the Snake and Columbia rivers where the nearly complete skeleton of Kennewick Man was found. These remains, containing a Cascade Phase spearpoint embedded in the left hip bone, were dated approximately 7,400 years B.C. These individuals are among those reverently referred to by Plateau peoples as the "Ancient Ones," and the tribal governments of the Inland Northwest's reservations have been embroiled in protracted legal struggles in federal courts fighting for their reburial as a sacred responsibility (P. Rice, 2001).

Based in large part on Palouse and other Indian oral traditions describing the massive floods, people, and creatures of these past ages, U. S. Secretary of Interior Bruce Babbitt ruled in favor of the tribes in 1999. Though still contested in court by scientists who contend that the cultural affinity of groups separated by such great time is unlikely, Babbitt's landmark decision affirmed that these stories, known to the Palouses as *walsákwit*, provide valid ancestral links between these prehistoric people of the Columbia Plateau and those living here today. The archaeological record does indicate that few humans probably lived in the region 10,000 years ago years ago but a thousand years later evidence of seasonal human occupation exits throughout the Columbia Plateau, from The Dalles to Hell's Canyon and from the lower Palouse River Canyon to Kettle Falls.

These first residents ranged widely using travel routes along Pacific shorelines and inland waterways to gather plant foods, hunt small and large mammals, and to find favorable salmon fishing sites after the great ice sheets melted. The beginning of a significant warming trend some 7,500 years ago, continuing until approximately 2,000 B.C., was accompanied by the appearance of fishnets and tackle assemblies along the Columbia and Snake rivers. The availability of salmon as a reliable staple of the native people's diet brought about more seasonal and regional migration patterns with pit-house villages appearing on the lower Snake River around 3,000 B.C. At that time King Menes united Upper and Lower Egypt to establish the first dynasty, the Sumerians were beginning to grow barley, and a thousand years remained before Abraham would leave Ur for the Promised Land.

An abundance of nephrite and diorite pestles along the lower Snake River and at the Marmes site dating from 3,000 B.C. suggests that the milling of roots and berries also came into widespread use at that time. Finely flaked projectile points show a gradual transition from use for hunting large prehistoric mammals with enormous Clovis spearpoints associated with the earliest occupation sites to those half the size for thrusting with an atlatl and finally, the beautifully crafted smaller arrowheads that came with the introduction of the bow around 500 A.D. I recall occasionally spotting artifacts of the latter sort during hikes in my youth along the Palouse River and Union Flat Creek. Invariably they were knapped into exquisitely symmetrical shapes and made from the widely assorted colors of semiprecious cryptocrystallines—yellow opals, banded agates, snowy chert, blood red jasper, obsidian, and transparent chalcedony.

Emily Peone told me that the Indians of her great-grandparents' generation were quick to adopt useful innovations from the first *Suyapus* (Whites) who came to the Inland Northwest. The name was likely derived from the hats worn by the early fur traders. Raised to a great extent by her own great-grandmother, Mary Owhi Moses, Emily recalled listening attentively in their cabin near Nespelem to her stories about times long ago. "Whenever we would take Mary with us to dig roots," Emily recalled, "whether toward the Yakima or Palouse, she could point out something special that had once happened on most any hill or in any valley. 'Here's where Chief Moses kept his horses in summer, there's where we traded with the King George's men [Hudson's Bay traders].'" Just as Eleanor of Aquitaine was considered "Mother of Europe" in the twelfth century, so Mary Owhi Moses served as an honored matriarch among the Columbia Plateau tribes during the nineteenth century. She was an especially venerated elder who had survived the cataclysmic events that shaped the region's history during an unprecedented lifetime of change.

Born in 1829, Mary Moses (Sanclow) witnessed the arrival of the first fur traders and missionaries to the Inland Northwest. She was the daughter of the Yakama Chief Owhi and first cousin to Chief Kamiakin—principal leaders with whom Governor Stevens negotiated the Yakima Treaty of 1855. Her brother was the warrior Qualchan whom Col. George Wright hung at Smith's Ford near Spokane in 1858. As a young woman, Mary became the youngest wife of the Columbia-Sinkiuse Chief Moses, whose political skills were instru-

mental in establishing the Colville Reservation in the 1880s. Emily Peone was one of dozens of descendants of Moses and Mary's children who lived on reservations throughout the Northwest. Mary Owhi Moses lived to the astounding age of 118 and spent her last years in Emily's household where she provided rare and unusually informative insight into events surrounding the wars of the 1850s and the tribes' transition to reservation life.

As I walked down Emily Peone's front steps when leaving her home in Nespelem, she grabbed a rootdigger that was leaning against the house and said, "See, the women also knew a good thing when they saw it! Mary grew up with one made out of wood, but look how they fashioned this one from hoop iron. Never gets dull!" She held it up and I nearly pierced myself feeling the tip. "Here, you take it," she said with a laugh and customary generosity. "I've got plenty and you're bound to run into some camas on the way back to my homeland" (E. Hunn, 1990; E. Peone, 1981).

Sacred Creatures and the Seasonal Round

At the dawn of the nineteenth century perhaps 2,000 American Indians lived in the Palouse Country for most of the year, frequenting various favored places to hunt, gather roots, pasture horses, and fish. Their numbers are difficult to estimate given the fluid nature of Plateau Indian culture; however numerous winter villages existed among the Sahaptin-speaking Palouse (*Paluspam*) and Nez Perce (*Nimiiipu*) tribes along the lower Snake River while Coeur d'Alenes (*Schitsuumsh*) and Spokanes (*Spukanee*) who Interior Salish languages also made extensive use of the northern region. As with most Indians of North America, the Columbia Plateau tribes had a close relationship with the natural world. Palouse Indian elder Mary Jim related that "the land was our religion. We considered the earth to be our Mother because it provided us all food. The Great Spirit (*Imepship*) had placed us on our Earth Mother (*Imephsha*) who blessed us with her nutritious roots, berries, and vegetables. The Great Spirit had created the deer, antelope, and elk, and these animals shared the earth with the Indian people." Like other Indians on the Plateau, the world of Palouse area tribes revolved about a yearly cycle or seasonal round that covered an immense territory. Beginning in the spring of each year, salmon swam out of the Pacific Ocean, fought their way up the great current of the Columbia River, and followed its tributaries upstream until they reached their spawning grounds in the Inland Northwest. Conditions were most favorable for fishing in May and from July through October.

The native peoples of the Palouse Country caught salmon by the thousands as these were part of the abundance given to them by the Creator. Both the physical and spiritual worlds were inseparable and both were derived from their relationship with the earth throughout the seasons. The spring renewal of life was strikingly evident in the resurgence of flow in the Snake and Spokane rivers and their tributaries. Fed by the melting waters of the Bitterroots and Blue Mountains, the Snake began to rise and carry with it a variety of debris from the high country. The animals felt the change as well, particularly the horses that still sported their heavy winter coats. Migration, trading, and raiding probably brought the first horses to the Inland Pacific Northwest by 1750. March was a time of much activity for the Indians who busied themselves in preparation for their journey onto the Columbia Plain. "We called this *Shai Tash,* 'Time to Move Out,'" recalled Mary Jim. "Those horses that were to make the trip out of the canyon were cut out from the herds. Many of these animals had not been ridden in some time, so the men mounted the skiddish ponies and rode them hard until they stopped bucking."

Men, women, and children alike then mounted the horses and began their jaunt to the root grounds while some family members remained along the rivers for the first salmon runs in May. For children like young Mary, traveling again and seeing the animals of the land was an exciting time. Linguistic indications of the Native People's intimacy with the natural world is evident in dozens of Sahaptin terms for plant species used for food, as medicine, or in fashioning baskets, mats, and other useful items. The Palouse and Nez Perce Sahaptin languages are among the most ancient spoken by Native Americans anywhere in the Western Hemisphere. Many Palouse names for birds were as much sung as spoken, in onomonopoetic mimicry of the creatures' calls—*áchay* (magpie), *miimím* (mourning dove) and *wawquilúk* (trumpeter swan), *khwalkwéhwai* (meadow lark), and a sentinel bird, *wawiyíkh* (whip-poor-will). Others were

known by their behavior or other distinct qualities including "dances together' (sage grouse), "traveler" (snow goose), and the prairie falcon, or "comes at you," America's only indigenous member of the Falconidae (M. Jim, 1979; E. Hunn and J. Selam, 1990).

Though not mutually intelligible, both Palouse and Nez Perce are members of the Macro-Penutian superlanguage family and are more closely related to Coastal Chinookan and even Mesoamerican tongues than Spokane and Coeur d'Alene Salish. Linguistic analysis have led some anthropologists to postulate that Sahaptin speakers may have descended from some of the earliest American Indian populations that migrated southward along the western Rockies at least 15,000 years ago before dividing into groups that continued south and west. Others chose to remain in the vast realm of the Inland Pacific Northwest where, according to their traditions, humans were formed from the body of giant creature and the land was prepared for their occupation by the Animal People.

The "winged seed" Lomatium family includes such familiar greens as parsley, dill, and celery. The nine species native to the Palouse, nutritious staples of the native diet, favored the shallow lithosols among rocky outcroppings. The appearance of blossoming Canby's lomatium, known to the Palouse and Nez Perce as *skolkul,* in late February and early March signaled the beginning of spring for Plateau rootdiggers. Union Flat Creek was called the Skolkul because of the four major rootgrounds found along its course (near present La Crosse, Wilcox, Union Center, and Colton). Among the other eight important tuberous lomatiums that grew along the Snake River and in the western Palouse were Gray's lomatium, or "Indian celery," Hamblen's lomatium, and yellow-flowered kouse (*L. cous*). Over twenty principal camas grounds covering up to several dozen acres each were located in the Palouse Country in vernal meadows at such places as Washtucna and Rock lakes, along Latah, Pine, and Union Flat creeks and the Palouse River, and in the fertile lowlands near present Colfax, the Pullman-Moscow area, and at the southeastern base of Steptoe Butte. Edible camas (*Q. quamash*) displays white or blue flowers and was gathered in vast quantities during early summer while the shunned death camas (*Z. venenosus*) presents yellow blossoms.

The rock rose, or bitterroot, also grew in the rocky soils of the western Palouse but was more abundant on the drier plains to the west. Along with the wild huckleberries that ripened in the fall on bushes clustered among the pines in the eastern Palouse, camas, kouse, and bitterroot were the four most important plant foods of the four Palouse Country tribes. Places favored by the Coeur d'Alenes and Spokanes for spring bitterroot and camas digging included the upper Palouse Country from *Nigualko* (Tensed) in the valley of the Palouse North Fork and northwesterly across the present Rockford, Spangle, and Cheney districts. Here the size of the roots and the ease of digging in the rich black loam attracted large tribal gatherings each spring (C. Piper and R. K. Beattie, 1914; S. Archer and C. Bunch, 1953; M. Jim, 1979).

Palouse area Indians gathered roots during their spring journey onto the Columbia Plain and Palouse Hills until the salmon began their movement up the Columbia River. When the bands learned of the spring run of the salmon, they returned to their permanent villages and prepared for fishing. Many varieties of fish were taken from the Snake and Spokane rivers and streams tributary to them including trout, whitefish, squawfish, suckers, chubs, and eels. Snake River white sturgeon were also fished although when mature some could reach twelve feet in length and weigh a half-ton—making them virtually impossible to capture. Three genera of the Salmonidae family of fishes were native to the Snake River including the genus *Oncorhynchus* with five species of Pacific salmon (Chinook or king, pink sockeye, humpback, silver or coho, and white-fleshed chum). *Salvelinus* members are the Dolly Varden, or bull trout, and brook trout, while the genus *Salmo* includes the anadromous steelhead and non-anadromous rainbow and cutthroat trout. With no major waterfalls for dip-netting on the lower Snake River, most salmon were taken by gill netting, weirs along small tributaries, or by gaffing spawning fish. Palouse area Indians also traveled to net fish at Celilo and Kettle falls, the two largest fisheries on the Columbia River. The annual catch of salmon and steelhead by Columbia Plateau tribes prior to White contact is conservatively estimated to have been 17,000,000 pounds. Fish accounted for approximately one-third of the Plateau Indian diet while roots and berries contributed about half. Game meat including venison and wild fowl substantially completed their nutritional needs (M. Jim, 1979; E. Hunn and J. Selam, 1990).

Salmon, however, were by far the most important fish to the Indians of the region. Besides being one of the most important sources of food, they held a special significance in the cosmology of the Indians. Most Plateau tribes of the Northwest held a thanksgiving ceremony in honor of the salmon as soon as the first fish was caught. All fishing in the area stopped when a man brought in the first salmon. It was cooked, usually boiled, and became the center of the rites. Everyone was issued a portion of water, to fill horn spoons or wooden vessels, and after a prayer was said, the water was drunk by all present. Another prayer was sung thanking the Creator for the fish. Everyone then took a portion of the salmon, ate it, and then took another sip of water. A lengthy prayer was sung and the remaining skeleton of the fish was returned to the water facing upstream. Once proper religious rites were completed for the sacred salmon, fishing resumed. Thousands of salmon were taken from the river, and each year they returned.

Fishing was very much a part of Plateau Indian lifeway as well as that of virtually all other Indians of the Pacific Northwest. The Palouse believed that the salmon runs began in the age of the Animal People. According to their legends Coyote had issued a challenge for anyone to break an immense elk antler. Various creatures tried including Eagle (*Khwayamayai*), Racoon (*Kalasya*), and Cougar (*Kwayawiyai*), but it was not until Salmon (*Nusuxya*) strained over the rack that it finally split with a thunderous clap. Burning with envy, the other competitors killed Salmon with their arrows but did not notice something fall from one of his wounds into the river. It was an egg that was carried all the way to the ocean where it eventually grew into another salmon. It later ascended the river to learn its origin and this journey began the cycle of salmon runs to the Palouse and other tribal domains of the Plateau. Coyote later taught the Palouse how to catch the salmon by using nets made of milkweed hemp (A. George; 1980).

After the spring and summer runs of salmon, many families left their villages to venture onto the Columbia Plateau or the lowland valleys in the Palouse Hills. They would travel to root grounds and camp to dig, hunt, and relax. Summers in the region were usually mild and dry. The children played games with a hoop and a pole or a bat and ball. Men and boys would practice and hone their skill as archers. One of the most enjoyable pursuits was horse racing. The Plateau Indians became great horse people soon after the introduction of these animals to the Plateau in the mid-eighteenth century, and men and women alike could care for and ride horses. They were well aware of the qualities that made a good horse, and they bred horses that were strong, fast, and smart. Although it is unlikely that they bred horses for color alone, some Indians prized the beautifully spotted Appaloosa horses (Palouse: *Mamin*, Nez Perce: *Tamslip*) and recognized their value as a medium of trade.

The late summer and fall were also important times to area Indians for hunting and digging, as well as for gatherings with neighboring tribes of the region. This time of the year also had a religious significance as the time when young people, boys and girls alike, were sent on their spirit quests. Youth from about the age of twelve went out alone to seek a spirit in remote places like the summit of Steptoe Butte. Similar places were located along the foothills and in the meadows of the Blue Mountains where tribal bands frequented fall hunting and berrying grounds. As the brisk autumn weather transformed the mountain slopes into fiery landscapes of red and yellow, young people sought their guardian spirits on such peaks as *Watniwash* (Spirit Mountain). *Taham Taham* (Cloudy Mountain) was avoided since the summit was a one-way portal to the Spirit World which humans were forbidden to enter. Animal People sentries clad in blue feathers and white bear hides stood high upon its slopes to warn seekers not to continue further into the foggy heights.

During the quest, a guardian spirit might come to them during a dream in the form of a wolf, cloud, bear, hail eagle, hawk, or other animal or natural phenomenon like hail or thunder. Protection and guidance could then be summoned for a lifetime through a song imparted to the seeker. After the youths experienced a few days of solitude, they returned to camp or elders of the tribe went to gather and feed them. The old men of the tribes, those of great wisdom, heard from the children about their experiences and interpreted dreams for the children who had now come of age. Such visions were not deemed fantasies but a deeply revered spiritual experience revealed through the imagination. The native peoples' specific knowledge of the regional landscape and its creatures informed their mythology and spirit quests. Human beings existed within a sacred circle of life that brought together past, present, and place in a nexus that transcended tense and tangibility (M. Jim, 1979; A. George, 1980).

Late summer meshed imperceptively with early fall and the bands moved gradually into that part of the seasonal round that took them to their favorite hunting grounds. The men killed larger game animals like deer and elk as well as grouse and water fowl. They prepared the meat for the coming winter while the women gathered berries and dug the last vestiges of camas and kouse. Wild gooseberries, thornberries, serviceberries, and blackberries were among the favorites of Palouse area Indians. Two varieties of elderberries were also picked, one from the prairie and one from the higher mountains. As the Indians moved their camps into the mountains where there was better hunting, the other variety of elderberry was picked. Also found in the higher country were the serviceberry, huckleberry, snowberry, and fireberry which sometimes were mixed with dried meat. The fireberry was so small that the Indians devised a small comb to pick the tiny fruit. Pine moss or bear-hair lichen was also collected in the high mountains, cooked underground like camas, and pounded into a fine treat that is still prized for its licorice-like flavor.

As winter approached, the many bands of Indians packed up their belongings and started on their journey back across the gentle valleys and rolling hills to their permanent villages along the Snake, Clearwater, and Spokane rivers. They were heavy laden with the prepared meat, berries, and roots. During the winter months family lodges became the center of much activity although the entire band usually gathered for the Guardian Spirit Dance. This was a sacred ceremony for Indians of the Palouse Country and demonstrated their affinity with their spirit guardians and the natural world. Because of inclement weather people spent much time inside or gathered around a communal fire along the river. While the women mended baskets and men repaired hunting and fishing gear or knapped new points, family elders shared their legends and tribal history with the children. Few could anticipate, however, the sweeping changes about to unfold as sailing vessels of exploration and trade from Europe and New England

Snake River Canyon   *Near Almota, Washington*

began appearing along the Pacific coastline. In September, 1805 a group of three dozen intrepid Americans and French Canadians, Nez Perce guides, and young woman with her infant son crossed Lolo Pass from the east.

Lewis and Clark and the Corps of Discovery

After an arduous trek across the Northern Rockies during which the Corps of Discovery was both befriended and rescued by Nez Perces, a name attributed to them by the Shoshones, Lewis and Clark entered the lower Snake River Valley in October, 1805. They named Potlatch Creek "Colter's Creek" for quick witted John Colter, one of Lewis's "nine young men from Kentucky" who all made the entire trip. Colter would earn fame for his legendary escape from Blackfeet Indians four years later when he was stripped of his clothes and received a brief headstart before given chase. Lewis wrote admiringly of the Nez Perces' horses which he described as "lofty, elegantly formed, active and durable.' He also noted some were colored "with large spots of white irregularly scattered and intermixed with the black-brown bay or some other dark color." In March, 1899 a surveyor found a Jefferson Peace Medal near the mouth of Potlatch Creek during railroad construction in the vicinity. One of the Corps of Discovery's Nez Perce guides through the region, Neeshnepark Keeook (Cut Nose), lived in a village near this place and was presented such a medal there by the captains during their return trip the following spring. This rare silver treasure, one of only about three dozen carried by Lewis and Clark, is now owned by the nez Perce Tribe and dis-

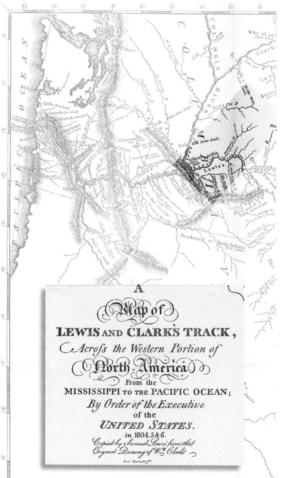

played at Spalding, Idaho's Nez Perce National Historic Park Museum. The explorers followed the Clearwater to its mouth near present Lewiston where the camped on October 10, 1805.

William Clark's diary entries for the next three days provide the first written account of the southern Palouse borderlands. On the 10th, he described the setting at this historic confluence: "We arrived at a large southerly fork [the Snake River] which is the one we were on with the Snake [Indian] nation. The country about the forks is an open plain on either side. The water of the south fork is greenish blue, the north [Clearwater] as clear as crystal. The Indians came down all the courses of this river on horses to view us as we were descending. The Pierced Nose Indians are stout, likely men, handsome women, and very dressy in their way. The dress of the men are a white buffalo robe or elk skin dressed with beads which are generally white, sea shells, and mother-of-pearl hung to their hair on a piece of otter skin. The women dress in a shirt of ibex [mountain sheep] skins which reach quite down to their ankles... ornamented with quilled brass, beads, shells, and curious bones."

On the following day the explorers continued on their quest to the Pacific: "We set out early and... passed a rapid at two miles. At six miles we came to at some Indian lodges and took breakfast. We purchased all the fish we could and seven dogs... for stores of provisions down the river. At this place [Almota] I saw a curious sweat house underground; with a small hole at top to... throw in the hot stones, which in[side] threw on as much water as needed to create the temperature of heat they wished. The country on either side is an

LEWIS & CLARK'S MAP SHOWING PALOUSE (DREWYER'S) RIVER, 1806

34

open plain and fertile after ascending a steep ascent of about 200 feet with not a tree of any to be seen on the river." On October 12, 1805 the party canoed nearly thirty miles and camped near present Riparia. *"We passed several stony islands today. The country as yesterday [is] open plains, no timber of any kind, a few hackberry bushes and willows excepted, and but a few drift trees to be found so that firewood is very scarce. The hills or ascents from the water are faced with a dark rugged stone."*

On the 13th the party passed the mouth of the Palouse River and Clark paid tribute to the useful presence of Sacajawea as a member of the epic expedition: *"The wife of Shabono [Charbonneau] our interpreter we find reconciles all the Indians as to our peaceful intentions. A woman with a party of men is a token of peace. We took all our canoes through this rapid without any injury. A little below passed another bad rapid [Texas Rapids].... Passed the mouth of a large creek [Tucannon River]. A little river [Palouse] in a starboard bend, immediately below a long bad rapid, in which the water is confined in a channel about twenty yards between rugged rocks for two miles above.... Here is a great fishing place, the timbers of several houses piled up, and a number of wholes of fishes. The bottom appears to have been made as a place of deposit for their fish for ages past."* The explorers' field map shows a village of tule-mat "cabins" on the west side of the Palouse River's mouth and burial "vaults" on the east side.

Three days later the explorers reached the great intertribal campground at the confluence of the Snake and Columbia rivers near present Pasco. A large gathering of native peoples greeted their arrival and the captains presented three Jefferson medallions to the assembled chiefs. One recipient was a Palouse leader named Ke Pow Han. Lewis and Clark incorporated the Palouse into their estimate of 2300 for the number of Nez Perce inhabiting the region below the Clearwater River. Many of the Palouse were likely encamped at that time on their fall hunting grounds to the southeast. By some peculiar coincidence a third Jefferson medal, one of a handful found along the entire transcontinental route, was also found in the region near present Wallula. The captains presented Walla Walla Chief Yelleppit, a "handsome Indian with a dignified countenance," the silver "token of

peace" near this place. This priceless artifact is now exhibited at the Oregon Historical Society Museum in Portland (G. Moulton, 1988).

Lewis and Clark called the Indians along the lower Snake the "Pelloat pallahs" in their journals though like so many other terms new to Northwest orthography, it was spelled in various ways. Appearing in the writings of frontiersmen in the 1830s was the word "Paloose" but the term "Palouse" in its present form is not found until the tribe was listed in the Yakima Indian Treaty of 1855. The notion that the word "Palouse" was derived from the French term *pelouse,* meaning "greensward or lawn" has no basis in 19th century accounts describing the region. The commonly held idea first appeared in print as an editor's footnote to a 1904 edition of the Lewis and Clark journals. French-speaking traders with the North West Company and others who first spied the rolling hills of pulsing grasses would have likely referred to it with the same French word for such a landscape that was lent to the English language—prairie. A description of the Palouse Hills published in French, an account of the 1846 Warre-Vavasour expedition, describes the region as *"une vaste prairie ondulante"*—a vast undulating *prairie.*

Lewis and Clark's Corps of Discovery included among its thirty-four members (counting Lewis's Newfoundland dog, Seaman) two French-Canadians who served as hunters and interpreters. George Drouillard was the most dependable of the hunters and behaved coolly under any crisis. Lewis and Clark named the Palouse River for their highly regarded companion and it bears the name "Drewyer's River" on their remarkably accurate 1806 map. The first person associated with the North West Company to reach the Pacific Slope was Corps' interpreter and the husband of Sacagawea, Toussaint Charbonneau. The verbose trader had apparently won the young Shoshone in a gambling game several years after she had been kidnapped at the age of twelve by Minnitaree raiders. She was only sixteen when Charbonneau took her for one of his several wives. Sacagawea gave birth to their son, Jean Baptiste, on February 11, 1805 while Lewis and Clark wintered among the Mandan Indians in present North Dakota. During the Corps' epic westward trek, she came to be highly regarded by the men for her kindness, occasional recognition of vital landmarks, and reassuring presence among the tribes which the group encountered (R. Thwaites, 1904; C. C. Todd, 1933).

In September, 1995 our Endicott-St. John Middle School was visited as it had been every fall for years by the regional representative for our communities' annual magazine sale fundraiser. I had worked with affable Tom Sharbono for years since his territory covered the Palouse Country and had always thought that with his strong build, dark complexion, and high cheekbones he could have made a threesome of John Wesley Jarvis's famous painting, "Black Hawk and Son." When I inquired about his previous life before helping supply the likes of me with *The Atlantic Monthly* and *Harper's Magazine*, he mentioned teaching near Mandan, North Dakota. Given that intelligence and the sound of his last name, I just had to ask. "Yes, I am," he replied with a soft smile. "My great-grandfather was Sacagawea's grandson, Joseph Charbonneau." I was stunned at the significance of such a heritage, and proceeded to learn much about Tom's efforts years earlier to help establish the Ft. Mandan National Historic Site.

I had always wondered about the fate of the expedition's youngest member, tiny Jean Baptiste, and what the family thought of the popular story that Sacagawea might have lived almost to the century mark on the Wind River Reservation in Wyoming. "I wish it were true," Tom sighed, "but Clark's records and our family accounts agree that she probably died from sickness in 1812. Her son, however, went on to have a long and incredible life." Clark had asked his parents' permission to adopt the boy, which they allowed, and he attended school in St. Louis. While still in his teens, Jean Baptiste guided Duke Paul Wilhelm of Germany on an excursion up the Platte River and was invited to join his family to study in Europe which he did from 1824

CHIEF KHALOTAS, 1855 (WASHINGTON STATE HISTORICAL SOCIETY)

to 1829. During that time the young American and toured North Africa where he probably saw the real "Pompey's Pillar" in Egypt for which Clark had named a promontory in Montana and was the basis of the nickname "Pomp" that he gave the boy. Jean Baptiste then returned to the Western frontier where he trapped with the likes of Jim Bridger and James Beckwourth. From time to time he would return to visit relatives in Montreal where he married Tom's great-grandmother, Charlotte Guery.

Jean Baptiste Charbonneau was the only member of the Corps of Discovery who ever returned to the Pacific Northwest. "He was heading from California to the Montana gold strikes in the spring of 1866 when he took ill and died in southeastern Oregon," Tom explained. "He's buried in the Jordan Valley at a place called Inskip's Ranch. I visit the place from time to time." When Tom returned to the school a month later to deliver his regular sales orientation to the students, we made arrangements for him to extend his stay and share his remarkable story and family memorabilia with all the middle school classes. The setting was our new school library, directly beneath a massive ivory colored bas-relief we had salvaged from the old Endicott School. Such three-dimensional works depicting pivotal moments in American history were once found in schools throughout the country, and this one gave the contractor fits getting it properly mounted in the wall. The image shows two buckskin-clad men with one pointing to crashing waves visible in the distance. Nearby stands a woman with a child carried in a sling on her back. Tom pointed to them to begin his presentation.

The romanticized scene is titled "Lewis and Clark Reach the Pacific" and whispers lines from Elmer Harper Sims's 1903 epic poem commemorating the 100th anniversary of the expedition, *Sacajawea and the Lewis and Clark Expedition*. The saga moves to the iambic rhythm of *Hiawatha*:

Swift they glided to the westward, down the Snake to the Columbia.
Here a wise and learned chieftain, very learned Yakima head chief,
Like the Nez Perce made an outline, of the country round about them.
Like the friendly Nez Perce tewat, marked the rivers and the trails,
Marked each mountain and each village, footprints pointed out the trails.

Again they floated down the river, down the deep and blue Columbia....
Here they heard the mighty breakers, only forty miles to seaward,
Roaring, surging, dashing, breakers, of the deep and briny ocean.
There upon a towering headland, when the sky was bright and pleasant,
They beheld the wondrous ocean, saw the open road to China,
Saw that vast expanse of water, stretching far away to westward.

Nor'Westers, Astorians, and "The Honorable Company"

Amiable relations continued with the European-Americans through 1811 when the Palouse "forced a gift of 8 horses" on British explorer-trader David Thompson who visited Palus in August. Enroute to the North West Company's Spokane House, he found the Palouse frenetic over his arrival and eager to trade. The irrepressible and diminutive Thompson was assiduous in his efforts to accurately map the regions he explored for the North West Company, founded in 1783 by Montreal merchants of Scottish ancestry, and became the greatest geographer of his time. Known to the native peoples as Star Man, for the sextant measurements he regularly took at night to precisely determine locations, Thompson's early years in the wilderness rendered him nearly blind in one eye. He attributed this condition to excessive smoke from reading by candlelight about surveying techniques as he recovered for nearly a year from a nearly fatal fall east of the Canadian Rockies when he was still in his teens.

The seriously broken leg left him lame for the rest of his life but did not deter him from eventually crossing the mountains and opening the Pacific Northwest to company interests. In a successful effort to find the source of the Columbia River, Thompson had crossed the Continental Divide in 1807 and established Kootenae House near

present Golden, British Columbia, the first Nor'Wester outpost in the region. Under his direction Spokane House was founded at the junction of the Spokane and Little Spokane rivers by Finan McDonald and Jacques Finlay in 1810. In the summer of 1811 Thompson ventured up from the lower Columbia and Snake rivers headed to Spokane House and reached the mouth of the Palouse River in August. On the way he noted the Snake River cliff's peculiar basalt formations, some appearing "like flutes of an organ at a distance" and others "broken or cracked by a violent blow." At Palus village the intrepid explorer-trader found dozens of Indians delighted with his arrival. They danced in his honor and gave Thompson eight horses and a leather war garment. He tried to repay their kindness with trade goods but the Palouses declined any compensation for their highly valued gift. Thompson then turned north and became the first explorer to traverse the western fringes of the central Palouse using the ancient route frontiersmen dubbed the Palouse Trail.

As always, he kept detailed field notes on his travels in which he described a open country where "there is often a few aspens, alder, a very rare fir along the brook, with much wild cherry and three sorts of currants" (J. B. Tyrrell, 1914). Thompson likely rode from the mouth of Cow Creek along the right bank of the Palouse River and Rock Creek to the foot of Rock Lake. He then veered north and followed the main trail that led to Spokane House. Cow Creek, incidentally, is one of the area's few waterways given a name by the fur traders by which it is still identified today. Some years after Thompson traversed the region, trappers spotted the curious sight of what appeared to be a cowhide hanging from a post near the stream's mouth.

FT. NEZ PERCES NEAR PRESENT WALLULA, 1859 (STEVENS REPORT)

The American response to economic opportunities on the Pacific Slope was the organization of the American Fur Company by New York financier John Jacob Astor in 1808. After months of planning, Astor dispatched an overland expedition that included Donald McKenzie, a 300-pound giant whose size matched his determination, and a rancorous group by sea that reached the mouth of the Columbia River after a voyage around Cape Horn. The Americans built Ft. Astoria in 1811 and Ft. Okanogan, near present Brewster, was established in the same year. Ft. Spokane was built in 1812 and in August of that year, the Astorians McKenzie, John Clarke, Ross Cox, and others traveled up from the lower Columbia and Snake rivers to the village of Palus, consisting of forty large tulemat-covered lodges, where they were welcomed by the "small and friendly tribe." The group divided at the mouth of the Palouse with Clarke and most of others continuing north to Spokane country to trade while McKenzie pressed further eastward along the Snake to establish a post among the Nez Perces.

Eighteen-year-old Ross Cox remained with the main party but became separated from them soon after they departed Palus on August 15. The account he wrote later of "the greatest ordeal" of his life portrays days of wandering along what came to be known as the Colville Trail. He later noted, "The country to the westward was chiefly plains covered with parched grass, and occasionally enlivened by savannahs of refreshing green, full of wild flowers and aromatic herbs, among which the bee and humming bird banqueted." On the 24th Cox pressed on through a "thinly wooded country," probably along Cow Creek. Here he camped near what "must have been an extraordinary nursery of wolves," more likely coyotes, that sounded such "loud and dreadful howling…, I never expected to the leave the place alive." He used rocks and a stick to ward off a night attack and hurried along for several more days only to encounter a lynx, bear, and "a murderous brood" of rattlesnakes. He finally stumbled into a camp of Indians camped near present Reardan who directed him to Ft. Spokane where he rejoined his companions. The young trader's vivid account of his perilous foray through the western Palouse appeared in his 1831 book, *The Columbia River*.

Donald McKenzie reached the mouth of the Clearwater River about the same time Clarke reached his destination and built the company's short-lived Clearwater Post across from present Lewiston. McKenzie then journeyed northward in the fall of 1812 on the Lapwai Trail to Ft. Spokane to consult with his associates. He became the first American to explore the eastern Palouse but did not leave any record of his journey along the base of the Clearwater Mountains' Thatuna Range. The first recorded foray through this area was penned by the eminent British naturalist David Douglas who spent several days of early August, 1826 in the company of Hudson's Bay trader John Work and the seventy-nine horses he was driving from Ft. Vancouver to Ft. Spokane via McKenzie's old post. The meticulous Scotsman described the Palouse's ubiquitous Douglas hawthorne, later named in his honor and the exclusive habitat of certain warblers and vireos, and eighteen distinct stem and blossom structures of lupine in the Inland Northwest. Such variation within a single species was leading Douglas and other prominent scientists of the era to find explanations for how such diversity through natural mutation could take place. Traditional church interpretations of Genesis held that fruits, flowers, and animals had remained fixed "after their kind" since the time of their creation.

The summer heat was stifling along the eastern Palouse trace, exceeding 100 degrees each day that left him "parched like a cinder" but the scientist with flowing white hair also pronounced "the undulating woodless country of good soil." This judgment was in stark contrast to his later descriptions of the barren landscapes along the Columbia River which he compared to Arabian deserts. Later at Ft. Vancouver, Douglas would read in a copy of the Royal Geological

CHIEF KAMIAKIN, 1855
(WASHINGTON STATE
HISTORICAL SOCIETY)

Society's Proceedings that his fellow countryman Charles Lyell proposed the earth was far older that the 6,000 years ascribed by many conservative theologians. Petrological evidence suggested to Lyell fewer indications of diluvial "catastrophism" than of a gradual "uniformitarianism" requiring millions of years to deposit fossil and mineral layers. Douglas would have seen exceptional evidence of both in the Palouse where he rode and strolled with his gold-headed cane collecting botanical samples a short distance between some of the continent's most ancient Eocene and recent Pliocene formations—terms coined by Lyell.

Primordial Steptoe Butte, surrounded by the loessal hills deposited but moments ago in geologic time and sheared off by catastrophic flooding to the west, would soon give its name to world science. In the 20th century, "steptoe" entered geological nomenclature as any ancient remnant surrounded by substantially more recent soil or rock formations. Unlike some others of his and later generations, Douglas, who had never been an especially religious person, actually found in the growing debate on earth's origins and his own discoveries reasons to hold in greater awe the work of "that Being, in whom all truth finds its proper lasting place" (W. Moorwood, 1973).

Early Palouse Country traders and explorers like McKenzie and Douglas often fed on the abundant wild fowl in this haven of sharp-tailed grouse that gracefully glided in formations on extended dihedral wings. The early settlers would soon hunt these birds, known to them as prairie chickens, to extinction. Later efforts, however, to introduce the ringneck pheasant, Hungarian partridge, both European species, Asia's chukar partridge, the American bobwhite quail, and other Galliformes were successful. Less welcome foreigners were the starling, English sparrow, and rock dove, or pigeon. The botanical diversity experienced by the native peoples and explorers of the eastern Palouse Hills can still be found at 800-acre Smoot Hill Ecological Preserve and at Rose Creek Preserve, a National Natural Landmark, both located about ten miles north of Pullman. The latter's twelve acres of fertile Palouse loam have never felt the plow and host over 300 native species of plants and animals. Self-reliant stands of aspen and red osier appear amid clusters of hawthorn and wild rose brambles to offer sanctuary to Western meadowlarks and red-winged blackbirds.

Other original inhabitants like mourning doves and killdeers sing plaintive tunes to smaller audiences of purple shooting stars and yellowbells as if celebrating the prairie solitude (D. Douglas, 1914; H. K. Buechner, 1953).

The belligerence of some American traders contributed to the geographic challenges of viable regional trade with the native peoples. In late June, 1813 a party of fur traders led by the ill-tempered Astorian John Clarke arrived at the mouth of the Palouse River enroute to Ft. Astoria from the Spokane River. In customary fashion, they were warmly received by their hosts at the village of Palus. While encamped there, Clarke displayed two small silver goblets to the Indians and invited their chief, Khalotas, to share some liquor. The next morning Clarke discovered that one of the vessels was missing. He immediately threatened "vengeance upon the whole tribe" if the article was not promptly returned. The chief called his villagers together and after a brief council the goblet was handed back to Clarke. But the traders immediately bound the arms and legs of the accused man. To the shock of the Palouses, they proceeded to hang him from a crude gallows quickly fashioned from his own lodge poles. Such arbitrary brutality elicited great outrage and several Indians hastily rode off to circulate the news. This first killing of an Indian by Whites in the Inland Northwest would cast pallor over relations between the two groups that would culminate in a series of armed conflicts later in the century (R. Cox, 1831).

The entry of the British Hudson's Bay Company into the Northwest fur trade marked the genesis of an enduring European-American presence and agriculture on both sides of the Cascade Mountains. After its merger with the North West Company in 1821, the company's leadership worked with monopolistic power to form "regular establishments" that would serve as more than exchange points for beaver and other peltries. Sir George Simpson, "The Honorable Company's" autocratic governor at York Factory on Hudson's Bay, was as interested in grain and growing seasons as in furs and supply routes. In 1824 he directed the construction of Ft. Vancouver on a verdant plain north of the Columbia River and appointed Dr. John McLoughlin to serve as the fort's chief factor and supervise company affairs throughout the newly formed Columbia

Department. McLoughlin undertook within two years to transform the region's mismanaged chain of thirteen posts into an expanded and profitable operation of twenty-two, while working to attain Simpson's goal of agricultural self-sufficiency. In its first year of operation in 1825, a small plot of bottomland was sown to wheat and in the next year barley, oats, Indian corn, peas, and potatoes were also planted. Initially the grain yields were low, which McLoughlin attributed to poor spring and fall seed wheat, but what did ripen he reported being "the finest I ever saw in any country" and within ten years approximately a thousand acres near the fort were in production (O. Winther, 1950).

Ft. Colvile (distinct from later Ft. Coville, a nearby military site) replaced Spokane House in 1825 as a center of trading activity on the middle Columbia. Following a tour of the region in 1824-25, Simpson recommended the location near scenic and strategic Kettle Falls, the greatest Indian fishery in the area and uppermost on the river, as a better place for trade and farming. After its construction under the supervision of John Work, another Canadian of Scottish descent, Andrew McDonald, was placed in charge of local operations. Though many of the traders did not share Simpson's exuberance for farming, McDonald persevered and by the end of the next decade, Ft. Colvile had grown to employ twenty men on a 400-acre farm and at the company store and gristmill. The first grain grown in the Inland Northwest, fifteen bushels of barley, was raised here in 1826 with seed from Ft. Vancouver and horses, cattle, and hogs from McLoughlin and abandoned Spokane House flourished on Big Prairie near the fort.

Wheat was likely planted the following year as grain production rose to 200 bushels in 1827. Larger areas were soon under cultivation at two nearby company farms yielding nearly 3,000 bushels of wheat, corn, barley, oats, buckwheat, and peas in 1832. Wheat soon came to be considered the company's dominant commercial as well as subsistence crop, especially after McLoughlin entered into an agreement in the late 1830s with the Russian-American Company to supply their fur trading posts in Alaska with flour and grain. Wheat became legal tender to British authorities in the Northwest with one bushel equaling one dollar. McLoughlin had taken great pains at Ft. Vancouver to build up a cattle herd which probably numbered about 100 head in 1825. Most of the animals were from Spanish stock obtained in California though McLoughlin also imported some Durham bulls from England to improve the breed. The two bulls and two cows McLoughlin parted with for Ft. Colvile in 1825 grew to a herd of some 200 by 1841 (J. Gibson, 1985; O. Winther, 1950).

Even languid Ft. Nez Perces, founded by Nor'Wester's in 1818 near present Wallula on the lower Columbia River, began to show signs of prosperity under McLoughlin's attentive guidance. Since the drier climate there did not foster agricultural development, the post came to specialize in horse breeding. In the 1820s there were usually between fifty to a hundred head at the fort and almost all were obtained from the neighboring Cayuse Indians, likely giving rise to the frontier synonym for a horse. A small cattle herd was begun around 1830 but these animals never numbered over fifty at the fort. However, Chief Trader Pierre Pambrum, a mixed-blood French and Indian native of Vaudreuil, Canada, did raise corn, potatoes, carrots, and other vegetables on fifty acres along the banks of the Walla Walla River for consumption by his family and a half-dozen employees.

Most company workers were unmarried *engagés* from Canada who had transferred voluntarily to new assignments in the Columbia Department. The chief factors and officers were usually of Scottish background and nominal members of the Anglican Church. French-Canadian ancestry predominated among the regular employees; most of them were *Métis*, or individuals with European-American fathers and Indian mothers, and virtually all were Catholic. Although many did not consider themselves settlers, their labor first tilled the Inland Northwest's soil and built its earliest frontier outposts. When the British were forced to forfeit their claims south of the present U.S.-Canadian border under the terms of the Oregon Treaty of 1846, some residents of the interior posts, like the Pambrum and McDonald families, chose to remain in the region and continue similar operations among the Indians and growing European-American presence. Ft. Nez Perces then came to be known as Ft. Walla Walla. A military post of the same name would be established twenty miles further east and give rise to the frontier town of Walla Walla (S. White and S. E. Solberg, 1989; T. Stern, 1993).

The principal fur-bearing animals actively sought by the traders were not native to the grassy hills of the Palouse area. However, the region was located between the three dominant points of early fur trading activity—the Hudson's Bay Company's Ft. Nez Perces near the mouth of the Walla Walla River, Astorian McKenzie's post at the mouth of the Clearwater, and Spokane House located at the junction of the Spokane and Little Spokane rivers. The natural triangular boundaries of the Palouse Hills were marked in ancient times by well-worn Indian trails embroydered with the imprint of horse hooves connecting these three points. They were extensively used by the fur traders to reach their posts. Exposure to the European-Americans resulted in devastating epidemics of smallpox and measles that took a heavy toll among all Northwest Indians, reducing the Columbia Plateau's native population by as much as two-thirds by 1850. In one village near Wawawai, the 1847 measles epidemic took all but one boy. Never a large tribe, the Palouse numbered about 500 in 1853 when Governor Isaac Stevens arrived in Washington Territory. At that time the Coeur d'Alenes numbered approximately 450, some 600 fewer than in 1780.

Blackrobes, Protestants, and the Star Brothers

The first "Blackrobes," or Catholic missionaries entered the region in 1841, led by the Jesuit Father Pierre De Smet after four visits by Nez Perces and Flatheads to St. Louis in the 1830s seeking the "white man's book of heaven." Father De Smet's humility was matched with an uncanny ability to engender the cordiality of Indians and Whites alike. Few persons have known such widespread acclaim amidst the trials of conflict between such widely divergent cultures. "No white man knows the Indians as does Father De Smet," President Lincoln was told when introduced to the Belgian priest by Thurlow Weed, "nor has any man their confidence in the same degree." Catholic missionaries responding to the "Macedonian Cry" for spiritual help led to peripatetic Father De Smet's founding of the Coeur d'Alene's Sacred Heart Mission in 1842. He was followed by such equally dedicated Jesuits as Joseph Joset, Nicholas Point, and Joseph Cataldo.

Subsequent work by members of the Oblate Order including Fathers Eugene Chirouse and Charles Pandosy at the request of the Yakama-Palouse Chief Kamiakin led to the building of St. Joseph's Mission in 1847 adjacent to his camp along Ahtanum Creek in the Yakima Valley. Unlike most Protestant missionaries, the Catholics generally believed that Christian conversion need not be accompanied by significant changes in the hunting and gathering patterns pursued for generations by the Indians. They did, however, insist on monogamy before baptizing an adult convert which was an unacceptable condition to some Indians on the Plateau. Sororal polygamy was not uncommon among men with sufficient means to care for more than one wife. Kamiakin's first wife, for example, was his second cousin, Sunkayee, and upon taking another, Kemeeyowah, daughter of a Klickitat chief, he also chose to become the husband of her three younger sisters. To Kamiakin the celibacy of the priests seemed more peculiar than plural marriage. Yet Kamiakin welcomed the Blackrobes and had all of his children baptized. His marital obligations remained a sacred bond, however, and the chief refused baptism until the hours immediately preceding his death in the Palouse Country many years later (E. Peone, 1981).

Kamiakin was probably born about 1800 to a Palouse father famed for horse racing, Tsiyiak, who had married Kamoshnite, the daughter of the prominent Upper Yakama (Kittitas) Chief Owhi, patriarch of the Weowicht family clan. Though he was primarily raised among his mother's people in the Yakima Valley, Kamiakin often traveled to the Palouse and camped at one of his family's four traditional campsites which included "Tsiyiak's Place" on a small lake about two miles west of Sprague Lake and on "Kamiak's Flat" at the foot of Rock Lake. Both bodies of water and the many pothole lakes in the western Palouse were seasonal homes to the now rare white pelican, trumpeter swan, whooping crane, and other migratory fowl. Narrow ledges tucked into mysterious Rock Lake's

KAMIAKIN FAMILY BEADED STAR

CHIEF SPOKAN GARRY, 1855 (WASHINGTON STATE HISTORICAL SOCIETY)

immense western cliffs provided one of the Northwest's few nesting sites for turkey vultures that could be seen for great distances circling high on vagrant currents of air where they were joined occasionally by the *khwama´* (high above), or golden eagle.

The Kamiakins also camped on the Palouse River north of present Endicott ("Kamiak's Crossing"), where native trout, whitetail deer, great blue herons, and other wildlife abounded, and at the village of Penawawa on the Snake River. (Though not a family campsite, Kamiak Butte was later named in the chief's honor by Colfax founder James Perkins, who thought the patriot chief should have a landmark bearing his name if Col. Steptoe was entitled to one.) Though Kamiakin directed some of his children to the "power mountain" *Eomoshtoss* (Steptoe Butte) for their vision quests, he acquired his *wyak* from the power of a buffalo seen a dream while taking his quest on the majestic but dangerous slopes of *Takhuma*, the "Mighty One," Mount Rainer. He would sing the song taught to him in the dream to summon strength needed in the battles that lay ahead in a life that witnessed nearly a century of cataclysmic cultural change.

As a member of the Weowicht clan, Kamiakin was treated with a deference that bespoke the family's unique ancestral ties to the two Star Brothers. Whether living near the mission or camping in the Palouse, he could point out *Khaslou*, the Evening Star, to his children and tell how his human wife gave birth in the ancient time to their ancestor at the foot of Chief Mountain, Miyowax, known today as Cowiche Mountain. Kamiakin was held in great esteem by both Indian and Whites throughout the Northwest and was described in regal terms by frontiersman Theodore Winthrop in his memoir, *The*

Canoe and Saddle. He was introduced to the legendary chief in 1853 by Father Pandosy after Kamiakin rode up to the men on a white stallion wearing a long green "robe of ceremony" with fine cloth patches "of all shapes and sizes…. He had an imposing presence and bearing, and above all a good face, a well-lighted Pharos at the top of his colossal frame." He was, Winthrop concluded, "every inch a king" (E. Peone, 1981; T. Winthrop, 1863).

Consistent with the Protestant policy of the American Board of Commissioners for Foreign Missions (1810-60), a joint creation of Congregational, Presbyterian, and Dutch Reformed denominations from the East, missionary couples were recruited in the 1830s to evangelize the Indians of the Pacific Northwest as the nation itself expanded westward. Most of those responding were conservative and Calvinistic in their theology who believed that progressive change among the tribes could best be undertaken through the proclamation of the Gospel, instruction in farming and animal husbandry, and opposition to "foreign influences" like Catholicism. The American Board's first efforts in the Northwest were led by Presbyterians Dr. Marcus and Narcissa Whitman, who founded the Waiilatpu Mission in 1836 near present Walla Walla among the Cayuses. The site's Cayuse name meant "Place of the Rye Grass" and was a scenic location that afforded good forage for the livestock and fertile land for the furit and grain Dr. Whitman hoped to raise at the mission.

The Whitmans were accompanied by their close friends Henry H. and Eliza Spalding who established the Clearwater or Nez Perces Mission of Lapwai on the north bank of the Clearwater River just above its confluence with the Snake. The two couples' children, Clarissa Whitman and Eliza and Henry Hart Spalding, were the first three American children born in America's Far West. In 1838 the nascent Protestant presence was reinforced by the arrival of Congregationalists Elkanah and Mary Walker and Myron and Myra Eells who were all directed northward where they launched Tshimikain Mission among the Spokanes near the mouth of the Spokane River. In the spring of 1838 Methodist Episcopal missionary Daniel Lee came from the Willamette Valley to build the Wascopam Mission on the tableland south of the Columbia River at The Dalles. The following year Lee reported that five acres were under cultivation yielding a considerable crop of potatoes and other vegetables as well as twenty five bushels of wheat. At each of these points the Protestant missionaries planted gardens and grain in order to be depend less upon the British Hudson's Bay Company for supplying provisions (J. Gibson, 1985).

A fertile tract of about sixteen acres at Waiilatpu yielded an abundance of corn and vegetables in 1837 and Whitman planted some of the ground to wheat in the fall. The next year's harvest produced some ninety bushels of wheat, three hundred of corn, and a thousand bushels of potatoes. A small herd of cattle, oxen, and horses were maintained in 1838 with Indian help. By 1842 the mission of the industrious Whitmans had grown to include two large adobe houses for use as a residence, school, and chapel, a sawmill, and two gristmills. The school was attended by young Cayuse, Walla Walla, and Palouse Indians. The Spaldings were essentially self-sufficient as well by 1843. But Whitman expressed another priority for the Americans' presence. "Our greatest work is to be to aid the white settlement of this country," he wrote to his parents in 1844, "and help to found its religious institutions." When immigrant travel commenced over the Oregon Trail to the Willamette Valley in 1841, American travelers found Waiilatpu to be an oasis on the vast dryland prairie after the strenuous trek through the Rockies. Many were as notably impressed with the mission's crops as with the Whitmans' hospitality and must have wondered what opportunities the surrounding landscape held. A number of the overlanders who finally reached the Willamette only to find the best lands already claimed may have recalled how the Whitmans spoke in most favorable terms of settlement opportunities in the fertile lowlands and hills to the north. Whitman and Spalding had explored this area in March, 1839 while examining a possible mission site at the mouth of the Palouse River (C. Drury, 1937; G. Himes, 1893).

One future Palouse pioneer who lived with the Whitmans overcame a series of unimaginable tragedies during her earliest years in the West. Matilda Jane Sager was just five years old when her parents, Henry and Naomi Sager, decided to leave Missouri in the spring of 1844 to seek a new life in the Oregon Country. The Sagers had six children under fourteen years old with Naomi carrying their seventh when they set out from St. Joseph in a large wagon train in May. She gave birth to a girl within two weeks of their departure but struggled for months to recover her strength. Shortly before reaching Ft. Laramie in late July, the couple's nine-year-old daughter Catherine fell from the wagon and suffered a severe bone fracture when the rear wheel rolled over her left leg. The family continued on after a brief rest at the fort but when crossing South Pass in August, Henry Sager contracted "camp fever" and died several days later. Naomi's health continued to decline the following week as she struggled to contend with her sorrow, the stifling heat, and suffocating clouds of dust. Sixteen days after her husband's passing, Naomi Sager died on the trail near present Twin Falls, Idaho.

When the wagons finally reached Waiilatpu in late October, 1845, the Whitmans were informed by the captain of the train that nobody with him could properly care for the seven children and that their father's death wish had been for them to remain together. In spite of their reluctance to take on such new responsibilities given the small community already existing at the mission, the Whitmans agreed to raise the children. The missionary couple had lost their only child, Clarissa, when she drowned at age two near the mission in 1839.

In July, 1847 the Whitmans hosted Canadian artist Paul Kane who painted a spectacular view of Palouse Falls, a sublime object to other frontier artists including Henry Warre, Gustavus Sohon, John Mix Stanley, and John Alden. Kane described his travels in the book *Wanderings of an Artist among the Indians of North America* (1859). Kane and Warre, both from Europe, provided vivid accounts of their visits to the falls sounding as mystical as an encounter with Celtic runes. "At one place the strata assumed the circular form," Kane noted, "and somewhat the appearance of the Colosseum at Rome."

Kane was guided to the falls by a Palouse chief "through one of the most sublime passes the eye ever beheld…. The water falls in one perpendicular sheet… from rocks of a grayish-yellow color, which rise to about 400 feet above the summit of the fall. Kane continued upstream to also sketch Little Palouse Falls, feasting on "delicious wild currants" and "much gratified with the surrounding magnificent scenes." But traveling in the July heat, the artist "never met with an animal or bird—not even a mosquito or a snake." In one of the first descriptions of the Palouse Hills, which Henry Warre saw from a high vantage point enroute to the falls in March, 1846, he described "… a vast undulating prairie, from whence the view was magnificent extending far into the distance & bounded by the Blue Mountains which were covered to the base with snow. The apparently rolling prairie is intersected by vast gullies of greater or less breadth & through one of these the Peloos River has its almost subterranean course."

Had Kane or Warre visited the falls during a frigid, clear February day, they may have witnessed one of nature's rarest phenomena. The month bore the Sahaptin name for the appearance of the year's first wildflower blossoms, "Buttercup Blooming Time." Sagebrush buttercups were known to the Palouse as "Coyote's eyes," an important element in tribal myth. The peculiar position of the sun in February shot brilliant rays at midday up the lower canyon sanctum striking the falls at hallowed moments as if the cenotaph deep inside the ancient Temple of Abu-Simbel. The combination of this light under distinctive climatic conditions at the head of the imposing basaltic colonnade created a

mesmerizing melee of colors. Deep reds and greens and yellows were refracted by rime ice clinging to the basalt cliffs flanking the falls and by prismatic mists arising from the pool beneath the narrow cascade of late winter. These spectral rays merged fantastically to create a shimmering rainbow halo suspended above the falls against February skies of lucent blue (P. Kane, 1859; H. Warre, n.d.).

In 1845 relations between the Whitmans and the Cayuses became increasingly strained. The Indians looked with suspicion upon the many wagonloads of Whites who were traveling through their lands likes bits of flotsam across the marine-like swells of grass. But they were carrying more than wooden trunks and cooking supplies. The Whites unwittingly introduced another series of communicable diseases that ravaged the area's tribes. When a measles outbreak in the fall of 1847 brought death to many Cayuses in spite of Dr. Whitman's efforts to inoculate them, some Indians believed the missionaries were deliberately acting to harm them. In a macabre scene witnessed on November 29, 1847 by Matilda Sager, her sisters, young Eliza

"SOURCE OF THE PELUSE"

THE PALOUSE HILLS FROM KAMIAK BUTTE, 1859 (STEVENS REPORT)

Spalding and others, a group of Cayuse men visiting the Whitmans suddenly brandished guns and hatchets and began killing the men who worked outside and some of the women. Marcus and Narcissa were struck down in the kitchen of their residence where Matilda watched helplessly as her two brothers were shot to death. Fourteen mission residents were murdered during the chaos. The survivors were held captive at the mission for a harrowing month of terror before a ransom of Hudson's Bay trade goods from Ft. Walla Walla purchased their freedom. Casualties from disease and exposure during the captivity included six-year-old Hannah Sager, Helen Meek, 8, daughter of famed mountain man Joe Meek and his Nez Perce wife, and Mary Ann Bridger, 11, daughter of Jim Bridger (J. Roth, 1998).

The murders created a sensation in the Willamette Valley. A volunteer army was raised to bring the perpetrators to justice and this response led to the Cayuse War of 1848-49 and the eventual destruction of the tribe. On June 3, 1850, five Cayuses accused of the Whitman killings were hung in Oregon City. The Sager sisters, Spaldings, and others were safely relocated to the Willamette Valley where many remained for the rest of their lives. However, following Matilda Sager's subsequent marriage to Matthew Faultz in the 1870s, the couple moved to Farmington in the Palouse Country. Here this indomitable woman wrote *A Survivor's Recollections of the Whitman Massacre* (1920), one of the few eyewitness accounts of her family's tragic experiences on the Oregon Trail and the Whitman Massacre, with an explicit description of the survivors' Indian captivity. Eliza Spalding went on to marry James Warren, son of frontiersman Hugh Warren, they later lived in Almota where she authored *Memoirs of the West* (1916). But the notion that the Whitmans knowingly sought to destroy the Indians by spreading disease lingered long with some Indian families. When asking a Palouse elder in the 1980s what she knew about Marcus Whitman, I was told, "He was that man who tried to poison our people."

The Interior Wars of the 1850s

With the extension of U.S. sovereignty over the Oregon Country in 1846, renewed interest was expressed by many Americans in the lands north of the Columbia River. The "Great Migration of 1843" had brought nearly 900 immigrants across the Oregon Trail to the sparsely settled Willamette Valley. Like the majority of later overland pioneers, most were from America's heartland, and some who ventured West on the historic 1843 trek like young J. A. Stoughton would later find their home in the Palouse. This first surge of immigration tapped the states from New York, Pennsylvania, and Virginia across to Iowa and Missouri. Most were descendants of European colonists who had come to America a century or two earlier. They came from rural areas and honored the values of faith, family, and farm. Some of the men also possessed skills as carpenters, livestock raisers, promoters, and businessmen and most couples tended to be active in church, local politics, and fraternal societies.

The women provided stability under frequently primitive conditions and filled the more private roles of mother, wife, physician, and moral guardian. These complementary functions were joined to create a culture centered on the family which often could number a half-dozen or more children. The Stoughtons were natives of Massachusetts who had relocated to Alabama in 1836. Dissatisfied with conditions in the South, they joined others in Missouri to undertake the six-month journey to the Willamette Valley. Like many others there, however, the Stoughtons would eventually relocate to the Palouse in order to unclaimed farmland.

Americans were attracted to the Pacific Northwest in unprecedented numbers during the 1850s on a quest for land, gold, and business opportunities. As early as 1850 disgruntled miners who had headed for the California gold strikes a year or two earlier were moving north again in their search for the precious metal. In the summer of 1850, Henry Spalding, who had moved to the Willamette Valley after the Whitman Massacre, wrote that "Great numbers went from country last June to explore the Spokane and Nez Perce countries for gold...." Further incentive for travel to the region came in the fall of 1850 when Congress passed the Oregon Donation Land Law, three years before treaties extinguished tribal land titles, in order to "provide for the survey, and make donations to settlers of the said public lands." This legislation granted every eligible citizen who had settled prior to 1852 a half-section (320 acres) while those occupying lands between 1852 and 1855 were able to obtain quarter sections. News of these liberal settlement provisions led to a pioneer exodus over the Oregon Trail, and in five years the territorial population rose from approximately 8,000 in 1850 to nearly 30,000. This dramatic increase led to the creation of a separate Washington Territory in 1853 and the appointment of General Isaac I. Stevens as governor. President Franklin Pierce also named Stevens Superintendent of Indian Affairs for the new territory and directed him to undertake an extensive survey for the proposed northern transcontinental railroad.

Beginning in 1853, survey teams under the direction of Territorial Governor Isaac Stevens were dispatched throughout the region to locate possible routes for the northern transcontinental railroad that would link Washington Territory with Minnesota and the East. A final determination was later made for the main line to enter Washington near Spokane and head southwest to the mouth of the Snake River thereby skirting the northwestern Palouse. However, information gathered through the surveys was used for the construction of the Mullan Road in the late 1850s and for subsequent railroad branch lines that tapped the Palouse grain district and eastern forests. Stevens himself traveled from Ft. Colvile to Palus in October, 1853.

While riding along the Snake guided by Chief Spokan Garry enroute to Olympia, Stevens met the Palouse Chief Witimyhoyshe who "exhibited a medal of Thomas Jefferson dated 1801, given to his grandfather... by Lewis and Clark." Despite the efforts of officials like Stevens and Catholic and Protestant missionaries to reconcile fundamental cultural differences, the surveys aroused Indian concern over control of their lands, and American zeal for development broke into open hostilities in the Pacific Northwest in the 1850s. Pivotal events during this decade of the "Interior Indian Wars" took place in the Palouse which served as the principal theater for the Edward Steptoe and George Wright expeditions of 1858. Territorial Governor Isaac Stevens and topographical engineer Lt. John Mullan directed the first thorough explorations of the Palouse Country during that period. While continuing on through the eastern Palouse near present Moscow, the governor described the surroundings as "a luxuriance of grass [and] richness of soil. The whole view presents to the eye a vast bed of flowers in all their varied beauty" (I. Stevens, 1860; Trafzer and Scheuerman, 1986).

An unexpected consequence of the railroad surveys was the discovery of gold in 1853 by the group working in the Yakima Valley. In the same year similar finds were made by Stevens's own party in the Bitterroot Valley. In order to avert an impending disaster caused by the anticipated flood of miners and in an effort to abolish Indian claims to interior lands sought for the railroad and settlers, Stevens called a grand treaty council near Waiilatpu in the Walla Walla Valley in the spring of 1855. Though attended by some 5,000 Nez Perce, Walla Wallas, Yakamas, and others, the Palouse were noticeably absent. A messenger was dispatched to their principal village at the mouth of the Palouse River but was told by their elderly Chief Khalotus that "his people were indifferent to the matter." The chief alone accepted the invitation to participate. During these meetings the Yakama-Palouse Chief Kamiakin, appearing "as a great sphinx," and other tribal leaders seemed unyielding when informed of Stevens' proposals.

The governor aggressively pressed the Indian leaders to accept payments and designated homelands in return for signing away most of their Plateau and mountain domains including the Palouse Country. To the assembled chiefs, however, the issue was spiritual, not economic. "I wonder if the ground is listening to what is said," challenged Young Chief of the Cayuses. Owhi responded, "Shall I say that I will give you my lands? I cannot…; I am afraid of the Almighty." Stevens was stunned and angered at what he had assumed would be a simple business operation. He needed his railroad and the Indians were in the way. After several weeks of apparent stalemate, however, the chiefs were induced to sign away over 45,000 square miles of their land in return for three reservations in the Yakima, Nez Perce, and Umatilla areas and extended time to make the transition. Kamiakin stoically signed for the Palouse as did Khalotus, primarily because they were threatened that they would "walk in blood knee deep" if they did not.

The leaders likely realized further negotiations were futile and may have signed only to gain more time to prepare for war. The Yakama Chief Owhi, Kamiakin's father-in-law, later stated that "the war commenced from that moment." Days later a group of Yakama women, including Kamiakin's relatives, were assaulted by a party of miners while digging roots in the Yakima Valley. Retaliation led to the murder of two White offenders followed by a number of skirmishes between the army and civilian volunteers against the Plateau tribes. When the elder Yakama chiefs Owhi and Teias sought peace on the military's terms in 1856, Kamiakin defiantly relocated to the Palouse Country never to return again to the land of his mother's people.

Gold strikes made in 1858 in the Colville Valley and on the Fraser River in Canada complicated the situation by renewing the onslaught of miners across restricted lands long before Stevens's treaties were ratified by Congress. The Palouse reacted by killing two miners headed north from the Snake on the Colville Trail in the spring and on the night of April 12, 1858 they raided livestock near Ft. Walla Walla. In an effort "to stop this thieving" and reassure the Colville miners with a personal visit and show of strength, Colonel Edward Steptoe and five companies departed Ft. Walla Walla after hearing that the hostile Palouse were near Alpowa on the Snake River. Finding only friendly Nez Perce there, Steptoe proceeded north to a point about eight miles northwest of present Rosalia. On May 16, 1858 several miles west of present Plaza, his detachment camped where they met a force of some six hundred mounted Palouses under Tilcoax, Chief Polatkin's Lower Spokanes, Coeur d'Alenes with Chief Vincent, and the Yakama firebrand Qualchan with other middle Columbia Indians. Kamiakin was probably not aware of the army's incursion until after the fighting had commenced.

Two days later the Indians forced the army to retreat to a small hill near present Rosalia where they were assailed throughout the day at what became known to the Palouse as the "Battle of *Tohotonimme* (Pine Creek)," to the Coeur d"Alene and Spokanes as the "*Hngwsuum* (Rope Making Place) Battle,"

and to military historians as the "Steptoe Disaster." The Palouse may have helped start the fight, for they were very hostile to the army. The Palouse Chief Tilcoax was present from the beginning of the battle, but Kamiakin probably did not arrive until the troops had been surrounded. Although seven of Steptoe's men were killed and thirteen others wounded, the command managed to escape at night and return to Ft. Walla Walla. One of the casualties, Private Victor DeMoy, had served in the French army and fought in the Crimean War. After sustaining mortal wounds early in the battle, DeMoy cried words that became synonymous with one of the U.S. Army's few defeats in the era of the Indian wars: "My God, my God, for a saber!" He asked to be left on the battlefield during the retreat armed with a fully loaded revolver. The hatred felt by the Americans after their losses in the Cayuse War of 1848 was minor compared to what arose after the Steptoe Battle. The Palouse were not only defiant and insulting, but had participated in attacks on the Steptoe command and killed American soldiers. The army set out to punish the Palouse and their allies.

Colonel George Wright organized a well-equipped expedition throughout the summer of 1858 and in mid-August departed Ft. Walla Walla with some 570 well armed troops. The army had been embarrassed by the Steptoe defeat, and Colonel Wright set out to avenge the death of Steptoe's men. The colonel crossed the Snake River near the mouth of the Palouse on August 25, but the Indians usually residing there had moved north. They kept their huge horse herds ahead of the military column trying to reach the relative security of the mountainous areas of the Coeur d'Alenes. A series of battles took place in which

THE BATTLE OF TOHOTONIMME (PINE CREEK), MAY 18, 1858, BY NONA HENGEN

the tribes, led again by Owhi, Kamiakin, and others were utterly defeated by the soldiers newer long range rifles and howitzers at the Battle of Four Lakes near present Cheney on September 1. Chief Kamiakin and his warrior-woman wife Colestah, clad in battle dress with her scarlet headscarf, fought together at Four Lakes until a cannon shell shattered a tree under which they were located. A falling limb broke Kamiakin's shoulder and he was taken to a camp near the mouth of the Spokane River for safe haven.

The Battle of Spokane Plains near present Fairchild Air Force Base four days later also ended disastrously for the Indians. Wright then overtook a herd of about a thousand Palouse horses on September 8 along the Spokane River near the present Washington-Idaho state line and shot virtually all of them. Wright continued eastward and forced a treaty upon the Coeur d'Alenes at the Cataldo Mission and then swung around Lake Coeur d'Alene to Latah Creek where Chief Owhi approached Wright's camp under a flag of truce to discuss terms of peace. He was immediately seized and shackled. Messengers were sent out demanding the surrender of his son, the notori-

ous warrior Qualchan, and Kamiakin. Chief Kamiakin was unable to be moved but Qualchan, still recovering from serious wounds inflicted at a recent skirmish on the Columbia River, boldly rode into Wright's bivouac with his wife, Whistalks, to seek his father's welfare. He was also summarily taken into custody although the effort required all the

THE BATTLE OF SPOKANE PLAINS, SEPTEMBER 5, 1858, BY NONA HENGEN

THE DEFIANCE OF WHISTALKS, SEPTEMBER 24, 1858, BY NONA HENGEN

strength of several soldiers. Fifteen minutes later he was hung as were several other Indians Wright had captured. Whistalks defiantly flung a beaded lance at Wright's tent and rode back to the Spokane River camp. The quiet stream would now bear the name "Hangman Creek."

Chief Owhi's daughter, Mary Owhi Moses, retold these traumatic events to her great-granddaughter Emily Peone in 1918: "About ten days after Qualchan was hanged and we were told the soldiers had left the camp…, my sisters and I ventured over to the campground. We found where they had buried Qualchan in a shallow grave covered with dust, grass, and sticks. The soldiers had taken his war bonnet and clothes. My sisters dug a deeper grave, took the body and wrapped it in a blanket, put moccasins on the feet and buried it again with some shells in the grave." The site is about sixteen miles southeast of Spokane near Smith's Ford. On his return trip to Ft. Walla Walla, Wright hastily called a "Palouse Council" on the Palouse River at the mouth of Willow Creek in order to hang several more Indians and threatened the annihilation of the tribe should they make any future trouble. The column then crossed the Snake River near Palus and as they continued on the south side toward to Ft. Walla Walla, two soldiers shot Owhi to death as he rode chained to a horse (M. Moses, 1918).

Chief Kamiakin and his family managed to escape to the mountains where they found sanctuary with Chief Victor's Flathead band. They returned to the Palouse Country in 1860 to live on the Palouse Rive at Kamiakin's Crossing. Here were found sufficient root grounds, wild game, and space to raise gardens and for his young sons to race their horses. Father Joseph Joset visited the chief and his family in November, 1861 at a place he identified as *Nihlikom*, possibly this ancient riverside campsite, and baptized five of Kamiakin's children (*Sacred Heart Mission Baptismal Register*, 1861). Kamiakin remained in the Palouse for the rest of his life in spite of later government offers to handsomely reward him for returning the Yakima Valley to establish order on the newly organized Yakima Indian Reservation. He steadfastly refused all such request, once even baring his ragged sleeves and telling the visiting agent he had never accepted anything in exchange for his lands and would never be poor enough to do so. Pivital events from the Steptoe and Wright campaigns are dramatically depicted on canvas in Nona Hengen's "Palouse War Series" on display in the Endicott-St. John Middle School Library. The collection is comprised of eleven large murals which took the Spangle artist six years to complete. Hengen is considered one of America's premier painters of horses, and notable scenes include "The Battle of Tohotonimme," "Colonel Wright's Snake River Crossing," "The Battle of Four Lakes," and "Horse Slaughter Camp."

The Northern Pacific Railroad Surveys

When Governor Stevens first entered the territory in 1853, he was surveying the northern route for a railroad that would link the eastern portion of the United States with the Pacific Ocean. His dream of a Northern Pacific line was shared by many visionaries and as settlers of the Oregon Country. Yet long before the eventual completion of the Northern Pacific Railroad in 1883, significant immigrant movement to the Palouse was taking place. Indian trails extensively crisscrossed the region and the major north-south routes had been known by trappers and traders for some time. Apart from the ancient paths along both banks of the Snake River, most Indian trails tended to lie on a northeasterly axis to expedite travel between the lower Snake and the domain of the Spokane and Coeur d'Alene tribes. A route known to the frontiersmen as the Colville Trail had been used for centuries by the Indians as the principal path from the Walla Walla Valley to the Colville area. Because it crossed the Snake River a short distance below the mouth of the Palouse River, Whites frequently encountered the Indians encamped at Palus. The first ferry on the Snake River began operating at this famous crossing after the Territorial Legislature granted the rights to Edward L. Massey in 1858. A year later the trail developed into a "road" as a crew under the command of Major Pickney Lugenbeel at Ft. Colville graded parts of it in order to improve transportation from Ft. Walla Walla (D. Meinig, 1968).

Stretching along the foothills of the Bitterroots in the eastern Palouse was the Lapwai Trail which led from Nez Perce country to the western shores of Lake Coeur d'Alene. The major route through the central Palouse was known to the settlers as the Spokane Trail. It was formed where paths along Penawawa Creek, Almota Creek, and other streams tributary to the Snake in that area converged on Smokle (Union Flat) Creek. From there it led northward to the land of the Spokanes, crossing the Palouse River near its northernmost point between present Endicott and St. John at the ancestral campsite of the Kamiakin family and skirted the base of Pyramid Peak, later renamed Steptoe Butte.

In his negotiations with the Indians in the 1850s, Colonel Wright had insisted that Americans be permitted to cross through Indian lands unmolested and the tribes, under duress, consented. Trails previously used for centuries by Indians were now thrown open to the Americans and soon developed into roads carrying the newcomers to "the land of milk and honey." Lt. John Mullan had been commissioned in 1858 to begin the first surveys for a military wagon road to link Ft. Walla Walla with Ft. Benton, Montana which marked the head of Missouri

River steamboat traffic. Since his work had been stalled by the Indian war, the ambitious young officer dispatched three advance parties in the summer of 1859 to explore the region ahead of his main column. Their objective was to locate the most practical route across the Palouse Country.

In the first recorded exploration of the central Palouse, Gustavus Sohon, in his capacity as guide, interpreter, and artist for the surveyors, traversed the course of Union Flat Creek in June, 1859 with two assistants and a Palouse Indian guide. The Indian was Slowiarchy, compliant headman at Palus. Sohon noted in his journey that there was a plentiful supply of grass along lower Union Flat Creek and ten miles above its mouth grew large stands of cottonwood, aspen, birch, pine, and brushwood. The view from Pyramid Peak he described as "rolling prairie, very much resembling a stormy sea" and densely wooded in the spurs of the Bitterroots. The abundance of these pioneer necessities—water, grass, and timber—interested many readers of Mullan's official report which described his road that arced northeasterly across the Palouse from present Benge and Lamont to the Spokane Valley at Dishman. It was published by the government in 1860 and widely distributed throughout the East necessitating a second edition. Both publications and Mullan's *Miners and Travelers' Guide* (1865) served to spark renewed interest in Northwest settlement opportunities now that the Indians had been pacified.

Stevens's official railroad survey report to Congress contained a wealth of information about the Inland Northwest's landscape, natural history, flora, and fauna. The extensive document also noted the presence of seven Indian farms along the Snake River from Palus to Alpowa "amounting to from 300 to 400 acres." At these places on sandy river banks and some islands, the Palouses and Nez Perces raised "wheat, corn, ...and vegetables of different kinds, and gained sufficient crops to encourage them in their labors." Also notable were the higher plateaus on both sides of the river that "produced fine grass that offered magnificent pasture grounds." The government's publication of the transcontinental railroad survey reports was illustrated with a series of rare color lithographs.

One based on Sohon's artwork titled "Source of the Peluse," an eastward vista from Kamiak Butte, is the first image ever made of the Palouse Hills. The original water color is held by the Yale University Art Gallery while Sohon's pencil and ink map of the Palouse, the first detailed chart of the region, is in the Library of Congress Sohon Collection (I. Stevens, 1860; P. D. McDermott and R. E. Grim, 2002).

Coeur d'Alene Relocation to Desmet

By the early 1860s Sacred Heart Mission on the St. Joe River had emerged as the center of Jesuit activity among the Coeur d'Alenes, and in the fall of 1866 Father Cataldo established the mission of St. Michael's on Peone Prairie near Spokane Falls. With each passing year of the decade both missionaries and tribal leaders became increasingly concerned about the level of immigrant traffic westward on the Mullan Road. The priests warned of the corrupting influences brought by whiskey peddlers and also noted that the best farmlands would be the first to be taken in the rich Palouse while the fields adjacent to the mission were stony and subject to recurrent flooding. The priests

SACRED HEART MISSION, DESMET, IDAHO, c. 1915 (MASC, WSU LIBRARIES)

advocated the tribe's transition to a more settled agrarian existence, and as early as 1863 Father Joset raised the question of their resettlement to the fertile and more sheltered Palouse River Valley. The periodic festival gatherings at the mission in later years provided opportunities to enunciate this advice to the entire tribe. "Those who are farming know by now," andrew Seltice remembered Joset preaching in 1864, "that the Palouse soil is the richest in all this land of yours. It is not only the best you own, but it is better than any land I know of. That is saying a lot, because I have been in many countries. Even on the other side of the ocean, I have never seen better soil anywhere than you have right here in the Palouse."

Given their ancestral ties to the Coeur d'Alene Lake area, the tribe's initial response to the priests' advice was cool. The Jesuits did not force the issue, however, and over several years tribal leaders came to share the view that relocation of their homes and the mission would be in their best interest. Several Coeur d'Alene families had been living for some time at traditional family campsites near present Oakesdale, Colfax, Plummer, Potlatch, and Tensed where the proposed mission site near present Desmet, Idaho was located. The scenic place had been a popular summer encampment for generations of *Schitsumsh* who found fish plentiful in the river, abundant game in the timbered slopes nearby, and a plentiful supply of nutritious roots. Although some members of the tribe began resettling southward in the late 1860s, the first significant relocation began in the spring of 1870. At that time the Andrew Seltice family built a cabin at the fork of Latah and Lovell creeks (present Tekoa). Others moving that year included Ignace Timothy (to present Plummer), Peter Wildshoe (to Tilma), and Massisla (near Worley). The families of See-mo Chimineme, Steptoe Battle veteran Andrew Youmas, Krato Nickodemus, and others went to the Moctelme Valley near the new Palouse River mission site (E. Kowrach and T. Connolly, 1990).

Although the severity of the first winter tested the group's resolve to remain in the Palouse, the following years brought a new prosperity to the tribe. Their devotion to the church came to the Holy See's Attention and the felicitous response from Pope Pius IX in 1871 is believed to be the only papal brief ever addressed to an Indian tribe. By 1876 most Coeur d'Alenes who had remained in the vicinity of the old mission joined the others in the Palouse Valley. A new Sacred Heart Mission Church was completed there in 1877 and in the following year a school began operation under the direc-

tion of a group of Sisters of Providence recruited from Vancouver, Washington. The cluster of buildings soon developed into the small community of Desmet which was surrounded by farmsteads spread across the verdant lowland. Sacred Heart Mission developed into a model mission under the supervision of Fathers Alexander Diomedi and Joseph Giorda. The mission also came to serve as the center of Catholic ministry to settlers throughout the Palouse Country. The priests in residence made frequent visits to congregations in Sprague, Oakesdale, Cheney, Uniontown, Colton, and Lewiston since the enormous area could not be adequately covered by the nearest diocesan priests from the Walla Walla parish.

Several Native American families like those of the Fishhook Jim family stubbornly clung to a few final outposts on the lower Snake River until most of them were also relocated to area reservations through a renewed government push for removal in 1905. Mary Jim remained with her family on the Snake River near Page until the construction of Ice Harbor Dam in the 1960s forced her to relocate the family to the Yakama Reservation. Today the original people of the Palouse Country remain in dispersion upon Northwest reservations. The Kamiakins, Poweens, and Felixes are on the Colville; the Jim, George, and Jack families on the Yakama; and the descendants of Wolf Necklace (Tilcoax) and Ernest Johnley on the Umatilla. Other Palouse and Nez Perce families whose ancestors once lived on the Snake reside today on the Nez Perce, Warm Springs, Coeur d'Alene, and Spokane reservations where elders like Carrie Jim Schuster, Lawrence Nickodemus, Virginia Beavert, and Adeline Fredin work to keep alive tribal traditions by their teachings, story-telling, and periodic visits back to the old homeland.

For decades members of the Coeur d'Alene tribe have commemorated the 1858 Steptoe Battle with the annual Memorial Warriors Horse Ride from Plummer to Rosalia. As has been customary for generations, participants in the May, 2000 *Hngwsuum* Ride witnessed a descendant of a Coeur d'Alene combatant raise a time-honored talisman from an exquisitely beaded sheath—the steel saber of an officer who fell near Private DeMoy during the fight. The memorial revisits and age when the native peoples of the Palouse Country were masters of a vast domain that safeguarded the bones of their ancestors. The land remains home for the descendants of the Animal People who's expressions can still be heard in a magpie's complaining call and read in the second glance of a loping coyote.

MARY JIM
PARKER, WASHINGTON

Mary Jim was one of the last Palouse Indians who once led a traditional life on the Columbia Plateau. Her grandfather, Fishhook Jim, was a headman on the lower Snake River whose brother was the famed Dreamer Chief Thomash. Despite enormous bureaucratic obstacles, both families acquired title to tracts of land along the river in the the 1880s through the Indian Homestead Act rather than move to a reservation. Mary was born about the turn of the century and spent much of her life living off the land's beauty, eating fish, deer, roots, and berries. Like so many of her people, Mary had a deep and reverent feeling for the earth and the abundance of food that was placed here by the Creator. She and her family lived on the river according to the traditions of their ancestors until the Ice Harbor Dam reservoir forced them to relocate in the late 1950s. She then her home on the Yakama Indian Reservation near Parker, Washington where she lived with her daughter and grandchildren. The following information was gleaned from interviews conducted by the author in 1980.

I am a Palouse Indian from Snake River where my people have always lived. God put us there and we prayed thanking Him for the river and the salmon and all good things. My father was Allíyua, Thomas Jim, and his father was Fishhook Jim. His Indian name was Chowatyet. My grandmother was Amtaloot who was from Priest Rapids. She was a relative to Smohalla. Her father was Him-tee-tsak-een, that means "Mouth is Stuck" in Nez Perce. He was related to Kamiakin and Grandmother taught me many things about how to live when I grow up. We lived about one mile from Page at village Tasawiks. There was a strong spirit in the river there; those who saw him became medicine men. It made a powerful song, "Shaa…, Shaa…." It left after the Shuyapo (Whites) came, musta went down to the ocean.

We would start to move in March. We would move to Soap Lake, dig certain kinds of roots. They used to dig skokul and some other roots, and then we used to move to Badger Mountain, all around

Douglas, and all over that big hill, Badger Mountain. And we used to stay there. That's where people used to gather, play stick games, dance the Washat, you know, the Seven Drum religion. We used to race horses by Badger Mountain. When we were done there, we moved back to Snake River, last of the May maybe, and then salmon came up the Snake River. We fished and got all kinds of fish. We got salmon and put it away. They used to dig a hole, big hole and put bunchgrass all around in it, then boards, then sticks. They buried that and nothing would happen. That's for our spring salmon and eels and other kinds of fish—sturgeon. They used to sell sturgeon. We also used to do digging around Colfax; Harry Jim took us up that way. In the fall we went over to Walla Walla to dig kouse. That's where we used to camp and dig. Then we went up the mountains to dig other kinds of roots. You baked some of them which turned black, almost like wild onions, but different. Then they cooked *tuna-winch-i-kunch*, tree moss, and they baked it and ground it. We traveled a lot. You ought to have seen them horses: packin', packin', packin'. No car at that time!

We used to go to Palus in the fall time after we worked the corn. We would stop at Khaiyous Kamiakin's place and my father used to get wood for them. He liked riding Appaloosy horses. We called them mamin. We also would go to the graveyard. I picked up some beads there when I was little and got a whippin! There were quite a big people there, and had a few houses and we would play. Chief Bones lived there and his daughter, Mityuitinmy, and son Pete Bones. We called him Hiyouwath. They were really Cayuses who moved up to Palus after that doctor (Whitman) tried to kill them all. He put stuff in them you know and made them sick. They killed him before he could do it all to them, but then the army came. They captured Chowatyet's brother, my uncle, Thomash. He was just a boy you know, maybe six or seven and they were shootin' everybody. But that army man (Captain Thomas Cornelius in 1856) took him away and sent him to school but he came back. He knew the Whiteman then and became a chief and powerful medicine man. He knew Smohalla. One time he told the White people who came, "You not gonna take my people, no, no reservation. My people want to keep their background. They want to stay here." And they took him (to Walla Walla) and they put him in jail. Pretty soon then tell him, "Thomash, you got a big head. You don't wanna move no place. Now you take your people back, and they gonna get homestead, and nobody's gonna bother them." And they came down and got a homestead on the other side of Ice Harbor. That's why we got that land. They wouldn't give it up and I don't either. They hand me money for it and I say I won't touch it, that land can't be sold no matter!

We also caught eels at Woweookemah where Coyote made Eel Place. His boat was made with a high stone in the middle where they would gather. He made it for the Indian people because he knew they were coming. *Spilyai* (Coyote) also taught us how to catch and eat salmon by the Snake River where the two Coyote Brothers lived. The youngest lived with five children on the north side by Palouse River but could not catch salmon like his older brother. So he told one of his sons to visit his uncle and find out what he used. The uncle said, "I am using kaamookii [milkweed hemp] that I gather and weave into a net." The boy crossed the river to tell his father but fell down so hard on the rocks that he forgot what his uncle told him. So on the next day Spilyai sent all five of his children so the message would not get lost.

Soon they all came running back saying over and over, *"Kaamookii, kaamookii, kaamookii."* They kept falling over each other while racing home and told their father who said, "I thought so!" They all then went to gather milkweed hemp to spin and weave into a net which Spilyai said was for the People who were soon to come and catch salmon there. He knew they were coming. He also taught his sisters how to bake salmon after catching the first one at Palouse Falls. He then said to his sons who had repeated the message from their wise uncle, "This land will also be the Repeater" for the People coming will holler here and have an echo. He turned them into stone as a reminder of this and you can see them at the top of the falls.

Now they built the dams and flooded our land and it's like choking off the blood from your heart. We don't need no more or we'll all die. The river's song is quiet now; you have to listen real careful to ever hear it. I want to reach out for my children and their children, because some now own no homes. And our land just wastes away without us. Sometimes I cry, feel sorry. Fishhook Jim has maybe two or three hundred children (descendants). Maybe young ones and they don't know what to do. They got no place to stay; the got no background; they got no land. That's why we would like to have a piece of our ground and have our horses again.

In the Shadow of Steptoe

North of Colfax, Washington

Chapter II:

THE PATHFINDERS AND EXILES

"Wawawai, yes, we used to have a campsite there and others all along the river.
All kind of fruit they raised—apples and peaches and plums and everything."
—Andrew George, 1980

After spending months and hundreds of thousands of dollars to garrison the chain of interior forts during the Indian wars, the army found it necessary in the early 1860s to divert its resources of men and materials to the East. In late December, 1860 South Carolina seceded from the Union and within weeks the country was embroiled in a national nightmare. Officers who had fought together against the Palouse, Yakama, and other Plateau tribes now found their loyalties divided between the Union and Confederacy. In the fall of 1862 Washington Territory mourned the loss of General Isaac Stevens who was killed while leading his men in a dramatic attack at the Second Battle of Bull Run. As the War Between the States put a tremendous strain on the resources of the Army's Oregon Department, its command found increasingly difficulties in dealing with disputes between Indians and settlers of the Inland Northwest. Everywhere the two groups mixed, trouble seemingly ensued. The alarming loss of promised Indian lands to settlers in the Colville district was brought to the attention of the Superintendent of Indian Affairs in 1862 and in the same year Fort Lapwai was built east of present Lewiston to keep the peace. The Palouse region seem to be encircled by brushfires of conflict yet at the beginning of the decade not a single settler lived between the Snake and Spokane rivers.

The area's first settlers selected homesites located in the western Palouse at strategic crossroads near sources of fresh water. In 1861 William Newman, a Canadian immigrant, built a cabin near the head of Sprague Lake at the junction of the Colville and White Bluffs roads. The latter was heavily promoted by the Oregon Steam and Navigation Company as its link between the Columbia River and the mines of western Montana and the Kootenai district. Newman's home served as a way-station for freighters and mail riders. In 1865 Henry Wind opened another roadhouse on the Colville Trail which was located on the lower end of Cow Creek below present Benge, Washington.

The rock corrals and stone foundation built in the shadow of the steep basalt cliff are still clearly visible from the roadside. In 1866 pioneer stockman Jack McElroy began raising cattle in the grassy coulees south of Newman's cabin and he was soon followed by Russell Bacon, Robert Potts, and William "Hoodoo Billy" Burrow.

The first settler in the Palouse Hills was George Pangburn, a twenty-seven-year-old bachelor from Walla Walla, who visited the area as early as 1862. He later squatted on unsurveyed land along lower Union Flat Creek south of present Endicott. Pangburn wintered in Walla Walla but returned periodically to farm, plant a small orchard, and raise hogs for the Lewiston. He lived in an earthen dugout south of the stream and in 1867 was raising wheat, corn, and oats on the flat. He built a twelve by fourteen foot log cabin in 1870 on the present August and Willene Luft farm where today a bronze plaque mounted on a basalt slab commemorates "The first known farm in the Palouse." About that same time Joseph "Kentuck" Ruark and his Indian wife settled near the mouth of the creek. Actually a native of Pennsylvania, "Kentuck" had also resided temporarily in Walla Walla before establishing his Palouse ranch. A settler named Knight squatted in 1864 on land near present Mica southeast of present Spokane. This site eventually developed into the famed "California Ranch" way-station operated by a colorful proprietor, Maxim Mulouin, as early as 1871.

Snake River Landings and Orchard Communities

The hamlets that appeared on the north side of the Snake River at the early ferry crossing sites in the 1860s and 70s, places like Palouse Landing (Perry), Penawawa, Almota, and Wawawai, became the Palouse Country's "ports of entry" for many of the region's earliest settlers. In 1859 Edward Massey began operating the "Palouse Ferry" a mile below the mouth of the Palouse River where the Colville Road crossed the Snake River. Massey sold his interest in the ferry to brothers William and Cyrus McWhirt in 1864 but in the following year John Silcott and John Harding purchased the operation. Business was brisk for Silcott and Harding who ferried army and civilian traffic traveling on the Colville Road from Walla Walla to destinations north of the river. Palouse Landing also became a principal destination of the Oregon Railway and Navigation Company's sternwheeler fleet that plied the fast waters of the lower Snake and Columbia rivers from Portland.

The Palouse Indians who stubbornly remained at the mouth of the Palouse were likely bewildered by the sudden surge in pioneer traffic across the land. The second ferry landing established on the Snake River was located about four miles upstream from Palouse Landing near the mouth of the Tucannon (*Tukwénenma*) River. Rights for the business were first secured by Isaac Kellogg in January, 1864 and operations began the following spring in partnership with Samuel Caldwell and James McAuliff. Soon afterward, however, Kellogg was killed in a gunfight near the Spokane River and Caldwell drowned with two other men after upsetting his canoe while the ferry was under repair. Four more miles upstream Michael Tormey established the Taksas Ferry in 1865 near the massive wood yard opposite Riparia where Lewiston steamers loaded fuel. The service came to known as the Texas Ferry and its connecting trail dubbed the Texas Road which continued northward through present LaCrosse, past Texas Lake, and skirted Rock Lake on the west to connect with the Mullan Road. The

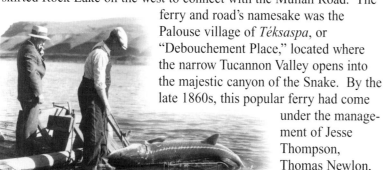

ferry and road's namesake was the Palouse village of *Téksaspa*, or "Debouchement Place," located where the narrow Tucannon Valley opens into the majestic canyon of the Snake. By the late 1860s, this popular ferry had come under the management of Jesse Thompson, Thomas Newlon, and T. M. Slocum (C. Kingston, 1951).

SNAKE RIVER STURGEON FISHING, c. 1900 (MASC, WSU LIBRARIES)

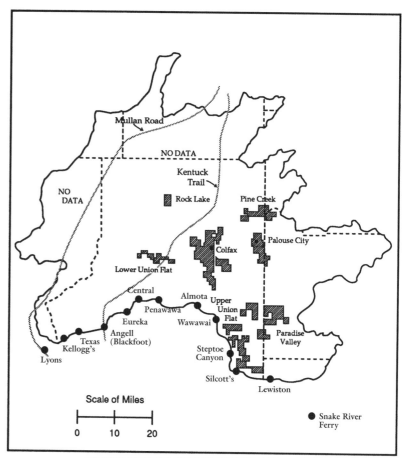

PALOUSE REGIONAL SETTLEMENT ENCLAVES, c. 1872

Thousands of miners, described as "a restless, shifting crowd," began redirecting their paths as reports of new strikes on the Little Blackfoot River in western Montana in 1865 led them to travel the recently charted roads across the Palouse. In that year, Ruark joined Thomas W. Davidson in operating Angell Ferry six miles upstream from Texas Ferry. In an effort to capitalize on the burgeoning traffic to the Montana gold placers, they renamed their site "Blackfoot Ferry" which linked Angell Ferry Road from Walla Walla with what they advertised as "the nearest route to the mines." The path crossed the heart of the Palouse region along portions of the old Spokane Trail and soon became known as the Kentuck Trail.

Moving to the vicinity of present Central Ferry in 1865 was Joseph DeLong, a bachelor originally from the Midwest. He had crossed the plains in 1862 and settled on the Tucannon River above Walla Walla where he farmed and raised livestock. In 1865 he joined Pangburn on Union Flat but relocated in 1867 to the scenic bottomland where the Kentuck Trail crossed the Palouse River after he found his missing cow grazing contently near the water. DeLong built a log cabin on a knoll of wild sunflowers that protruded from the northern bluffs and he sold provisions to immigrants traveling along the trail. For protection from area Indians he also fashioned a wall of talus in a rockshelter overlooking the river's bend.

Steam navigation on the Snake River was inaugurated in 1859 by two army supply runners who had sailed the waters from Celilo to Ft. Walla Walla during the Indian wars using small scows. Frontier entrepreneurs R. R. Thompson and L. W. Coe decided that the Idaho gold strikes made that year would justify an investment to build a steamer. That year they had the shallow draft sternwheeler *Colonel Wright* built at the mouth of the Dechutes River which Master Leonard White then nudged fifty miles up the Snake on her first test run. Business soon boomed with all the mining excitement above Lewiston as the ship made as much as $2,500 per run on passenger fares alone for the weekly two-day trip from Celilo. Freight was shipped during the first decade at rates varying from $60 to $80 dollars per ton. Over the next twenty years a fleet of ships like the gleaming white *Okanogan* and *Spray* were acquired and built by the O. R. & N. Co. and did a brisk business in upriver traffic. They returned with ever increasing loads of grain each summer and fall. With the completion of the company's

ALMOTA, WASHINGTON, 1889 (MASC, WSU LIBRARIES)

rail line from Walla Walla to the Snake River opposite Riparia in 1881, the vessels were needed only to run upriver from the south shore railhead. Vessels belching forth billowy clouds of black were seen almost daily from Riparia to Lewiston during the spring and summer carrying loads of immigrants and supplies. (R.V. Mills, 1947).

Snake River rafters and riverboat pilots found the most daunting of the seventeen rapids between Lewiston and the river's mouth to be Palouse Rapids.

Beginning four miles above the mouth of the Palouse River, a series of basaltic outcroppings stood like a monstrous spine that created a watery obstacle course leading to the "chute." Here the channel narrowed for the river to descend six feet in a three-quarter mile stretch of billowy foam. In 1861, fifteen-year-old William Polk Gray accompanied his father, missionary William H. Gray, on a grueling forty-day rafting expedition upriver using a capstan and rope to pull a load of merchandise from Wallula to Lewiston. The same year Samuel Clemens was serving as a cub pilot on the Mississippi gaining experiences that would culminate in the creation of Huckleberry Finn two decades later. Young Gray also met first-hand the perils of life on the river but the efforts of father and son confirmed the viability of river commerce in spite of the hazards. While floating a raft of lumber and skiff downstream from Lewiston on a September return trip, Gray encountered Palouse Rapids with all its force. "I sent the raft into the center. The current was so swift it sent us into the eddy. The forward part of the raft went under water. The skiff...started to float off but I caught the painter and got aboard. About a half-mile below the rapids our skiff was suddenly lifted out of the water by the reappearance of the raft." The party was surprised at the sight of both burden and raft that "had gone with the current and, oddly enough, had appeared directly under us." The teenager's experiences on the Snake left him with the resolve that "no combination of wood, iron, or water" would ever scare him again. Gray went on to serve as a cub pilot on the sternwheeler *Yakima* and eventually made a career on the Snake River where he regularly visited landings from Riparia to Lewiston—the Hannibal, Missouri of the Inland Pacific Northwest.

John Silcott relocated to a crossing eight miles west of Lewiston in 1861 to establish a ferry at historic Red Wolf's Crossing and another at Lewiston the following year. He married the daughter of the noted Nez Perce leader, Chief Timothy, whose people lived in the vicinity. Silcott sold his interest in Palouse Ferry to Daniel Lyons, a forty-three year old native of Limerick, Ireland, in 1872. Lyons had immigrated to the United States in 1847 and following his marriage to Anna Wright in 1854, the couple moved west in a series of peregrinations that led from California and British Columbia to Walla Walla and Palouse Landing. The site came to be known as Lyons Ferry and following Daniel's death in 1893, their son, Perry, established a small community nearby and continued to operate the ferry for over thirty years. (Lyons Ferry was later acquired by W. J. Cummings and eventually by Nye and Ruth Turner who operated this last ferry service across the Snake River until its closure in 1968.)

Two dozen miles upstream from Lyons Ferry in the vicinity of Penawawa, pioneer stockmen began grazing vast herds of cattle in 1870 on the steep grassy slopes of the Snake River canyon. In 1872 C. C. and Sarah Cram moved to Penawawa from the Walla Walla Valley and with the help of their son, William, established the Penawawa Ferry, which the family operated into the 1880s. Cram, a veteran of the Interior Indian Wars, became an active promoter of Palouse Country settlement and built a substantial portion of the Territorial Road from Pataha to Penawawa and northward to Union Flat in the 1870s. This route became one of the primary arteries for travel from Walla Walla and Dayton to Colfax and Spokane. A fellow veteran of the Indian campaigns, Iowa native Alexander Canutt also settled in Penawawa with his wife, Sallie, and their family in 1872, as did George and Nancy Smith. In the following year, Emsley and Mary Fincher arrived in the fledgling settlement to begin a large sheep raising operation. Like most of the Snake River ferry landings, Penawawa in the 1870s boasted several saloons, a hotel, and freight warehouses. Area pioneers credited Canutt with the introduction of irrigated orcharding to the valley and the family's holdings expanded when sons John and Joseph obtained property adjacent to the original ranch.

Fourteen miles upstream from Penawawa was the frontier river settlement of Almota where Civil War veteran L. M. Ringer settled in 1872 though rancher Edward Johnson was raising cattle and horses in the vicinity a year earlier. In 1873 Ringer was joined by his wife, Sophia, and their children and the family established a general mercantile business. Located at the northernmost point of the Snake River, Almota was soon transformed into a bustling pioneer community with O. R. & N. Co. warehouses, two hotels, a saloon, gristmill, and another cable ferry service across the river. Joining the Ringer family in 1872 was Henry Hart Spalding, son of the famed Congregational missionaries to the Nez Perce, Henry Harmon and Eliza Spalding.

Following the 1846 Whitman Massacre, Spalding and his parents had moved to Oregon's Willamette Valley. Henry Hart missed the land of his youth, however, and decided to return east of the Cascades in the 1860s to settle in the Walla Walla Valley before moving to Almota. He acquired 1200 acres of land adjacent to the river and established one of the largest orchards in the valley with vast plantings of apple, pear, peach, and other fruit trees as well as wine grapes and grain.

Area orchardists like the Spaldings, Canutts, and others formed a horticul-

FELIX WARREN AND PULLMAN BOY SCOUT TROOP, c. 1920 (MASC, WSU LIBRARIES)

tural society to better raise and market their fruit and these efforts contributed to the successful promotion of the "Palouse Apple." The origin and name of this Red Bellflower variety was attributed to Joseph and Susanna Arrasmith, natives of Indiana, who settled in 1874 on the Palouse River several miles west of present Palouse. The succulent fruit's red skin with lemon yellow stripes was selected for its taste as sauce, in pies, and for cider. Our family knew the Palouse Apple as Grandmother Scheuerman's *Schnitzel Apfel* with one tree of the species inhabiting the orchard behind our house. The colorfully stripped fruit was gathered each fall and derived its German name from the hundreds of "pieces" she carefully sliced and dried each fall for year-round consumption. A special holiday treat that ensures a complete family Christmas holiday week is her *Schnitzel Soupa*, a peculiar fruity concoction of cooked apples, apricots, raisins, and prunes served hot and mixed with sweet cream just before serving.

Also a hardy survivor of Northwest winters, the Palouse Apple became the most widely raised variety in area orchards like those of the Arrasmith's neighbors to the north, Lewis and Mary Love who emigrated from Missouri in 1881 to homestead south of Garfield. Love was an innovator who tried his hand at raising numerous varieties of fruit and grain. Nearby Elberton boasted the world's largest fruit dryer in the 1890s with a daily capacity of 1,800 bushels of fresh fruit. An enormous dryer for prunes was built in the tiny settlement of Diamond and another large facility that took a variety of fruit was built in Colfax. Large orchards also flourished from 1890 to 1910 in the eastern Palouse from Potlatch to Kendrick. The Palouse Country held approximately 300,000 fruit trees in 1910 but subsequent severe winters and the economic challenges of fruit production led to a gradual decline in production. Within two decades

most large orchards in the Palouse Hills had been removed and planted to grains (W. Lever, 1901; *Spokesman-Review*, June 17, 1909).

The year 1877 in Almota witnessed the alliance of two of the Palouse Country's most colorful and prominent families as Henry Hart Spalding married Mary C. Warren. The Hugh Warren family had journeyed westward over the Oregon Trail in 1865 to settle in the Prescott area. Mary Spalding's brother, Felix Warren, became a legendary stagecoach driver for the Northwestern Stage Company on the Territorial Road from Walla Walla and Dayton via Pomeroy and Almota to Colfax. This route was an important company spur penetrating the Inland Northwest from its main route between Kelton, Utah and Portland, Oregon via Pendleton. When just twelve years old, Felix Warren had an abrupt introduction to his life's work. The boy's father, who served as wagonmaster for the Missouri emigrants, fell gravely ill in the Rocky Mountains. Young Felix took over the reins and continued leading the wagon train all the way to Walla Walla. In later years Warren frequently overnighted at the Spalding's palatial home, which came to be known as Almota House, after a long day's run at the reins atop his Concord coach. In the evenings he often regaled passengers, relatives, and friends with stories of battles against the elements, wild animals, and notorious outlaws. Clad in fringed western garb and broad-brimmed hat with a neatly trimmed moustache and goatee, Warren was a gifted teller of tales and looked every bit the part he played in Palouse Country frontier lore.

The O.R.&N.Co.'s only other north shore landing below Lewiston in the 1870s was located at Wawawai, eight miles southeast of Almota. The community was named for the ancient Indian village of the same name near which homesteads for raising livestock were established by William Winter, John Gould, James Root, and others in

THE INTERIOR GRAIN TRAMWAY, c. 1900 (MASC, WSU LIBRARIES)

1875. The first apple and soft fruit trees were likely planted by Isaiah Matheny the same year with large orchards established soon afterward on both sides of the river below Granite Point by Sewell Truax. A large warehouse for fruit, sacked grain, farm implements, and other commodities was constructed in 1877 by Matheny and Colfax businessman and miller John Davenport. Ferry service at Wawawai was inaugurated by John Kanawyer in 1885. Stone was also quarried form the ancient Miocene fissure at Granite Point several

TABER FAMILY HOME AND ORCHARD AT ALMOTA, 1889 (MASC, WSU LIBRARIES)

areas of dangerous rapids between Lewiston and Riparia. Eventually an O.R.&N.Co. demolition crew began working from the steamer *Wallowa* to remove the most treacherous outcropings in the river and the thunder of downstream blasting eventually came within earshot of the remaining villagers at Palus. Inexorably the crewmen approached Palouse Rapids. After several days of blasting, the crew moved four more miles upstream to tame Texas Rapids using the same method.

miles upstream and hauled to such burgeoning townsites as Colton, Pullman, Moscow, and Colfax where it was used for foundations and façades in many commercial buildings. (J. Cruthfield, 1973).

Grain trader Aaron Kuhn built a second warehouse in the 1880s and began seeking a better solution to the problems his clients encountered in transporting their wheat by wagon down the steep grade of the winding Canyon Road that led from Pullman and Colton to Wawawai. The entrepreneur eventually financed the construction of the mile-long Interior Grain Tramway, an immense project that when completed had the peculiar appearance of a ski lift carrying sacked grain down the slope on wooden benches. At the lower warehouse the sacks were unloaded and stacked to await steamship transport to the railhead at Riparia for shipment to the Coast. When working properly, some 2,000 sacks of Palouse grain took the twenty minute ride down the tramway each day. In an average year, as many as 150,000 sacks were transported to Wawawai warehouses using this method.

The decade of the 1880s also witnessed the first biweekly runs of the *Annie Faxon*, *Almota*, *Harvest Queen* and other O.R.&N.Co. steamers that could reach speeds of eighteen miles per hour on upstream runs and return with up to eighty or more tons of grain and other freight. Their daring pilots continued to navigate the seventeen

Colfax's *Palouse Gazette* reported in 1885 that farmers were rapidly fencing their lands to control damage from roaming livestock. In doing so cut across miles of trails freely used by Indians since time immemorial to reach root grounds and traditional hunting areas. While most farmers tolerated the diminishing travel by Indians through the area along the few routes still open to them, and often traded their produce for salmon. Others did not. They greatly objected to "Indian trespassing" and brandished weapons to impose the new order of the day. In at least one case, such a confrontation ended in the murder of a Palouse that was never reported to authorities.

In the late 1890s William and Mary LaFollette, Palouse pioneers of 1877 who also farmed near Ewartsville, acquired several hundred acres of land adjacent to the river and divided by Wawawai Creek. The LaFollettes built a sawmill and devised an extensive irrigation system on their property and planted vast tracts to fruit, principally shipped to Portland for distribution, as well as strawberries, grapes, rhubarb, asparagus, and melons which were marketed to communities above the river bluffs. As the LaFollettes' enterprises prospered, William acquired adjacent properties and was later elected to Congress. For the next seven decades, families throughout the Palouse made festive outings in late summer or early fall to the Snake River

*Lewiston Grade Vista**

North of Lewiston, Idaho

orchard communities to spend a day picking tree-ripened fruit for home-canning to meet winter needs.

Provisioned with picnic lunches, young and old would join together to gather the finest produce in a harvest sequence beginning in June with Mount Morincy pie cherries, Bings, and Royal Anns for canning. Apricots, nectarines, and Hale peaches rippened in July followed by pears in August. Midsummer apples were also picked at this time including green Transparents for applesauce and Rome Beauties, a dessert favorite of railroad chefs on the region's early lines. Smaller crabapples, excellent for jelly, and pears were also picked in August. Fall apples included Jonathans, Red Delicious. Ripening last of all were the Winesaps and Winter Bananas, two of the finest baking apples. Friendships between orchard and farm families were renewed annually as boxes and baskets were weighed at wholesale prices on ponderous iron scales and then carefully loaded for the return home (M. Lautensleger, 2003; J. and K. Kromm, 2003).

Settlers in the Hills

Blacksmith James Hall obtained backing from Lapwai businessman W. A. Caldwell to establish a cattle ranch near the head of Hatwai Creek north of Lewiston in 1868 and later constructed a cabin of hand-sawn planks. That same year twenty-year-old Riley Knight hauled lumber from Dayton to build a cabin on Thorn Creek northwest of Steptoe Butte. After three years on the isolated prairie, Hall had second thoughts about continuing his operation since a fellow with his smithing skills could find employment almost anywhere. He decided to leave and the place was acquired in 1871 by Michael and Elizabeth Ruddy, immigrants from eastern Canada. The Ruddy family built onto the house which later served as a stagecoach and mail station until it passed into the hands of Orville Collins. The original home has remained in the family ever since and is likely the oldest residence in the southeastern Palouse.

In 1869 T. A. E. "Doc" Philleo established a ranch several miles northwest of present Spangle where he found ample open rangeland and access to a small lake later named for him. Several miles due east of the lake was a wooded flat surrounded by small lakes chosen by Cyrus Turnbull for his homesite. In the 1930s the original ranch was acquired by the federal government to form the nucleus of the Turnbull National Wildlife Refuge for migrating Canada and snow geese, swans, ducks, golden eagles, and other migratory fowl. The area has grown to cover 15,500 acres and also serves as an important sanctuary for beaver, river otter, the Palouse Country's largest elk herd, and ten species of bats including nocturnal big browns and the long-eared myotis (J. Philleo, 1979; R. Kirk and C. Alexander, 1990).

A September, 1869 issue of Portland's *Morning Oregonian* reported that the Palouse Country was "finally attracting the attention of settlers." The first significant surge of immigration to the area took place between that year and 1871 when a number of settlers like James and Jennie Ewart located on Union Flat Creek in what later became known as the Ewartsville district. Most of these early settlers were Americans from the upper Midwest and Northeast although nine were Irish immigrants like the McNeilly brothers who had come to the northeastern United States in the 1840s and moved on to the western gold strikes. As was the case with Ewart, a Civil War captain in the Illinois Volunteer Calvary, their loyalties had been with the North and the stream was dubbed "Union Flat Creek" accordingly. The 1870 federal census listed 116 settlers residing on Union Flat and at the time of Whitman County's creation in 1871 about 200 were living within its boundaries.

Natives of South Carolina and Georgia like the Alfred Holt family settled along the neighboring stream north near Plainville (the present Palouse Empire Fairgrounds near Colfax) in 1872, which resulted in it being named Rebel Flat Creek. Soon veterans who had fought against each other in the Wilderness Campaign,

GERTRUDE COSSITT IN HOMESTEADER TENT, c. 1890 (MASC, WSU LIBRARIES)

Chickamauga, and in other Civil War battles found themselves neighbors in the Palouse. An immigrant presence was also found along Paradise Valley by 1870 in the vicinity of present Moscow. On a foray through the area in August of that year, census-taker C. P. Coburn

COLFAX, WASHINGTON, 1889 (MASC, WSU LIBRARIES)

Georgia Donner Babcock was a child of five when she set out with her family in April, 1846 from Independence, Missouri in a wagon train headed to California led by her father and uncle, George and Jacob Donner. At Ft. Bridger their group of ninety decided to take the little-known

encountered two prospectors, William Powers and Frank Points, as well as Kentucky native John Buchanan who had begun raising livestock to the consternation of local Indians who prized the unspoiled root grounds of the verdant valley. In 1872 Civil War veteran "Major" R. H. Wimpy and his wife became the first settlers on Hangman Creek when they established a farm about seven miles southeast of present Waverly (W. Lever, 1901).

Other Palouse pioneers came in search of peace and possibility after experiencing nineteenth century American tragedies every bit as disturbing as the Whitman Massacre and Civil War atrocities. An old photograph of Rock Lake City shows blacksmith Joseph Lee standing behind his anvil and clutching a white-hot horseshoe with long-handled pliers. His thick apron and debris-laded floor portray the life of hard labor known to men of his trade. Lee's parents had joined the Latter-Day Saints in 1832 just two years after the church was founded and the family witnessed the murder of Joseph and Hyrum Smith in June, 1944 in Nauvoo, Illinois. The Lees crossed the Great Plains in 1849 bound for Utah but Joseph and his wife, Mary Ann, relocated to the Palouse where they raised a family of thirteen children in the Rock Lake area. The Lees soon became acquainted with neighbors who had overcome unimaginable horrors about the same time they had lived in Utah.

Hasting's Cutoff south of Salt Lake but rather than saving precious time, the desert heat considerably slowed their progress and the group did not reach the foot of the Sierra-Nevada Mountains until late fall. An abnormally early winter struck as they began climbing the range and they became snowbound near the shores of a lake where they endured frigid weather and famine. Fully half of the party perished in the mountains, and only because some of the survivors resorted to cannibalism. But the others including members of Georgia's family displayed bravery of the highest order and were eventually rescued. In later years she moved from California to the Palouse where she took an active part in managing one of the largest ranches in the Rock Lake area in partnership with her son, Frank B. Babcock (F. Patterson, 1996; M. Trunkey, 1976).

Many of these immigrants had first lived for a time in the bustling settlement of Lewiston where land seekers and freighters made connections to travel northward on John Silcott's ferry. His landing a short distance downriver became the beachhead for the impending European-American invasion onto the Palouse prairies and eastern mining districts. Following the boomtown excitement of the previous decade that brought recurrent waves of miners to its muddy streets, Lewiston at the dawn of the 1870s was experiencing an awkward adolescence. Its population had stabilized at about four hundred, but a civic pride foreshadowed steady growth and was reflected in the replacement of false fronts and canvas roofs with substantial frame structures. Saloons and hotels still predominated along Main Street but the town now also boasted a doctor's office, drug store, and school.

Although most Lewiston residents were native-born Americans from the East, fully one-third were foreign-born with Chinese, Germans, Irish, and Canadians predominating. Lewiston in 1870 was home to a much more ethnically diverse population than other inland Northwest communities with its citizenry also including natives of Sweden, France, Mexico, Chile, and the Philippines. Within months some would ascend the imposing bunchgrass covered bluffs north of the river and join the handful of others to make a lifelong home in the Palouse. William Ewing, a Lewiston butcher from Pennsylvania, would soon establish a ferry crossing near the future site of Palouse City; drayman Michael Leitch would found the settlement of Leitchville at an important stage stop southeast of present Pullman; and Hungarian-born Jacob Kambitch was making plans to homestead in Paradise Valley near present Moscow.

Belleville, Paradise Valley, and Three Forks

In 1870 settlement began at present Colfax where James Perkins and Thomas Smith built a twenty-four by sixteen foot log cabin at the base of a bluff near the confluence of the Palouse River's North and South forks. A testament to frontier construction, the building remains as the oldest structure in the Palouse Country and is on the grounds of the Perkins House National Historic Site. First known as Belleville, Perkins suggested the name Colfax for the hamlet to honor Vice-President Schyler Colfax of Crédit Mobiler notoriety. Settlement also began at Farmington in 1870 and the following year pioneers located near present

Moscow, Palouse, and Rosalia. Growth was steady if not rapid between 1870 and 1872 as settlement expanded along Union Flat Creek and the Palouse River at Colfax. Other pioneers located during this time along Rebel Flat Creek, Pine Creek, Four Mile Creek (near present Viola), near present Genesee, at the foot of Rock Lake, and at present St. John and Spangle.

The majority of these families were native-born Americans who had journeyed to the Oregon Country after the Civil War but shared the experience of one immigrant group that "found all the land taken up in the Willamette Valley and ...heard there was still plenty of good land in the Palouse Country." Immigrant traffic to the region through Walla Walla was observed by the editor of the *Walla Walla Union* who noted in April, 1871 that the "country between the Snake and Spokane Rivers seems now to be the favorite region with stockraisers, and the valleys that skirt the small streams in that section are fast filling up with this class of settlers. We are told that no less than 500 head of cattle have been taken across the Snake River at the different ferries since last fall (F. Yoder, 1938; W. Lever, 1901).

In the summer of 1871 brothers Almon and Noah Lieuallen, natives of Tennessee who had crossed the Plains to Oregon in 1867, brought a herd of cattle from Lewiston to Paradise Valley and built cabins for their families about three miles northeast of present Moscow. The area was also dubbed "Hog Heaven" since razorbacks delighted in rooting up the camas fields and other native tubers. The Nez Perce name for the area was *Taxt Hinma*, or "Place of Deer Fawns." Within a year the Lieuallens followed to the area by George Tomer, Thomas Tierney, John Russell, and enough other families to justify the creation of Paradise Post Office. A school was also erected in 1872 near Almon Lieuallen's home and adjacent fields of flax. Further down the valley and later in the decade, a small enclave of settlers clustered near the

DANIEL BOONE FAMILY PICNIC NEAR PULLMAN, c. 1920 (MASC, WSU LIBRARIES)

Boone's Farm Spring   *East of Pullman, Washington*

confluence of the Palouse River and Dry Fork and Missouri Flat creeks. Named "Three Forks" by pioneer residents, the land that would later become the Pullman townsite was first claimed by Daniel G. McKenzie in 1877. Arriving in the vicinity a year later was Indiana native Daniel W. Boone, named for his famed frontiersman ancestor, who came with his wife, Amelia, after a brief sojourn in Oregon. A general mercantile was built in 1881 by Orville Stewart and M.D. Lee and in the following year Northern Pacific Railroad surveyors laid out the town on property acquired from McKenzie.

Most pioneers during the first decade of settlement lived next to streams or good springs in order to supply domestic needs and to maintain their livestock. Wood was needed not only for fuel and building material but also as fence rails since barbed wire was not invented until 1873. Western yellow pine provided the best lumber but large stands were found only along the mountainous eastern uplands, down both Palouse River forks, along Union Flat Creek and near the scabland channel northeast from Rock Lake. Many families camped for weeks or even months in tents until they obtained enough logs or lumber to build a home. Some primitive habitations were little more than holes dug into leeward hillsides with crude shelters erected over them. When sufficient preparations had been made for construction, the typical house in the Palouse hinterlands resembled the small box-house measuring from twelve by fourteen to sixteen by twenty feet. Often a "lean-to" was added to one side to extend the sleeping area. Glass windows were a luxury and many families waited weeks for floorboards since the demand for lumber usually exceeded the supply from local mills. Well-drilling equipment was operating in the Palouse by 1878 to expand the possibilities for locating a homesite and the silhouettes of windmills against crepuscular skies soon appeared across the Palouse horizon.

Frontier Living and Trade Centers

The journals and account books kept by Joseph DeLong at his Palouse River ranch and store provide a rare glimpse of life on the Palouse frontier during its earliest years of settlement. Journal entries record information essential to pioneer self-sufficiency under such scribbled headlines as "Smallpox Cure," a concoction of sugar, foxtail, and zinc sulfate, "Recipe for Preserving Green Fruit," and "Grasshopper Poison." Related knowledge of value clipped from early issues of the *Walla Walla Statesman* and *Palouse Gazette* was safeguarded between the small, lined pages of his hardboard bound books providing the mathematical formula "To Measure Hay in Ricks," stories about Lincoln and Grant, and favored verse: "Let live forever grow, and banish wrath and strife; So shall we witness here below, the joys of social life." Perhaps to advance social relations with the travelers and neighbors who frequented his place, DeLong also found time to jot down riddles. One favorite of this thinly bearded soul with kindly mien was in rhyme: "I went to walk through a field of wheat, and there found something good to eat. It was neither fat, lean or bone, I kept it till it ran home (an egg)."

Most folks with whom DeLong most often shared such wit and practical knowledge were families of those who later settled near him on the pine covered slopes of the Palouse River Valley. Names frequently appearing in his account books include Ben Davis, Frank Smith, Steve Cutler, Link Ballaine, and E.E. Huntley. These families came to DeLong's store to visit, collect mail, and procure staples, often on credit. DeLong's inventory included eggs, onions, coffee, sugar, and baking powder; soap, sarsaparilla, and tobacco. He also stocked hardware supplies like nails and wire, and such curatives as oil of anise, oil of bergamot, and sulfuric of ether. DeLong and his neighbors spent considerable time building and repairing split rail fences to hold in their livestock and also experimented with a variety of grains and fruits to determine those best suited to Palouse soils and climate. The Palouse River bachelor planted hundreds of apple trees along the river obtained from Walla Walla nurseries as well as pear, cherry, plum, prune stock, grape vines, and currant bushes. Summer visitors to his store could always expect a good supply of Tall Pippins, Yellow Bells, Northern Spy and other apples as well as soft fruit and vegetables which he sometimes traded for salmon with Indians who seasonally passed along the old trails along the river. Ben Sissom, who settled a short distance upstream from DeLong in 1867, was credited with seeding the first wheat along the river (J. DeLong, 1863, 1866, 1887, 1891).

The early American and Canadian settlers were primarily subsistence farmers and stockmen who raised cattle, sheep, and hogs. The virgin sod of dense bunchgrass crowning a fibrous root system was broken in the heavy, wet bottomlands by long-sheared breaking plows, primitive disks, and harrows fashioned from bushes or wooden teeth. A two-horse team pulling a single shear plow could turn a half-acre per day while a larger three-horse triple shear gang could cover two acres in the same time. The laborious task of breaking virgin sod, however, almost always required a single shear plow, steady strong hands, and a cooperative horse. Stands of hawthorn and wild rose were widespread along some draw bottoms and stubbornly resisted the pioneers' attempts to burn them out and plow through the roots and sod.

The early farmers experimented with flax, rye, and spelt, a primitive grain used for livestock feed. Sufficient moisture in the bottomlands usually allowed two cuttings of alfalfa and such grasses as clover and meadow fescue in June and September. Small cleared patches were seeded in the spring by hand broadcast to oats, barley, and wheat. The crops were usually cut with a scythe or cradle to hold the cuttings. The grain was trampled out by horses or flailed in the ancient manner and often yielded sixty bushels per acre in the early 1870s when not frostbitten. The settlers planted orchards and large gardens and gathered wild currants, huckleberries, gooseberries, and serviceberries for canning. Trout were abundant in the clear waters of the Palouse River where the pioneers also hunted doves, grouse, and waterfowl.

Meeting the physical needs of large Palouse families was a substantial undertaking in the pioneer era that required considerable planning, planting, and processing. Provisions stored for winter and spring were substantially home-grown or traded locally since trips to even Colfax or Oakesdale for bulk foods meant paying premium prices that many families could not afford. A family with even six children commonly required butchering five hogs in the fall and canning or smoking the pork, five hundred pounds of flour, and a ton of potatoes— about twenty gunny sacks or the product of one to two acres. At least a hundred pounds of sugar was needed for canning hundreds of jars with fruit and vegetables, another hundred pounds of dry beans and peas, and in some cases a substantial amount of popcorn. Two coffee grinders were commonly stored in pioneer Palouse households. Since coffee beans were usually green when purchased, they were oven-roasted for grinding. Those for whom coffee was a luxury sometimes roasted wheat or barley kernals until dark brown to brew an acceptable substitute. Those for whom coffee was too much of a luxury to afford sometimes roasted wheat until dark brown to brew an acceptable substitute. The other machine was for crushing wheat berries to be mixed with rolled oats or dried fruit for a boiled breakfast "mush." To immigrant English, the variable mixture was called porridge, while the early Germans knew it as *Hirsche*, from the German word for millet. They sometimes joked that it was "*nicht fuer essen aber fressen!*" (not for eating but for grazing).

From the earliest days of settlement women pickled a variety of garden and orchard produce with a medley of spices in earthenware crockery ranging in size from five to ten gallons. Cucumbers were crocked with salt and dill, tomatoes in water with herbs, and peaches with sugar and cloves. Potatoes, carrots, and beets were stored in root cellars that were often dug into an adjacent sidehill and connected to the house by a porch. Milk, cream, and butter were made throughout the year and chickens and eggs were readily available if they were also raised. These needs required farmyards with barns, chicken houses, hog sheds, vegetable cellars, smokehouses, granaries, and other outbuildings in order to substantially maintain pioneer self-sufficiency. Most families also pastured one or two dairy cows to supply milk, cream, and butter.

Land was claimed through several means. The liberal provisions of the 1862 Homestead Act promised 160 acres of public land to qualified adults who lived on their property for five years and improved it. Others purchased relinquishments from those who came as speculators or who wanted to leave after laboring under the difficult conditions. Land prices in the early 1870s ranged from $1 to $2 per acre. Timber cultures provided a quarter section to those who wanted to plant ten acres of trees, few of which, however, survived the dry climate. Preemption claims involved a substitute payment to the government of $2.50 per acre for the five-year residence requirement. Many early settlers merely "squatted" on the parcel they desired until compelled to gain legal title to the property. This became possible only after the 1871-73 federal land surveys were completed in the Palouse by teams bearing chains, rods, stakes, and brass optical instruments. The work was directed by L.P. Beach, David Clark, Henry Meldrum, and others who labored from spring to fall to measure and mark township and section lines. A vast checkerboard grid was inexorably imposed upon the compliant Palouse like a net cast on a slumbering creature, and without regard to the region's unique topography (W. Yeager, 1961).

The first trading centers emerged in the Palouse Country in the early 1870s to provide lumber and milled wheat. Those who settled on lower Union Flat Creek found little quality timber in native groves of cottonwood and willow and even eastern Palouse settlers lacked facilities to process their stands of higher grade timber. Promotional material sent out at the time by a Portland immigration bureau had warned, "The greatest difficulty which the settler will encounter in taking up a farm is the comparative absence of timber. There are groves of cottonwoods, birch, alder and willow along the watercourses, but pine, fir and tamarack must be transported as a general fact from the mountains." In October 1871, the first sawmill in the Palouse Country was built at the fork of the Palouse River near present Colfax by former Midwesterners James Perkins, Hezekiah Hollingsworth, and Anderson Cox. Cox also intended to build a flour mill in Colfax but died near Dusty in 1872 while on a trip from Portland to obtain the necessary equipment.

Over 60,000 bushels of wheat were raised in the Palouse in 1872 but the *Portland Oregonian* lamented the fact that "this amount will not any more than supply the settlers with seed for this year and yet, strange to relate, they have no thriving mill between the Snake and Spokane Rivers, a vast area of country, uninhabited four years ago but now dotted all over with the improvement of energetic farmers and some of the land already in a high state of cultivation." In 1873 Joseph W. Davenport arrived from the Willamette Valley to construct a flour mill in Colfax and the local farmers warmly responded by pledging 5,000 bushels of wheat for processing. By 1877 other flour mills were operating at Palouse, where James "Modoc" Smith had settled in 1873, and at Almota. A second sawmill had been constructed in Colfax along with others in Palouse and near Moscow. A horse-powered model was used by James Ewart on Union Flat but the machinery was relocated to the Palouse River near Elberton where a larger

sawmill was constructed in 1878. Other early sawmills were located at Moscow, Pine City, and Rockford.

One of the smaller operations that survived the economic pressures of the era was Oakesdale's Barron Flour Mill. This five-story steam-powered facility was built with mortise and tenon construction in 1890. The facility was purchased by Pennsylvania native and second generation miller Joseph C. Barron in 1907 who introduced the popular "Sweet Home" brand. The mill is a National Historic Site and Barron's son, Joseph, still operates a smaller mill in an adjacent facility. He is responsible for coining the popular brand name "Nutrigrain" that was acquired by Kellog's in 1982 (F. Gilbert, 1882; W. Davenport, 1925; R. Swanson, 1958).

Among Latah County's earliest pioneers, David Notman had heard about the legendary grasslands of the Inland Pacific Northwest while ranching on Big Thompson Creek north of Denver, Colorado. In 1873 he joined a group of friends and relatives who had come in a dozen wagons from his old home in Arkansas. They had decided prospects for the future were better risked in the uncertainties of this new land than in the grim realities of subsistence farming in the South. The Arkansas families included those of J. M. Woody and cousins John P. and John Freeze. Their trek began on April 4, 1873 in Benton County, Arkansas, and ended seven months later with their arrival on August 3 in Walla Walla. Notman continued north across the Snake River later that month to Deep Creek northwest of present Potlatch. The Freeze families remained in Waitsburg-Dayton area until 1876 when they joined the Notmans and others to form a rural community later known as the Freeze district. Others in the original group from Arkansas including J. M. Woody were among the first settlers further west from the Freezes in the Farmington and Garfield areas.

Ranching in the Western Palouse

The earliest ranchers in the Rock Lake district were John Eaton, another veteran of the 1855-56 Indian Wars who arrived in 1870 after helping to operate the Kentuck Ferry for two years, Thomas May, and the William and Minnie Henderson family. The Henderson home, a two-story whitewashed frontier Gothic structure built in 1872, survives as one of the oldest houses in the Palouse

*Divine Protection**

*Freeze Church Summer**   *North of Potlatch, Idaho*

69

Country. A guest of the Hendersons in the 1870s described the interior of the one-room house that measured sixteen by twenty feet in no-frills terms. "Two corners were occupied by beds, a third by a cook-stove, and the fourth by a table. In addition, there were a cradle, several chairs and benches, cooking utensils, and a limited supply of dishes." Residing at the foot of Rock Lake was the legendary Chief Kamiakin with his four wives and their children.

Once the Northwest's most influential Indian leader, the old chief had been reduced to near poverty but never surrendered his pride. He remained adamant about living in his ancestral homeland rather than accepting liberal government inducements to move to the Yakama Reservation. He deeply mourned the passing of his first wife, the warrior-woman Colestah, companion at his side during the wars of the 1850s who had died at the family's Palouse River camp near present Matlock Bridge in 1865. The Kamiakins raised cattle, horses, and large gardens on Kamiak's Flat at Rock Lake where the chief's youngest son, Peopeo Kahow Not, known to Whites as Cleveland Kamiakin, was born in 1870. Seven years later the venerable chief sensed his time was near and asked that Father Joseph Caruna, a Jesuit priest from the Coeur d'Alene mission, come to baptize him. During the years of his stay in the Palouse, Kamiakin had frequently traveled to the mission to have his children baptized. He died the day after his christening in April, 1877 (E. Peone, 1981; T. Connolly, 1988).

The passing of one of the Northwest's greatest patriot chiefs went unheralded in the regional press, military bulletins, and reservation reports that had so often commented on him over the years. Local rancher friends Jack McElroy and John Eaton helped the family bury Kamiakin on a grassy bench several hundred yards southeast of the lake. Most family members gradually drifted onto the Colville, Yakama, and Coeur d'Alene reservations. Only Kamiakin's eldest son, Weeatkwal Tsicken, remained in the area at the village of Palus until his death in 1886 from a horse fall. Family members returned to the gravesite in 1878 to rehabilitate Kamiakin's body in accordance with tribal custom but were outraged to find that the grave had been opened. Bones including the skull had been removed by Charles Sternberg who was one of several scientists collecting fossils and anthropological specimens in the West for the Philadelphia Museum of Natural History. The sons reburied their father at a secret location on the broad flat on the other side of the lake. The missing remains of the great chief have never been located (L. West, 1927; C. Trafzer and R. Scheuerman, 1986).

In 1873 Henry Halsey settled further east in the upper Pleasant Valley district beyond present St. John where an ancient Indian trail leading from the Palouse River to Steptoe Butte crossed the stream. Halsey established a livestock operation and built a log cabin that became home to pioneer cattleman George Howard nine years later who then disposed of the ranch's 2,600 sheep and acquired nearly a section of adjacent land. Later improvements were made to the ranch with the help of his wife, Emma, including the construction of a larger log home, complete with upper story gun ports, which has been kept in excellent condition to this day. On the southwestern Palouse frontier Mullan Road packer Thomas Benton Turner and his wife, Martha Jane, settled in 1871 at the confluence of Union Flat Creek and the Palouse River to raise livestock and sub-irrigated gardens and grain. Ten miles downstream, Devonshire, England natives Albert and Ernest Hooper arrived in the same year where the small community named for them later emerged. The brothers also brought a young black named Zanzibar, perhaps for his homeland, whom they later assisted in homesteading property on the Palouse near their property. He was an excellent swimmer but drowned after getting entangled in a rope he was using to lead one horse from another that he was riding across the Palouse River (R. Howard, 1996; M. Fronek, 1973).

The family of Andrew Jackson "A. J." and Melvina Smith established several ranches in the western Palouse after the area was first scouted by one of their sons, Andrew, in June, 1876. The Smiths had overlanded on the Oregon Trail in 1865 and settled in the Willamette Valley but eventually sought more open spaces where they could both farm and raise livestock. Andrew returned with favorable news about settlement opportunities north of the Snake River and persuaded his parents and brothers John and Virgil to relocate in 1880. A. J. and Melvina settled on upper Downing

Creek near present St. John, Virgil established a ranch on lower Downing Gulch, and John settled several miles to the east near Matlock Bridge, Kamiakin's Crossing, on the Palouse River. This scenic area was about two miles below DeLong's ranch where the steep river bluffs were dotted with yellow pine and was the northernmost point on the Palouse River. The bridge was located on an important route known to the pioneers as the Spokane Trail that led through the Palouse Hills following an ancient Indian trail.

Matlock Bridge was named for the first settlers in the vicinity, Missouri natives Preston and Kerlista Matlock who established a ranch on the river in 1872 and whose daughter, Sarah, later married John Smith. The brother who began the Smith family's exodus to the Palouse, Andrew, settled at Pine City in 1880 and operated the flour mill established there a year earlier by Anderson Edwards. At peak capacity in the 1880s, the mill could turn out sixteen barrels of flour a day, or approximately 100 bushels. Other early Pine City area settlers included Peter and Annie Carlon, William and A. E. Davis, all in 1878, and Adam and Marinda Kile in 1881. Having surveyed much of the region prior to settling, former stagecoach driver James Gordon and his wife, Mary, claimed land in the Four Corners district north of present Malden in the late 1870s (R. Smith, 1960).

Settlement of the region by the mid-1870s was still restricted, however, to small bottomland farms while stockmen maintained increasingly large cattle herds and flocks of sheep on the hills and breaks of the Snake River and in the Channeled Scablands. In 1871 the *Walla Walla Union* reported that over 5,000 head of cattle had been taken across the Snake River since the previous fall into "the favorite region of the stockraisers." The paper also covered the rise in immigrant traffic from the Willamette Valley to the Palouse Country. The *Union* reported in the spring of 1872 that "most of those that are going there have more or less stock, and are attracted thither by the well merited reputation of the country for stock raising." The herds of several individuals grew to over a thousand head on the unfenced prairies of the Palouse where, by the end of the decade in Whitman County alone, 45,000 cattle shared the range with 58,000 sheep. The stock typically wintered in the milder pas-

tures in the western portion of the Palouse or in the sheltered Snake River Valley and were driven to the superior eastern ranges of Idaho in the summer.

By the turn of the century Pendleton's famous Hamley Saddlery Company was creating saddles uniquely suited to the needs of Snake River ranchers and cowboys. Nicknamed the "Bear Trap," the Hamley Snake River model was considered a work of art and practicality by Palouse Country bronc-busters. Traditional styles with a low cantle in back and high horn for tying off a lariat made for a dangerous combination in some circumstances. Cowboys riding on uneven ground or slopes to rope wild horses for breaking and uncooperative cattle at branding time could sometimes be thrown up and nearly impaled or crushed if they landed on the protruding horn. A pioneer ranching family near Sprague suffered the double tragedy of Tom Lakin's death in 1905 in a horse accident followed by the fatal fall of his uncle, George Lakin, some years later. The Hamley Snake River featured a low cantle and horn with high front swells made of wood blocks covered with leather. Mounted inside a "Bear Trap," with thighs pressed hard against such supports, a cowboy felt secure. Palouse Country native Dan Luft was among Hamely's foremost saddlemakers at the company shop in Pendleton where exquisite leather inlay on company designs made Hamleys some of the most coveted saddles in the country—a tradition that continues among ranchers and collectors (B. Kromm, 2003).

The Nez Perce War of 1877

The Palouse Country's "Indian Scare" of 1877 brought panic to pioneer families north of the Snake River and led to the exile of one of the largest Native American bands that had sought to retain a traditional way of life in the region. Many settlers in the Palouse during the 1870s were perplexed at the presence of so many Indians who continued to winter in villages along the Snake River. They traveled throughout the hills in spring and summer to traditional root grounds and hunting areas favored by their ancestors for generations. To many Whites, the Indians had lost the wars of the 1850s and as signatories to the Stevens treaties should be confined on the

CHIEF LOOKING GLASS
(WASHINGTON STATE
HISTORICAL SOCIETY)

Yakama, Umatilla, and Nez Perce reservations. However, a number of Palouse Indian bands never felt obligated to these agreements since their leaders had not been present at the Walla Walla treaty councils. Many Indians had lived peacefully for generations along the Snake River above Lewiston from Alpowa to Wawawai. Local headmen included the venerated Dreamer priest, or *tewat*, Husishusis Kute, a warrior who had been severely wounded in General Wright's campaign of 1858, and Hahtalekin, or Red Echo, chief over civil matters. Husishusis Kute was a revered orator who adhered to the traditional Washani religion and believed his people should be able to travel unmolested throughout their ancestral areas along and above the river. The treaties had specified, after all, that the tribes be able to fish and hunt at their "accustomed places." He was angered by the displacement of his people's winter villages as pioneer settlements appeared at the mouth of Penawawa, Almota, and Wawawai creeks in the 1870s and by occasional attempts of some ranchers to raid the band's vast horse herds that roamed freely along the unfenced grassy river bluffs from Penawawa to Lewiston (L. V. McWhorter, 1952; M. Ochs, 1991).

For these reasons, Husishusis Kute and Hahtalekin had much in common with Idaho and Oregon's non-treaty Nez Perce who were led by Chief Joseph, Looking Glass, and White Bird. Members of these bands actually lived in areas promised to them in the Nez Perce Treaty of 1855. However, after gold strikes in the mountains in the early 1860s, pressure from White miners and settlers prevailed upon the office of Indian Affairs to force a renegotiation of that agreement in 1863 through which the Nez Perce were com-

pelled to surrender an additional 320 square miles of land for about eight cents an acre. Nez Perce bands in the newly ceded areas did not sign and refused to accept the legitimacy of this "Thief Treaty." Government officials were petitioned by settlers in 1876 to remove these Indians to the reservation. In November of that year, Nez Perce Agent John Monteith at Lapwai was ordered by the Secretary of the Interior to convene a council of non-treaty Indian leaders in order to arrange for their relocation to the Nez Perce Reservation.

The five commissioners appointed to negotiate the agreement, who included General Oliver Howard, met in council with area Indian leaders at the Nez Perce Agency in November, 1876 but found the chiefs of no mind to move. Joseph expressed their convictions by saying, "The Creator, when he made the land, made no marks, no lines of division or separation on it." The earth was "too sacred… to be sold for silver or gold…. We love the land; it is our home." The commissioners left in frustration and blamed the Indians' intransigence on the religious influences of Washani leaders like the old Nez Perce spiritual leader Toohoolhoolzote, and Husishusis Kute of the Palouse. They recommended to the Interior Secretary that such individuals be immediately required to live on the reservation or, in the event of noncompliance, they be exiled to Indian Territory (present Oklahoma).

General Howard's forces at Fort Lapwai were to be put at the agency's disposal in the event of any resistance, and in January, 1877 Monteith received orders to move the non-treaty bands to the reservation "in a reasonable time," which he defined as being by April 1. Given the need for the chiefs to consult with all their people and move their livestock during spring flood season, they urgently requested a second meeting with Monteith and Howard that was held at Lapwai during the first week of May. Husishusis Kute, Hahtalekin, and the Nez Perce leaders again attended only to witness another stormy exchange between Howard with Joseph and Toohoolhoolzote. When the latter asked rhetorically, "What person pretends to divide the land, and put me on it?" Howard exclaimed, "I am that man! I stand here for the President, and there is no spirit good or bad that will hinder me…." He ordered the Nez Perce leader to be immediately jailed and then asked the others for their decision. With great reluctance, the chiefs consented to move. "We were like deer," Joseph later explained. "They were like grizzly bears" (Chief Joseph, 1879).

The Palouses were to be given lands near the agency but Howard offered little compromise on the timetable, giving the bands thirty-five days, or until June 15 to complete their relocation. Husishusis Kute was particularly dismayed by this requirement given the time needed for his people to gather their Snake River horse herds. The Palouse leaders returned to their camp near Wawawai deeply angered over their circumstances but set about to gather their people and horses in anticipation of the deadline. As June approached it became obvious that summoning all the families, many of whom were then digging camas across the northern Palouse region, and rounding up the herds would be an impossible task. Among the Nez Perce, three young members of Joseph's Wallowa band killed four settlers on the Salmon River on June 14 in retaliation for the recent murder of one of the warriors' father. All four victims were known to have acted hostilely towards Indians but news of their deaths stunned Joseph when he learned of the violence the following day. Joseph advised a meeting with Howard to explain the situation for which he felt the rest of the band should not be held accountable. But the chief's counsel was spurned by a large number of younger braves whose patience with the peace talk of the older leaders had worn thin.

In the meantime, sixteen members of White Bird's band, emboldened by news of the fighting, attacked other miners and ranchers along the Salmon River while Joseph, oblivious also of these depredations, led the rest of his people to join White Bird in White Bird Canyon where both leaders hoped to somehow resolve the

sudden turn of events through a council with General Howard. But Whites fleeing in panic from the area pleaded for the general at Fort Lapwai to attack the non-treaty Indians and a company of soldiers was dispatched to White Bird Canyon on June 17. Ignoring a truce flag sent by the chiefs, the soldiers fired upon a nearby group of Indians to open a brief but violent exchange that left thirty-four soldiers dead while the Nez Perce did not incur a single fatality. These events set in motion the epic Nez Perce War of 1877 which put the entire Inland Northwest into a state of hysteria as White residents had no idea in which direction the warring Indians might head. Memories of the Custer Massacre a year earlier were fresh in the minds of the general public and if the Indians' reasonable intention was to join Sitting Bull in Canada, their most direct route could be north through the Palouse Country.

The period was especially desperate for newcomers to the area like Riley and Rachel Hatley, William and Susan Doty, Abraham and Virginia Haynes, and Wilson and Anna Mraz who had just homesteaded that year south of Three Forks (present Pullman). The citizens of Colfax received word that "400 Indians, more or less, traveling in a body had killed eighty persons on the Clearwater, and were coming toward Colfax, sweeping all before them." Volunteer troops organized and settlers rushed to the nearest towns for safety in numbers. Sixty wagons of panic-stricken people around Colfax fled their farms to seek refuge in the schoolhouse while stockades were hastily built at Palouse, Pine Creek (Farmington), Willow Springs (Cheney), Pine Grove (Spangle), and Four Mile (Viola). Three separate structures served to protect the residents of Paradise Valley near Moscow—Forts Russell, Howard, and Crumerine. A large number of families living

NEZ PERCE AND PALOUSE AT LAPWAI, c. 1910 (MASC, WSU LIBRARIES)

along the Snake River congregated at Penawawa where they constructed an elaborate fort out of wool bales awaiting steamer transport, complete with gun portals and corner standouts. Unfortunately for the residents of these confined quarters, cholera outbreaks appeared in several of the makeshift forts which forced many of them to find lodging elsewhere or risk returning to their homes. For one settler, the decision to leave would prove to have fatal consequences.

The pioneers had grounds for seeking safety in numbers. On or about June 22, the same day General Howard took to the field with 500 troops, two Palouses who were likely from Huishuis Kute's band headed north toward a large gathering of peaceful Palouses, Coeur d'Alenes, and Spokanes camped at *Elposen* (present Tekoa). They sought recruits to ally with the non-reservation bands facing the Whites but encountered settler John Ritchie at his cabin near present Farmington and killed the man. The two then continued on to *Elposen* with Ritchie's horse and reported that they had attacked two Whites and taken one of their mounts. Their demeanor and inquiries betrayed another explanation and Chief Seltice (1810-1902) of the Coeur d'Alenes confiscated the horse and spurned their presence. An Indian was dispatched to investigate the incident with two Whites from Colfax who were in the area to discern the feeling of the northern tribes. They eventually came upon Ritchie's cabin and found his lifeless body on the bed inside, shot in the chest and with an axe wound in the head. They concluded that Ritchie had been murdered and both Indian and White leaders pressed diligently in the newly volatile climate to prevent further hostilities in the area. Ritchie's body was taken to Farmington and interred as the first grave in the community cemetery (C. Trafzer and R. Scheuerman, 1986).

Sixteen Upper Palouse families under Husishusis and Hahtalekin joined the non-treaty Nez Perce bands on the South Fork of the Clearwater following an unprovoked attack, not countenanced by Howard, by a group of soldiers and trigger-happy Mount Idaho citizen volunteers on Looking Glass's village on July 1. Looking Glass, who had kept his people out of the fighting and urged peace with the army, was residing within the new reservation boundaries near present Kooskia when the cavalry unit under Captain Stephen Whipple attacked the village. Many of Looking Glass's people were related to members of the Palouse band and the army's senseless actions that morning drove these groups into alliance with Joseph and White Bird. The united non-treaty bands soon sought to escape their homelands altogether by fleeing from Weippe Prairie over the Lolo Trail to Montana and onto the Northern Plains. One of the first to fall during the campaign was Chief Hahtalekin, shot to death at the Battle of the Big Hole on August 9 in a fight that also claimed his son, the warrior Pahka Pahtahank (Five Fogs).

Following a heroic three-month struggle and a dozen battles and skirmishes over 1200 miles of rugged terrain, the Indians were finally captured in the Bear Paw Mountains near Canada in early October, 1877. Chief Looking Glass was slain the day before the decimated Indian force surrendered on October 5, 1877. When Joseph handed his rifle to General Nelson Miles, he knew in his heart the words he spoke to the sky and all who could hear him: "My heart is sick and sad, our chiefs are dead and the children scattered everywhere.... From where the sun now stands, I will fight no more forever."

During the previous night, Chief White Bird managed to lead a remnant of able-bodied Nez Perce and Palouse survivors to sanctuary among Sitting Bull's Sioux in Canada where the renown Salmon River chief died several years later. One of the exiles, Waaya-Tonah-Toesits-Kahn, later known to Whites as Jackson Sundown, was only fourteen at the time of the war and returned after the turn of the century to live near Lapwai where he became a legend in rodeo circles. Tall, lean, and with handsome features, Sundown was known for wearing brightly colored shirts and scarves and shaggy orange Angora chaps with black spots. The very prospect of his participation in an event was often enough to cause other hopefuls to withdraw from competition. He became the first Native American to be named World Champion Bronc Rider at the 1919 Pendelton Round-Up. Alexander Proctor and Charlie Russell used Sundown as a model for some of their finest bronze sculptures.

Joseph and Husishusis Kute were among the few leaders to survive the entire ordeal and were exiled with the other 416 forlorn prisoners to Fort Leavenworth in Indian Territory, known to the Nez Perce and Palouse as Eekish Pah, the "Hot Place." They were eventually transferred to the Quapaw Agency and finally to the Ponca near present Tonkawa, Oklahoma to live among other tribes banished from their homelands to the dry plains of the Midwest. Nearly a third of the Nez Perce and Palouse exiles died there from malaria and other health disorders (L. V. McWhorter, 1953).

In an epic display of stealth and daring, the Palouse warrior Pahala Washeschit (Five Shades) made the decision to undertake the thousand mile trek back to his homeland. He escaped alone and traveled for weeks to reach the upper reaches of the Snake River which he then followed to the Palouse Country. Fearing he would be arrested if found off the reservation, Five Shades came to reside among relatives who were living in the Thorn Hollow district on the Umatilla Reservation where he became a highly respected Washani leader. Taking the name "Star Doctor" in the years after his legendary journey, perhaps an allusion to his means of reckoning directions during the legendary months of nighttime travel, he later became a popular figure at the Pendleton Roundup where he was known to Whites as George Lucas. At such special events, Star Doctor usually wore traditional buckskin clothing adorned with fox and wolf furs and crowned his head with a brightly flared porcupine roach.

In January, 1879, Chief Joseph journeyed to Washington, D. C. where he delivered an impassioned two-hour speech in Lincoln Hall to a vast audience of congressmen, cabinet officials, and other political leaders. He recounted the injustices done to his people and cited specific agreements that had been abrogated by the government and had led to the war. He spoke of the false terms of surrender offered to him by General Miles. Officials were moved by Joseph's oratory and congressional intervention eventually enabled the Nez Perce and Palouse who survived in Indian Territory to return to the Pacific Northwest in 1885. Under the leadership of Husishusis Kute, the remaining 268 exiles finally boarded a train in late May bound for the Northwest and arrived on May 27 at Wallula

Junction where they were divided into two groups. Nearly half were directed to Lapwai while the others continued with Joseph to the Colville Reservation (C. Trafzer and R. Scheuerman, 1987; I. Patrick, 1981).

Traditionalists like the Palouse Husishusis Kute who were sent to the Nez Perce Reservation soon found antagonisms directed against them by the Christian Nez Perce, who were disaffected because lands were being given to the newcomers as well as by their insistence on following the old ways. Restrictions were placed upon Washani religious practices by agency staff who felt their continuation was detrimental to Indian commission policies of acculturation. For this reason, Husishusis Kute relocated to the Colville Reservation where most of Chief Kamiakin's sons, Tomeo, Tesh Palouse, and Skolumkee and other Palouses had clustered along the river near the settlement of Nespelem. Here the Palouse leader and Chief Joseph lived out the rest of their days. The Nez Perce-Palouse campaign remains the story of an American tragedy as dramatic as Xenophon's March of the Ten Thousand. The war is a subject of study by military academy cadets both in the United States and abroad. A defeat accomplished only by the army's vastly superior numbers, the Indians' tactics serve as a classic example of successful guerrilla warfare and evasive action techniques.

Following the death of Joseph and Husishusis Kute around the turn of the century and the passing of Tesh Palouse (1857-1932) and Tomeo (1856-1935) in the 1930s, leadership of the Palouse band on the Colville Reservation fell to Chief Kamiakin's youngest son, Cleveland (1870-1959) and then to the chief's nephew, Charley Williams (1879-1969), the Palouses last designated hereditary chief. A remarkable series of Palouse and Nez Perce portraits were among those painted by Worth Griffin who was hired in 1924 to teach art at W.S.C. in Pullman and who became the principal organizer of the summer Nespelem Art Colony in the 1930s. Griffin also painted a series of Palouse Country "historic characters" including Felix Warren, Garfield businessman Winchester Oliphant, Hooper rancher Peter McGregor, and Jenny Kenny, an early settler and wife of a veteran of the 1858 Steptoe campaign. Griffin was critically commended for works that depicted both the documentary and inherent creative values of his subjects. His orange ocher and olive green earth tones—shades of dawn and dusk—were favored colors by the Palouse and Nez Perce whose arrows and sallie bags were decorated as uniquely as ancient cartouches.

Some of the most expressive images of Indians living at that time on the Colville Reservation were painted by colony member and Adams County native Anne Maybelle Harder who was majoring in art at Pullman. Her mother, Anine, remembered the days when some 200 Palouses pitched their tipis near the Harder home, and she "never got tired of watching them." Harder's portraits were characterized by Fechin-like splashes of bright cadmium yellow and vermillion. Her mother, Annine Harder, remembered the days when some two hundred Palouses pitched their tipis near the Harder home, and she "never got tired of watching them." Most of Griffin's portraits today are safeguarded in the W.S.U. Department of Fine Arts' vaults while those by other colony artists like Harder may be found in collections ranging from the Northwest Museum of Arts and Culture in Spokane to the Smithsonian (E. Peone, 1981; J. J. Creighton, 2000; A. Harder, 1960).

The proud heritage of the Palouses has been carried to another generation besieged with alcoholism and alienation by elders like Alumti Kamiakin, Cleveland's wife who was raised near Penawawa, James Selam, and strong-willed Mary Jim and daughter Carrie Jim Schuster, natives of Page on the lower Snake River. For years they have gathered every spring near the mouth of the Snake River for name-giving and offering thanks to the Creator for the year's first salmon and roots, and heard Emily Peone, whose sparkling countenance hinted at her kinship with the Star Brothers. Andrew George (White Eagle) was a native of Palus who found mystery in the ordinariness of nature. He was known to Indians throughout the Pacific Northwest for his powers of healing, and as a storyteller and spiritual leader.

In 1989, Washington's centennial year of statehood, Governor Booth Gardner presented Andrew George the state's first Ethnic Heritage Award which named the aged Palouse a "Living Treasure." The special event held in his honor at the Seattle Center was attended by members of his family and leaders in government, the arts,

and entertainment industry. Following the day's whirlwind festivities, Andrew slowly made his way down a sidewalk adjacent to the Space Needle and was asked what he thought the most memorable part of the day had been. Without hesitation, he joyously replied, "A bird was singing in the trees here earlier; it was unlike anything I've ever heard."

Spotted Horses and Rodeo Champs

The few remaining Indian families who resided on the Snake River after 1877 were determined, like Chief Kamiakin who died that year near Rock Lake, to remain in their ancestral homeland and avoid removal to area reservations. Most of them had established friendly relations with White settlers in the river communities and sometimes worked the orchard harvest seasons while still fishing and tending their dwindling horse herds. Many of the animals abandoned by the Palouses who had joined the Nez Perces were caught by area horse traders like Walla Walla's "Cayuse" Brown to sell in Canada where they brought up to $8 a head. Many others were eventually destroyed by local farmers when they strayed across fenced areas and trampled crops.

Smaller herds of the finer animals were safeguarded by the families of Yusyus Tulekasen (Something Covered in Blue), brother of Hahtalekin, who remained near Wawawai, Husishusis Poween (Shot in the Head) at Almota, Poyakin at Penawawa, and the blonde-headed Chief Husishusis Moxmox, and Weeatkwal Tsiken (Young Kamiakin) at Palus. During an inspection tour of the lower Snake and Columbia regions in 1878, General Howard made an unexpected suggestion to agency authorities: Indians who remained off the reservation in these areas and lived in peace with the Whites should consider filing claims for unpatented lands under the terms of the recently enacted Indian Homestead Act. The idea was not popular with many citizens in the territory, but the Indians at Palus were among the first to respond after fuller explanation and encouragement by their friends, local ferryman Daniel Lyons and ranchers George Hunter, A. G. Lloyd, Jack Pettyjohn, and Hans Harder.

One of the prime movers among the Palouses in the effort to legitimize their rights to ancestral lands was Husishusis Kute's nephew, Juk Lous, known to Whites as Sam Fisher, who encouraged the others to join together in a collective registration of claims (C. Relander, 1956). Fisher had grown up along the Snake River tending the horse herds of his father and relatives and developed a passion for both life in the valley and quality breeding stock. He was thirty-two years old when his famous shaman uncle returned from exile in 1885 and had been living with Husishusis Moxmox's band at Palus. Since settlers had homesteaded or purchased most lands further upriver, the unclaimed and relatively remote canyon from Palouse Falls to the Snake seemed the most practical place to raise horses and fish and hunt without encountering the fencelines of any surly Whites. Working under the provisions of the new legislation and with competent counsel, Fisher and the band were able to acquire a substantial tract of over 1,500 acres along both sides of the lower Palouse River in the 1880s. This area, which was later expanded to 2,650 acres, though semi-arid and rocky, gave the Palouses complete control over the entire lower canyon below Palouse Falls. Their claims would be recurrently contested in court by envious ranchers who also sought the land, but with legal assistance from Lyons, the Pettyjohns at Starbuck, and the McGregors of Hooper, Fisher and his people were eventually able to secure title to their claims.

In return for their benevolence, Fisher offered the men horses from his herd while Meatu Kinma, the daughter of Teewa Teenaset (Chief Bones), presented their wives with exquisitely imbricated baskets and finely detailed and colorful beadwork. The Palouse band's most treasured relic was their silver-inlay red catlinite peace pipe, said to have been traded several generations earlier by Sioux Indians on the Plains for fourteen of the Palouses' finest horses. An extensive collection of these items is housed today at Whitman College's Penrose Library in Walla Walla. Other important material culture collections of eastern Plateau Indians are found at the Nez Perce National Historical Park in Spalding, Idaho which displays the remarkable Spalding-Allen Collection originally sent in 1841 by Henry Spalding to a mission sponsor in Ohio. This priceless array of early tribal clothing, weapons, bags, and other artifacts was acquired by the Nez Perce Tribe in 1996 following a public fundraising campaign supported by a major grant from Mrs. Walt Disney, who grew up in Lapwai, Idaho. The Chap C. Dunning Collection, described as "the best single collection of local Indian material in existence," displays outstanding examples of Spokane and other Plateau Indian basketry, costume, horse gear, cornhusk bags, and other items at the Northwest Museum of Arts & Culture in Spokane. Traditional Coeur d'Alene twined and beaded bags and ceremonial clothing can be seen at Cataldo, Idaho's Old Mission State Park Museum (C. Trafzer and R. Scheuerman, 1986).

In addition to a horse's intelligence, disposition, and sure-footedness, of special appeal to Sam Fisher was the distinctive spotted pattern in stock that came to be known as Appaloosa. Their name was derived from their Palouse homeland and in widespread use throughout the region as early as the 1870s. He gelded and used a "powerful medicine" to ensure the breed's distinctive spotted blanket markings which were beautifully evident on such Palus herd stallions as Calico Sam and Knobby. Other Appaloosa patterns include snowflake, white spots on gray, and leopard, or dark spots against a lighter coat. To Fisher, one Appaloosa was worth more than a "truckload of other horses" and at times he ran well over a hundred head along the lower Palouse River Canyon.

Fisher's prized animals became well known to other Indians as well as ranchers and cowhands throughout the region who purchased them for work with cattle, pleasure riding, and as rodeo stock for such premier events as county fairs and the Pendleton Roundup. Fisher's knowledge came to be highly regarded by area horsemen who made the effort to find him, admired for his horse raising experience and for his tenacious efforts to honor his people by maintaining a presence at Palus. Until his death in 1944, Sam Fisher and his wife, Helen, a survivor of the Nez Perce War, were also stewards of the tribe's ancient burial ground near their simple home. He freely traded his knowledge with local ranchers, most of whom raised draft horses for farm work, like Phillip Cox whose Cherrydale Stock Farm near Hay was famous for producing the area's finest Percherons, Emery and Frank Gordon who began raising horses in the Pampa-Rock Springs area in 1884, and Herb Camp of LaCrosse (F. Roe, 1955; E. Metzker, 2003).

Old friends from the river communities and Palouse Hills who knew the value of fine horse flesh also bought many of their favorite animals from Fisher. National rodeo star Faye Hubbard and his brother, Fern, grandsons of Wilcox pioneers Goalman and Nancy Hubbard, acquired some of their most beloved stock from Fisher including Faye's Ole Rex, a gray stallion with black spots. "We ran wild horses with him in Oregon, 'dogged' off him in Canada, roped off him all over the country," Hubbard later recalled. "He was just all-around useful and as tough as he was good-looking." Hubbard went on to earn honors as World Champion Bulldogger at the 1939 New York World's Fair Rodeo where he met Broadway composer Kay Swift. The unlikely friendship led to the couple's marriage and subsequent move to Cougar Rock Ranch near Bend, Oregon where they raised Appaloosas and other horses used by fellow Palouse Country native Enos "Yakima" Canutt and film makers of popular Hollywood Westerns. Hubbard and Swift's quixotic relationship was chronicled in her autobiographical novel *Who Could Ask For Anything More?* that appeared on screen in the 1949 RKO production *Never a Dull Moment*.

One of John and Nettie Canutt's sons from Penawawa, Yakima Canutt won international acclaim as four-time World Rodeo Champion beginning in 1917 and as the principal developer of Hollywood's "film fighting" and action stunt techniques. He acquired his nickname after winning the Pendleton Roundup competition while still in his teens. Some impressed observers in the stands remarked that he rode "like a Yakima." Claiming "I can't remember a time when I wasn't on horseback," Canutt worked with such notable directors as John Ford and Stanley Kubrick on dozens of movie epics including *Stagecoach*, *How the West Was Won*, *Ben Hur*, and *A Man Called Horse*. Canutt was presented an Academy Award in 1966 for his unique contributions to the industry and was later inducted into the National Cowboy Hall of Fame. Canutt's Hollywood experiences influenced his younger cousin, Colfax native John Crawford, to become an actor and he also starred in several Western films and the popular television series *The Waltons* (M. Terrell, 2003; O. Drake, 1997).

Almota rancher Floyd Hickman purchased a mare from Sam Fisher that became the dam of Old Blue, named for the shade of this beautifully varnished roan. Servicing up to a hundred mares annually and living to his mid-thirties, Old Blue was considered to have had more influence than any other studhorse in the Palouse for upgrading the quality of the region's Appaloosas and gave Hickman his favorite horse, famed Toby I. Other prominent Appaloosa breeders in the area were George Adair of Potlatch and Moscow's George Hatley who was a prime-mover in the formation of the international Appaloosa Horse Club. Others included Palmer Wagner, Roy and Zaidee Parvin whose Fourmile Appaloosa Ranch was located between Colfax and Pullman, Les Sauer of Dusty, and Lester Riley of Riley's River Ranch and Chet Lamb near Central Ferry. Due in large part to the tireless efforts of Palouse Country residents George and Iola Hatley, the National Appaloosa Museum and Heritage Center opened in Moscow, Idaho in 1974. The facility features exhibits on the breed's use by area tribes and as champion show and rodeo stock. Toby I, overall performance winner of the first National Appaloosa Horse Show in Lewiston a generation earlier, and Hatley's own Toby II were both descended from Sam Fisher's native Palouse herd (P. J. Wagner, 1999; G. Hatley, 1954).

ANDREW GEORGE
LEWISTON, IDAHO

While conducting interviews on the Yakama, Colville, Nez Perce, and Umatilla reservations in the 1970s for a book on the tribes of the Columbia Plateau, my co-author Clifford Trafzer and I would often be told, "You really need to ask Andrew George about that." Time and again when our interests led to some obscure but important matter relating to Native American history and culture, we were directed to Andrew. Each visit to one of the area's reservations provided an opportunity to visit the widely regarded Palouse-Nez Perce elder but recurrent trips to homes of his relatives invariably ended with the news that he had just left for a name-giving ceremony at Warm Springs, a pow-pow in Saskatchewan, or ministering to the needs of old friends on the Coast. We began to wonder if Andrew George was a phantom of some kind. Finally in November of 1980, another recent sighting led us to try finding him. A crude map made by a friend led us down a long lane near Toppenish where Andrew was resided at the home of his daughter and grandchildren. After we knocked and were allowed in by a small girl, a small man of great age shuffled into the room from a long hallway. Legendary storyteller, healer, and spiritual leader Tipyalanah Khikhi (White Eagle) had a bright smile on his face, and without introducing ourselves, he said, "I've been expecting you for a long time."

When I remember it is like a dream, you know how it is, as if it happened long, long ago. There was a time when I was not sure that all I saw in my mind had actually taken place; it seemed more like a vision of the way things once were. It is in that way that I remember leaving our home at Palus, where the big bridge is. We were all loaded onto that steamboat somewhere about 1908 that took us upriver to the Nez Perce Reservation. My parents never liked to talk about it much. I was just a boy but still can see it as if in a dream. I used to see Palouse Falls I my vision and I would ask myself, "Were you really at that place, Andrew?" It was only a distant memory but everytime I would see a falls like Multnomah or somewhere else, I saw it clearly in my mind and knew the falls back above Palus were real.

I was born on the upper reaches of the Palouse River in Idaho and lived in that country and on the Snake River until they took us away. We looked all through those old brown and faded agency records to find out when I was born but could never find anything. The date of my enrollment, that's the date of my birthday! I could have been born in the early Nineteens or maybe in the Eighteens; I think maybe in the Eighteens. There is something else I wondered about in my visions. I saw a place up on a mountain where we lived and I saw us sledding down the hill. In the valley below there was a white church. Then one time when we went up to Welpinnit, I can speak Spokane and Coeur d'Alene, we drove over to a store and on the way back I saw a sideroad going up into the trees. I said, "Let's take a little drive and go up there and see the country around here." We went up the road and soon came to a place where we could look down into a beautiful valley where I saw a white church—it was the one in my dream.

Our history and truth was written in the ancient rocks. You cannot read it all in a book or understand it all, you can only see some of it. Steptoe Butte, a power mountain, is that place where it was dry land on top when the great flood happened here. Indians knew these things too, just like it says in Genesis even though we did not have the Bible. You see, the same truth is everywhere. The salmon are wise and sacred and understand this truth. We should never kill all the fish or dam up all the rivers. That would be like closing off your arteries one at a time stopping the free flow of the life force. Eventually you would die. After Salmon had a fight with the jealous Animal People who did not possess his strength, they killed him with an arrow that had a flint point. You can still find this point in the head bone of every salmon. When a salmon egg hatched out in the ocean and Young Salmon began his first migration back to our land, he got into a fight with Rattlesnake because he refused to give him one of his fangs. Salmon took his great tail and started beating the head of the snake which is why Rattlesnake's head is very flat. Salmon never got the fang but he did get some of his power and poison. If a salmon bites you today you get a sore arm and break out. That is from the poison that Salmon got from Rattlesnake. I heard many of these stories from Cleveland Kamiakin and other elders and I listened carefully so I could tell them exactly as they did.

God provided everything we needed in our Earth Mother. We kept track of time based on this sacred cycle of blessing:

February is *Ah-lah-tah-mal*, the Time When Buttercups Start to Bloom;

March is *Lah-te-tahl*, the Time of Flowers Beginning to Bloom;

April is *Ka-ke-tahl*, the Time of Digging Kah-ket;

May is *Up-pa-ahl*, the Time of Digging Kouse;

June is *Tus-te-mah-sah-tahl*, the Time of Digging in Higher Places;

July is *Ti-yal*, or Mid-summer;

August is *Wa-wa-mi-ka*, or Chinook Coming to the Headwaters;

September is *Pe-kun-ma-i-kah*, or Salmon Spawing Time;

October is *Hoph-lulh*, the Time of Falling Yellow Needles;

November is *She-le-wahl*, the Time of Drying Game Food;

December is *He-ek-we*, when Deer Embryo Begins to Form; and

January is *We-lu-pup*, Stormy Winter Cold Time.

At a great gathering of the Animal People on the Snake River long ago, the trickster Coyote challenged anyone to outrun him in a race northward to Spokane country on the following morning. Coyote was always boasting about his speed and was certain that nobody could possibly defeat him in such a contest. One by one, Blue Jay, Marmot, and others stepped back. To everyone's surprise, both Turtle and Coyote's aunt, Magpie, said they would take Coyote up on the bargain. Now at that time, the land between the Snake and Spokane rivers was a broad prairie and even though Coyote could not believe that anyone could be faster, he made a plan to be absolutely sure he would win. While the rest of the Animal People danced and sang into the evening, he ventured onto the prairie and scooped all that land up into the endless hills that you can see today. Coyote knew he could simply leap over them in several bounds while Turtle would have to go up and down them one at a time and that Magpie would grow weary of such a long flight.

That night, however, Turtle called his five younger brothers to scout the route since Coyote had a reputation for being mischievous and they discovered that Coyote had changed the land. Turtle then sent his brothers out onto the hills where they line up in a row on the highest points between the two rivers. The next morning, Coyote, Magpie, and Turtle lined up near the village of Palus and took off at a signal given by Blue Jay. Coyote leaped high over the first set of hills leaving Turtle slowly crawling up and down each slope far behind while Magpie madly flew past him. But when Coyote began his second jump, he was surprised to see Turtle was on the hilltop ahead of him. He pressed ahead with great effort only to find Turtle right across from him when he landed. He then bounded as far as he could only to find Turtle at his side again. Coyote began to tire.

Meanwhile, Magpie was also beginning to slow down, after setting off in a fevered flight. He was high enough to see Coyote and Turtle far ahead. Realizing that Coyote had changed the land and that the Turtle Brothers had all joined in the contest, Magpie complained in screams and screeches which is why that still sound that way today. *Achay! Achay!* Coyote bounded ahead with all of his strength two more times and fell completely worn out when he reached the finish. But there was Turtle on the other side looking rested! Turtle had outwitted Coyote at his own clever race across the hills!

Today Coyote is unrecognized, unwanted, unprotected—a victim to wanton destruction by civilized man. Yet God made Coyote and he had plenty to eat long before sheep or cattle came into the country here. He had no worries until the White man came and destroyed his dinner table—rabbits, sage hens, prairie chickens, and many other fowl of the sage, even destroyed my vegetation. These are the reasons for Coyote's wrath but he will never be destroyed because God created him and in the time of judgment he will be the last to die. The Bible tells us to care for all of God's creation, not kill it off or dam it up and destroy things so we can live better.

I am going to be going way over to Battle Fort in Canada soon to see a monument in honor of an unknown Nez Perce warrior from Chief Joseph's band who made it to Canada after the war in 1877. Some of my relatives went there but most with Joseph were sent to Oklahoma where they didn't fare very well. The story of the Canadian Nez Perce isn't known much; some were killed by Canadian troops in 1885. It's a history untold but if I live to have the time I will try to learn more about these warriors. You see our people are spread out from Canada to Oregon and I am often asked to help out in their affairs so I can't say for sure when we might meet again. I hope it is soon.

Chapter III:

THE AMERICANS AND CANADIANS

*"We took butter, which sold for seventy cents a pound, up to the Hoodoos, also eggs and garden stuff.
This with hay at $4 a ton and shingles at $2.50 per thousand made our living in those early days."*
—Anna Person, 1923

Settlement by immigrant farmers was taking place to such an extent on that by 1880 a government official observed that "the best pasturage of the territory...is rapidly passing into the possession of the farmers." By 1884 the number of cattle in Whitman County had been reduced by over half, to 20,000. The Palouse farmers were slowly discovering the fertility of the hills. The alluvial soils on the bottoms were actually inferior to the aeolian deposits of the hills since the former were poorly drained and were much slower to warm in the spring. Soil temperature is an important factor in seed germination and damaging frosts often settled on the bottoms due to the downslope flow of cool air. One immigrant to the Palouse in 1874 observed many others "leaving the country because the people thought they could not grow crops and fruit" (Yoder, 1937).

One early Idaho settler warned that while entry fees and commissions were nominal, the costs of improving new lands could be staggering and the labor burdensome. He stated, "It is one of the severest struggles a poor man with a family can undertake in his lifetime to settle upon, pay for government land, and support his family all at the same time. He may try it and fail after much deprivation, toil and hardship. As a rule, in these territories, to conquer a piece of land and fence it, making it in any way valuable, and paying the necessary fees to land offices is worth all the land is worth" (J. Chase, 1880).

The Transition from Stockraising to Farming

Locating a potential farm site in the Palouse remained a formidable task throughout the 1870s. Travel expenses to the region were not inconsiderable as prospective settlers had to make allowances for ferry service, meals, and other costs on the journey. Once in the Palouse, a pioneer could spend weeks or even months in search of a favorable homesite. For these reasons many men chose to leave their families while scouting the land and often remained alone on their claims for an extended time to see if permanent residence would be economically feasible. When his family joined the Palouse settler, all able members were needed to contribute to the success of the venture. This was particularly true with the European immigrants as the expense and distance of the migration precluded hopes of a return to the homeland. Isolated on the Palouse prairies, pioneer families began writing to their relatives and friends in back East or in Europe to interest them in moving to the Northwest. Many joined their kinsmen in the Palouse Country where numerous rural communities emerged associated in name with an area of Eastern origin—Tennessee Flat, Missouri Flat, California Flat, Minnesota Flat, New York Bar, and Texas Ridge.

The Nez Perce Indian War of 1877 had only temporarily interrupted the flow of immigrants to the Palouse Country. By 1878 the population of Whitman County had risen to 3,700, and in 1879 the Federal Land Office in Colfax transacted more business than any other district office in the entire nation. Clearly, a land rush of significant proportions was taking place. In the spring of 1879 Colfax's *Palouse Gazette* announced "Immigration has commenced again, every boat up the Snake River is loaded with passengers for the Palouse Country, hotels are crowded, and people seeking land or business locations may be seen in every direction." That year nearly 18,000 acres were under grain production with almost half in wheat. Composite land claims for the 711 farms in Whitman County totalled 144,207 acres. Immigrants were flocking to the eastern Palouse as local advice deemed the best land lay within the twenty-mile strip west of the Idaho-Washington border.

Some banks would not loan money on farmland located west of present Diamond because of the greater risks involved in farming the drier districts. The Potlatch River country was heralded in promotional literature as "the most fertile country in the world,...well wooded, well watered." Palouse farmers were raising an average of three hundred bushels of wheat and seventy bushels of rye by 1880 for which they usually received from twenty-five to thirty cents per bushel at the Snake River landings. By the late 1880s prices rose to forty and occasionally fifty cents a bushel. Most of the grain was shipped to commission merchants in Portland before local buyers began operating later in the decade. The population of Whitman County and Nez Perce County (which included present Latah County) swelled to 11,179 in 1880. At this time the overwhelming majority were native-born Americans (82%). The largest foreign-born elements were the Germans (numbering 229), Irish (228), Canadians (209), and Scandinavians (156).

Joseph Delong's notation of "E. E. Huntley" in his account books likely referred to Elmer E. Huntley whose mother, Phoebe, brought her three children on a two-month covered wagon trek to the Palouse in the spring of 1880 following the death of her husband in Marion County, California. Originally from Maine, the Huntleys settled near present Thornton, Washington. Among their nearest neighbors were Marion and Louisa Baker who had homesteaded two miles west of present Sunset in the summer of 1872. Mrs. Baker was also the wagonmaster on their family's trip to the Palouse from Eugene, Oregon while Marion followed with the cattle and horses. In 1886 the Bakers' daughter, Nettie, married Elmer Huntley. A distant cousin of the Huntley clan who had lived in Indiana and Missouri, William Huntley, relocated to the Endicott area in 1884. Equally proficient with a ledger book and breaking plow, Huntley acquired 10,000 acres of farmland in the area through purchase and lease over the next fifteen years and established a chain of mercantile stores in Endicott, St. John, and Colfax in partnership with his brother, George Huntley.

Maine native Reuben Prince settled near the Bakers and Thornton Huntleys in 1878 and induced his brother in California, Nathaniel, to join him on unclaimed land adjacent to his farm. Nathaniel's wife had just recently died, leaving him to care for their three young children so the offer of family assistance appealed to him. But three years after their arrival in the Palouse, Nathaniel also died and left the care of his orphaned sixteen-year-old son, Henry, and two younger daughters in Reuben's care. The three determined children chose to remain at home and work to prove up on the homestead themselves, a goal they realized five years later. Neighbors George and Margaret Comegys, also Palouse pioneers of 1878, settled southeast of present Thornton where the Territorial Road crossed Thorn Creek. The grand scenery of the Comegys's new home inspired them to name it Belle Mead (Beautiful Meadow), where they remained for a decade before moving to Oakesdale where Comegys joined financier E. H. Hanford in establishing the Oakesdale Commercial Bank. Comegys represented area citizens in the 1889 Washington Constitutional Convention where he played a leading role in drafting the new state's constitution (R. Huntley, 2003; W. H. Lever, 1901; A. Erickson, 1994).

Among the earliest settlers in the vicinity of Steptoe Butte were Tennessee natives J. P. T. and Mary Minerva McCroskey who arrived with their ten children in 1879. The family first squeezed into a one-room cabin at the southern base of the butte until the family constructed a larger twenty by twenty foot residence several weeks later. J. P. T. was a prodigious letter writer to relatives and friends back in Rockville and elsewhere in the Volunteer State extolling the fertility and availability of land in the area. With ten children, peacocks and prairie chickens, cattle and horses, the McCroskey ranch was, like many others in the Palouse, a beehive of activity throughout the year outside where labor was contributed by all in the fields and tending the livestock. Around the house the family carefully placed vast plantings of fruit and ornamental trees, raised a large garden, and passed evenings discussing the political issues of the day and lessons being taught at school.

With the completion of a spacious and gracefully designed two-story home in

B. W. DAVISON HOMESTEAD, 1885 (MASC, WSU LIBRARIES)

the 1890s flanked by broad rows of dogwood trees and evergreens, the McCroskey ranch became a Palouse Country showplace. J. P. T.'s correspondence campaign succeeding in inducing dozens of other Tennesseans to emigrate to the Palouse where many settled on what became known as Tennessee Flat near Steptoe. Some pioneers credited McCroskey with leading more settlers to the region than any other one person. The McCroskeys' youngest son, Virgil T. McCroskey, later donated land to create Steptoe Butte State Park (1946) as well as Idaho's Mary Minerva State Park in 1955. The Idaho tract's native landscape covers 4,400 acres and stretches nearly a mile from Mineral to Huckleberry peaks to offer incredible vistas of the eastern Palouse (M. Reed and K. Petersen, 1983; J. Howell, 2001).

From Draw Bottoms to Hilltops

Rosalia-area pioneer A.J. Calhoun sewed both the flat and hills on his Spring Valley property in 1877, noting that, "If the hilltops wouldn't raise decent crops the country wouldn't amount to much." Congregational missionary George H. Atkinson rode from the Snake River through the Palouse Country to Spokane in May, 1879 and noted the gradual change taking place in the region as farmers were slowly discovering the viability of growing crops on the hilltops. "Here and there the plow runs up the slopes and over the hills, opening the lighter or more reddish soils. The harvests of wheat from the uplands are proving to be the best." In a letter to the editor of the *Spokan Times*, Atkinson predicted "that the homestead which crosses the small valleys and takes in a larger portion of the hills will be the most valuable." Crops were gradually planted higher and higher on the slopes and, contrary to previous speculation, frost damage was generally minimal. The farmers soon found it impractical to plow "up and over" the steeper hills due to the strain on the animals and the resulting erosion problems. They devised a method of "backlanding" for tillage. In this process, the farmer began his field operation slightly above the base of the slope and followed the contour of a group of hills completely around to the point of beginning. Successive passes followed the same curved pattern and gradually worked the soil up to the top of the hills.

Such experiments proved successful and in the spring of 1879, the *Palouse Gazette* reported on this most significant development:

Our own observations have been confirmed by the experience of farmers that the hill lands prove to be best for all kinds of grain. While being about the country for the last ten days, it was noticed that grain is looking unusually well for this time of year, many hills so high that it would seem impossible to cultivate, being covered with a fine stand of wheat. The bottoms grow too heavy straw, are more subject to frosts, and being usually more effected by late spring rains, the crop cannot be sown so early as on the uplands, and consequently cannot be harvested before the fall rains set in. These ideas are mentioned for the benefit of new settlers, who, seeing that the bottom lands have been taken first, may think the hills or uplands have been rejected, while the latter are now generally preferred by those who wish to make grain growing their principal business.

Greater acreages were steadily brought under cultivation, and the region's agrarian economy was further stimulated by the opening of the grain export business through Snake River navigation in 1876. One factor inhibiting development prior to this time was the relative isolation of the Palouse from the larger marketing centers on the more populated Pacific Coast. The opening of shipping facilities at Almota by the Oregon Steamship and Navigation Company in 1876 enabled the Palouse farmers to export nearly 10,000 bushels of wheat to Portland while "four threshers, three sulky plows, three reapers, three headers, fifteen wagons and 100 tons of produce were unloaded there." In the following year other shipping warehouses were constructed at Wawawai and Penawawa on the Snake River. The volume of river traffic significantly increased in 1877 as Henry Spalding, proprietor of shipping at Almota, recorded 1,000 tons of produce exported from the town. Deliveries to Almota that year included 500 tons of merchandise, 195 new wagons, 95 sulky plows, 100 Noble plows, 10 threshers, and a variety of other agricultural equipment. The Palouse, once synonymous with bunchgrass and wild horses, was now becoming a haven for prospering colonist farmers. In early 1880 there were only about 20,000 acres under cultivation in Whitman County. By the end of the decade, however, that figure had risen to nearly 750,000 as European-Americans had claimed virtually the entire farming district (though some areas in the western Palouse remained unplowed until 1920).

Baled and Ready   *Northeast of Albion, Washington*

Many families in the countryside gathered to help build enormous barns that were needed to store hay and protect livestock and farm equipment during the Palouse's snowy winters. As unique in design as the people who built them, many today lie in twisted hypotenuses of weathered wood defeated by decades of wind and rain, others remain as vital and impressive as the year they were raised. The classic red walls of Thera's Adam Daubert barn have proudly stood for nearly a century and the unusual Max Steinke (Dechenne) round barn west of St. John and the T.A. Leonard barn east of Pullman were constructed to simplify the task of feeding horses from the spacious hay lofts. The gleaming white horse stables trimmed in green of the McCroskey place near Steptoe Butte look as ready for use as when J.P.T.'s Tennessee relatives raced their animal nearby and the enormous dairy barns adjacent to Moscow's U.of I. remain among the largest in the Pacific Northwest.

The population of the Palouse nearly tripled in the 1880s as the completion of the Northern Pacific Railroad facilitated immigration to all parts of the Pacific Northwest. By 1890 the population of Whitman and Latah Counties reached 28,282. Of that number approximately 2,000 were foreign-born and one-third of these were from England and Canada. Among the one million Canadians who came to America in the 1880s were two Scottish-Canadian brothers, Archie and Peter McGregor, who claimed homesteads on Alkali Flat near present Dusty in 1883. To earn extra income they later herded sheep for ranchers along the Snake River and in 1885 they acquired a small flock of their own. The McGregors invited other family members from Sydenham Township on Ontario's Lake Huron to come West and in 1886 their brother, John, relocated to Whitman County. A fourth brother, Alexander, followed in 1900.

The industrious McGregors increased the size of their flock into one of the region's largest and pastured them on the winter ranges along the lower Palouse River until the annual summer drives to the eastern mountain districts. Pooling their profits and business acumen, the brothers entered into lucrative grazing leases and purchase agreements with the Northern Pacific Railroad covering 25,000 acres in the southwest corner of Whitman County. In 1902 title was secured to the leaseholds which gave the McGregors control of an agricultural empire seventeen by twenty-one miles. The McGregors continued to run sheep for decades, brought large tracts of pastureland under irrigation, developed a substantial dryland grain farming operation, and later expanded their enterprises into wheat research and fertilizer production (A. McGregor, 1982).

The Rustler War and Law Enforcement

Ranchers like the Huntleys, McCroskeys, Ochses, Benjamin Manchester, Lucius and Lillis Smith, and others in the central and western Palouse were harassed by livestock rustlers in the 1880s and early '90s which led to the organization by some fifty men of the Stockmen's Protective Association in 1892. A February issue of the *Colfax Commoner* that year reported that fifteen head of horses belonging to Lafayette Wright of Sprague were found in Valley City, South Dakota! Another four hundred stolen earlier from D. A Flewerree of Colfax had still not been located. Association members worked to break up a notorious horse thieving operation headed by William "Big Bill" Masterson who had established a ranch in Palouse Cove between present Ewan and Winona. The narrow box canyon sheltered natural springs and a small lake and was flanked by large basaltic columns to form an ideal hideaway for stolen livestock. The herds were moved eastward at night beyond Pine City and Farmington to be sold in north Idaho and Montana. The Stockmen's Association joined with local marshalls to eventually put an end to the depredations in the summer of 1892 when over two dozen rustlers were captured including the Williams and Cooper gangs.

Masterson's operation, however, continued to thwart the efforts of the ranchers. Standing six feet, four inches tall, Masterson was imposing outlaw who wore a heavy mustache and, according to an acquaintance, was "uncouth, profane, insolent, and overbearing." He was also a crack shot and suspected of murdering Slowiarchy the Younger, son of a Palouse Indian chief, in a dispute over a horse. Masterson's son-in-law and accomplice, Ed Harris, was arrested for selling stolen livestock in Montana in July, 1892 and brought to Spokane by train enroute to Colfax to stand trial on the charges. In an attempt to free Harris, Masterson intercepted the party at the Pacific Hotel in Spokane where a gunfight erupted during the night in which deputy

Charley Miller killed Masterson after the outlaw wounded Pine City sheriff Luke Rawls. Harris was then taken to Colfax and later sentenced to an eight-year term at the state penitentiary in Walla Walla. He escaped not long after his imprisonment, however, but was never seen in the area again. The Palouse Country Rustler War had come to an end (M. Ochs, 1989; J. Smith, 1975).

Most Palouse Country communities could not afford the services of a local constable so law enforcement in most places from 1870 to 1900 was left to city marshals in Colfax and Moscow who were periodically assisted by deputies. Their efforts to maintain domestic tranquility were often challenged by distance and the brutal circumstances of pioneer life. Colfax's *Palouse Gazette* regularly reported during the 1880s and 1890s in lurid detail on cases involving gunfights and murder as well as occasional "crimes of infamy." Three episodes of vigilante justice led to the overpowering of deputies on night shift at the Colfax jail and the lynching of the accused offenders. The first victim was a man convicted of an 1884 Pullman murder but some locals felt the wheels of justice did not grind fast enough for proper restitution. The grisly scene was repeated at a double lynching for two horse thieves in June, 1894 who were unceremoniously tossed out an upper window of the Colfax courthouse. The same venue was used in January, 1898 for a man held on a Farmington charge of murder and theft. The area's only legal hanging, which drew a large crowd, took place near the Colfax courthouse on March 25, 1898.

J. A. "Brooks" Mackay and Joseph Canutt were Colfax's marshals for most years from 1888 to 1915 and became colorful Palouse area legends in their own time. Standing six feet tall and weighing two hundred pounds, Sheriff Mackay exhibited a rare balance of terror and tolerance depending on the situation. An old acquaintance later elaborated on Mackay's approach: "On Saturday nights, instead of jailing the drunk farmers, Brooks, who knew them all, would take each one to his own team and wagon, slap the team on the rump and head them for home…. There were some tough customers reluctant to go, however, and Brooks could lead them off, two at a time, with a chain around the arm of each one. He used guns as a last resort. His main defenses were a strong right fist and a billy-club…. He was fearless" (*Palouse Gazette*, August 22, 1884; *Colfax Commoner*, June 8, 1894; W. Lever,

1901; *Colfax Gazette*, July 13, 1972).

Villard, Tannatt, and the Columbia & Palouse Railroad

A native of Bavaria, Henry Villard came to the United States in 1853 and labored for several years at various occupations before studying law in Carlisle, Illinois. He then worked in the offices of several influential United States senators from the Midwest. Having a talent for journalism, he reported on various political campaigns for several newspapers, and these experiences led to personal acquaintanceships with Abraham Lincoln, Horace Greeley, and men in the highest circles of American and European business. He became interested in the subject of railroad securities and finance and in 1873 joined a German protective committee which had heavily invested in Ben Holliday's troubled Oregon and California Railroad, as well as the Oregon Central and the Oregon Steamship Company. In 1874 Villard journeyed to Oregon as a representative of a committee to investigate the situation. He later noted that the trip changed the course of his life: "I felt that I had reached a chosen land, certain of great prosperity and seemingly holding out better promise to my constituents than I had hoped for (H. Villard, 1944)."

To bolster the region's developing transportation industry, he was supplied with the distinction of "Oregon Commissioner of Immigration" and by 1875 had established offices in Boston, Topeka, and Omaha that cooperated with the main Northwest Immigration Bureau in Portland in directing immigrants to the Pacific Northwest. The duty of railroad officials there was to provide these new arrivals with employment on construction crews or sell them railroad land on which to settle. Special displays were circulated of Northwest grains, fruits, and vegetables; large advertisements regularly appeared in English, German, and Scandinavian newspapers throughout the country and thousands of circulars extolled the Pacific Northwest as containing the "best wheat, farming and grazing lands in the world" (J. Hedges, 1930).

Villard observed that geographically the central artery of transportation throughout the entire Northwest was the Columbia River and assumed that whoever navigated the great river and controlled the railways along its course would virtually monopolize transportation east

Fall Patterns

Steptoe, Washington

of the Cascades. He journeyed into that region for the first time in May, 1876 and stated later, "It was at that early date that a plan arose through the organization of the Oregon Railway and Navigation Company." Within a year, Villard's clever manipulation of several indebted concerns led him to the presidency of all three Northwest transportation lines previously operated by Holliday. In 1878 Villard formed the Oregon Improvement Company to facilitate the construction of his network and to arrange for the orderly settlement and exploitation of his holdings in the region (E. Bryan, 1936).

The man selected by Villard to be the general agent of the new company was Thomas R. Tannatt, who later arranged for colonization in the Palouse by Volga Germans and other immigrants. Ultimately, Tannatt acquired a large estate in the Palouse near Farmington for himself. He was a native of Manchester, Massachusetts, was a prominent New England figure and retired brigadier general who had commanded Union forces south of the Potomac in 1862. During the defense of the capital he became acquainted personally with President Lincoln. After the war Tannatt became interested in developing railroad land grants in the Pacific Northwest. He wrote a letter to Villard in 1877 in which he offered several suggestions to aid in the westward settlement of immigrants. Impressed with the advice, Villard appointed Tannatt the eastern agent for the Oregon Steamship Company in 1877. In the following year he began directing the immigration program for Villard's other Northwest transportation companies. After the formation of the Oregon Improvement Company in 1878 Tannatt was elevated to the position of its general agent and his offices were transferred to Portland.

Realizing the vast untapped agricultural potential of this region, Villard's Oregon Improvement Company purchased 150,000 acres (the odd sections in fourteen townships) from the Northern Pacific in the center of present Whitman County. These lands were carefully selected and Villard intended to build his Palouse line directly through this district and populate it with dependable colonist farmers. The lands varied in price from $5 to $10 per acre and sold on a six-year installment plan at seven percent interest. In March, 1881 General Tannatt relocated his office to Walla Walla in order to be closer to the Oregon Improvement Company's operations in Eastern Washington. He made frequent trips to the company lands in the Palouse and began arranging for their settlement. Villard took a personal interest in this program of colonization which he outlined in the following 1881 stockholders report:

A regular land and emigration department has been organized, the lands fully surveyed and appraised, 5,000 acres are now being broken up. The plan is to divide the lands into farms not exceeding

*Rosalia Railroad Bridge**

Rosalia, Washington

160 acres, to fence and improve no more than 40 acres upon each quarter section, erecting thereon plain but substantial dwellings and the necessary outbuildings, so as to be able to offer farms ready for immediate occupancy at reasonable rates to incoming settlers. The Oregon Railway and Navigation Company is extending its system of roads right through these lands, and there is every assurance that our land operations will be successful and will result in a large profit to the company.

In 1881, Tannatt began developing these properties with the assistance of A. A. Newberry, the Oregon Improvement Company's Colfax agent. Their crews methodically traveled from section to section in a special train of "six wagons heavily loaded with agricultural implements, tents, commissary stores, etc., forming the best outfit of the kind" that had ever entered the Palouse. Local farmers also found temporary employment by leasing their teams and a new market for their produce. The new work force turned to plowing and seeding 20,000 acres of company lands under Tannatt's capable management. For fencing and construction in the area, three million feet of lumber was stored at the company flume at Dayton and delivered to the Palouse in the spring.

Villard's massive investment in the region contributed to the virtual economic transformation of the central Palouse from grazing to farming. In addition, the marketing potential of the entire region was enhanced since the railroad allowed Palouse farmers to capitalize on growing European demands for Northwest grain exports. Exporting of Palouse wheat had begun as early as 1868, but had been limited to that which could be transported on the Oregon Steam Navigation Company down the Snake and Columbia Rivers. In 1879 only half the crop was shipped before navigation closed in December for the winter. Railroad transportation would thus insure a more dependable system of grain delivery throughout the year to both foreign and domestic markets. The

Palouse Gazette in November 1881 observed, "A few not engaged in agriculture will dislike to see so large an area of grazing country broken up; but this is a narrow consideration, compared with the standing it will give our farming lands and the stimulus it will bring to our country." To begin populating the sparsely settled area with immigrants, the company also hired a number of writers "to go over every section of the country and give its true merits to the world, in newspapers, pamphlets, (and) magazines...."

At the dawn of the century's ninth decade, an air of peculiar expectation seemed palpable throughout the Palouse Country. The early '60s had witnessed the first penetration of the region by a scattered group of stockmen and subsistence farmers, mostly bachelors from the Walla Walla and Lewiston areas, who risked a beginning on the Palouse frontier. The completion of federal land surveys in the region by 1873 provided legal means for the pioneers to legitimize their claims which gave significant impetus to the first real surge of immigration. Families began homesteading on the unbroken prairies north of the Snake River and clustered along the fertile bottomlands of its course from Wawawai to Riparia that earlier had only known the presence of pithouse and mat lodge villages.

Surveys for the first railroad route through the Palouse had been undertaken as early as 1869 by such pathfinders as Levinius Swift whose meanderings through the hills enabled individuals like him to find some of the most favorable sites to settle. After completing his work, Swift returned with his wife, Cornelia, to purchase land from the railroad for $2.50 per acre on Rebel Flat near present Diamond. Here they planted a small orchard and several black walnut trees along the stream, some of which still remain to this day, and began turning the rich sod of the bottomlands. The prescient prose of Walt Whitman in the 1870s suggested in effusive terms the possibilities that awaited those who dared venture onto unclaimed landscapes like the Palouse. In the provocative essay

COLUMBIA & PALOUSE IMMIGRANT TRAIN, c. 1895 (MASC, WSU LIBRARIES)

"Democratic Vistas," Whitman wrote, "We presume to write upon things that exist not, and travel by maps yet unmade, and a blank. But the throes of birth are upon us…. It seems as if the Almighty has spread before this nation charts of imperial destinies, dazzling as the sun…."

When the sun appeared above spring skies of the Inland Northwest in 1881, work began in earnest eastward from Palouse Junction (Connell) where the O.R.&N.Co.'s Columbia & Palouse branch line advanced from the main N.P.R.R. transcontinental route. The sounds of rock blasting, road grading, and spike driving were a prelude to a new period of immigration to the region. Providing its subsidiary with title to 150,000 acres of prime farmland in present Whitman County alone, the cash-strapped Northern Pacific was eager to promote the sale of its Palouse properties along the proposed route and plat a number of existing and future and townsites. Those members of the earlier vanguard who had attempted to settle in the area prior to 1880 only to "bust" from the inability to turn the stubborn sod, withstand the Indian scares, or contend with the sheer loneliness engendered by such isolation, decried the region in unmistakable terms. The Palouse was "no place to take women and children," "unlivable wild country," and a "frosty land of such hills where no crops can grow."

As grading continued northeast to Kahlotus and Washtucna in 1881, the Northern Pacific's promotional department and affiliated Oregon Improvement Company aggressively campaigned in the regional and national press to change public perception of settlement prospects in the region by heralding its agricultural potential. Soon newspapers from Lewiston and Walla Walla to Oregon City were replacing their accounts of "foolish journeys to the rainbow's end" with testimonies of the Palouse Country's "inexhaustible soil up to eight feet deep" and recurrent high yields "without irrigation" of "never failing crops." These articles and railroad broadsides specified the liberal terms under which the Northern Pacific was prepared to part with its vast tracts, arranged in checkerboard formation on alternate 640-acre sections where prices ranged from five to ten dollars per acre.

Villard's grandiose scheme for his railroad empire also reached fruition in late 1881. He had come to the realization that direct rail-

way connections to the East were imperative if the Pacific Northwest was ever to be actively involved in the commerce of the nation and settlement of European immigrants. With this in mind, he had embarked secretly in December 1880 on collecting an unprecedented $8,000,000 "blind pool" from his financial supporters in order to purchase the controlling interest in Billings' stalemated Northern Pacific Railroad. In less than year his request was actually oversubscribed and on September 15, 1881 he was elected president of the Northern Pacific. Work on both ends of the line again resumed and his dream of a northern transcontinental under his personal control rapidly approached reality.

The editor of the *Palouse City Boomerang* extolled the virtues of the region's burgeoning economy while seeking to depict the area's unique topography in favorable terms: "The surface of this country looks as if it had been… ruffled, tucked, puckered and puffed, with several rows of trounces." The unforgiving steep slopes were now being characterized in terms of comfortable bedding. The stolid farmers who remained did come to realize the Palouse's relatively mild winters coupled with wet springs and dry summers provided an ideal climate for growing soft white wheat. By the fall of 1882 the railroad had passed through LaCrosse and Winona to Endicott and in 1883 extended along Rebel Flat to Colfax. Levinius Swift's original survey had bypassed a Palouse River canyon route into Colfax in favor of the more advantageous path from Mockonema Flat to Guy (Albion). For decades the rumor persisted that Colfax City Fathers raised $20,000 to successfully bribe the Columbia & Palouse's chief engineer into redirecting the line down the three degree slope to Colfax, the steepest grade along the entire system (F. Yoder, 1938; *Palouse City Boomerang*, September 20, 1882).

N.P.R.R. President Henry Villard had become the sower, casting forth seeds of settlement with his Columbia & Palouse line moving further inland week after week. As in the parable, some seed took root on fertile ground where communities large and small were platted that remain vital throughout the next century, some fell among stones to sprout for a few years and perish by the wayside, and others like Plainville seemed to vanish before the maps bearing their location were even printed. Changes in company management and financial difficulties periodically stalled further progress in the early '80s but Pullman and Moscow were both reached by 1885 which sparked great celebrations. The first train was clad in red, white, and blue bunting and arrived in Pullman to the music of the community brass band. Speeches were given at the newly completed depot proclaiming a new era for town and region while unimpressed grizzled workers prepared to lay the next stretch of ties and rails to Moscow where their arrival in September met with more music and a volley of G.A.R. cannon fire.

PULLMAN, WASHINGTON, 1889 (MASC, WSU LIBRARIES)

the lower Snake was built at Central Ferry in 1924. Ferry service was begun at this point by twin brothers Alvin and Alfred Hastings, natives of Pataha Flat, in the spring of 1895. The operation was taken over by Robert Young in 1917 and continued until the bridge was built. This route became a principal thoroughfare for travel from the Palouse to Dayton and Walla Walla (B. Kromm, 2003; E. Hastings, 2003).

The line extended eastward from Moscow toward Juliaetta in the late 1880s while the main Columbia & Palouse line turned north from Pullman as grading proceeded at an aggressive pace to Garfield, Farmington, and Tekoa which were linked in 1886. Two years later the line completed the master circle route by building from Farmington to Oakesdale and southwesterly to St. John down to the junction at Winona. General Tannatt found the area around Farmington to be among the most pleasant in the region and retired to a large farm there in 1888. He often employed as fieldhands newly arrived immigrants from Europe like Jacob Adler who remembered the general as being "a stern but fair" taskmaster. He also served as a member of the Pullman college's first board of regents (J. Adler, 1973).

Work began in the next century on the Union Pacific's plan to tap the Palouse grain district. By then reorganization of the railroads led to the U.P.'s control over the Oregon Railroad and Navigation Company which built a line connecting its parent company's railhead opposite Riparia on the Snake River with the Columbia & Palouse at LaCrosse. The river was spanned at Riparia by the O.R.&N.Co.'s massive Joso Railway Bridge which was completed in 1914 after four years of construction. Named for local sheepman Leon Jaussaud, the bridge is 4,000 feet long and 280 feet high making it the tallest bridge in the entire Union Pacific system. The first highway bridge across

Townbuilding: Real Estate, Religion, and Roundhouses

Many of the Palouse's first communities had already emerged as small rural trading and postal centers before the rails came to their doorstep. These places became the nexus of country life where both economic and social exchanges were made in a forum of hospitality. Many town names honored their founders including (Albert J.) Hooper, (Edward T.) St. John, and (William) Spangle. Others were named for the eastern hometowns of their first inhabitants or surveyors such as Fairfield and Farmington (Minnesota), La Crosse (Wisconsin), Genesee (New York), Winona (Michigan), Waverly (Iowa), Malden (Massachusetts), and Moscow (Pennsylvania). Samuel Neff, who named Moscow, was also said to have favored the word because Russia's capital sounded like a scenic and holy place—fitting for a new community in "Paradise Valley." Many towns platted along the route were given names of such railroad company officials as vice-presidents Thomas F. Oakes(dale) and Daniel Lamont, directors Benjamin Cheney, John Sprague, and William Endicott, and sleeping car magnate George Pullman. The namesakes of other communities were of Indian origin—Latah, Washtucna, Kahlotus, and Palouse. Tekoa was named by its postmaster's wife, Mrs. Daniel Truax, for the imagery presented by the biblical reference in II Samuel to the "city of tents" (R. Hitchman, 1985; J. Monroe, 2003).

The surveyors who platted Palouse Country townsites laid out

91

standard checkerboard patterns of streets and lots in accordance with the lines of the federal land surveys. In many cases the locations of rivers and streams, steep hillsides, and additions by landowning developers conflicted with rigid conformity to the cardinal directions. Streets occasionally turned at odd angles or twisted along peculiarities of the terrain. In addition to the colorless alpha-numeric rules for naming streets, Palouse area communities commonly featured the two categories of names used across the country—trees and presidents. Perhaps life along Elm, Chestnut, Walnut, and Ash brought hope to local residents that deciduous stands of such non-natives would soon shade their grassy homesites. Over half of the region's communities also contain streets named for Washington, Adams, Jefferson, and Lincoln. Only the name Whitman, in tribute to the martyred missionaries Marcus and Narcissa, is accorded such honor on as many street signs in the area. Tekoa also originally honored Jackson and Taft, Colton favored McKinley and Harrison, and Garfield platted Monroe and Cleveland. Town founders also received such recognition including McConnell and Lieuallen (Moscow), McKenzie and Neill in Pullman (Kamiaken Street runs through the center of town), Greif (Colton), McCoy (Oakesdale), Loomis (St. John), Shindler (Malden), and Manring (Garfield).

Between 1899 and 1910, seven hamlets and sidings along the Washington, Idaho & Montana Railroad line east of the company town of Potlatch paid tribute to the Ivy League. Tiny Princeton, located closest to Potlatch, probably inspired the designations, though it had been named in 1896 by founder Orville Clough in honor of his original home, Princeton, Minnesota. The hamlet served as a stopping point for the Palouse-Hoodoo (Woodfell) stagecoach. Harvard, platted in 1906, was named by founder Homer W. Canfield, who owned considerable property along the W.I.&M. route. Vassar appeared in 1907 but its name may also have been in tribute to James R. Vassar, a Civil War veteran who had settled nearby on Vassar Meadows. Yale, Purdue, and Wellesley soon appeared along the railway although among schools in the West, only Stanford was accorded similar status in the eastern Palouse though Inman A. Stanford had settled earlier in the vicinity. Like Mount Hope and Staley, most of these have more letters in their names than residents. Still other Palouse community names

owe their origins to an obvious local quantity, quality, or geography as with Hay, Dusty, and Rockford.

The first commercial enterprises in the region were the sawmills and gristmills that were built at Colfax and Palouse City in the 1870s and by the end of the decade pioneer businessmen had established general mercantile stores at these and other sites where settlers clustered. These businesses brought relief to families who had previously depended on long annual treks by wagon to Walla Walla for household necessities. Samuel Neff established a general store in Paradise Valley in 1873 but sold his business about two years later to Almon Lieuallen who moved it to a new location at the corner of First and Main streets. William Ragsdale's general store opened in Palouse City also in the 1870s, and in the next decade more than a dozen others were established in the region including Lippett Brothers of Colfax, Moscow's McConnell and Maguire, Stewart and Lee in Pullman, and Huntley Brothers which operated stores in Endicott, St. John, and Colfax.

The aroma of spices and coffee mixed with the scent of fresh leather in the stores' cavernous interiors where farmers, ranchers, and timber workers could procure everything from flour, corn meal, and sugar, the latter selling for as much as 25¢ a pound, to kerosene, window panes, and squirrel poison. Horehound hard candy and licorice found their places near bolts of gingham, calico, and linen. Reflecting the needs of a nascent business class, some stores even advertised suits by Hart, Shaffner & Marx though such sartorial needs by Palouse farmers were generally restricted to church functions. Other businesses soon followed the mills and mercantile stores with most early Palouse communities having blacksmith and livery services, a meat shop, saloons, lumber sales, dentist and real estate offices, a train depot, local bank, and grain warehouses.

Among the first structures erected in each town was a school and church and in several communities the pastor also served as the first schoolteacher. Rev. Cushing Eells, son of pioneer Spokane missionaries Myron and Myra Eells, worked with Rev. George Atkinson of Portland as a circuit-rider to organize the earliest churches and several schools in the Palouse. The indefatigable "Father Eells" joked that he covered a district from the Snake River to the North Pole and toiled to be a good steward of divine blessing. He subsisted on 37¢ a week and

Little Kamiak Butte Sunset*

North of Pullman, Washington

traveled everywhere on his beloved sorrel horse, Le Blond. The region's first organized church was Colfax's Plymouth Congregational (1874) followed by others in Cheney and Sprague. Moscow's Zion Baptist Church (1876) was among the first of its denomination in the area and other early congregations in many communities included Catholics, Methodists, Methodist-Episcopals, Christian, Presbyterians, and Lutherans.

MOSCOW, IDAHO; 1889 (MASC, WSU LIBRARIES)

Oakesdale, Palouse, Moscow, and Sprague boasted opera houses in the 1890s featuring plays by such traveling professionals as the Graham Company Players and the Curtis Comedy Company. National figures like the hatchet-bearing crusader Carrie Nation came to rail against "evil of all kind including tobacco and alcohol use" while other stage guests included hypnotists, professional wrestlers, and musicians. At the turn of the century, these structures also served as the regions first silent film theatres (*Palouse Republic*, April 14, 1905).

Virtually every town had fine lodging and meals available at hostelries like Moscow's Barton House, Juliaetta's Grand Hotel, the Hotel McMichael at Spangle, the Palace in Pullman, Almota House, Duff's Hotel in Colton, and Colfax's Ewart House. Many featured second-story ballrooms beneath proud mansard roofs. Perhaps the Palouse's most elegant lodging was at Waverly's extravagant Harbottle Hotel, a palace on the prairie built in French Empire style. The ornate three-story brick edifice came with the local sugar beet factory but seemed to be brought from New Orleans cane country. In these places, large gatherings of couples danced the Virginia Reel and other quadrilles as well as more formal minuets and waltzes to the accompaniment of popular Palouse Country musicians like the Cy and Andy Privett String Band. Among the most famous inns far and wide was James A. "Cashup" Davis's grand Steptoe Butte Hotel. Visible for miles around, the substantial two-story structure perched at the very top of the butte opened in 1888. Guests first met a wide entry exhibi-

tion hall displaying dozens of grain sheaves creatively displayed across the walls and in floor vases. The hotel offered stunning vistas of the Palouse landscape enhanced by views through a brass telescope in glass enclosed turret crowning the building. Rumor held that a careful observer could use the instrument to spot buildings in Walla Walla.

Rock Lake City boatbuilder and hostelier Willis "Dad" Evans had a similar vision for a lakeside destination resort. Evans and his wife, Emma, opened the Cliff House in 1903 on a rocky tongue overlooking the southwest shore of Rock Lake where he also offered tourists Sunday afternoon excursions to the head of the lake in a coal-fired steam vessel thirty feet long for $1.50, twice the daily room rate. Sprague area pioneers organized the Merrie Crew Boat Club in the 1880s for sailboating on Colville (Sprague) Lake. John and Francis Kebla acquired lakefront property about 1910 and built Sprague Lake Resort—a sprawling complex of cabins, a dance hall built on stilts over the lakeshore, store, and park. Tons of sand were hauled to create a scenic beach and dock for their tour boat, *Silver Star*. For years the resort served as the site of one of the Palouse Country's most spectacular Fourth of July celebrations. Accommodations were available even in the smallest Palouse Country settlements where travelers could find respite at the Hotel Lamont, Hooper's Hotel Glenmore, and Texas City's Hotel Stewart where late night poker games were occasionally known to end in gun-play.

Two nefarious businessmen used Endicott's Hill Hotel to plot the murder of a local country doctor who threatened to close a house of ill-fame operated by the pair. Many such "parlor houses" were located in the Palouse in the late 1800s, especially in the larger railroad and logging communities were some had as many as a half-dozen. The doctor in Endicott also acquired the area's first Model T Ford franchise and was expected to unload a shipment of vehicles when they arrived by rail in the summer of 1914. The conspirators placed gunpowder in

Summer Patterns   *South of Oaksdale, Washington*

a cylinder of one of the cars but a recent German immigrant from Russia in need of employment was hired to drive the vehicles down from the flatcar. When he turned the ignition switch an enormous explosion ripped through the engine sending debris flying in all directions. The hapless driver was killed instantly when a piece of glass struck his temple, leaving a destitute family in a strange new land. The case went unsolved for nearly a century.

The economic vitality of several communities was based to a great extent on a single enterprise. In Cheney, Pullman, and Moscow, the three state institutions of higher learning ensured an abiding employment base as did the location of county seats in Colfax for Whitman County in 1871 and Moscow for Latah. For years residents of Moscow had lobbied for a separate county in the northern part of Nez Perce County, headquartered in faraway Lewiston. Through the extraordinary lobbying efforts of Congressional representative Willis Sweet, and businessmen Charles Moore and William McConnell with other Moscow political activists, the new county was authorized through Congressional mandate—the only such case in American history. McConnell derived the name "Latah" from the Nez Perce words *La-kah* (pine) and *Tah-ol* (pestle) to mean "Place of Pines and Pestles" (J.R. Monroe, 2003).

The bitter struggle between Cheney and Spokane for county seat status and the contested 1880 election outcome resulted in the notorious night theft of county records from Spokane to assure Cheney residents that their city would attain the honor and reap the subsequent benefits of employment. The victory, however, was short-lived. The 1886 county election definitely proved the balance of population power had swung east and the books and jobs were returned to Spokane. Sprague was designated Lincoln County's seat of government when the area was detached from Whitman and Spokane counties in 1883 but only after Harrington and Davenport accused the town of submitting votes from children, train passengers, and the cemetery. Several years later the honor was won by more centrally located Davenport.

In 1899 Fairfield businessman E. H. Morrison established the Washington State Beet Sugar Company and arranged for a $500,000 investment to construct a three-story processing factory in Waverly after determining that the crop could be grown profitably in the area.

The facility employed four hundred seasonal workers and 150 others to operate the factory in two shifts which processed up to 6,000 tons of beets annually. Complications plagued the operation of the complex extraction machinery, however, and some farmers found more familiar grain production to be less labor intensive and more commercially viable than raising beets. Within ten years the company was forced to curtail operations. In some area communities, the railroad continued to provide relatively high-paying jobs long after the rails

PERKINS HOUSE, COLFAX, WASHINGTON, 1889 (MASC, WSU LIBRARIES)

decade. This number was second in the Palouse Country only to Moscow's population of 2,000 where the "Merchant Prince of Idaho," William McConnell and his wife, Louisa, served as two of the area's greatest boosters. McConnell used his considerable political influence in the legislature to locate the state university in Moscow. He went on to serve as Idaho's third governor from 1893-95 and in the U.S. Senate. The story of life in Moscow (Opportunity) during the 1890s is evocatively portrayed in Carol Ryrie Brink's juvenile novel

were laid through the region. Roundhouses for servicing and repairing the massive steam engines and railway cars were established on the main Northern Pacific transcontinental line at Sprague in 1882 and at Farmington in 1886 by its subsidiary, the O.R.&N.Co. (Gl Leitz, 1994).

Tiny Malden was designated a division point by the Chicago, Milwaukee & St. Paul Railroad (the Milwaukee Road) in 1906 for its Idaho-Cascade route which swelled its population from a few dozen at the turn of the century to 800 at the end of the decade. At these points the railroad employed dozens of mechanics and repairmen and housed its crews of engineers, stokers, brakemen, conductors, and other personnel. The abandoned C.M.&S.P. line is now the Milwaukee Road Trail Corridor. The former S.P.&S. Railroad has been converted to the Columbia Plateau Trail for hikers and bikers and runs 132 miles from Fish Lake to Pasco via Lamont, Hooper, and Washtucna.

Boom and Depression

Designated headquarters for the N.P.R.R.'s Sandpoint-Pasco Division in 1881, Sprague was rapidly transformed from Newman's original stagecoach stop and scattered flat of a few dozen houses at the head of the lake into a small city of 1,700 residents by the end of the

Caddie Woodlawn, winner of the 1936 Newberry Award for the nation's outstanding contribution to children's literature. Born in Moscow in 1895, Brink went on to write a trilogy of critically acclaimed adult novels about the area including *Buffalo Coat* (1944), *Strangers in the Forest* (1959), and *Snow in the River* (1964).

Colfax's population swelled to 1,650 by 1890 while Pullman and Cheney, still awaiting college faculty and enrollments, numbered 868 and 647, respectively. Palouse Country businessmen like James Perkins and William McConnell built magnificent homes from the flourishing enterprises they established by supplying area residents with pioneer necessities, lending farmers money to acquire larger acreages, and by marketing grain and livestock. Evidence of their success is displayed in 19th century Victorian repositories of communal memory that serve as portals to the past and expressions of civic pride. These timeless works by patient craftsmen include such masterpieces as Garfield's R. C. McCroskey House, Tekoa's A. B. Willard Home, and the residence of R. J. Howard in Rosalia with its distinctive rooftop cupola. James A. and Minnie Perkins's home in Colfax (restored by the Whitman County Historical Society) is a rare example of pioneer Italianate architecture, while the E. H. "Hanford Castle" overlooking Oakesdale displays a blend of 19th century styles crafted in brick and stone. The William and Flossie Sanborn home in Sprague is the mirror image of an identical brick Victorian structure originally used for offices across the street. Both were erected by a local railroad official in 1880.

A cornucopia of 19th century architectural style and composition is strikingly evident along Mosow's Fort Russell Historic District of over one hundred structures northeast of the city's downtown area. The McConnell Mansion itself is a lesson in structural eclectics generally conforming to Eastlake style but incorporating elements of Victorian and Queen Anne architecture. The McConnells' daughter, Mary, was raised in the home during the years it served as the city's social center and she later married Senator William Borah. Mary McConnell Borah died in 1976 at the age of 106 and the home was substantially restored to its original condition with many interior furnishing from the family to serve as headquarters and museum for the Latah County Historical Society.

The neighboring "House of Seven Gables" is a two and one-half story fairy tale chalet built for pioneer flour mill owner Mark Miller. The manor features stained glass windows and upper story notched purlins thrusting through wide carved bargeboards. The Jerome Day Mansion was built for the son of silver magnate Henry Day with both men providing the principal financing for Moscow's Idaho Harvester Company. Henry Day had made a fortune with F. M. Rothrock and others in the 1890s as principal shareholder in the Silver Valley's Hercules Mine near Mullan, Idaho that produced $85,000,000 worth of ore during its first twenty-five years of operation. Jerome Day spent lavishly on the residence that was built in Queen Anne style with Colonial influences evident in the metal crenellations and white columns along the lengthy curved veranda. Nearby Butterfield House is one of the Palouse Country's few examples of Georgian Revival architecture; another can be seen in the elegant lines of brick Colfax Post Office with distinctive cream-colored window trim and arches. Moscow also has one of the Pacific Northwest's few original Carnegie Libraries which was built in Spanish Mission style with funds endowed by the famed industrialist Andrew Carnegie to improve public education throughout the country and especially in rural areas that could not afford to build such an edifice.

Many Palouse Country historic structures did not survive the region's "great fire era" that devastated large portions of many towns including Colfax (1881, 1882, 1891), Pullman (1886, 1888, 1890), Palouse (1888), and Moscow (1890). Oakesdale (1892) and Kendrick (1893) did not escape the scourges and other conflagrations also struck Troy (1893), Sprague (1895), Farmington (1897), Endicott (1905), and Lamont (1910, 1913). Communities located in lowland areas like Rock Lake City and Sprague or on the banks of the Palouse River as with Colfax and Palouse also periodically experienced destructive floods.

From Moscow's magnificent mansions to the simple John Kelly log cabin built near Oakesdale in 1872, the grounds of Palouse homesites hosted capacious coves of colorful plantings. Most were brought by Palouse pioneers from the East or purchased from nurseries in Walla Walla. Blossoming General Jacquimonts and Paul Neyrons appeared in rose gardens and rows of colossal scarlet-blossomed hollyhocks and trumpet-flowered hybiscus guarded homes and outbuildings. Virginia creeper vines embraced walls with southern exposure while white Catalpa flowers, one of the few ornamentals bearing its Native American name, appeared in front yards in springtime. Successful country flower gardeners all had their secrets for raising blooms in such abundance and variety. Our Grandma Johns watered houseplants only from containers filled with crushed egg shells, her enormous begonias were always started in pots lines with potato peelings, and coffee grounds were worked into the compost along the border of the yard for the brightest yellow and orange nasturtiums.

As in boomtown Lewiston during the 1860s, walking the boardwalks of Sprague in the 1890s provided lessons in pioneer cultural diversity as one could hear conversations in an babel of foreign tongues. While most early residents like Iowa natives Matthew and Mary Brislawn and Nathaniel and Harriet Davis of Illinois were American born, other early settlers represented virtually every European nation. The Davises came to Sprague in the '90s where Nathaniel's milling skills readily led to his employment at one of the town's gristmills. About the same time the Olaf Petersens arrived from Denmark to homestead in the vicinity, as did Swedes like Nils and Vendla Anderson and Robert and Adrina Franseen, and Robert and

Emily Potts and John and Anna Costello from Ireland. Christian and Louisa Kintschi emigrated from Switzerland while Jacob and Anna Stromberger were German-speaking immigrants from Russia's lower Volga region. Many other families in the area came from Germany, Norway, and England.

Sprague also became home to the Palouse's only colony of emigrants from Portugal's Atlantic Azores that consisted of the Anthony and George Pereia, Frank and Manuel Silva, and Joseph and Manuel Simas families. Many of the men worked as herdsmen for area ranchers like F. M. Rothrock and the Harders before saving sufficient capital to acquire their own land. In the early years of the 20th century, brothers John and Marcus Escure, Basque natives of the Pyrenees Mountains of northern Spain, settled southeast of Sprague where they eventually established sprawling Rock Creek Ranch for raising cattle, sheep, and other livestock. Combining Old World values of frugality and hard work with progressive ideas on rangeland capacity and animal nutrition enabled the Escures to expand their holdings to cover 15,600 contiguous acres. The entire ranch was acquired in the 1990s by the Bureau of Land Management and as the Rock Creek Area provides valuable native habitat for threatened species including black- and white-tailed jackrabbits and the rapid chattering burrowing owl.

F. M. Rothrock and Harry L. Day used their Hercules Mine earnings to launch a number of regional commercial enterprises. Rothrock was a rancher at heart and his preferred endeavor became operating the Hercules Ranch which he and Day established in 1914 on the shores of Sprague Lake. Within several years their holdings expanded to 20,000 acres where vast herds of Shorthorn cattle and sheep pastured for marketing throughout the region. Rothrock made his headquarters the sprawling fourteen-room Hercules Ranchhouse where prominent Northwest cattlemen and prospective buyers

were entertained on the white-pillared veranda during exhibitions in the adjacent show pavilion. Rothrock also acquired nearby Golden's Racetrack to add to his holdings which became one of the area's most popular scenes of competitive horseracing. Emblazoned in bronze upon a massive basalt slab at the Hercules's main entrance was Rothrock's personal creed: "Agriculture is the foundation of all prosperity; livestock is its cornerstone." The ranch continued under Rothrock's management for twenty years before he sold his interest and operated Spokane's Union Stockyards. In 1937 he began an enduring tradition by organizing the first Spokane Junior Livestock Show.

Neither Day nor Rothrock were immune from the effects of the Panic of 1893 and subsequent five years of economic depression that engulfed the entire nation. In the words of Enoch Bryan, recently appointed president of the state's new Land Grant college at Pullman just two years earlier, "The Northwest had come up to the very moment when the storm broke, in the full tide of prosperity." Exhibits showcasing Idaho and Washington's "fisheries, minerals, giant trees, grains, fruits, and wheat farms... had astonished and delighted" crowds from across the nation that visited Portland during the 1892 World Columbian Exposition. Almost overnight in the early spring of 1893, however, Northwest wheat prices that had hovered for some years around 40¢ a bushel fell to 30¢ and within nine months sunk to 18¢—far below the cost of production. The situation unfairly came to be associated with the 1892 election of Democratic candidate Grover Cleveland. Seeds of the disaster had actually been planted several years before that fateful year as tens of thousands of newly claimed farmland acres were coming into full production in the Palouse and other rural districts throughout the West.

Overproduction of grain in the early 1890s depressed commodity prices and farm income

PALOUSE COUNTRY PIONEERS, c. 1910: MRS. S. B. OLIPHANT, ELBERTON, '73; C. E. KETCHUM, MALDEN, '70; O. V. BRIGSON, ELBERTON, '70 (MASC, WSU LIBRARIES)

while mortgage rates and payment schedules remained constant. For these reasons the problems of the decade especially affected farmers who had financed land purchases through local banks from the original landowners or the railroad. Unsound banking practices and reckless railroad spending had already leveraged the nation's economy and when mortgage payments could not be met on homes and farms across America, foreclosures brought family evictions. Widespread loan defaults resulted in bank failures at the same time thousands of railroad miles went into receivership. In late 1893 the lines of the Northern Pacific, Union Pacific, and the O. R. & N. Co. all came under new ownership. Complicating the situation in the 1890s was a significant increase in silver production from new mines in the mountain states like those in northern Idaho. The production of silver in the United States had increased by 65% between 1880 and 1890 while the amount of gold produced over the same time fell by almost exactly the same proportion. The Silver Purchase Act of 1890 authorized the treasury department to acquire excess silver as its price fell against the value of gold bullion.

The final blow to the precarious situation for many Palouse farmers came in the summer of 1893 when incessant rains substantially ruined the grain harvest. August days that had not experienced more than a trace of moisture in pioneer memory suddenly wrought devastation upon what was expected to be a bumper crop. To many residents in the region, the unprecedented failure of crops dashed their last hopes of making a living, but with unemployment growing everywhere few other options were open for relocation. An air of despair swept upon the land like a biblical plague that persisted until federal intervention began boosting grain prices and farmland values in 1898. Despite state elections in Idaho and Washington in 1896 favoring Democrat William Jennings Bryan, G.O.P. nominee William McKinley narrowly won the popular vote and electoral margin.

Many Palouse farmers came to attribute the welcomed changes to Republican policies after McKinley took office in 1897. Active reduction of federal revenue over expenditures had taken place, however, during the administration of fellow Republican William Henry Harrison from 1889 to 1893. Such practices helped fuel the crisis in the first place. The new prosperity and reorganization of the northern railroads under the efficient management of J. P. Morgan and James Hill led to the region's "Great Decade of Progress" from 1897 to 1907. Gold discoveries in Alaska sent forth a stream of placer miners in 1897 and brought new reserves to the precious metal into treasury coffers in the same year that Australia and New Zealand sent over fifteen million dollars worth of bullion to purchase wheat from the Inland Northwest. Wheat prices in the Palouse shot up to 75¢ a bushel leading to a rise in immigration and land values. Farmers who had survived the depression of the '90s were delighted with the new prospects but sought every possibility to secure and further improve their situation. New attention was paid to scientific improvements in agriculture advocated by personnel serving under presidents Bryan and Franklin Gault at the Land Grant colleges' experiment stations in Pullman and Moscow (E. Bryan, 1936; *Palouse Gazette*, May 17, 1897).

The Palouse Press, Folk Arts, and Sporting Events

As the Northern Pacific's "immigrant trains" brought recurrent streams of newcomers to the Inland Northwest in the 1880s and 1890s, the new transportation networks facilitated the export of grain and other produce from the Palouse. Communities throughout the region slowly prospered and newspapers appeared in virtually each one to inform a growing readership of local events and boost the virtues of settlement in the vicinity. Area political contests, social affairs, school events, and economic issues affecting life from Spangle to Uniontown and from Genessee to Washtucna were regularly featured in the Palouse press. Performances of the Lamont Mandolin Orchestra and the Uniontown Brass Band were announced and reviewed next to news from Seattle on grain exports to China, Japan, and Korea, markets important to Palouse farmers, and national headlines on the controversial agrarian policies advocated in the Cleveland and Harrison administrations. Pioneer businessmen L. E. Kellogg and C. B. Hopkins had published the first newspaper north of the Snake River with the inaugural issue of the weekly *Palouse* (Colfax) *Gazette* on September 29, 1877. The *Spokan Times* appeared two years later.

Several other local papers were established before the end of the century including the *Moscow Mirror* (1882), *Pullman Herald* (1888), *Sprague Advocate* (1888), *Palouse Republic* (1892), and *Fairfield*

Standard (1895). The early Palouse press generally issued weeklies in which editors made clear their political affiliations. Moscow's readership was large enough in the 1890s to allow three competing weeklies—the *Mirror, Times-Democrat,* and *North Idaho Star.* Over one hundred different newspapers in thirty-six towns were published in the Palouse between 1877 and 1920. Several communities have had more than six weeklies during this period but rarely with more than two in publication at any one time. The widest variety of news, though often short-lived, was found in Juliaetta (*Advance, Enterprise, Gem, Potlatch, Register*), Oakesdale (*Advocate, Breeze, News, Observer, Sun, Tidings, Tribune*), and Tekoa (*Advertiser, Blade, Globe, Manitou, Sentinel, Topic*). Others that appeared for smaller circulations included the *Elberton Wheatbelt, Ewan Telephone, Malden Register, Valleyford Enterprise,* and *Thornton Tidings.* Some papers did not hide their small-town informality; the ephemeral *Winona News* announced publication beneath its banner "whenever something happens." An extensive collection of these newspapers is filed at the Palouse Boomerang Print Museum in Palouse.

Something newsworthy did happen every June in the Palouse to inaugurate the arrival of summer. Hundreds of residents from far and wide gathered for up to three days over June 21st along the Palouse River at Elberton for a special event that combined pioneer family picnicking with Chautauqua presentations and evening revival campmeetings. During the day couples waited in line and gazed upward in awe at hot air balloon ascensions while children scurried up and down the wildflower meadows playing Run Sheep, Run and Fox and Geese. The grand affair invariably included a game of baseball with teams drawn from communities throughout the region.

The origins of the Palouse Empire Fair date to April, 1887 when a fair association was organized in Whitman County by James Perkins and others to raise capital stock of $20,000 to build a respectable park, horseracing track, stables, and exhibition buildings. The Latah County Agricultural Fair was organized in 1888 and held annually near Moscow's Mountain View Park. The Whitman County site was selected along the Palouse River a mile north of Colfax and the first fair was held there the following October. Residents throughout the region flocked to the event which featured a variety of both commercial and

agricultural exhibits. The *Palouse Gazette* reported, "Horseshoes, honey, a new sack sewing needle, a rare collection of birds' eggs, the new Domestic sewing machine and the latest hats were among the exhibits of the first county fair, which opened on October 4 and lasted five days. So many livestock were brought in that carpenters worked all night to erect additional sheds." Show cattle included Durhams, Holsteins, Herefords, and Jerseys and numerous draft horses with their colts were represented. One noisome pavilion displayed caged turkeys, geese, chickens, and ducks along with a cornucopia of fall vegetables including a newsworthy twenty-five pound beet. An enormous brightly colored pyramid of rare flowers was arranged and an array of "lovely things that only the mind of woman can conceive and her deft fingers fashion" wax and paper flowers, and an enormous brightly colored pyramid of rare flowers, crochet, and needlework.

The traditional designs favored by some quilters hinted at places of origin for many Palouse families both foreign and domestic—Irish Puzzle and Dresden Plate, Ohio Star and Kansas Sunflower. The only patterns known to be indigenous to the Pacific Northwest are Oregon Trail and Lewis and Clark. Certainly among the most unique quilts ever fashioned in the Palouse is one of cream-colored calico bearing signatures in red floss of 276 pioneer residents of Moscow. Included among the names are Lieuallen, McConnell, and Adair with stitched identification showing it was "Made by the Ladies Industrial Society of the Baptist Church of Moscow, Idaho, May 8, 1897." The remarkable creation is displayed at the Latah County Historical Museum in Moscow.

Carnivals were added to the fair in 1903 and Grange exhibits were shown in 1907 with first prize awarded the remarkable sum of $125. Due to problems with recurrent flooding on the Colfax site and the public's demand for other locations to showcase the region's bounty, the fair was held in Garfield for several years during the Twenties and in other communities the following decade. In the 1948, Charles McSweeney, Hugh Huntley, and Byron "Bo" Henry acquired thirty-one acres of property on the Palouse Highway along Rebel Flat near Mockonema to establish the more permanent Palouse Empire Fairgrounds and the half-mile Mockonema Downs racetrack for pari-mutuel betting (*Palouse Gazette,* October 7, 1887; A. Repp, 1989; J. Henry, 2003).

*Palouse River Sunset**

North of Endicott, Washington

Area newspapers also reported on sporting events that took place at the area's two Land Grant colleges and Palouse residents came to look upon one game with growing interest year after year following the inception of the "Battle of the Palouse" in 1893. The annual game pitted the football squads of W.S.C. and the U. of I. playing against each other in an era devoid of padding and goal posts. Featuring the "old style" offense of mass formation and a center rush of players clad in baseball pants, the teams faced each other for four brutal quarters on a muddy field in Moscow. Though the Cougars managed the most wins in the grudge match's first decade of play, the teams' first meeting ended in a 10-0 Idaho victory.

The year 1893 also marked the appearance of a small booklet written by Massachusetts college physical education instructor James Naismith titled *The Official Guide to Basketball*. Naismith had devised the game to overcome the boredom associated with calisthenics and specified in the guide the size of the ball, backboard position, height of the basket, and rules of play. Within ten years the game had caught on at W.S.C. where Cougar coach Fred Thiel added it to the p.e. program to be sustained under legendary Cougar coaches J. Fred "Doc" Bohler and Jack Friel. The first Palouse Country high school teams were organized in Colfax where a girls team began playing in 1902 followed a boys squad two years later. The more experienced females bested their counterparts in their first game played against each other in 1904.

In the winter of 1905-06 Endicott and Garfield played the first small town game in an Endicott grain warehouse after the local team had moved all 2,500 wheat sacks into another facility across the street over Christmas vacation. The hosts won the game 9-3 in a "gymnasium" featuring two long shelves to hold six coal lamps, protected by hogwire, and a wood floor that inflicted frequent slivers whenever someone fell. Teams were soon organized in Palouse (1906) and St. John (1910) to create the first area league that was comprised of both boys and girls teams. Since dribbling was prohibited in Naismith's original rules and no ten-second line violations existed, scores were extremely low in the early years of the game. Out-of-bounds fights over possession were also frequent as referees usually awarded the ball to the person who bested others in a struggle for the prize. Spectators

found these skirmishes to be some of the more entertaining aspects of the game—especially when most of the players sped after a loose ball down a stairway or in a darkened corner for which many early area gyms were notorious.

In the second decade of the century basketball spread to virtually every school in both Whitman and Latah counties with new high school teams organized in Pullman, Moscow, Colfax and in smaller communities like Johnson, Hay, Pine City, and Thornton. Even at dozens of the one-room country schools that dotted the rural Palouse, young boys and girls tossed up balls of tied rags into an iron hoop nailed to the side of the building. The transition from traditionally outdoor sports to the more controlled atmosphere of indoor basketball continued to be difficult, however. As one newspaper noted in 1915, "Sunset's idea of a basketball game and ours differ pretty materially. If we are going to play football we want to get out doors and call it by its right name. But perhaps we don't know what basketball is anyway." The first Whitman County high school basketball tournament was held at W.S.C. in 1922. No distinctions were made among teams on the basis of school enrollment and the tourney was won by the local Pullman club. The critically acclaimed film *The Basket* (1999), substantially filmed in the western Palouse near Lamont features the story of rural basketball and one-room country school education against the backdrop of World War I.

Private academies were established by Colfax Baptists in 1876, later Colfax College, under the tutelage of Leoti West whose enrollment of seventeen students for the fall term swelled to a hundred by the following June. The United Brethren in Albion founded short-lived Edwards College in 1885. However, only Uniontown's St. Andrew's Parochial School, also established in 1885, and St. Joseph's Academy in Sprague (1886) survived as alternatives to public education in the Palouse into the 20th century. Both Catholic schools established outstanding reputations for their academic programs and attracted students from as far away as Alaska and California. (Upper Columbia Academy near Spangle was established by the Seventh-day Adventist Church in 1945 but traces its origins to an academy founded by the denomination at Viola in 1917.) During the first two decades of the 20th century, over one hundred country schools operated in the

Palouse, a legacy of Jefferson's plan establishing a school in every township, in addition to the larger community schools.

Lancaster native Glen Miller enrolled at Cheney Normal School in 1919 to obtain a degree in education and served as a teacher and administrator in schools at Sunset, Ewan, and St. John. Miller's hometown had the distinction of being perhaps the only Palouse community with two names—Lancaster to most locals, Willada to the railroad and mapmakers. Over the years he and his wife, Beulah, who met at the Sunset school, provided local residents with generous services ranging from hair-cutting to dance lessons and eventually Glen added the additional task of leasing farmland near Ewan which he worked at night. The Millers were eventually able to purchase their first farm that led to the establishment of the Miller Land & Livestock Company. During the couple's lifetime their holdings came to include 27,000 acres of Palouse Country grainfields and rangeland, making the Millers the largest private landowners in the Inland Northwest. My first encounter with Glen was at the Palouse Empire Fair in the 1970s where I happened upon him and ubiquitous Uncle Ray Reich discussing the finer points of fence-building. Glen was making a point with such gestured enthusiasm that I did not find it incongruous that someone who had spent a substantial portion of his life driving a Caterpillar tractor and on horseback still gave his grandchildren tap dancing lessons (G. and C. Miller, 2003).

Years later when our community voted to construct a new school, we sought to incorporate a number of pieces from the original structure and someone mentioned that Glen had salvaged the school's original cast iron bell which had been used for decades to announce the beginning and end of classes every weekday. Due to the deterioration of the belfry portico, the bell had been removed and sold at auction to a local resident and later acquired by Glen. I volunteered to seek the return of the relic for remounting in the new structure and visited the Millers at their home on the old Hugh Huntley place. (Regardless of current residents, farms in the Palouse are usually known by the name of some distant owner from the pioneer past.) After driving a couple miles down a dusty gravel road, I approached the unmistakable entrance to the Miller residence as it was obvious that Glen was interested in collecting more than just land. A Texas longhorn steer stood staring at the road and the Miller house was surrounded by enormous cast bells securely mounted to iron cradles and other frames built to hold objects of substantial weight. The largest bell of all, from a mission church in Oregon, rested on a flatbed trailer parked along the yard. After explaining our interest to the Millers, they generously offered to donate the community treasure back to the school where it remains in the courtyard to this day.

Secret Societies and Lodges

In addition to annual gatherings at special events like the Elberton summer celebration and county fairs, Palouse residents also found social and practical benefits from membership in a variety of fraternal and benevolent lodges and auxiliaries. Most were organized in the region after settlers who had been members in the Midwest and East came to reside in Palouse area communities. These societies provided opportunities for fellowship between townspeople and their rural neighbors and membership, by invitation only, usually entailed elaborate initiation rites, secret ceremonies for degree advancement, and service for civic improvement. Among the organizations most active

PALOUSE COUNTRY KNIGHTS OF PYTHIAS AND PYTHIAN SISTERS CONFERENCE, c. 1920 (MASC, WSU LIBRARIES)

in the Palouse in the late 19th century included the two largest in the nation. The Free and Accepted Order of Masons was heir to the medieval guilds of stone masons and cathedral builders, and their women's auxiliary was known as the Order of Eastern Star. The Shrine Club and The Daughters of the Nile were philanthropic Masonic affiliates. The Independent Order of Odd Fellows also had its origin in Europe as did its affiliated Daughters of Rebekah Lodge, founded in 1851 by Colfax's namesake, Vice-president Schuyler Colfax.

The village of Colfax also hosted the Kamiak Tribe of Order of Redmen and Women's Order of Pocahontas. Other societies with widespread membership in the Palouse included the Woodmen of the World and Women of Woodcraft, originally established as a life and health insurance company; and the Grand Army of the Republic, formed for fellowship among veterans of the Civil War. Also active in the region were the Maccabees, Elks, Improved Order of Red Men with the offices of great sachem, great senior sagamore, great prophet, and great keeper of wampum; and the Knights of Pythias, led by a chancellor commander, masters of arms, works, and exchequer, and inner and outer guards. A Memorial Day visitor to virtually any cemetery in the Palouse will find freshly cut flowers beneath gravestones on which are engraved epitaphs containing such inscriptions as G.A.R., K.of P., and I.O.O.F.

As a boy growing up in the Palouse, I was aware that in the pioneer past local chapters of the Knights of Pythias and Pythian Sisters had met on the top floor of the Wakefield Building, a large brick structure in the center of town. There was an air of mystery about the place since the outside locked door leading upstairs had high windows that revealed an immense cobweb-laced stairway that seemed to stretch far into the darkness of some inner sanctum. A cousin, Jim Lust, had access to the door key and attempted to frighten us for some time with tales of skeletons hidden away in the Knights' chambers. Old enough to defend a measure of bravery, I joined several friends in slowly climbing the stairs late one afternoon. We made our way past any vestiges of defending commanders and inner guards to a room with large wooden plaques bearing long gray spikes. Our docent informed us that these had been used to test prospective candidates for

the order. He pushed against one set made of immovable iron and told us to strike the other plaque with full strength. For good reason we refused. He proceeded to hit the other spikes which bent backwards since they were fashioned from some kind of rubber.

We then continued into the main hall, shrouded in gloom from parchment-colored window shades, and spotted an ebony casket on a dais at the front of the room. A chill swept up my spine and we saw that the box had no lid. We moved as a group to view the contents, reason telling me to expect a practical joke, but as we stepped onto to landing, our eyes first spied the skull. One more pace revealed an entire human skeleton—just as we had been promised, but we collectively decided against a more thorough investigation of what I might have believed were the remains of Damon or Pythias himself. We never learned whose bones made the building their home.

The Grange Movement and Soil Conservation

The roots of another organization popular among early Palouse Country residents ran deep into America's rural history. The Patrons of Husbandry, or Grange, was an agricultural fraternal society organized in 1867 as a result of President Andrew Johnson's and journalist-farmer Oliver Hudson Kelly's efforts to develop means for reconciling the animosities that persisted between the North and South after the Civil War. The term Grange was derived from a word used in the Middle Ages for a country manor with barns, stables, granaries, and other structures necessary for husbandry, or agriculture. Grange organizers in America were familiar with the Masonic Order and used the lodge as a pattern for much of their structure and ritual. The role of each local Grange officer was associated with an occupation on a typical English estate including a master, overseer, steward, chaplain, gatekeeper, and other offices.

The Grange movement was envisioned to be progressive and women were equally represented in the leadership with designated titles drawn from Greek mythology—Ceres, the goddess of grains; Pomona, the goddess of fruits; and Flora, the goddess of flowers. The Grange was organized with officers at the local, county (Pomona), state, and national levels with seven farm implements used as symbols in the formalities of each degree. The plow, for example, "should teach us to drive the plowshare of thought diligently through the heavy soil of ignorance," the hoe "is emblematic of that cultivation of the mind…, thus promoting the growth of knowledge and wisdom," while the "ancient and honorable" sickle "speaks of peace and prosperity, and is the harbinger of joy. It is used not merely to reap the golden grain for the sheaf, but, in the field of mind and heart and soul, to gather every precious stalk, every opening flower, every desirable fruit." The Horn of Plenty and Bible were all-encompassing symbols representing the values of harvest blessing and godly wisdom.

A panoply of problems faced Northwest farmers when the first Granges were formed in Washington (1873) and Idaho (1874). The region's Grangers deplored the excessive profits made by several farm implement manufacturers and artificially high freight rates charged by the Northern Pacific Railroad. Putting into practice their preachings about citizenship activism, the organization sought every legal means to improve their economic plight by lobbying state legislatures and Congressional regulatory commissions. Their efforts brought concessions from manufacturers and the transportation industry which enhanced the role of the Grange in both states. Local farmers assembled in James Ewart's log cabin to organize the first Grange in the Palouse in 1897. Two years later others were established at Whelan near Pullman and at Spangle (Pine Grove). In 1903 the State Grange Session was held in the Palouse for the first time when Pullman hosted the event. The warm reception given participants by W.S.C. President Enoch Bryan was calculated to foster stronger bonds between the region's farmers and the land grant universities.

Nearly twenty Granges came to be organized in the Palouse with most located in smaller communities like Ewartsville, Whelan, Dusty, Winona, and Pine City as well as near Moscow and Pullman. Grange halls were built in these and other areas in response to state campaigns to ensure the viability of the movement. In 1918 the state organization formed the Grange Wholesale Warehouse Company, later known as Grange Co-op Wholesale, which combined the purchasing power of smaller Grange cooperatives to more economically market equipment and petroleum products to farmers. The prime-mover behind this important effort was Pullman-area Granger William Smith. A dozen years later the state Grange cooperative merged with the Midwest's

Farmers Union Central Exchange (CENEX) to create one of the nation's largest agricultural supply enterprises that integrated ownership of oil wells and refineries with bulk handling and services at the regional and local levels.

Grangers were also well-known for campaigns aimed at educating youth and the general public about the importance of agriculture to all segments of society. No visit to Palouse Country county fairs was complete without viewing Grange displays fashioned in intricate designs of rural scenes using multicolored mosaics of grains and legumes. Exhibition themes focused public attention on the significance of agriculture in daily life and evidenced Grangers' spirit of fellowship and hard work. The *Pacific Grange Bulletin* (later the *Agricultural Grange News*) began publication in 1908 to better coordinate activities within the organization and to feature prose and poetry by rural authors that merited publication. Sara Archer penned the following lines to commemorate one of the earliest agricultural fairs in Spokane:

Another year of garnered hopes, of bending boughs on orchard slopes;
Of stubble-fields where Ceres reigns, of bursting barns and
stagg'ring wains;
The tardy sun seeks southern skies; and Hesperus is quick to rise.

The Washington and Idaho Granges also used their growing influence to fight for rural electrification and conservation practices. Efforts to bring electrical power to the farm were greeted with widespread support and eventual success following the organization of public utility districts and Columbia River hydroelectric dams a generation later. The Grange campaign to promote an ethic of land stewardship was rooted in moral principle and enunciated by Grange enthusiast Theodore Roosevelt. The president visited the Palouse in April, 1911 and addressed an enormous audience at Moscow from a platform made of Palouse wheat sacks. Using the White House as his "bully pulpit," the president had earlier proclaimed, "The conservation of our natural resources and their proper use constitutes the fundamental problem which underlies almost every other problem of our national life. Unless we maintain an adequate material basis for our civilization, we cannot maintain the institutions win which we take so great and so just a pride; and to waste and destroy our natural resources means to undermine this material basis...."

Roosevelt went on to define stewardship of the land in terms that balanced principle with practicality: "Conservation means development as much as it does protection. I recognize the right and duty of this generation to develop and use the natural resources of our land; but I do not recognize the right to waste them, or to rob, by wasteful use, the generations that come after us." The Country Life Commission appointed when Roosevelt was in office to investigate the major problems confronting rural America concluded that the tillage practices followed by many of the nation's farmers could better be described as "mining." Soil fertility was at risk throughout the country and especially in highly erodible regions like the Palouse Hills. The commission's report concluded that the situation "has now become an acute national danger.... (*Palouse Republic*, April 14, 1911; Commission quotations in T. Salutos and J.D. Hicks, 1951).

Roosevelt's reasoned ethic of land stewardship for sustainable agriculture was promulgated by Granger leadership that sought to alter farming practices throughout the nation that threatened the country's most precious resource—fertile topsoil. The Palouse Hills had acquired one of the most unenviable reputations as an area where an average of twenty-five tons of topsoil per acre eroded away annually resulting in the loss of nearly 20,000,000 tons of soil each year. Erosion rates were serious throughout the cropland area but the most serious damage occurred on the steeper slopes of the south-central Palouse. Unprotected summer-fallow or newly planted fields were extremely vulnerable to water erosion in the fall as rills formed after even moderate rains to drain the water. The frozen surface soil in early spring was

equally at risk from rainfall that could not be absorbed but washed down in muddy masses of dislocated loam. The epochal forces of nature that required a millennium to form one inch of fertile humus could be washed away in a single day's heavy rainfall on an unprotected Palouse sidehill. In just two generations such neglect transformed the dark chestnut earth on many slopes into the exposed pale clods of clay nubbins.

The Palouse Country's legendary "inexhaustible soil" once heralded by railroad promoters and land speculators was, in fact, a fragile but priceless patina overlaid upon significantly less organic subsoil. Over half of the entire Palouse region's soil erosion was taking place on the steepest 25% of the basin's cropland. The magnitude of the problem not only decreased the fertility of the land but significantly contributed to the degradation of fish and wildlife habitat and the formation of massive silt deposits in the Palouse, Snake, and Columbia rivers. Grangers worked together with soil scientists at the region's colleges to identify and advocate measures to moderate the crisis. Grange publications, extension service bulletins, and farmer workshops recommended several practices that could be expected to reduce Palouse erosion rates by over half without significantly reducing income—divided slope farming, greenbelts along streams, and planting trees on the steepest hillsides (G. Norwood, 1988; USDA, 1978).

Perhaps the Grange's erudite founder O. H. Kelly had perceived deeper significance in what the goddesses Ceres and Pomona represented than their common association with nature's bounty. The ancient Greeks were among the first civilizations to note with grave concern the effects of unbridled farming on once fertile landscapes above their Corinthian shores. Kelly read Plato who

**FROZEN SUBSOIL SHEET EROSION (TOP)
AND RILL AND GULLY EROSION (BOTTOM)**

*Palouse Canola**   *South of Glenwood, Washington*

regarded the environmental changes of Hellenic Greece with alarm as noted in the famed philosopher's dialogue with Critias. "What now remains of the formerly rich land is like the skeleton of a sick man," he observed, "with all the fat and soft earth having wasted away and only the bare framework remaining…. The soil was deep, it absorbed and kept the water in the loam, and the water that soaked into the hills fed springs and running streams everywhere. Now the abandoned shrines at spots where formerly there were springs attest that our description of the land is true." But most of Plato's countrymen would not hear of exchanging their ingenuity and diligence for understanding and conservation. Soil erosion continued at an alarming pace in ancient Greece and degraded the waters of the northeast Mediterranean, weakened the region's economy, and forced the Greeks to plant their grains and vines on the increasingly marginal soils of Attica's highest slopes. The great British historian Alfred Toynbee wrote that this lamentable situation significantly contributed to the fall of Classical Greek civilization.

UNIVERSITY OF IDAHO ADMINISTRATION BUILDING, MOSCOW (MASC, WSU LIBRARIES)

Some Palouse farmers began to speak of agriculture in terms of living on sustainable topsoil interest rather than spending hillside capital. Yields may have been slightly lower than their neighbors but the benefits over time far outweighed and more than paid for any inconvenience or limitations. The federal government was slow to respond with financial incentives for conservation practices which hampered efforts by Grangers and other interest groups to preserve the basis of the Palouse Country's vitality. However, landmark congressional acts creating the U.S.D.A. Agricultural Adjustment Administration (1933), the Soil Conservation Service (1935). The A.A.A. introduced subsidy payments to farmers who voluntarily reduced their production acreage by 15 to 20 percent. They would be guaranteed a parity price for their crop as the plan successfully intended to reduce commodity surpluses

that had depressed grain prices for years. Counties were assigned wheat allotment inspectors to assist interested farmers in complying with the terms of the act. The S.C.S. was heir to the soil conservation initiatives undertaken in the Republican administration of Democrat F.D.R.'s presidential uncle, Theodore Roosevelt.

Peter and Maude McGregor's son, Maurice, returned in 1923 to the family's sprawling Hooper ranch following graduate studies in finance at New York University and was appointed to the A.A.A.'s first Washington State board of supervisors in 1933. McGregor had long expressed concern about the problems of farms surpluses and soil erosion. In the early 1930s he noted that the family cropland was "approaching a critical stage" and required soil rebuilding if the enterprise was to be viable for future generations. Under Maurice's leadership, the McGregors implemented a series of innovative conservation practices including the planted of crested wheatgrass on depleted areas, streambank protection, and the elimination of stubble burning. He expressed deep concern over what W.S.C. scientists termed area farmers' "lack of appreciation of the seriousness of the situation" and "attitudes of indifference" regarding soil loss. The decade came to represent one of the most significant shifts in agricultural practices for those willing to change traditional approaches since the introduction of mechanized farming in the previous century. Farmers like the McGregors turned to stubble mulch summerfallowing to build cropland humus and provide more land cover to protect topsoil. Three generations of "clean fallowing" in which the stubble of the early tall wheats was completely plowed over and recurrently weeded left vast tracts at the mercy of the elements.

In September, 1930 Pullman was designated one of the U.S.D.A.'s first ten Soil Erosion Experiment Stations in cooperation with the two land grant colleges in the vicinity under the leadership of William

Rockie and Paul McGrew. Following the organization of the S.C.S. in 1935, soil conservation enabling acts were passed in Washington and Idaho to fund state committees that would work in cooperation with the new federal agency. The Pacific Northwest's first conservation district, North Palouse in west central Whitman County, was organized in January, 1940 as one of a dozen districts in the Washington and Idaho Palouse. Five-member district farmer supervisor committees and staff conservationists worked together to promote the new minimum tillage "trashy fallow" techniques, reduce stubble burning, and encourage tree and native grass plantings on highly erodible slopes and marginal farmland. In the spring of 1942, a group of state S.C.S. staff members including State Conservationist Harry Carroll (Pullman), Regional Conservationist G.B. Swier (Spokane), agronomist Veryl Kaiser (Moscow), and W.R. Spencer (Fairfield) arranged a tour for interested farmers and state officials of soil and water conservation practices on the McGregor Land and Livestock Company ranch near Hooper. Following this inspection, the Washington Association of Soil and Water Conservation Districts was formed in May, 1942 at a meeting in Ritzville. Key Palouse Country leaders at the state and national levels in these strategic efforts to improve farm management practices have included Ervin King, Lars Nelson, Verle Kaiser, Russ Zinner, and Read Smith (O.A. Camp and P.C. McGrew, 1969; D. Roe and R. Riehle, 2003).

College Communities and the Agricultural Experiment Stations

The institutions of higher learning established in the Palouse in the 1890s made unprecedented contributions to the region's agricultural development as well as to the general education and culture of residents throughout the Pacific Northwest. Both Pullman's Washington State University, originally Washington Agricultural College (1891), and the University of Idaho at Moscow (1892) were established under the provisions of

the 1862 Morrill Land Grant College Act and the Hatch Agricultural Experiment Station Act of 1887 which obligated them to serve the interests of area rural populations through liberal arts education, vocational training, and agricultural research. Eastern Washington University's roots were in the creation of Cheney Normal School, a teacher training college established in 1890, which equipped hundreds of young educators for the rigors of service in the one-room country schools and stately community brick structures throughout the Palouse and greater Northwest. The Cheney Normal School Heritage Center, established in 2000 is the renovated one-room Jore School located in the center of the E.W.U. campus. The historic building showcases the heritage of rural education inside the traditional wainscoted country school walls where young people once studied on pine floors with chalk slates and copybooks.

W.S.U. was birthed in a rectangular building known as "the Crib," built of brick from clay dug at the summit of College Hill where the structure stood for many years. Located between present Holland Library and Compton Student Building, a portion of the original wall was incorporated into the library's south face. Castlellated Thompson Hall, built as the college's original administrative building in 1894, is now a National Historic Site. The University of Idaho's flagship structure was the imposing Administrative Building. Although destroyed by fire in 1906, the classic design of its 1909 replacement in Tudor Gothic style set the architectural standard for further construction on the university's scenic 450 acre campus. In 1908 the prestigious Massachusetts landscape design firm Olmstead Brothers was hired to give a New England nuance to the school's sweeping grounds (K. Petersen, 1988).

The populations of the "college towns" soared as these three schools successfully expanded their programs and enrollments. Pullman more than tripled its numbers between 1890 and

THOMPSON HALL, W. S. U., PULLMAN, WASHINGTON (MASC, WSU LIBRARIES)

1910 by increasing from 868 to 2602 residents, and the most significant growth elsewhere in the region over the same period took place in Moscow (2000 to 3670) and Cheney (647 to 1207). Cheney also benefited from its strategic location on the main line of the Northern Pacific Railroad and became a major grain warehousing and milling center. F. M. Martin, a former implement dealer, established a flour mill at Cheney in 1908, the F. M. Martin Grain and Milling Company, that became one of the largest independent mills in the Pacific Northwest. Cheney's first mill had been built in 1880 by Colfax's John C. Davenport. Milling was highly skilled trade that required a long period of apprenticeship. The massive milling stones were usually imported from France or Belgium. Running twenty-four hours a day, early Palouse Country mills could produce up to seventy-five bushels of flour. F. M. Martin's son, Clarence Daniel Martin, inherited the Cheney business and owned it until selling to the National Biscuit Company (Nabisco) in 1943. Beginning in 1931, Martin also served two terms as governor of Washington and worked to promote new grainland conservation efforts introduced by the state and federal departments of agriculture. Most other milling operations in the Palouse either closed or were merged in a series of consolidations that climaxed with the formation of General Mills, Inc. in 1928 (J. Fahey, 1986).

The agricultural experiment stations established in Moscow in 1892 and in Pullman the following year were first met with a measure of skepticism by area farmers and ranchers who were suspicious of outside experts yet several forward thinking residents of the Moscow and Pullman areas joined together to purchase acreage large enough for test plots near both schools. Within several years the research teams won over considerable numbers of their constituents by respecting them for overcoming the challenges of life the Palouse frontier and by demonstrating the practical results of scientific methods for improving crop and

livestock production. In 1893 Louis F. Henderson, whose mentor had been prominent naturalist David Starr Jordan, arrived in Moscow to head up plant sciences at the experiment station and teach at the university where his classroom readings from Shakespeare were almost as well known as his research in plant pathology.

Agronomist W. J. Spillman arrived in Pullman to serve on the college's faculty in 1894. The most commonly grown wheats in the Palouse at that time were Little Club, named for the shape of its head, and Pacific Bluestem, both tall, low protein varieties. But Spillman found most farmers planting their crops in the spring rather than risking winterkill, to which early plantings of these two grains were susceptible. This practice resulted in severe wind and water erosion on fallow lands and the growth of unwanted thistles, cheatgrass, Jim Hill mustard, and other invasive weeds. Spring planting generally failed to develop the secondary root system needed to absorb available moisture and good stands often lodged, or were knocked flat, after moderate rains while the heads shattered in brisk winds. Spillman initiated an ambitious wheat breeding program in 1899 and found that offspring from crosses of various parent stocks created a variety of characteristics in the second generation.

William Spillman's pioneering research independently paralleled the groundbreaking work with peas, a single chromosome species, by the 19th century Austrian biologist Gregor Mendel whose Mendelian laws first explained the basic principles of heredity and gave rise to the field of genetics. Spillman worked with the more complicated triple chromosome sets in wheat, crossing over 300 pairs, to select plants in each generation with the most desirable characteristics. The decade of Spillman's tenure in Pullman also witnessed the introduction of several wheat varieties by the U. S. Department of Agriculture and private Eastern breeders. Each, however, experienced problems in the region. Red Chaff was often damaged by Palouse winters,

SPILLMAN FARM HERITAGE WHEATS
(l to r): PACIFIC BULESTEM, HYBRID 128, GAINES

Early Baart did not yield well, Fortyfold and Jones Fife shattered easily, and Russian Red, actually of English origin, was of such poor milling quality that it brought considerably lower prices (D. Meinig, 1968).

Following Spillman's departure in 1902 for a position with the Department of Agriculture, the wheat breeding program was capably continued by Claude Lawrence. Finally in 1907, a series of promising hybrids which he and Spillman had developed was released to area farmers for commercial production. One variety in particular, Hybrid 128, proved to be the most winter hardy and productive. Results of the program's research in the Palouse and other experiment station recommendations were more fully disseminated among area farmers following the enactment of the Smith-Lever Act of 1914 which established an agricultural extension service cooperative among the federal, state, and county levels. The work of the county extension agents facilitated rural education in farm management practices, home economics demonstrations, and 4-H programs (S. Jones, 2003).

Lawrence and others patiently worked for years with their experimental varieties in Pullman and Moscow and released the soft red winter variety Triplet in 1918. However, like other varieties of the time, its kernels became infested with the black fungus "smutting bunt" which drastically reduced yields and the quality demanded by shippers and millers. Plant geneticist E. F. Gaines had begun breeding for resistance to bunt in 1915 at the Main Experiment Station in Pullman. This research led after nine years to the release of the hard red variety Ridit, followed by the soft white club wheat Albit in 1928. The scientists also took into account farmer concerns about marketability since the hard classes were used domestically for breads and breakfast cereals while most of the whites were for pastry flours and export to Asia for making noodles.

Continued problems with smutting, the appearance of the fungal disease rust on wheat leaves and stems, and a proliferation of varieties for marketers to grade led to the organization of the Cooperative Western Regional Wheat Improvement Program in 1930. Funded by Congress through the Department of Agriculture, eleven states participated in the program which was administered in the Palouse by Gaines, Vogel, and plant pathologist O.E. Barbee in Pullman and V. H. Florell and C. A. Michels at Moscow. The two teams worked closely together to develop more and larger nurseries by acquiring additional lands adjacent to the experiment stations and in areas of various microclimates and soil classes across the region. These efforts led to the development of more specialized soft white wheats like Brevor and Omar for areas of high rainfall, semihards for intermediate lands, and hard reds for low rainfall areas. In the 1960s Vogel introduced the semidwarfs Gaines and Nugaines for resistance to lodging, and yields often exceeded 100 bushels per acre. For his distinguished contributions to plant genetics that also gave rise to the "Green Revoluton" of vastly improved wheat production in Central America, India, and Sudan, Dr. Vogel was awarded the National Medal of Science in 1975 by President Gerald Ford. Due to the enduring efforts of the college experiment station staffs, their allied cooperative extension service agents, and local farmers, the Palouse Country became and remains the highest yielding dryland grain district in the world (E. F. Gaines, 1941; O. A. Vogel, 1973).

Oroville Vogel was known to a wider community in the Palouse and beyond for his involvement in the affairs of the United Methodist Church and as a principal force behind the organization of FarmHouse Fraternity chapters at W.S.U. and U. of I. One week after the White House formalities, Dr. Vogel was on his knees at the Pullman fraternity laying new hallway carpet he had helped procure. Never one to stand on ceremony and imbued with a servant's heart, Dr. Vogel devoted substantial personal time and funds to help new families moving to the community through the church, farmers asking for weekend field-crop inspections, and college students in his classes and at FarmHouse. Unlike many of his predecessors who moved on to positions with the U.S.D.A. or private industry, the Vogels, who had no children of their own, chose to make their life in the Palouse. "How could I leave the family we have all around this area?" he once quipped to a colleague who knew of other lucrative offers that came Vogel's way. He often stood alongside new FarmHouse members and recited their pledge to seek "…the best in lines of study as well as in life… and give promise of service to others and to the world." Orville Vogel's kindness, service, and scholarship gave living expression to his creed.

*Palouse Country Barn Canola**

North of Genesee, Idaho

A Department of Forestry was established at the University of Idaho in 1909 under Charles H. Shattuck who created the first college arboretum west of the Mississippi by planting some 300 different varieties of trees near the campus. Known today as the Shattuck Arboretum and Botanical Garden, many of the original plantings of oak, beech, chestnut, fir, and pine from around the world survive amidst lilacs and peonies on sixty-acres along the south rim of the campus. The trees are evidence of Shattuck's efforts to find species that could adapt well to conditions in the Palouse and be used for research on conifer disease resistance. The department was elevated to college status in 1917 under Dean Francis G. Miller who was induced to migrate across the border from W.S.C. where he had served there as head of the forest department. The practice of the two schools enticing professors from one to the other was not uncommon and generally represented a rivalry far less damaging than the Vandals' periodic theft of Butch, the Cougar mascot, from his cage on the Pullman campus.

Under Miller one of the nation's largest college forests was acquired one parcel at a time through tenacious effort and considerable political maneuvering to obtain the necessary funds for purchase and as gifts from the state. The tract eventually grew to cover 7,000 acres in the Moscow Mountains just north of the city where extensive research was conducted on productivity, insect infestation, diseases, and other aspects of forest management. Edward J. Iddings and Cuthbert W. Hickman were also hired at the university to strengthen the college of agriculture, where the two pioneered important work on Palouse area cattle raising, horse breeding, and legume production. Dry peas were first introduced to the eastern Palouse about 1910 and slowly became an important alternative crop while dry beans were introduced with less success about the same time in the Genesee district. The Palouse would eventually supply 90% of the dry peas and lentils consumed in the United States with the nation's largest genetic stalks of these legume varieties located at the U.S.D.A. Plant Introduction Station in Pullman (R. Gibbs, 1962).

Cradles, Threshers, and Combines

The period from 1880 to 1920 also witnessed a revolution in agricultural mechanization in the Palouse. A determined farmer with a single shear "footburner" plow could break out only about forty acres of land each year, usually after the thick native grasses had been burned off. A seemingly Sisyphean struggle still loomed ahead, however, as the thickly fibrous root system penetrated the ground for two to three feet. To prepare a seedbed, farmers devised crude harrows by pounding long nails or wooden pegs into wide beams. The first seeding was done by hand broadcast, considered an artform by a pioneer farmer, who moved at a measured pace with a sack slung over their shoulder, to cover a swath about fifteen feet wide. The field was then harrowed again to cover the seed and the farmer prayed for rain and for an early sprout that would root the grain and create a ground cover before winter. The introduction of the shoe drill in the middle '80s greatly improved plant emergence as the seed was placed evenly at a calibrated depth beneath the soil and the implement could be connected to a harrow to smooth out the ground. Threats from weeds, especially cheatgrass, as well as rodents and uncooperative weather could still do considerable damage to a promising crop.

The arduous task of summer harvest was first done using a primitive cradle, or scythe connected to long wooden ribs that would hold several hand swathings to then be dropped in the stubble and tied into larger shocks. The calloused hands that knew this labor then either flailed the cuttings or, more often, winnowed them first by tamping down a circular area to form a hard surface and spreading the stalks across the area. Teams of horses would then trample the stalks for at least two hours before the straw was removed with pitchforks. The seed was carefully shoveled with as little dirt and roughage as possible into burlap "gunny" sacks to be eventually dumped and thrown into the wind "to separate the wheat from the chaff" (and dirt). An entire family might harvest only two acres in a day and hope for favorable winds from which might be gleaned seventy bushels of grain.

A few farmers could afford to purchase small mechanical fanning mills but these were expensive and required considerable strength to turn the internal blades for sufficient wind to clean the grain. In the early 1880s small, horse drawn reaper-binders appeared in the Palouse that could deposit grain bundles on the ground that were then hauled in wagons to large stationary separators, or threshers. These reapers increased harvest output 10-fold over the hand scythe method.

Threshers were first introduced in the 1840s and powered by several teams of horses tied to rotating sweep bars on the ground that turned a tumbler rod attached to the machine. The system experienced numerous breakdowns and the horses used for this work were soon replaced by coal- or wood-fired steam engines (M. Ochs, 1991; F. Garrett, 1979).

Larger headers with twelve foot sickle bars and reels were introduced in the middle 1880s. These three-wheeled contraptions were pushed by horses or mules behind the header and driven by a "header puncher" who steered by means of a rudder wheel connected to a board between his knees. His hands guided the lines to the horses and operated a lever to adjust the height of the sickle that cut the grain which fell onto a wide and rapidly moving canvas draper, reinforced with hardwood slats. On the downhill side of the header was a sloped elevator on which the draper carried the cuttings upward and dropped them into a header box wagon, built with one side lower than the other to fit under the elevator. In addition to the wagon driver, a loader worked inside the wagon to equally distribute the grain with a pitchfork in a laborious routine considered one of the most strenuous of the entire operation. Another header box would move into place when the other was full and the loader would jump into to it to continue working while the other header box was driven to the thresher, a beehive of harvest activity.

At a centrally located area in the field, usually near a country road, a small army of workers moved continuously amidst the cacophony of roars and whistles from the steam engine, thresher, derrick table, and horse-drawn wagons. Successful farmers treated their livestock with the attention demanded by resources so vital to work and sustenance. Family members of all ages often made pets of bummer lambs, runt piglets, abandoned calves and other offspring without mothers to tend them. But few farmstead relationships between owner and creature were more special than those between a farmer and his beloved draft horses, usually Belgians, Percherons, or Clydesdales. Weighing as much as one ton each, these gentle giants bore affectionate names and evidenced dispositions and capabilities unique to each one that were taken into consideration when arranging teams for pulling heavily loaded wagons and weighty field implements. One of

the most delightfully told and illustrated stories about these memorable creatures is Spangle artist-author Nona Hengen's *Plodding Princes of the Palouse* (1984).

As many as two dozen experienced workers were needed for stationary thresher operations, and it was not uncommon to see women from the family driving teams. The overall harvest operation was supervised by the "straw boss," often the owner of the thresher and engine who rented their use out to area farmers. He handled the hiring of the core crew from reliable acquaintances and relatives and other helpers from the several thousand "bindle stiffs" who converged on the Palouse from Spokane and other cities each summer looking for harvest employment. The boss also worked with the farmer to determine the sequence of areas and fields to be cut, and oversaw all aspects of the workers' myriad responsibilities. Teamsters were needed to drive the two or three headers that usually comprised an outfit's contingent, and others for handling the two-horse teams that took the three or four header boxes back and forth to the threshing area from the headers.

The wagons were unloaded into large piles by the driver and a "spike pitchers," another demanding role, and a "stacker" who properly arranged the grain into two or three high piles. A "forker" then set to work on a large platform mounted on a wagon called a "derrick table," named for a high four-beam derrick that rose some fifteen feet above it. At the top of the poles a pulley was suspended through which a rope ran connecting to a "derrick team" of six to eight horses to a six-pronged steel Jackson fork. The forker positioned the Jackson onto one of the piles and yelled to the "derrick team driver" to move the horses ahead so the fork's load could be hauled to the table and dropped with a trip rope. In later years the main pulley rope was connected to a net in the bottom of the header box wagon that could lifted to deposit the load directly onto the derrick table, which eliminated the need for the Jackson fork.

Two "hoedowns" then used hoe-shaped forks to carefully guide the grain at a measured pace onto a long canvas feeder that led to the thresher's gnashing mouth, out of which long metal fingers moved back and forth to pull in the grain. This grueling work usually went in shifts with two hoedowns replacing the other pair in half-hour shifts. These workers determined the maximum rate of intake by listening to

Retired to Reuse

North of Colton, Washington

the growl of the metal monster. They had to be careful not to choke the creature by plugging it up with too much grain which risked breaking a drive chain or shaft, or the laborious task of extracting the partially digested stalks by hand from inside the tightly jammed innards using every possible contortion of limb and colorful language. This chore, usually attended to by several of the younger workers, was especially unpleasant if the straw was infested with countless miniscule spines of scabrous tarweed, actually a Palouse native, that stung like fire if touched.

A rapidly rotating cylinder with rows of short steel tines was narrowly mounted above a set of stationary iron "concaves" with large teeth to shatter the kernels out of the heads. The particles then fell through a series of rocking sieves to an auger at the base of the machine and into a storage bin. The sieve action combined with the effects of a wide-bladed fan created a virtual wind tunnel through which the straw and chaff were blown out the back of the thresher. These tailings were stacked by to "straw pitchers" until a long and powerful "wind stacker" pipe was introduced after the turn of the century that blasted the straw twenty feet away to form a pile. Other important needs of the thresher were tended to by an "oiler" who kept the moving parts well lubricated and assisted the mechanic, or "separator man," in maintenance work.

The inner workings of the thresher were turned by an enormous rubber drivebelt, at least sixty feet long and crossed in the middle, which ran from the steam engine's power wheel to deliver up to forty horsepower on the 1890s Case, Rumley, and other models to the machine's main pulley. The huge engines were ponderous steamers, some up to twenty feet long, and tended pridefully by an experienced engineer. The long distance from the thresher was a fire prevention

measure. The fireman's job was considered one of the most exhausting of all, and certainly the hottest. Both workers earned the crew's highest wages. The fireman rose at 4 a.m. to clean out the ash pit and boiler flue soot and light the firebox with straw. When sufficient pressure was reached, he blew the whistle to wake the rest of the crew who usually slept outside in their bedrolls with their feet toward the strawpile. During the day he had to constantly fuel the flames, usually with straw brought to the fireman by a "straw buck" who used a pitchfork to provide a steady supply from the main pile behind the thresher to the engine. A "water buck" was in charge of the cigar-shaped wooden water wagon, carrying up to 500 gallons and a hand pump, that kept the steam engine and horses supplied.

The wagon also remained close in case a fire broke out—a farmer's worst nightmare, to douse any flames in case a spark escaped from the engine, or a malfunctioning thresher bearing. Exploding boilers were rare but ever a risk and accidents were not uncommon among forkers and hoedowns who were sometimes hit with moving equipment. Navigating a header box on steep slopes could also be very difficult as well as and hazardous, since the horses tended to drift downhill while the wagon remained on course. America's longest serving Supreme Court Justice and Eastern Washington native William O. Douglas remembered driving a header box in the southwestern Palouse when it struck a rock and started to tip over. He jumped free just as the wagon tumbled down into a ravine (W. O. Douglas; 1974, T. Keith, 1976).

Twirling sprockets run by flat chains turned the cylinder, fan, augers, and other components that howled throughout the day. A mechanic was needed to keep thresher properly operating, a "roustabout"

to run errands, gather the enormous foodstuffs necessary for the crews consumption, and facilitate communication among the workers. A "sack jig" filled gunny sacks with the grain while two nimble-fingered sack sewers sitting on two grain sacks raced to close the bags using long steel sack needles flared at the end. They formed a corner "ear" on the left side of the sack, rapidly tied it off with two half-hitch loops, and then moved across the top with nine lightning stitches before closing it off with an identical ear on the right side. Weighing about 140 pounds each, the sacks were then stacked nearby to await loading by a teamster onto flatbed wagons with short sideracks. The wagons were often hitched together in a group of two or three to be pulled by eight-horse teams to local warehouses and outside storage platforms. Here men carefully arranged the sacks into formations that could reach several stories high. During a good fourteen-hour day with eighteen workers, an experienced threshing crew running two headers could harvest about sixty acres and fill 1,200 sacks with 2,700 bushels of grain (F. Garrett, 1979; M. Ochs, 1991).

Such intense labor and long work hours generated enormous appetites. One of the surest ways to keep a good crew was to ensure they were well fed with plenty of fresh meat and potatoes, vegetables, and applesauce. Sometimes workers were also treated to fresh fruit desserts. A portable cookshack was used by women who toiled from the predawn hours to feed the workers up to five times each day— breakfast by 6 a.m., midmorning lunch break, dinner at noon, afternoon lunch break, and supper after 8 p.m. The men ate in shifts behind screened windows, on long narrow benches and tables. The abundance and quality of harvest food was legendary among most crewmembers, who considered the cook's job even more demanding than their own, and a matter of great concern to farmers' wives and other women who often assumed this responsibility. Pulitzer prize-winning author H. L. Davis, raised at The Dalles, portrayed a threshing crew's harvest season his novel, *Team Bells Woke Me and other Stories.* Nard Jones's *Wheat Women (1933)* presents another perspective in one of a triology of novels about the hopes and cynicisms of pioneer life east of the Cascades.

By the early 1890s implement manufacturers like Holt, Deere, and McCormick were combining reapers and threshers to make "combines" which in the hilly Palouse could require as many as thirty-two head of horses to be pulled and powered by massive drive chains from large metal-cleated side wheels. The first one to make an appearance in the Palouse Country drew crowds of gawkers throughout the region to the farm of "Wheat King" Lillis Smith near Endicott in the summer of 1893. A reporter from the *Palouse Republic* proclaimed Smith's Holt "the seventh wonder of the world" that seemed to require "all the horses in the neighborhood… to drag the great machine over the hills and through broad fields of ripe grain."

Such complicated contraptions of chains, sprockets, and cogs still required sizeable crews. A driver was needed to direct teams of up to thirty-five horses or mules from a seat perched precariously out in front of the machine while trying to minimize the animals' trampling down standing grain. Just harnassing the herd could take several hands a full hour in the early morning and late evening. A "header tender" stood behind on a wooden deck to raise and lower the cutting platform according to the slope and height of the grain. This area was shared with a machinist, who served as the overall boss of the operation and controlled the combine's rack and pinion leveling mechanism with a lever in front of the bulk tank where up to fifty bushels of clean grain could be stored. A single sack sewer sat on a bench beneath the bulk tank where the kernels fell through a downspout into burlap sacks that were sewn shut and stacked nearby until six to eight could be dropped onto the

CORRICK, DAVIS, AND GILLESPIE HARVEST NEAR PULLMAN (MASC, WSU LIBRARIES)

117

ground. This process still required wagons for collecting the sacks and transportation to local warehouses.

A number of inventive minds devised improvements for the machines, usually built in the Midwest or California, so they could function more efficiently on the steep slopes of the Palouse Hills. Given the amount of capital needed to launch such enterprises, the equipment's relatively high cost, and the limited market, only a few of these enterprises prospered including Moscow's Rhodes Harvester and Idaho National Harvester companies, the Colfax Harvester Company, and the Dunning-Erich Harvester Company of Harrington. Farmers and manufacturers modified their combines to be pulled by tractors and powered by a separate engine after these became available at the turn of the century. Such improvements increased the harvest to forty-five acres a day.

By 1920 the economic benefits of mechanization in the Palouse were becoming more pronounced given the costs needed for hired help and to maintain livestock throughout the year. This substantially reduced farmers' reliance on draft animals and thousands of horses and mules were sold in order to purchase combines, trucks, tractors, and the larger field implements that accompanied them. These changes also meant less need for additional workers during the harvest season which angered those laborers from area cities who had come to depend on the seasonal employment. Protests also came from leaders of the Industrial Workers of the World (Wobblies) who tried unsuccessfully to organize their labor. These conditions across the Inland Northwest provided the backdrop for the 1919 Zane Grey novel, *The Desert of Wheat*.

For younger harvest hands like William O. Douglas, earning money to study at Whitman College, conditions for seasonal workers in the Palouse during this period would deeply influence a distinguished career in jurisprudence. While harvesting on the Ralph Snyder ranch near Washtucna, Douglas fell into the company of a transient crew that included an I.W.W. member whom he only knew as Blacky and who befriended the rookie wagon driver. What Blacky lacked in ambition, he made up for in kindness and compassion, but also evidenced "a desperate loneliness." Douglas had always based his judgments on the Puritan work ethic that held prosperity in life was the result of proper moral choices, and that society's malcontents were victims of their own unrighteousness. As a scrawny lad suffering from the lingering effects of polio, Douglas had read the journals of Lewis and Clark and become acquainted with Indians on the Yakama Reservation near his birthplace. He knew from these experiences that valid exceptions existed to the principles so widely affirmed in the wider culture.

Douglas's experiences with the itinerant bindle stiffs in the Palouse formed fuller understandings in his inquisitive mind. "Many of these wanderers had real grievances," he observed, "and responded by protesting, sometimes crudely, sometimes eloquently, that their plight was serious, the injustices heaped upon them real. They sang, they swore, they did outrageous things at times. But they were seeking a place of some security in a free society." By his own account, these formative years in the sweltering harvest fields of the Palouse Country forged ideas that greatly shaped William O. Douglas's liberal ideas and years of service on the nation's highest bench, the longest Supreme Court tenure in American history (W. Douglas, 1974).

The next generation of Palouse farmland innovators led to significant improvements in tillage and harvesting equipment and fertilizing methods. In the early 1920s Claude Calkins founded the Cheney Weeder Company in Spokane and introduced an implement containing a long, narrow square rod that turned beneath the ground to clear summer-fallow fields of weeds and help conserve moisture. Like some other major farm equipment manufacturers located in the Midwest, the John Deere Company came to have a special interest in adapting their machinery to

RHODES HARVESTER NEAR MOSCOW (MASC, WSU LIBRARIES)

118

the unique topography of the Palouse. Regional manager Elray Woerman, based in Moscow, organized a committee of area farmers headed by Endicott's Conrad Hergert, who had established one of the first John Deere dealerships in Eastern Washington. Hergert had an amazing talent for visualizing complicated solutions to a variety of structural and mechanical problems ranging from the custom bracing of church steeples to establishing company standards for early diesel tractor carburetion. The company brought Woerman and Hergert to their Moline, Illinois headquarters to help design the first hydraulic mechanisms for a new generation of combines that were to be self-propelled (J. Lally, 2003).

James Love and Horace Hume of Garfield invented the tined combine pick-up reel and floating cuttterbar to better capture downed and shorter grains and fragile legumes which reduced crop loss during dry pea and lentil harvest from fifty to ten percent. In the neighboring community of Palouse, R. A. Hanson devised a revolutionary mercury board automatic combine leveling system. This device gave rise to the R. A. Hanson Company which and later relocated to Spokane to become an international provider of some of the world's largest earthmoving and construction equipment. Hooper's Sherman McGregor used a plow to devise a liquid nitrogen applicator that placed fertilizer behind the plowshares and several inches beneath the surface of the ground for greater plant absorption rates that resulted in significantly higher crop yields. To improve the process without turning over the soil, thin steel shanks were soon fashioned to replace the plowshares and the equipment eventually carried tanks for phosphorus and sulfur as well to create a "triple shooter." McGregor's ideas and industriousness launched The McGregor Company, the Palouse Country's largest independent agribusiness and significantly contributed to the development of related technologies throughout in the West (S. McGregor, 1972; J. Leonard, 2003).

The Trend Toward Native-Born American Predominance

Native-born European Americans continued to be the most populous group in the Palouse at the 1900 as the total population of Whitman and Latah Counties reached 38,811. Although the rate of growth never reached the phenomenal pace of the 1880s, the healthy 29% increase of the 1890s was strongly reinforced by another 26% rise by 1910. That year the two-county area's population peaked at

52,098—the highest of any decennial year. 90% of the people were native-born Americans but significant numbers of European immigrants continued to settle in the Palouse during the first two decades of the twentieth century. Relative to the total population, however, immigrant numbers declined after 1910 when they constituted 10.4% of the region's populace. European emigration was interrupted in 1914 with the outbreak of the First World War.

The unsettled international situation was concurrent with final settlement on open but marginally productive public lands on the western periphery of the Palouse. Few immigrant farmers came to region after 1915 as its economic base remained overwhelmingly agricultural. Farm labor needs were generally met by self-sufficient families, and few opportunities for new employment existed in the small agrarian communities. The area experienced a 5% decline in numbers between 1910 and 1920 as the population of Whitman and Latah Counties fell to 49,415. The trend would continue for several decades as farm mechanization and economic conditions allowed fewer farmers to acquire larger holdings.

The Palouse's American Indian population had been largely displaced by 1890, great measured squares marked in fences had been placed on its rolling terrain, and the land thoroughly peopled with families from virtually all states in the Union and every European nation. Bolstered by geographical and cultural advantage, native-born Americans predominated by the end of the century and though children of the foreign-born often grew up bilingual since the language of the public schools and local government institutions was English. Most churches associated with a European homeland offered an additional service in English during the First World War as the region's growing second-generation of European-Americans contended with both internal and external pressures to "not be different." New identities emerged in the region as dozens of vigorous rural communities in Whitman, Spokane, and Latah Counties boasted a two-story brick school, state bank, churches, and mercantiles while local newspaper editors bore frequent witness to the "fulfilling of pioneer dreams" in the early years of the new century.

ANNA PERSON
PALOUSE, WASHINGTON

Mrs. Anna Person was born in Indiana i n 1849 and came West with other Midwesterners after a series of moves that led to her family's settlement on Chambers Flat near Palouse, Washington in 1882. Her recollections of pioneer life were published in the Spokesman-Review, *May 15, 1923.*

My first western move was from Indiana to Illinois, and then seven years later we really started on the western trail. My mother was born in Kentucky; her parents moved to Indiana when she was but a little baby. Her maiden name was Woody, and she was born June 5, 1827, and my father, Hiram P. Burch, was born December 13, 1826. I was born in Green County, Indiana, May 1, 1849, and was married to Joseph A. Cisney on July 30, 1868, at the home of my parents, Mr. and Mrs. Burch. Mr. Cisney was a veteran of the Civil War and served three years and three months. He was wounded in the battle of Vicksburg under Grant. He never fully recovered from the effects of this wound and died from the effects of it February 23, 1898. Our first child, Arvilla Pearl, was born January 7, 1871, near Salsbury, Indiana.

I remember the comet in the sky before the war, and as I remember it seemed larger than Halley's Comet of a few years ago. I remember people prophesied war. My father, who was never strong, was exempted. Almost every week we would hear of someone we knew being killed or wounded, and it seemed terrible to my child mind. I met Mr. Cisney after the close of the war. He was never strong and wanted to move west in hopes of better health, so we moved to Illinois and lived seven years near Lafayette, where Ruby Arzellia was born January 12, 1878. We lived on a farm until she was one year old, when we started west again to Cherokee County, Iowa, and lived five miles from Cherokee one year. We had a terrible storm that year and several people were killed.

The following March, we started to move west again. We had one cow, a team of mules, and one horse, and two wagons. I drove the horse hitched to the light wagon. Our party consisted of brother John Burch, now of Deer Park, Mr. Cisney, our two little girls and myself. The night

before Easter, 1882, I shall never forget, we had such a terrible storm, thunder and lightning. We were directed to a farmhouse we had to cross a field to reach. They came over. They had a small boat and the men folks went out and caught some nice fish. We met some people that we traveled with as far as Bismarck, North Dakota. The men went hunting in some timber along the Missouri River. One of the men had some greyhounds, one the color of a deer; he shot it thinking it was a deer. He felt so bad over killing his dog he could not sleep that night. However, they got a deer that same day and Mr. Cisney brought it home on a horse. While we were camped here the men found a skeleton.

We came to the James River in Dakota, where we camped out at what I supposed was a logger's camp. We got such nice fish there, bullheads, I think they called them; they had to be scalded before we could clean them. We moved on to Sioux Falls, where we camped for a few days. My brother would play the banjo and sing while people would gather at the hotel to hear them. While at Miller he painted the hotel and while we were here we had our first Indian scare. About noon one day word was brought into town that the Indians were on the warpath and were killing men, women, and children and for every one to come to the hotel and bring ammunition and guns. Mr. Cisney had gone away on business, so I asked my brother what to do. He laughed and said it was only a report, so when Mr. Cisney came back we stayed in camp. All night long we could hear people coming into town for protection. The next morning we hear it was only a false report, that some White men wanted a claim that another had taken for a home. These men dressed as Indians, painted and feathered, came down to the home to scare them away. I can tell you I did not sleep that much that night.

The Hoodoo mines were very active in those days; there were hundreds of Chinese and a few White men at work there. One man by the name of Williamson struck a pocket of gold, where they took out hundreds of dollars in a few days. They were not long in getting it out, but they had a gay time while it lasted anyway. we took butter, which sold for 70¢ a pound, up to the Hoodoos, also eggs and garden stuff. This with hay at $4 a ton and shingles at $2.50 per thousand made our living in those early days.

Hoodo Mountains Vista   *Southeast of Potlatch, Idaho*

*Spring Twilight**

From Kamiak Butte

Chapter IV:

THE IRISH AND BRITISH

*"Following the marriage, Katherine Jane moved out to the farm and there Edward presented her with a wedding gift—
a hand-dug well out her back step!"*

—Leonard Devlin, 1980

Surveying the uninhabited brown-green expanse of bunchgrass in the shadow of steep bluffs and looming pines, Catherine Whelan startled her husband and four sons by announcing, "Here we will stay!" Encamped in October, 1869 on lower Union Flat Creek with a cattle herd destined for hungry miners, Irish emigrants Nicholas and Catherine Whelan had been searching for a permanent home since their arrival in America some two decades earlier. Considering the broad valley near present Wilcox ideal for stockraising, Nicholas assented to his wife's plea to end their perigrinations and the Whelan homestead became the first of many in the Palouse to be filed by Irish. The region's first British resident was likely a Welchman named John Williams who lived a short distance upstream from the Whelans in 1871.

The case of emigration from Ireland demonstrated how inextricably intertwined are the forces of "push" from the Old World and "pull" toward the New. According to historian Marcus Hansen, the periods of greatest immigration to the United States coincided with the time and areas of liveliest American industrial activity. Emigration from Ireland was due in large measure to the great economic stress within that country during the nineteenth century. The single most important factor in Ireland was the relation of the citizenry to the land. In 1849 five-ninths of the Irish population was directly dependent on the soil and society was generally arranged into a four level social pyramid. The landlords were numerically the smallest class, constituting less than one percent of the total population, but they possessed the majority of the farmland. Beneath the landlords was the leaseholding class (2.5 percent of the population), who generally resided on large grazing estates while arranging for the tillage of arable lands through an oppressive class of middlemen. These people often rented lands themselves or subdivided them and offered annual tenancies and short leas-

es at notoriously high rents. Those who actually labored on the farms, the tenants, formed by far the largest social class in Ireland in the 1840s and were divided into three sub-classes: small farmers or annual tenants who rented their lands from the middlemen, cotters who existed from year to year on a small plot which was rented on an eleven-month basis, and agricultural workers who usually had no land at all.

The nature of the land system in Ireland had debilitating effects on the masses of tenant farmers. Small plots were rented temporarily at exorbitantly high rates while laws regarding improvements on the land delegated the resulting profits to the landowners and not to the improvers themselves. These problems were compounded in the 1840s when further subdivision of tenant lands among a father's sons was not economically viable. Since it was customary for the eldest son to inherit, the other children were forced to go elsewhere to find economic security. Ireland at mid-century, however, had little industry so the system "predisposed it to disperse population" which led to massive and prolonged emigration. The Irish Potato Blight first struck in 1846, but the people had already developed a tradition of emigration. The vast majority journeyed to America where news of employment in the industrial cities of the East was attracting thousands of workers. The effect of the famine of 1846-1848 swelled the number of those immigrating to American shores in 1848 to 151,000 and this increased to over 219,000 in 1851—the most ever to emigrate to the United States in a single year from Ireland (A. Schrier, 1958).

The Pioneering Palouse Irish of Union Flat
Nicholas Whealen was among those who emigrated before the famine. He came to the United States as a young man in 1842 and settled in Illinois, a state which boasted one of the highest concentra-

123

tions of Irish-born residents. He then crossed the plains to California a short time later and engaged in mining for three years, then returned East to Pennsylvania and married Catherine O'Neil, a native of Wexford, Ireland, in 1854. The day after their marriage the couple embarked around the Horn by steamer to the northern California mines and settled in Siskiyou County where they remained for eleven years. Large numbers of immigrants had been attracted to the California strikes and the Whealens found themselves in the company of many Irish and English, some of whom would later relocate to the Palouse Country. William, Andrew, and Robert McNeilly lived in nearby Trinity County, California, where they had arrived in 1859. William had come from Ballybrack, Ireland, nine years earlier indentured to a Pennsylvania blacksmith in Stratsberg. After learning this trade he journeyed with his brothers to the California mines.

By the 1860s, however, most of the placers there had been thoroughly worked and expensive equipment was needed to continue operations. Many people decided to travel north where new strikes were reported early in the decade in eastern Washington Territory (present northern Idaho and western Montana). The lower Snake and Clearwater wilderness in 1860 was suddenly transformed into a whirlwind of frontier activity as the *Colonel Wright, Tenino,* and other steamers transported hordes of eager men from Portland to the jumping-off points of Wallula and Lewiston: 15,000 in 1861; 24,000 in 1862; and 22,000 in 1863. Miners were flocking to new deposits found along the Coeur d'Alene, Clearwater, and Salmon Rivers in present Idaho and along the Blackfoot and Bitterroot Rivers, and Jefferson Basin and Gallatin Valley (the Bannock district) in what is now western Montana.

The dramatic increase in the region's population led to a strong local market for livestock and agricultural produce. Many coming up from the California mines had witnessed the same situation before and decided more money could be gained by supplying the miners than by digging with them. About 1867 Nicholas and Catherine Whealen and their four sons joined others like the McNeilly brothers in heading north, settling in the Waitsburg area north of Walla Walla to begin raising cattle for the new Lewiston markets. The Whealens drove large herds over the mountains where buyers paid in gold, which during the

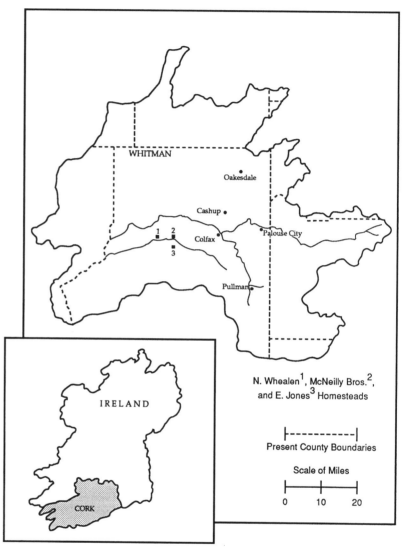

N. Whealen[1], McNeilly Bros.[2], and E. Jones[3] Homesteads

Present County Boundaries

Scale of Miles

0   10   20

COUNTY CORK, IRELAND AND UNION FLAT, WASHINGTON, c. 1870

return journey, was buried each night beneath the wheel of a wagon. The family decided to move to the Palouse while pasturing a herd on Union Flat near present Wilcox in October, 1869. Catherine announced that the place afforded everything they could ever want and

124

Palouse Perspective

Union Flat Creek

that she was determined to stay after their many years of wanderlust. Nicholas consented and remained to secure the property while the rest of the family returned to Waitsburg for the winter and prepared to move the following spring.

In February his family joined him on Union Flat to establish one of the earliest homesteads in the Palouse. Eventually each of the sons also homesteaded and the family acquired several sections of land in the vicinity. Due to the scarcity of good lumber, the Whealens lived in a sod house for the first year. These structures were not uncommon in the Palouse where the densely matted sod was up to ten inches thick. Sometimes the selected homesite was dug to a depth of two or three feet with sod sides extending the walls to a height of about six feet. The settlers then constructed small pole framed roofs which they covered with wild rye grass stalks. A thin layer of dirt was then spread over the grass. The floors often remained earthen until hewn logs could be laid over them (R. Whelan and L. Kissler, 1980).

The only other Irishman in the Palouse Country in 1869 had also stopped along Union Flat Creek that year and decided to make it his home. Edward T. Jones, a native of County Louth, Ireland, immigrated to Wisconsin as a young boy with his parents, Patrick and Catherine Devlin. In 1862 Jones enlisted in the Union army and following the Civil War, he travelled to San Francisco, arriving in 1867. Later in the year he journeyed north to Oregon's Umpqua Valley but the damp climate there prompted another move. In 1869 he rode across the Cascades and scouted the Yakima and Walla Walla valleys before coming to the Palouse in May. The spring's luxuriant growth of bunchgrass was as high as his horse's belly and he recalled that "it waved like the waves I had seen on the ocean." Apart from the Indians who passed through the area frequently, Jones found no other sign of habitation in the vicinity with the exception of an abandoned dug-out in which a miner traveling through the area had lived during the previous winter.

Jones traveled to the fork of the Palouse at present Colfax where he met James Perkins and Hezekiah Hollingsworth and became the first sawyer in their new Colfax mill. When operational, it could cut three to four thousand board feet per day in two shifts and greatly contributed to meeting the demand for building material in the region. Jones soon earned enough money to invest in the sheep business and over several years built up an enterprise of 20,000 head in five bands (L. Jones, 1980).

Conflicts with cattlemen were rare during this early period on the unfenced Palouse prairies. These grasslands were ideal for raising sheep and a number of individuals acquired vast flocks. Their movement to the distant markets at Lewiston and Walla Walla, however, did sometimes lead to violent incidents with cattlemen living along the route. W.F. Hickman, a fellow sheepman and neighbor of Jones, described in a letter headed "December 4, 1872, Union Flat, Washington Territory," a journey he took the previous summer in which he helped bring two bands numbering over 1,000 head through the Walla Walla Valley to the Palouse. It is among the earliest letters in existence from the Palouse Country.

We went thiew Walla Walla Valley and city we thot is a nice country. We stop on 6 day of Sept on east bank of Snaik river sixteen miles off and right on the south sid of the Palouse river where our sheep is now. And am about 35 or 40 miles east of them on the Tenawaze [Penawawa] creak. I have taken up a homested and air living lik two coans again. This is a fine grass country. And soil is good....This is one of the ruffest hilley countrys I eaver saw but some good leavel valey. I think this is a very good country for stalk [stock]..."

Such communication did much to encourage further settlement on the unbroken Palouse prairies.

Leaving the northern California mining district late in the 1860s, the McNeilly brothers had turned to supplying the needs of the miners by running a pack train from Walla

COLFAX, 1910 (MASC, WSU LIBRARIES)

Walla over the Kentuck Trail to Fort Colville. The trail crossed Union Flat Creek three miles north of present Dusty and on one trip through the area William decided that he "wanted to settle there among the pines." He permanently located on a tract of land neighboring the Whealen homestead and was joined by his two brothers who homesteaded nearby. Together they brought in a herd of cattle and became successful stockmen. However, due to the scarcity of timber, they found it impossible to stack enough rails to fence their land and, like others in the area, turned to the arduous task of digging ditch fences. These were about four feet deep and three feet wide with the excavated dirt thrown along the outside of the ditch to fashion a low wall of intimidation. Remnants of these trenches are still visible in some places and they provided an effective way to enclose stock, but they required constant maintenance and were eventually replaced with wooden rail fences which in turn gave way to those made with wide-banded barbed wire (W. McNeilly, 1980).

News spread rapidly about the blossoming settlement along Union Flat Creek, which was known until the early 1870s by its Indian name, "Smokle" Creek. In 1870 two Irish-born brothers, Frank and Owen Dowling, also settled in the present Wilcox district. Like the Whealens and McNeillys, the Dowling brothers had worked in the mines though their experience had been in the Salmon River district where they labored for about seven years at "Fabulous Florence" and in the Warren area. On Union Flat they engaged in raising stock and farming and soon became acquainted with many of the other Irish families in the area. A genuine spirit of pioneer cooperation and congeniality developed among the Irish community. Frank Dowling later married another native of Ireland, Annie Dunagon, and two of their children married into local Irish families.

CASHUP DAVIS RANCH AND WAY STATION NEAR STEPTOE, 1880 (MASC, WSU LIBRARIES)

Marriage between children of the first generation of emigrants from the same country occurred frequently in the Palouse. Of the fourteen foreign-born immigrant farming families who had settled in the Palouse by 1871, seven were Irish. All of them had congregated in the present Wilcox district along Union Flat Creek where other families from the Emerald Isle continued to settle through the decade. Among the first of their number to homestead on the Palouse River was Peter Feenan, also a native of County Cork, who first traveled to the area on horseback from San Francisco in 1877 after hearing about the legendary hills from a fellow Irishman. Feenan resolved to acquire land on the north side of the river near present Diamond and homesteaded a quarter-section there in 1880 within weeks of acquiring American citizenship and his marriage to Annie McSweeney, whom he had known from his youth in Ireland (K. Knittel, 1993).

Origins of the Palouse English Community

James A. "Cashup" Davis was one of a small number of English immigrants in the area but realized the great potential of the land for supporting livestock. Davis, born in 1815 in Hastings, England, had crossed the Atlantic in 1840 and lived for thirty years in the Midwest before crossing the Plains. He settled near present St. John in 1871 where, like many Palouse pioneers, he constructed a combination sod and frame house for his family which was built into a hillside. Bunchgrass blocks were used for walls and the structure was divided into two rooms by a curtain of flour sacks. Davis soon built up a large cattle herd and in 1873 wrote to his son, William, who had remained in the Midwest, favorably describing their new life in the Palouse:

The country is one vast pasturage of grass. Its fattening qualities

Cashup Flats Storm

Cashup, Washington

are unsurpassed by any in the world...Cattle are fat all the year. I have eight horses, and I have not fed any grain since I have ben here and not more than two hundred pounds of hay...These valleys run from 50 to 160 acres and from 5 to 50 miles long. There are some claims on each side of me just as good as mine that I think are worth money. They are very pretty and level but they will be gone in the spring, if not before. The country is fast settling up.

The ambitious Englishman continued with an optimistic plan for achieving financial success through his ranching efforts.

Now you figure on 500 sheep and their increase for seven years, even calling the wool at seventy-five cents a head, and the increase one dollar in a country where you do not have to feed them all the year, with thousands of acres of pasture without even to pay the taxes on, then you look at cows, your increase and your butter at $40 a week, and this is in good besides your calves, say fifteen calves out of twenty cows at $10 a calf, then your hogs from your grain and milk and your land for nearly nothing.

Davis concluded the letter to his son with a prediction that the cattle and sheep market would remain good throughout the region "for years." This assessment proved to be the case as coastal demands spurred high beef prices during the 1870s, and by the middle of the decade new markets surged in the upper Midwest leading to immense drives across the northern Rockies. A gregarious man who always sought new opportunity, Davis sold his farm and relocated about fifteen miles east in 1875 at the base of Steptoe Butte where he and wife, Mary Ann, built a large home and general store on 1600 acres bought from the railroad. Their place evolved into a waystation for stagecoach passengers traveling through the region. The site later became known as Cashup in tribute to the man whose nickname indicated his preferred terms of business. His dream to build a splendid hotel on top of the Butte was fulfilled after years of arduous labor but the enterprise proved impractical because of the remote location and maintenance expenses (R. Johnson, n.d.).

Other English-speaking immigrants also settled in the western Palouse during the 1880s including one family whose members had struggled to make a home in England, Australia, and California. Their global travels began with William Swannack's decision to leave his native England at age twenty-one for Australia and join thousands of his countrymen who were immigrating to that continent for economic betterment. He eventually acquired a farm near Perth and in 1870 married Hannah Nicholson, a native of Shelby, England. Fifteen years and eight children later, the Swannacks decided to journey to San Francisco after hearing about the Homestead Act and rumors of available land in the States more suited to agriculture and cattle ranching. Finding the best land already taken or too expensive to purchase in California, they began investigating settlement opportunities elsewhere and learned about extensive railroad tracts for sale in the Sprague-Lamont area of Eastern Washington. They relocated to the territory in 1886 and settled near Lamont. Eventually Swannack helped his sons acquire ranches in the vicinity with much of the land was purchased from the Northern Pacific Railroad (J. Swannack, n.d.).

Strapped with increasing financial pressures in the early 1890s, the Northern Pacific aggressively promoted sales of its vast holdings in the Pacific Northwest. The railroad was instrumental in the formation of the Eastern Washington and Northern Idaho Bureau of Immigration in 1894. The bureau established a central office in Chicago to distribute literature throughout the East and Midwest about Spokane, Colfax, and other communities supporting the project. The Northern Pacific ran special colonist sleepers divided into family sections with a kitchen at one end of each car. Soon entire trainloads of immigrants were arriving in Spokane and the Palouse where they were conveniently met by local land promoters handing out colorful pamphlets extolling the virtues of the region and describing liberal terms of purchase (J. Fahey, 1986).

The Eastern Palouse Irish

A small enclave of Irish immigrant farmers also settled during the 1870s and 1880s in the central Palouse Pleasant Hills district east of present Oakesdale. The group included Robert and Thomas Murphy, natives of County Antrim in northern Ireland, Alexander Tomilson, Thomas Norton, and Charles Woods. The Murphy brothers, sons of a tenant farmer in Ireland, immigrated to America about 1865 and found temporary employment in New York, Chicago and St. Louis. They eventually joined a wagon train and rode horseback to California where they farmed for several years and became naturalized citizens. In the middle 1870s they sold their California property, traveled to Portland, Oregon, by steamer and then walked over 400 miles to Cheney, Washington, in order to work on the construction of the Northern Pacific Railroad line. While in the Cheney area they learned the railroad was offering Palouse land for sale at $1.50 per acre.

A number of Irish laborers decided to take advantage of the opportunity. The Murphys, Tomilson, and others bought half-sections of virgin land near present Oakesdale. Many of these families were instrumental in later establishing the Oakesdale Presbyterian Church. Later, other Irish families settled in the same area including the Warwicks and Kilpatricks. Patrick Sheahan, an Irish emigrant of 1860, served in the Illinois Volunteer Infantry during the Civil War before moving to Portland in 1869. After farming at several different places in the Northwest during the 1870s, he settled on land about six miles west of Oakesdale in 1881 and in 1889 platted the town of Thornton, which was established on his property.

The Palouse Irish were responsible for colorful ethnic contributions to the region's legends. The Irish reputation for being quick-tempered was typified by an early settler in the eastern Palouse near Genesee, Idaho, John Robert Coffee, whose first of several reported scrapes was in Levi's Store where he went after an Englishman named H.B. Hodgins. Coffee was armed with a pair of nail pincers and managed to tear off a portion of Hodgins' ear before the men were parted. (As often the case in frontier skirmishes, the reason for the fight became not important enough to remember.) Later, in a running battle with a Scotsman named Fitzgerald, Coffee tried to pull his adversary from his horse. Fitzgerald responded by firing a revolver at him—hitting his own horse instead—and then rode away on the wounded animal with Coffee in pursuit. Boarded inside his cabin, Fitzgerald was safe until morning when Coffee, unable to break through the door, began firing his revolver through a window. He could not hit his target, however, and left with a vow to return.

Fitzgerald swore out a warrant for Coffee's arrest and a posse was formed. Riding to his ranch, the lawmen asked Mrs. Coffee for permission to search the house. She pleaded for time to dress properly, and while these gentlemen obligingly waited, Coffee rode away from the barn at a gallop. He was picked up the next night as he boarded a steamboat at Lewiston, Idaho, jailed, and fined $500. A few years later Coffee was killed by a man named Stephens who worked for him, in a dispute over wages. Mortally wounded though he was, Coffee managed to wrestle the pistol away from Stephens. This was all witnessed by a neighbor, James DeHaven. Coffee chased Stephens around the barn, firing and missing until the gun was empty. Then he walked into the house and said to his wife, "Well, he has killed me," and went to bed. Although Stephens turned himself in to the sheriff, Coffee refused to give any information on the fight and died four days later. Stephens was exonerated.

The major Latah County Irish community was northeast of Genesee about a dozen miles from Moscow where the predominant families carried the names Keane, Linehan, Kinnier, Magee, Mullaley, Driscoll and Cunningham. Later to be named Lenville, the area was first settled by two Irishmen, Tom Linehan, followed by Patrick Kinnier. Many Civil War veterans, most from the Union side, moved in and it was nicknamed "soldier neighborhood." In 1882 Len Nichols built a store and a year later Kinnier set up a competing store one-half mile east. Because the latter's business was better stocked, Nichols was forced to close. The town took roots around Kinnier's store but ironically became known as Lenville. Other enterprises followed, including a chop mill and blacksmith shop where many of the early day wagons in the area were built. Mail was delivered from Genesee by horseback. Although there was a strong Irish Catholic influence, the Lenville Church, built in 1897, was reserved for use by all Protestant denominations and its revival meetings drew from a large area. Land for the church was donated by Kinnier, himself a devout Catholic.

Lenville school politics were stormy. The location of the first school building, in dispute because it had to serve a large area, finally was chosen one-quarter mile east of the Kinnier place. Not satisfied with that decentralized site, men from the lower section of the district came one night with horses and wooden skids to pull the school over to the Scott Ross Ranch. The county school superintendent was asked to intercede in the theft, and he suggested that the large district be divided into the Yellow Rose and Fairview districts. The compromise

Red Barn   *North of Johnson, Washington*

did not satisfy everyone in the Fairview District. The issue again was precise location of the school, and fights broke out on the day that school directors were elected. As feelings grew hot, Tom Linehan is reputed to have climbed into a wagon to fight another man. Kinnier, who was an election judge, had to conceal the ballot box under his coat to protect it when an uproar arose that some had voted illegally. Lenville also became a center of entertainment, dancing, and sports. A group of young men—Mike Mullaley, Will Kennedy, Art Linehan, Joshua Armstrong, Percy Kinnier, and Ed Armstrong—rented the old Nichols' store building for $8 per year and opened it for dances. They also had a baseball team and sponsored horse races and prize fighting. The disintegration of Lenville as a business community began before 1910, as travel to the larger nearby towns became easier because of road improvements and the automobile (J. Platt, 1975).

Many Irish were more fun-loving than their pious neighbors on the Palouse frontier. When John "Jack" Driscoll, who had come in 1850 to the Troy, Idaho area from New Brunswick, Canada, decided to take a wife, he made the mistake of not consulting her on the house he was building on Driscoll Ridge. When work was completed, he showed it off to the woman, a Miss Mullaley of Genesee, and she broke their engagement. The house had a huge living room, perfect for dances, a tiny dark kitchen and bedrooms so small that there was not room for more than a bed. Driscoll never married. Because social life in the early days often revolved around neighbors—whoever they happened to be—there was not always agreement on when to end the party. Historian Ann Nilsson Driscoll explained that at some events where both the

Irish Catholics and English Methodists were invited "the entertainment would start out with parlor games such as skip-to-my-lou, winkum, and fruit-basket upset, but later in the evening the Irish would bring out their fiddles and start dancing. When the music started, the Methodists would gather up their children and depart for home, and for the Irish the party had just begun." John Quinn, a Driscoll Ridge Irishman who often drank too much must have believed after one binge on election day that the party really was over for him. Several young men who found Quinn passed out put him in a coffin and placed lighted candles about it, simulating an Irish wake. They apparently wanted him to believe that everyone thought he was dead. When he came to, Quinn survived the fright and managed his habits well enough to live to age eighty-three (A. Driscoll, 1970).

By 1880, the Irish in Whitman County, predominantly farmers, constituted the largest European foreign-born element (148, or 14 percent of the total foreign-born population). In Nez Perce County they numbered 80 individuals (10 percent of the total foreign-born) but most there were either soldiers at Fort Lapwai or miners. About 100 in the region at that date were from Great Britain. By 1890 the number of Irish in Whitman and Latah Counties had increased to 284 but the trend was reversed in the following decade as the 1900 census registered 257. This rate of decline continued and by 1920 their numbers had fallen to 147. Although they have been among the smallest ethnic groups in the Palouse since the early 1900s, the Irish and British played a major role in opening the region to later settlement by other European immigrants.

ALBION, WASHINGTON, c. 1915 (MASC, WSU LIBRARIES)

LEONARD DEVLIN
DUSTY, WASHINGTON

Leonard Devlin is a descendant of one of the Palouse Country's first settlers, Irish immigrant Edward T. Jones, who came to the area in 1868. Jones was raised on the original family homestead southeast of Dusty and returned to farm after attending Stanford University in the 1940's. Long a student of the region's history, Devlin is also a gifted storyteller who recounted the following narrative for the author in 1989.

Adventure had come early for my Irish-American Grandfather Devlin whose family had settled in Wisconsin. When the war to save the Union was underway, Edward's father joined with General Grant and moved south. Young Edward Thomas had to be in on the glory, so he did what other youths had done—lied about his age and changed his name to "Jones." He was only fourteen when he was captured a year later. Taken by Confederates to plantations on the Amazon in South America, he later found his way north to San Francisco by sailing from the coast of Peru. When cholera was discovered aboard his ship, all on board were quarantined and held for six weeks during the months of August and September, 1865. Following his release, Edward he hurried north to the Umpqua Valley in Oregon where family friends had settled following the gold rush of 1849. There he learned the lumbering trade and while he liked the woods and the wilds, the chilly damp weather made him ill. By 1868 he was moving again, this time to the territory north of the Columbia River. He was searching for something and he had a dream to fulfill. I don't know that he had it firmly in mind but everything seemed to fall into place.

There was plenty of time for Edward Jones to scout the area. One of the big drawbacks of the water-powered mill at present Colfax where he first worked was that it could not take the fluctuations of stream flows of the Palouse. So he had time to move about. He had ridden by the present homestead and had been impressed by it and as time went by became more interested. The horseshow basin gazed away toward the east, it was protected from the howling north winds

by the range of hills and the hot summer days by hills to the west that shadowed the ranch site. It had the greater benefit in that a number of springs flowed down the meandering flat of what was to be called Alkalai Flat Creek. So he chose this site and applied for a homestead and a little later for a timber culture. When he met a sprightly young lady, a very diminutive girl named Catherine Jane Fincher, he began to have other ideas and began to work on a house was, of course, required by the Homestead Act of 1862. He began occupation which was required about three months a year but he could still do that and fulfill his work at the mill in Colfax.

In any event, in 1873 on November 1 in Colfax, Catherine Jane Fincher became the bride of Edward Thomas Jones. His family had begun a search for him. The Devlin family had heard through relatives in the Umpqua Valley that heir eldest son Edward was alive and had ventured to the United States from South America and had made his way to the Washington Territory. It was Edward's younger brother, John Devlin who came West and discovered his brother living near Colfax. The two of them got along very well and worked shoulder to shoulder, of what Edward Thomas was to achieve might be to some degree at least ascribed to his warm relationship with his brother John. John would eventually take a homestead of his own at the edge of the Jones farm and by the early 1870s the two sisters, Margaret and Bridgett, and the mother and father, Patrick and Catherine Devlin, moved west to be with their family.

The two girls found ready employment in Penawawa. There was always need for able hands in the family. Patrick and Catherine took a homestead just east of the one that John had taken for himself. So the Devlin clan was reunited at last. Grandfather Devlin in his way tried to persuade his son Edward to take back the Devlin name but he was stubborn and determined man. Having married his bride under the name of Jones he refused to do so. He would make his life to the last day as a Jones rather than a Devlin. Nonetheless the relationships remained amicable and my father grew up under the tutelage of his grandfather, Patrick Devlin, especially so when Edward was taken off at an early age because of illness. Following the marriage, Katherine Jane moved out to the farm and there Edward presented her with a wedding gift—a hand-dug well at her back step! Indeed it was his pride that she would not have to get wet in order to get water. He ordered in a pump and the dug well remained there for years and years during the period when the family was coming. These were very hard times. There was no money; barter was the usual form of trade. While he could earn a meager living as a sawyer at the mill, because of the diminished stream flows he was often without employment. However, there was a ready demand for his carpentry skills and as new settlers began making their way to the Palouse country, he traveled almost daily from homestead to homestead helping settlers erect a roof over their house.

Farms at that early time like ours could have a milk cow; in fact we had three at one time. Rye hay was grown in the fall, it was the only grown that would survive the high alkalinity. The sheep bands were taken into the Blue Mountains in the summer and down in elevation in the wintertime and that meant they didn't need to receive great quantities of hay, indeed the native hay was not very nutritious. One settler who brought in a hundred head of cows and had driven them all the way to Union Flat Creek thinking to pasture them on the perennial ryegrass found that before the year 1888 was over that he had lost all but twenty of his cattle. The nutrition simply was not there to support them. The sheep enterprise expanded and was aided and abetted by the good fortune of the Devlin family for the two Devlin girls, Margaret and Brigett, met and very soon married two very industrious brothers, Patrick and William Codd, who had determined to go into business in Colfax.

They had by this time become very competent in the business of felling timber although that really was not their great love. In some winters when Hez Hollingsworth was unable to run his mill because of icy conditions, the two boys would leave their wives and go down the rivers to the Willamette Valley and in that milder climate they could find employment for two to three months in the most bitter time of the year and then come home with money for the needs of the farmsteads. John was building a home and, of course, both boys were trying to help their father, Patrick with the erection of his home. In any event, the Codd Mill became a boom, it kept the family together. After Edward passed away the district decided that a new and bigger school was in order and they decided to locate it right no the boundary of the Jones farm. Professional carpenters were hired to put up the schoolhouse and it was quite an impressive building. It is still standing today, one of the last one-room schoolhouses I presume in the state of Washington. While the school belfry is no longer there, nonetheless it was in its own time and fine edifice and gave an opportunity for the children to go to school from the time they could attend by horse or cart. In the erection of this building one of the carpenters working on the steeple turned and looked down at Grandfather Devlin and said to him, "Mr. Devlin, didn't one of your daughters marry a Codd?" All the lumber for the school was being hauled out from the Codd Mill. And in the words of my father who never forgot it, the old Irishman looked up and said, "One married Pat Codd and the other married Bill be God!"

Chapter V:

THE CHINESE AND JAPANESE

"He told me America was Gum Sam, the 'Land of Golden Mountains,' and that those who worked hard could return to China and enjoy a good life with their savings."

—Owen Eng, 1989

Born in the village of Teishan in China's populous southeastern province of Guangdong, longtime Cofax resident Owen Eng remembers well the stories his grandfather, Ken Hock, would tell of his early years in Gum Sam to which he first journeyed in the 1860s. Ken had worked as a rice farmer in the district south of Canton but joined thousands of his countrymen in seeking to acquire enough wealth to ensure a better life for his family in China. Rumors depicted America as a land where fortunes could be made in little time as the relative value of American money was said to be worth ten-fold back in China. With such prospects Gum Sam offered hope in stark contrast to life in China during the mid 1800s where the future held a lifetime of endless toil in the fields. The early Chinese immigrants to America, therefore, were unlike Europeans or even other Asians who sought permanence in the new land. Most Chinese journeyed across the Pacific only as a means to an end—a better life for themselves and their families back in the homeland.

Troubled Times in the Heavenly Kingdom

Mid-nineteenth century China was a land in tumultuous transition. For over two hundred years the country had been ruled by the oppressive Ching Dynasty which sought to maintain Manchu domination over the Chinese peoples through the carefully structured "banner system" of tiered military controls, the preservation of strict social codes, and a distinctive provincial government structure that featured Manchu generals wielding authority over Chinese governors and district administrators. Despite this foreign super-structure imposed on the Chinese bureaucracy, the Ching emperors of the eighteenth and early nineteenth centuries developed relatively effective means of political administration and during this period the empire reached its greatest geographic extent.

Although the Chinese had been an agrarian people for generations with limited ties to foreign trade, trans-Pacific commerce was inaugurated in 1779 when the British explorer-trader James Cook entered the port of Canton with furs from the Pacific Northwest coast and was surprised to see the Chinese offer as much as $120 worth of goods for a single pelt. This event helped to spark a global trade network tied together by the vast sailing fleets of the Europeans and enterprising Yankees whose ships annually plied the waters off the present Washington and British Columbia coastlines to gather furs for Canton and other burgeoning Asian market centers. Chinese silks, spices, and porcelain were then traded for profit in Europe. During this same period Jesuit and Dominican missionary efforts, begun in the late 1500s, flourished with perhaps 300,000 Christians in China by the early 1700s, and the population of the entire country reached approximately 200 million by mid-century. In contrast, Europe's most populous nation at that time, France, had a population of only twenty million. By the 1850s, however, the Chinese population hit 450 million and a combination of religious, political, demographic, and other factors sparked the beginning of an unprecedented immigration of Chinese to the United States.

The first in a series of regional revolts against Manchu domination began in 1850 after the charismatic leader Hung Hsiu ch'uan announced the creation of a "Heavenly Kingdom of Great Peace," or the Taiping Tien Kuo. A former Confucian scholar who became greatly influenced by Christian missionary literature, Hung assumed the role of messianic deliverer who organized a massive popular uprising against the Ching emperor from the Taiping capital of Nanking. From their base in southeast China, the Taipings brought a third of China under their control by 1860 and forced the emperor to flee to Mongolia. At this juncture the rhetoric and success of the intensely

*Rolling Palouse Summer**

South of Moscow, Idaho

nationalistic Taipings aroused the concern of the Western powers.

The British, in particular, feared that a Taiping government might limit their extensive commercial interests including their exploitive trade in opium which the Taipings felt was partly responsible for the moral decay of the nation as well as the economic collapse in the southern provinces. Accordingly, the British decided to lend military support to the exiled Manchu emperor and dispatch General Charles "Chinese" Gordon to lead forces against the Taipings. With these changes power gradually returned to the Manchus and by 1864 the war that had ravaged China for nearly fifteen years was over. Likely the most catastrophic civil war in human history, some twenty million Chinese died in the revolution. To compound this tragedy, a series of natural disasters struck southeast China in the 1850s resulting in extensive flooding along the lower Yellow and other major river systems and recurrent destruction of the rice crop (S. Leibo, 1982).

Chinese Labor in the American West

Peasants experiencing the debilitating effects of life under these conditions likely found stories about life in the Land of Golden Mountains worthy of more than mere retelling. Some inquired about opportunities for travel and work in Gum Sam around port cities like Canton where representatives of various American commercial enterprises established headquarters. They, in turn, arranged agreements between American labor contractors and Chinese agents who were paid to assemble "coolie gangs" for transport to America. (The term likely owes its origin to the word "kuli" which referred to a burden bearer in British India.) The British, Spanish, and other Europeans had engaged for decades in the forced recruitment of Chinese laborers for their colonies throughout the world from Cuba to India.

Chinese laborers lived in virtual enslavement. With popular uprisings in the coastal provinces surfacing against their recruitment methods in the 1850s, the European merchant community in China reformed their policies and established programs of voluntary recruitment subject to government inspection. Many peasants like Owen Eng's grandfather, Ken Hock, headed for the United States to enter into a kind of indentured service through which a portion of their wages in America would be kept by the Chinese coolie trader while

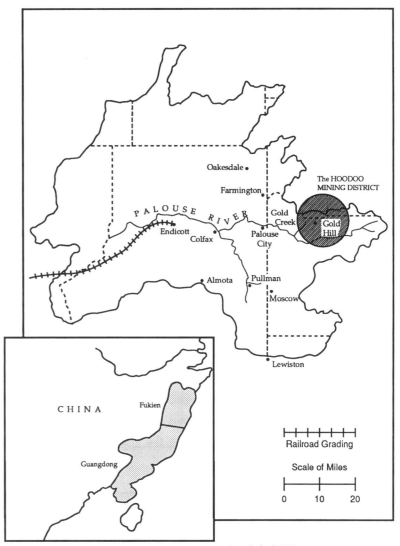

**GUANGDONG AND FUKIEN PROVINCES, CHINA
AND THE EASTERN PALOUSE MINING DISTRICT, 1882**

the remainder could be saved and sent home. In characteristic fashion, Ken returned three times to China with his savings and remained to live in Teishan after his third trip. A son, Gin Sing, chose to remain in

137

Rolling Palouse Winter*

South of Moscow, Idaho

California and later relocated to the inland Pacific Northwest (O. Eng, 1989).

Nearly 2.5 million Chinese immigrated to North and South America or elsewhere in southeast Asia between 1840 and 1900. Probably the first Chinese to the West Coast were three individuals aboard the Bard Eagle which journeyed to California in 1848. Hard workers were needed for labor in the newly found gold strikes on the American River and American traders communicated this to Chinese labor contractors at several major port cities in China. While only about a thousand Chinese were in California by 1851, during the following two years 43,000 journeyed to the new land which was becoming known to people in both hemispheres as truly a "Land of Golden Mountains." Since emigration directly from China to the United States was illegal until the Treaty of Burlingame in 1868, virtually all were young men and most were from Guangdong Province since the area was adjacent to the British controlled port of Hong Kong.

Accustomed to either rice farming or life in the urban coastal cities, work in mining camps of the Western frontier evoked little familiarity with the homeland for the Chinese laborers who flocked to the region. Accordingly, merchants and workers from the same geographical areas in China banded together to form benevolent societies, or tongs, which served the cultural, social, and business needs of the community. Over time these associations evolved into the famous Six Companies which maintained diplomatic ties to the Chinese Imperial Government and provided legal and medical help to their members as well as arranging for burial of the dead or the interment of remains in China. Important in the Chinese experience in the Palouse Country as elsewhere in the region, the societies also became the contracting agencies for coolie labor and provided interpreters for work gangs which operated throughout the Pacific Northwest (L. Hildebrand, 1977).

Chinese had been present in the region since the late 1850s when they followed other miners from California to the gold strikes of the Colville district. Placers had been found in the summer of 1855 on the Pend Oreille River near present Metaline Falls, Washington and by July newspapers on the Coast were reporting the discovery. While relatively few Chinese worked east of the Cascades in the 1850s, the dis-

covery of gold on Canada's Fraser River in 1858 brought some 2,000 of them to Fort Victoria within a year. The late nineteenth century Chinese experience in the Palouse can be characterized by three labor-related phases: mining (1860s-1870s), railroad construction (1870s-1880s), and the development of service-related businesses (1880s-1900). Hostility toward the Chinese was evident in the Palouse and elsewhere in the Northwest throughout the 1880s and 1890s. The anger and fear of European-Americans was expressed in local newspaper editorials in Spokane, Whitman, and Latah Counties and in murder and arson. Many felt justified by the widespread belief that Chinese aliens working in the gold placers of surface gold deposits were expropriating the country's wealth and sending it to Asia. Moreover, the coolie gangs used to build the Central Pacific and Northern Pacific Railroads were thought to be taking jobs away from European-Americans.

In fact Asian labor was often preferred by company owners for various frontier enterprises largely because of the reputation the Chinese earned as industrious miners who worked many California placers after the Americans left. They were also responsible for building the Central Pacific Railroad from California to Utah in the 1860s. Seemingly at his wits end when faced with construction through a treacherous stretch in the Sierra Nevada Mountains, railroad magnate Charles Crocker's company lieutenants hired a party of fifty Chinese who promptly completed the cut with picks, shovels, and wheelbarrows to the amazement of the engineers. This incident "permanently revised their opinion of the Chinaman's endurance" and led to Crocker's famous remark that a people capable of building the Great Wall could certainly handle a railroad. Thousands of Chinese laborers were subsequently hired by the C.P.R.R. through the Six Companies in San Francisco until the completion of the line in 1869. When construction began on Pacific Northwest railroads in the 1870s, labor contractors again turned to the Six Companies to meet their needs (S. Kung, 1962; B. Sung, 1971).

Phase One: The Chinese and Palouse Regional Mining (1860s-1870s)

Rumors circulated as early as 1856 that gold had been found on the South Fork of the Clearwater River in present Idaho and these stories were confirmed when Elias Pierce and Seth Ferrell made a significant discovery there in 1858. Two years later, in August, 1860, Pierce and a dozen other miners located a rich placer on Canal Gulch near present Pierce, Idaho while others found color at Gold Creek near the headwaters of the Palouse River. Before 1860 European-American settlement east of the Cascades was largely composed of military personnel, settlers, and miners in the vicinities of Forts Colville and Walla Walla. But when the news rapidly spread about the Clearwater strikes just when the Fraser and upper Columbia placers were playing out, a series of muddy boomtowns appeared in 1860 on the Clearwater as Lewiston, Elk City, and Florence were born. Thousands of goldseekers followed by merchants, traders, and whiskey peddlers flocked to the new mining district and by 1862 the Oregon Steam Navigation Company was operating a fleet of boats from Portland to Lewiston carrying passengers, food stuffs, and building supplies. The *Yakima*, *Tenino*, *Spray*, *Okanogan* and other steamers were soon making regular runs on the upper end of the network and served as the chief link between the Clearwater diggings and coastal cities. The 1860s also witnessed the first European-American settlement in the Palouse Country where a few adventurous souls like George Pangburn and Joseph DeLong began raising livestock for the new markets to the south.

The vast area of the Washington Territory east of the Cascades, virtually uninhabited by European-Americans at the dawn of the decade, teemed with approximately 30,000 Whites by 1863. Few, if any, were Chinese. The majority of the newcomers were miners who were brought by the excitement on the Clearwater while others fanned out across the tributaries of the region's major rivers to make additional strikes, usually followed by shortlived workings, on Cottonwood Creek, the upper Salmon in the Florence district, and on the Little Blackfoot River in present Montana. In 1862 renewed interest in the upper Palouse Country was focused along the streams at the southern base of the Hoodoo Mountains where miners dubbed the tiny rivulets bearing the precious metal with such names as California Gulch and Eldorado Gulch. While these may be suggestive of previous experiences or expectations, the names of adjacent streams like Poorman

Creek and Greenhorn Gulch suggest less fortuitous origins.

Although some Chinese may have entered the Clearwater and Palouse mining districts early in the 1860s, references in the regional press to their presence do not appear until the spring of 1865. The pattern of Chinese immigration to the Palouse is consistent with the general cycle of their movement in the West which featured initial placer discoveries and subsequent workings by impatient European-Americans who often terminated their efforts within a couple years or even months after the sluicing of gravels yielded all the nuggets deemed large and plentiful enough for the effort. Seeking to avoid racial animosities and imbued with an industriousness and frugality that had won them the respect of America's railroad builders, the Chinese typically entered a field after most others had lost interest. With fine-screened wooden rockers and pans they would carefully rework the gravels to glean smaller nuggets and fine gold.

The Chinese were also known to devise ingenious sluicing operations using wooden flumes or long diversion ditches to open new placers. Mining historian William Joseph Trimble visited the Palouse Country on numerous occasions around the turn of the century while conducting research on his authoritative *The Mining Advance into the Inland Empire*. He observed that while the Chinese were "debarred from the camps so long as claims paid 'wages' or better, they were welcomed later to buy the claims, once washed, which no white miner would consent to touch.... It was seldom the Chinaman worked for the white man, but he often paid large sums for his claim—as high in some cases as $8,000—and he paid in cash, or the white owner of the claim took out of the sluice boxes each Saturday night a certain amount until paid.... Undoubtedly America owes considerable to them for saving treasure which might otherwise have been wasted" (W. Trimble, 1919).

On March 1, 1865 the *Portland Oregonian* reported that the "first installment" of Chinese had reached Walla Walla enroute to the Snake River and Orofino mines. An earlier issue reported, "testimony of Chinese agents, [that] a very large number of Chinese miners may be expected in the Upper Country in the coming season." Estimates of the projected number varied from 2,000 to 5,000. The numbers indicated that a movement of significant proportion was about to be undertaken. Judging by such terms as "installment" and "agent," the influx was likely orchestrated by Chinese contractors working for the Six Companies in San Francisco. Typical of those who came in the first wave of 1865 were two seventeen-year-old boys, Mah Young and Pun Loi. The pair had arrived on a sailing vessel in San Francisco the previous year where they stayed for several months before taking a steamer to Portland and walking four hundred miles to Lewiston and Pierre City. Owen Eng's father, Gin Sing, followed a similar route much later but periodically returned to China to visit his family. Mah and Pun, however, remained in the Clearwater Mountains mining district for six decades until their return to China in 1923.

While some Chinese may have worked independently or under contract to hire, most Chinese working in the inland Northwest during the 1860s were employed directly by other Chinese. The majority undertook the backbreaking labor to eke out a living with daily wages of fifteen cents customary. Contractors were obliged to feed and clothe their employees, but most miners were provided with little more than a blue cotton jacket and pants and a straw hat—hardly appropriate for the mountain winters. They subsisted primarily on rice brought by muleskinners, beef and pork procured from area cattlemen, and vegetables which many raised themselves. To allay the difficulties of life on the frontier, many engaged in the illegal trade and smoking of

KAMIAK BUTTE, c. 1920 (MASC, WSU LIBRARIES)

opium, a vice learned from enterprising European traders in China.

Gin Sing related that living conditions for Chinese miners in the upper Palouse gold districts were primitive; they lived in log cabins, tents, or crude dugouts. A typical North Idaho miners' cabin was described in 1863 as about ten by twelve, "the roof extending eight feet from the main building, a pile of pitch wood to the left of the door; over the wood hangs a fore and hind quarter of beef." Along one wall inside the one-room structure were "stored any amount of provisions, over which are fixed two bunks above the other. To the right of the fireplace stands a small table...and still to the right is a goods box nailed to the wall for a cupboard, which is filled with all kinds of cooking traps. On the right hand side of the room is the window, one pane of glass constitutes the size, under which is placed the dining table." Distinctively Chinese items uncovered in recent archaeological excavations in the region include pottery shards from rice whiskey jugs, soy sauce bottles, brass coins, and opium tins. The same research indicates that even in the mountains Chinese abodes were sometimes surrounded by small vegetable gardens and berry patches, often terraced and irrigated (J. Fee, 1987).

The efforts of European-Americans to wrest the yellow metal from the lower Clearwater placers were largely aborted by 1869 and the Chinese who took over the work there have been credited with saving Lewiston from a complete economic collapse as its population already had shrunk from several thousand to several hundred. The availability of Chinese gold helped stabilize area businesses which in turn generated opportunities for some Chinese to enter service-related employment in support of the nascent middle and merchant classes. With approximately 500 residents in 1870, Lewiston showed signs of recovery due in large measure to the local Asian populace which at that time numbered almost one third of Lewiston's total population.

An extensive "Chinatown" developed along lower "D" Street down to the river with numerous laundries, restaurants, and shops. Later a joss house, or temple, was built graced with a beautifully scalloped entry, door casings, and interior accouterments that remained there until the structure was demolished in 1959. An inscription carved next to the entry in Chinese characters read, "The Emperor's virtues are far reaching and profound, flowing to this foreign land."

Evening Light Moscow Mountain

North of Moscow, Idaho

Communication among extended families was possible via the extensive Six Company network in the West and many early Chinese residents of Lewiston informed their relatives in California about conditions in the Northwest. In this manner Gin Sing first heard about the region through a cousin who was residing in Lewiston.

The Chinese planted extensive vegetable gardens on the north edge of town to provide the local populace and steamboat traffickers with fresh produce. Soon they were also working as porters and cooks aboard legendary paddlewheelers like the Almota and Tenino. Passengers enroute along the lower Snake in the late 1860s and 1870s could frequently glimpse groups of Chinese miners busily working their equipment on the river's sandy bars. A contemporary newspaper account on their methods along the Snake River reports that hundreds were at work on the bars where fine gold was painstakingly extracted by the "Celestials" from rockers at the edge of the water. "The pay dirt is carried in baskets, sometimes a distance of one hundred yards. The rockers have an upright handle to them which the worker operates with one hand and gives a rocking motion to the machine, while, with a long handled dipper he ladles water into it with the other hand. The dirt and gravel run off with the outflowing water and the minute particles of gold adhere to a piece of blanket or coarse cloth fixed in the bottom for that purpose. They make from $1 to $1.25 per day on the average, which amount the white miner scorns...." As late as 1879 three hundred Chinese were reported still to be engaged in mining on the lower Snake from its mouth to Almota. Many remained into the 1890s to tend orchards and gardens at Almota, Penawawa, and other Snake River communities.

Mining interest near the headwaters of the Palouse River was rekindled in the Gold Hill district along Jerome Creek in the middle 1870s and Camp Grizzle developed into a thriving settlement of Chinese and other miners from 1874 to the early 1880s. The site's namesake was Griswold's Meadow located near the mouth of Strychnine Creek where colorful John Griswold and his Nez Perce wife had settled in the early 1870s. By 1874 the camp boasted numerous cabins, a blacksmith shop, post office, and saloon. About ten miles downstream a flour mill was erected in 1874 by W. P. Breeding who platted the townsite of Palouse City the following year. A sawmill was built there in 1875 and a thriving community developed over the next two years as settlers in the treeless western Palouse purchased considerable lumber in Palouse City while the needs of miners in the Gold Hill, Hoodoo, and Moscow Mountain districts spawned numerous mercantile and supply businesses widely patronized by the Chinese.

Chinese were drawn to upper Palouse mining areas in great numbers in the late 1870s and, if not engaged in service-related endeavors in local communities like Palouse City, Moscow, or Farmington, they usually worked in the placers as part of labor gangs with one to several dozen workers. While some Chinese worked independently for developers like Adam Carrico, who employed as many as 200 on his East Gold Hill property, most Chinese labor gangs remained part of the vast network controlled by the Six Companies in San Francisco. As elsewhere in the West, day-to-day local operations were directed by a Chinese supervisor who was periodically visited by a company representative. Traveling the Chambers Brothers stage line monthly to Camp Grizzle, for example, one company official stayed in the log cabin hotel there while arranging to collect the gold dust each time and return to San Francisco. Chinese businessmen also sought to negotiate long-term leases on gold bearing property on the upper Palouse in order to secure control to lands in an enterprise often complicated by conflicting land claims. Prominent Palouse City financiers A. A. Kincaid of Northwestern Pacific Mortgage Company and J. G. Powers of Security State Bank handled several of these transactions in the 1880s for Charles Yet & Company (R. Waldbauer, 1986).

Chinese employment opportunities and restrictions in railroad construction and mining during the 1870s and 1880s were indicative of the peculiar nature of Northwest labor relations at that time. The Northern Pacific Railroad, anxious to complete the first northern transcontinental, was eager to hire the Chinese workforce that had distinguished itself in the construction of the Central Pacific. Organized labor, however, charged that the Northern Pacific was exploiting the Asian workers by paying "coolie wages" while providing jobs to foreigners at the expense of unemployed Americans. At the same time politicians with significant constituencies in the mining districts were pressed hard to limit Chinese competition in placer development.

Sounding an alarmist note in July, 1885, the *Moscow Mirror* reported that the Chinese were purchasing numerous claims and "if the work is continued the pig tails will in short time own the whole Palouse mining belt...." The article also implied, however, that the miners were willingly abandoning their workings, likely enroute to yet another rumored Eldorado.

Restrictive legislation in Washington Territory was evident as early as January of 1864 when the Legislature passed "An Act to Protect Free White Labor against Competition with Chinese Coolie Labor and to Discourage the Immigration of the Chinese in the Territory." This law established a quarterly six dollar Chinese Police Tax on every Asian in the territory with local law enforcement officials receiving 25% of the receipts as an incentive for collection. Subsequent legislation in the 1860s somewhat moderated the tax burden and guaranteed a degree of civil protection. Chinese were allowed to own property though most gained access to land for vegetable farming, mining, or other uses only through leases usually offered to them at exorbitant rates.

By 1880 the Asian population was the largest single foreign-born group in the Palouse Country with 530 Chinese residing in Whitman County and 198 in Nez Perce County which included present Latah. Accordingly, they represented 39% of the total foreign-born and 15% of the entire population in the two-county area. Virtually all were male. Their relatively large numbers, distinctive culture that tended to isolate them from the predominate European-American society, and regional economic factors combined to create a climate of suspicion and hostility toward the Chinese in the Palouse during the early 1880s. Reflecting the nascent Yellow Peril sentiment espoused nationally in labor and political circles, these tendencies were fueled by editorials in Moscow, Colfax, and Palouse newspapers appearing under such headlines as "The Chinese Curse" and "Shake the Chinese." Such articles branded the Chinese "obstreperous heathens," and, ironically, "lazy and shiftless." The effect of these conditions and the injustices directed against the Chinese during this period reduced their population in Whitman and Latah Counties to just 183 in 1890. This was not, however, until they had also labored to construct the earliest railroads throughout the Palouse Country giving the region its critical commercial link to coastal and international grain markets.

Phase Two: Chinese Labor and Palouse Railroad Construction (1870s-1880s)

The Northern Pacific Railroad first extended employment opportunities to Chinese in the spring of 1871 when 750 were hired to begin grading the line and laying track from Kalama to Tacoma. Upon completion of the task in 1873 some 2,000 had been procured through San Francisco for this purpose. Financial panics and changes in corporate leadership stalled construction through eastern Washington until 1879 when work commenced on the famed two hundred mile "Pend Oreille Division" between Ainsworth at present Pasco and Sandpoint northeast of the tiny hamlet of Spokane Falls. For this massive undertaking on one of the final links along the Northern Pacific's long-envisioned route, labor gangs were recruited through prominent contractor Kwang Tae to clear the route, pile ballast, and lay the rails. Estimates of the Chinese work force ranging as high as several thousand for the construction period 1879 to 1883.

Kwang's organization was directly linked to Six Company interests in San Francisco and the workers they supplied again lived up to the Chinese reputation for diligence and productivity. The main line skirted the northwestern periphery of the Palouse where proximity to the railroad with a monthly construction payroll as high as $20,000 brought a boon to local economies and assured a future to emerging townsites at Ritzville, Sprague, and Cheney. The Chinese working from these points were paid 85 cents a day in 1880 while European-Americans received $1.75 for the same grading and surfacing work. Track layers brought down two dollars per day and teamsters could earn as much as eight. Wherever possible railroad builders sought to obtain materials and provisions locally. Ties and trusses were purchased from sawyers in Lewiston and Palouse City while area farmers provided vegetables, meat, and other commodities.

With locomotives from Philadelphia, steel rails from England, German financing, and laborers from Ireland and China, the Northern Pacific's march across the inland Northwest was truly an international effort. The construction plan for the main force of perhaps one thousand workers involved organization suggestive of a military campaign. The army of laborers was commanded by a field superintendent for the Pend Oreille Division which was usually divided into "camps" of

*Manning Bridge Winter and Spring**   *West of Colfax, Washington*

about one hundred men under the immediate supervision of a fore-man. Most camps would be engaged in preparation of the roadbed along successive one to two mile increments while any remaining gangs usually had to contend with special challenges encountered along the route like bridging for coulees, cutting through hilly summits, or the blasting and removal of massive basalt formations. One 1,200 foot cut through solid rock near Palouse Junction required the persistent efforts of sixty men and thirty teams of horses for two dust-choking, back-breaking months. The nature and conditions of the work led to a strike by tracklayers on the line in the spring of 1881 as European immigrant workers sought a fifty cent increase in daily wages and the Chinese held out for a raise to two dollars a day. Management met most demands half-way and work soon resumed.

Construction of the Columbia and Palouse through the western Palouse often required efforts of herculean scale as Chinese laborers moved massive fractured basaltic boulders from cuts sometimes blasted to depths of thirty feet. Although railroad reports shed little light on worker safety records, blasting and landslide accidents were said to claim the lives of many Chinese who were buried in obscurity along the western Palouse route or in unmarked graves in local town cemeteries. Continuing largely with Chinese labor the Columbia & Palouse line extended to Colfax in 1883 and Moscow in 1885. In the following year the railroad stretched northward to Garfield, Tekoa, and Farmington, and by 1889 the central Palouse was encircled when the Columbia & Palouse progressed southwest to Oakesdale and St. John, meeting the original stretch at Winona. By the summer of 1891 the line to Moscow had been extended to Juliaetta via Troy and Kendrick. Extensive construction of area branch lines employing Chinese workers was also undertaken during this period including the Oregon Railway & Navigation Company link between Riparia and Lacrosse in 1888 and its line from Farmington north to Rockford and Spokane. Also completed in 1888 was the Northern Pacific's Spokane & Palouse Railroad from Spokane southward through numerous towns including Rosalia, Oakesdale, Pullman, Moscow and Genesee. A small Chinese presence was noted in virtually all these communities as late as 1894 where, likely aware that railroad construction in the area was nearing completion, some began laundries, raised vegetable gar-

PULLMAN WASHINGTON, c. 1900 (MASC, WSU LIBRARIES)

dens, or entered domestic service.

The renewed anti-Chinese sentiment expressed in the regional press in the early 1880s reflected a growing national resentment of the Chinese presence as foreign influences were said to be imperiling traditional American values and economic opportunities. Echoing racist themes prominent across the country, area newspaper editorials continued to characterize Chinese as unchristian, unclean, and undercutting fair wages. A national campaign based on such principles launched by the Workingman's Party of California sought nothing less than the total exclusion of Chinese from the country. Despite intense lobbying efforts by the major railroads, the Chinese Six Companies, and civil rights advocates, Congress enacted the Chinese Exclusion Act in 1882 citing the government's opinion that "the coming of Chinese laborers to this country endangers the good order of certain localities...." The law prohibited for ten years the further importation of Chinese laborers and forbade Chinese naturalization. It contained a clause permitting renewal which was exercised in 1892. Further extensions and subsequent exclusionary legislation effectively eliminated further immigration of Chinese laborers to the United States until the original

146

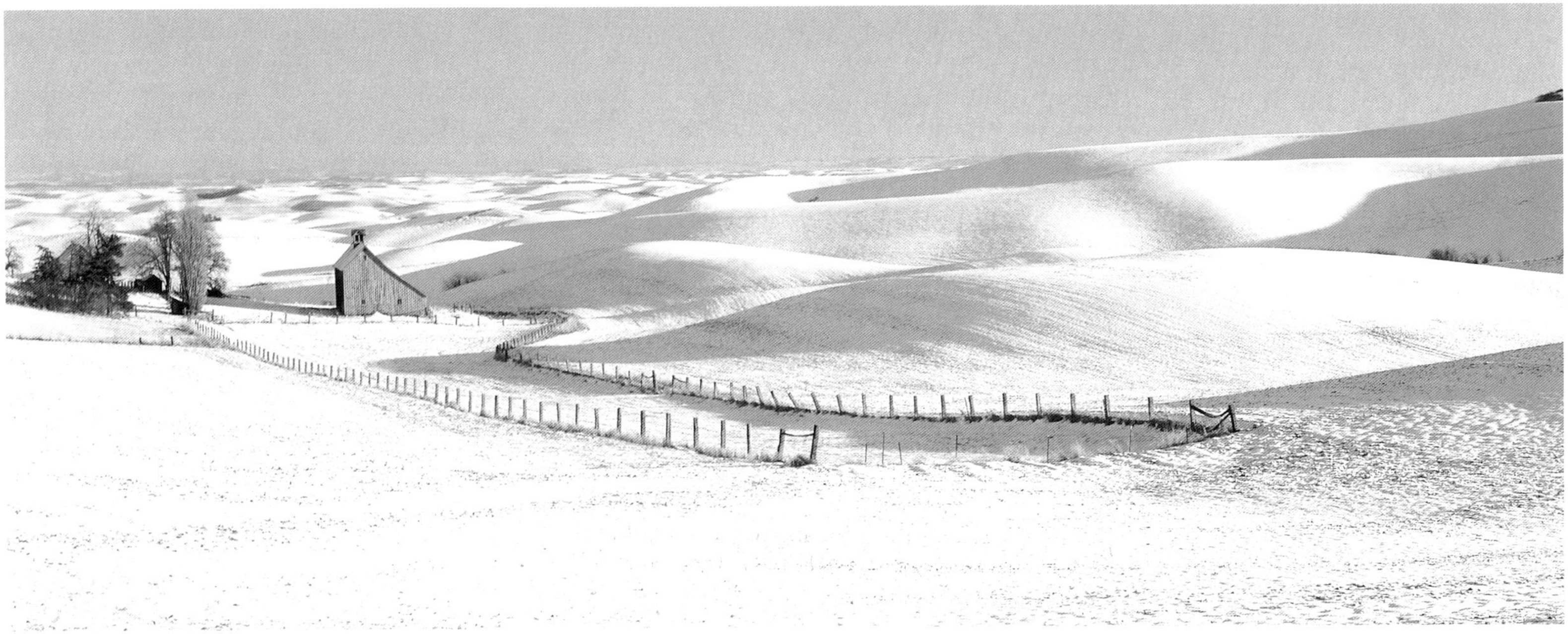

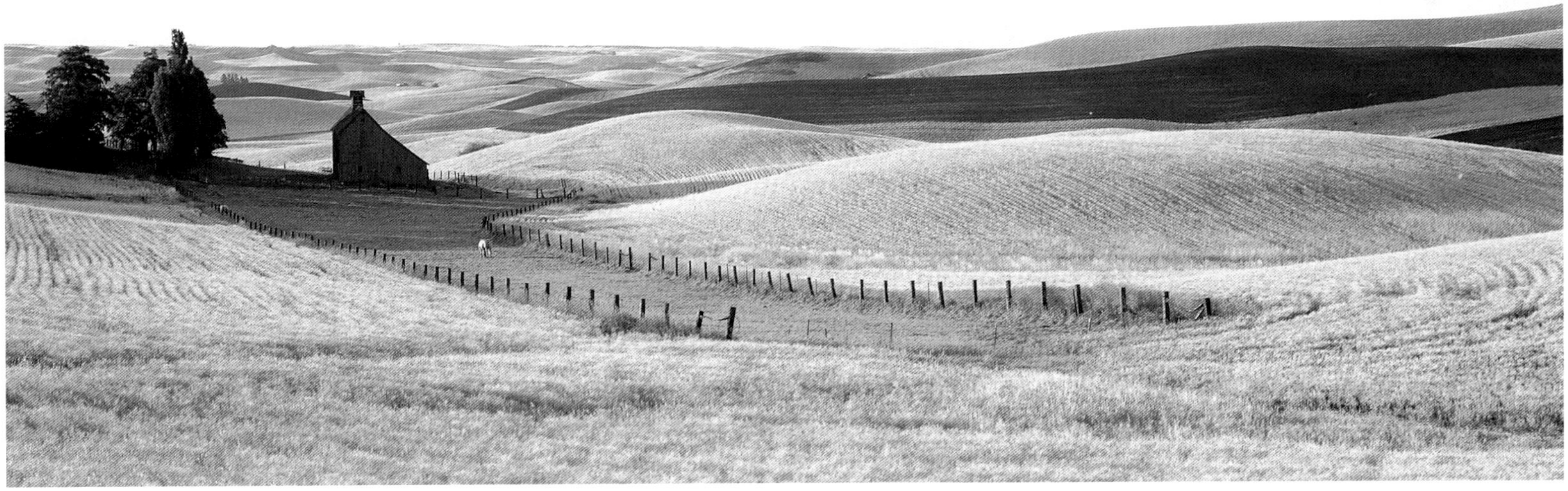

*Palouse Country Barn/Winter-Summer** *South of Moscow, Idaho*

act's repeal during the Second World War through a bill introduced by Washington State Senator Warren G. Magnuson.

If the recurrent anti-Chinese diatribe appearing in area newspapers helped fan the fires of racism, the passage of the Exclusion Act likely contributed to a wave of violent assaults directed against the Chinese throughout the Palouse. The Inland Pacific Northwest was the scene of some of the worst atrocities against the Chinese in the West. In the fall of 1884 three Chinese miners were slain near their cabin on the Palouse River a dozen miles east of Palouse City. The suspect in the case, who was observed purchasing supplies in Farmington with gold dust shortly afterward, was later tried and acquitted. Subsequently he confessed to the crime. Strychnine Creek, located a few miles upstream from the murder scene, was said to have been named after a group of Chinese were poisoned there by Americans seeking to take over their diggings. The body of a murdered Chinese miner found floating in the Snake River at Penawawa on June 5, 1887 provided the first evidence of the Deep Creek Massacre which claimed the lives of thirty-one Chinese miners from Lewiston. The men were brutally murdered in their camp some fifty miles above Lewiston about a month earlier and the slaughter was later proven to have been commit-ted by Americans seeking their gold. The outrage was widely reported in the national press and led to a diplomatic exchange between Washington and Peking on the protection of Chinese aliens in the United States and reparations for such crimes (D. Stratton, 1983).

European-Americans were given virtual free reign in the Palouse mining districts in the spring of 1890 after district court judge Willis Sweet at Mount Idaho ruled in an Elk City case that Chinese had "no rights whatever on mining lands," making any titles or leases to prop-erty by Chinese invalid. The Chinese were stunned and many in the area had already negotiated and paid for long term leases on Palouse River placers. Denied legal recourse they either acquiesced or soon were forced out by jubilant citizens. Within a year few, if any, Chinese miners remained. Most likely left the region entirely while some sought other employment in Palouse area communities. Even there many were harassed through renewed enforcement of the Chinese poll tax. Three Chinese living in the town of Palouse in 1892, for example, were arrested for failing to pay the tax. Perhaps in protest, two had

enough money to cover the charge but chose incarceration instead.

Prospects with the railroad were not without risks either during this time. In February, 1888 indignant residents of Tekoa demanded that all Chinese leave the city in protest of their employment for the construction of the O.R. &N.Co. line. Likely unaware of these events, a solitary Chinese inquired about work at the company office in town several days later but was seized by a hostile crowd and immediately hanged. Other protests were made in Rosalia the same year and eight Chinese were expelled from Colfax in February, 1889 for the same reason. Similar incidents took place in Spangle, Fairfield, Garfield, and Moscow. Sensitivities to the "foreign presence" were heightened by the Depression of 1893 and ensuing high unemployment. Viewing the problem from a socialist perspective, an editorial reprinted in Moscow's *North Idaho Star* reasoned that, "If the workman had free access to natural opportunities and owned what he produced, he would have no fear of the Chinaman as a competitor. This was the condition of things our forefathers contemplated when they declared this country to be an asylum for the discontented of all nations, and until the American workman is returned to that happy state, I hold that he has a right to protect himself from invasion by any person or class, by what-ever means may be found necessary; peaceably if he may, forcibly if he must."

Phase Three: The Palouse Chinese and Rural Community Services (1880s-1900)

The rural communities of the Palouse substantially benefited from the arrival of the railroads as the region's towns experienced a building boom in the 1880s. However, with the completion of Chinese labor contracts, and expulsion from the mining camps, the few Chinese who chose to remain in area communities congregated in enclaves desig-nated "Chinatowns." Never as populous as Lewiston's famous district of the 1880s, Palouse Country Chinatowns were nevertheless colorful neighborhoods with small shops and laundries but they also were charged by the larger community with harboring vice and corruption under a shroud of mysticism. Colfax's Chinatown, located in the vicinity of Main and Canyon Streets with tightly clustered back alley lodgings along the riverfront, probably did not exceed one hundred

Shades of Green   **From Kamiak Butte**

and fifty residents at its peak in the late 1880s. Most Chinese worked in adjacent wash houses, small shops, or at the Chinese Gardens just west of town where about a dozen Chinese tended vegetable plots and sold fresh produce locally.

The periodic arrests in the neighborhood by Marshall Mackay did little to alter the citizenry's generally low opinion of the residents. The *Palouse Gazette* carried reports on charges ranging from opium smuggling and illegal gambling to cockfighting and disturbing the peace when Chinese New Year's celebrations got out of hand. In April, 1892 the *Colfax Commoner* decried a "large opium-joint" said to be located on Main Street near the Railroad Avenue bridge. "The rooms are divided off into smoking apartments and each table bed is provided with a complete opium-smoking outfit." Claiming that paraphernalia might harbor "the germs of leprosy," the editor urged local police to use "rigid measures" to punish both keepers and visitors. That same spring the newspaper reported the murder of Twin No at the hands of fellow railroad section hand Ah Loy in Endicott.

That the Chinese community experienced more than its share of conflict was due in large part to the "bachelor society" that denied Chinese a stable family life in America. In the Palouse as elsewhere in the Northwest, the Chinese community during the late nineteenth century was overwhelmingly male as both custom and later United States law militated against women immigrating to the country with their husbands. For this reason many married men like Owen Eng's father, Gin Sing, endured trans-Pacific crossings on several occasions. Finding conditions there little changed during the closing decade of the nineteenth century, Gin invariably returned to the American West to work as a cook and laborer in various mining camps and towns. The few women who did come usually were brought illegally for servitude. Intermarriage with Caucasians was strongly condemned. By 1900 Chinese males outnumbered Chinese females in Washington 26 to 1 and the average ages of both groups continued to climb since the Chinese Exclusion Act had effectively prevented family perpetuation (E. Erickson and E. Ng, 1989).

The absence of conventional social and cultural institutions led to the formation of organizations similar to fraternal orders known as tongs, from a Chinese term for hall or meeting place. Although organized in cities to help meet the social and economic needs of a group ostracized from the larger society, tongs in America also came to be associated with illegal activities and public fears over the designation of geographic spheres of foreign influence. These viewpoints surfaced in the 1893 trial of Lee Doon in Colfax who was charged with the attempted murder of Charlie Lee, a popular cook at Colfax's Baldwin Hotel, a heated argument. The Colfax Commoner reported the trial preliminaries in lurid detail which featured oaths of Chinese incantations and the sprinkling of blood from a half-dozen decapitated chickens. Through the proceedings the public learned that the men were members of rival tongs and that organization representatives from Tekoa, Spokane, and Walla Walla had been in Colfax offering advice to both parties.

The *Commoner* observed that, "This bloody association of Mongolians has recently terrorized San Francisco with a series of horrible assassinations" and speculated that similar events might transpire in the back streets of Colfax before a tong war would end. The jury ultimately found the defendant guilty and the judge, lamenting that the case had attracted so much attention, sentenced Lee to a single year in prison. Bloodshed was averted and paranoia over the anticipated tong war soon subsided. As in other pioneer communities, however, Chinatowns in the Palouse were also susceptible to calamities given their usual frame construction and proximity to the waterfront. According to Gin Sing, Lewiston's Chinatown was virtually wiped out by fire in 1883 and similar devastation was visited upon Colfax in 1881 and 1892. The flood of 1893 also forced many Chinese to abandon their neighborhood. Colfax's Chinatown never fully recovered from the effects of these final disasters.

Moscow's Chinatown emerged in the middle 1880s and consisted of several laundries, small shops, and apartments in the vicinity of Jackson and "A" Streets. The wash houses regularly advertised their services to "renovate and rejuvenate garments" in local newspapers with the most operating at any one time being four in 1886 under the proprietorships of Git Wing, Sam Lee, Sin Chin, and Wah Lee. As in Colfax, Moscow's Chinese found employment cooking and cleaning at various establishments like the Hotel Moscow, Hotel Del Norte, and in restaurants and saloons while others worked as domestic servants. By 1890 the populations of Colfax and Moscow had reached 1,649 and 2,000, respectively. On the fertile bottomland adjacent to both cities, Chinese took advantage of consumers' needs by tending large vegetable gardens and carrying fresh produce around the towns in characteristic balanced basket fashion on six-foot hardwood poles to sell throughout the spring and summer (P. Wegars, 1986).

Other Chinese in the Palouse worked in gardens and orchards at Almota, Wawawai, and elsewhere on the Snake River where, following initial plantings in the 1870s, the trees reached maturity in the Eighties and Nineties. During the peak work seasons in summer and fall Chinese would pack baskets of cherries, apples, and other fruit, carry it in traditional style to receiving wagons, and prepare the fruit for shipment from the packing houses to coastal and Eastern markets. Both Almota and Wawawai had their "China Houses" in the 1890s. A former two-story hotel in Almota met housing needs while the former Jesse Burgess home in Wawawai served as a popular residence for members of the local Chinese labor force and provided havens for others in transit across the region (E. Gay, 1975).

With the passage of the Geary Act in 1892, Congress extended the exclusionary provisions enacted ten years earlier and added a requirement that all Chinese possess an identification certificate indicating their length of residence in the country or face deportation. The provision was aimed at expelling Chinese laborers who had managed to enter the country during the previous ten years. These developments were strongly endorsed in the Colfax Commoner which also carried the story of the Chinese deportation from Bonners Ferry, Idaho on June 6, 1892 where citizens met to demand "the removal of the Chinese already here and positive exclusion. . . hereafter." That night about fifty were forced on two Great Northern boxcars and taken away.

The impossible task of registering all Chinese under the Geary Act fell to Internal Revenue collectors who reported 105 Chinese in Colfax in 1894, twenty in Pullman, and lesser numbers in Palouse City, Oakesdale, Garfield, and Winona. These political initiatives served the purposes of organized labor and nativist advocates by renewing anti-Chinese prejudice and sparking a new wave of persecutions and boycotts. A November, 1893 issue of the Commoner recommended "no better way of settling this vexed question than by a united boycott against these pig-tailed heathens in every city and community on the coast. With such a boycott in force it would not be very long until a large majority could be compelled... to return to their native land, or to emigrate into eastern states and cities where the evil of their presence are [sic] not now understood."

The combined effects of the public outcry for their removal, widespread harassment by ill-tempered citizens, restrictive legislation, reduced employment opportunities, and natural disasters in the Palouse caused a Chinese exodus from the region in the 1890s. While the seemingly low number of 183 Chinese appears from the 1890 census for Whitman and Latah Counties, this number dropped to just 114 in 1900 and to only twenty-two in 1910. During that decade Chinese labor gangs joined Greeks and Italians to construct the Camas Prairie Railroad along the river's north bank from Riparia to Lewiston. The Chinese population declined to its lowest level in the two-county area in 1920 when only fifteen were counted but rose to thirty by the end of the next decade. Several Chinese families from Spokane and Lewiston like that of Owen Eng's later reestablished restaurant businesses in Colfax, Pullman, and Moscow beginning successful enterprises that have continued in operation to the present time.

The Palouse Japanese Community

Although the size of the Japanese community in the Palouse has always been small relative to the entire population, their number in the two-county area nearly equalled that of the Chinese in 1900 (114 Chinese, 107 Japanese) and exceeded other Asian groups during the first several decades of the twentieth century. These circumstances were likely in response to the Chinese exodus from the region in the 1890s during which time the first Japanese settled in the Palouse to assume

ORIENTAL CAFÉ, PULLMAN (MASC, WSU LIBRARIES)

roles as vegetable farmers, railroad workers, and laborers. Effectively sealed off from Western contact from the expulsion of Dutch traders in 1640 to the reception of Commodore Perry's historic mission in 1853, the Japanese people did not experience the tumult of European partition and fratricidal wars as was known in nineteenth-century China.

Japanese society was cohesive and stable although the collapse of the Tokugawa Shoganate in 1868 ushered in a period of sweeping political change. The restoration of authority in the Meiji emperor led to the end of samuri rights, the reorganization of land in prefectures, and access to foreign ideas and international trade. Concurrently, new economic policies tended to adversely affect Japanese farmers at a time when the nation was overwhelmingly agrarian. Changes in land tenure led to unemployment in some areas. Deflationary pressures reduced prices for rice and other commodities, and a series of natural disasters wreaked havoc on the population and crops in central Honshu, the main island of the Japanese chain. For these reasons, thousands of Japanese chose to relocate to Hawaii in the 1880s where they worked as contract laborers on sugar plantations.

With the annexation of Hawaii by the United States in 1898, Japanese workers there were able to immigrate to the West Coast where they found higher paying jobs in railroad building and the timber industry while others established small farms. Soon Japanese were journeying directly to the Pacific Northwest from the homeland which, as with most immigrants, was an experience both poignant and auspicious. These twin themes were eloquently expressed in a poem written by Kenji Abe, a Japanese immigrant in Pullman who first found employment on the railroads in 1906 (G. Nomura, 1988).

In his "Ode on Leaving my Home Town," Abe wrote:

Over the horizon of the wide Pacific
Entertaining high ambitions,

*Palouse Pastels**

East of Colfax, Washington

I looked for eternal happiness.
Great love..., huge efforts...,
Large land..., vast sky...
I survey my future path.
On my two shoulders I bear a mission;
In my heart hope swells.
Goodbye, my home country.

With the Chinese increasingly driven from their homes in the Palouse in the 1890s through exclusionist legislation and public harassment, small numbers of Japanese began entering the region. In some instances they were hired for section gangs as railroad construction and repair work continued through the eastern Palouse. Although the Japanese government was influential enough to prevent Congress from enacting exclusionary legislation directed against its people until 1924, both Japanese and Chinese were included under appellation "Asian" or "Mongolian" that connoted undesirable status to many European-Americans during this period. Among the Japanese, moreover, no ethnic labor-contracting organizations existed like the Chinese Six Companies to facilitate their employment in the country.

Japenese without independent initiative or personal contacts were often at the mercy of such businesses as the Northwestern Employment Agency and All Nations Employment Agency, both with offices in Spokane, which despite the latter's name, spurned Japanese workers in favor of Northern Europeans. "Scandinavian Labor is our Specialty" proclaimed its letterhead. Nevertheless, when the growing labor requirements for the enterprising Potlatch Lumber Company exceeded the usual supply, the employment agencies found Japanese workers for the firm. The lumber company was organized in 1903 by Weyerhaeuser interests and was headquartered in Potlatch, Idaho where timber from the massive white pine stands from the Clearwater and Bitterroot Mountains were milled. Japanese laborers were hired in 1902 to construct the Potlatch Lumber Company's Washington, Idaho & Montana line from Potlatch eastward tapping prized timber and hardrock mining districts. Others were employed that same year on railroad construction in eastern Spokane and Whitman Counties.

Japanese in the Palouse also engaged in truck farming after the turn of the century, occasionally hired out for farmwork, and began food and service related business in several communities. A Japanese restaurant opened in Palouse in 1907 and others followed in Moscow and Pullman. Although legislative and cultural circumstances continued to contribute to the decline in the Chinese "bachelor society" population after 1900 in the Palouse, the number of Japanese rose from 107 at the beginning of the century to 126 a decade later. Perhaps more interested and willing to engage in farming than other Asians who immigrated earlier to the Palouse, most Japanese arrived only after most agricultural lands had already been claimed. Accordingly, their population also steadily declined after 1910 and fell to sixty-seven in 1920.

The problem of land ownership by Japanese was further compounded in the 1920s when, during another era of nativistic fervor, the Washington State Legislature passed the anti-Japanese Alien Property Bill in 1923 to specifically prevent Japanese farmers from owning land. The legislature also petitioned Congress to include Japan on the list of immigrant excluded nations. The Immigration Act of 1924 legitimized this sentiment and denied naturalization rights to the Issei, those immigrants born in Japan. Due in part to these developments, the Japanese population in Whitman and Latah Counties dropped to just forty-eight in 1930 and stabilized near that level until events during the War years further reduced the number of one of the Palouse Country's most industrious yet maligned minorities.

OWEN ENG
COLFAX, WASHINGTON

Familiar to countless patrons for his masterful culinary talents, Own Eng worked in Colfax restaurants for decades until his retirement in the 1970s. He provided the following interview in 1989 with assistance of historian and translator Eddy Ng.

My father and grandfather came to America long before I was born and they lived in San Francisco and other places in the West. My father, Gin Sing, stayed in America although he returned to China about three times to see his family in the village of Teishan, where I was born in 1911. It is a rice farming area located a short distance south of Canton. My grandfather's name was Ken Hock and after working as a laborer for a long time, maybe with the railroad, he decided to come back to his home in China. I remember him well in my youth there for we all lived together in one big house. He told me America was *Gum Sam*, the "Land of Golder Mountains," and that those who worked hard could return to China and enjoy a good life with their savings.

I decided to go to the United States by myself in 1933 when I was twenty-two years old. I was married and had a son and a daughter but the work there was very hard and I thought my life would be better in America. But the laws would not let me bring my wife at that time and so it happened that we became separated for fifty years! First It was the laws here until the war and then after the war the government in China changed and would not allow it. Finally in 1974 she was able to join me.

I crossed the ocean in a British ship in 1933 but it was not easy for me to live on the boat with seasickness and everything. I went from Canton to Hong Kong and then across the Pacific to Seattle. This trip took nearly a month and I brought only a blanket. At that time my father was working in Orofino and we had written to each other so he came to Seattle and waited there to meet me. He had left San Francisco about 1905 after the big earthquake and first moved to Lewiston. He had a cousin who had gone there earlier. Their folks were from the same are a in China. He worked in a restaurant there for a while and then went to Orofino where there were mining camps in the old days. My father had a little restaurant there and I went to work right away and helped him and learned about the work. There were not many Chinese in Orofino and he decided to move back to Lewiston in 1935. We worked in the Majestic Restaurant which was well known as a fine place in Lewiston's Chinatown. There were Chinese laundries, shops, and restaurants and some small vegetable farmers....

A few years later I came to Colfax. In the 1930s there were a few Chinese in Colfax mostly working in the hotels. Others grew vegetables in the Chinese Gardens outside of town along the river. Maybe there were a few other Chinese in Pullman and Moscow. I didn't stay very long the first time and went on before and after the war to work in restaurants and hotels in Great Falls, Montana, Spokane, and Seattle. Spokane had a small Chinatown at that time down along Washington Street. Then in the early 1960s I returned to Colfax and went to work for Pete Eng at his restaurant where I cooked for many years. My wife, Yuen Kam, finally joined me here about ten years later. I am glad that I came to Colfax; it is a nice place to live.

Chapter VI:

THE EMPIRE GERMANS AND SWISS

"She feared the Indians, the coyotes, the treelessness..., the horses and cattle roaming, the wide open, unfenced country—
in fact, everything about the new life was terrifying to Mother."

—Bertha Williams, 1975

Of the more than twenty million European immigrants who entered the United States during the nineteenth century, by far the largest number came from the German Empire. In contrast to emigrant groups such as the Irish and southern Europeans who largely spurned a life in rural American, many Germans actively sought it. Given the long history of German immigration to the United States beginning with the first great wave in the 1830s, German families understandably among the first to settle in the Palouse Country. The number of those coming to the Palouse steadily increased from the time of their arrival in the early 1870s, and by 1900 they constituted the largest foreign-born element in the Palouse.

Many factors in nineteenth century Germany influenced decisions to emigrate: over-population in the farming districts and high unemployment in the cities, rapid industrialization in the middle of the nineteenth century which left thousands of artisans destitute, failure of the potato crop in southwestern Germany in 1846-47, and the social revolutions of 1848. Many of the first German families settling in the Palouse Country emigrated during the late 1860s and early 1870s. This period corresponds to the time of the great wars of Prussia and the resulting turmoil in the various German states experienced until being molded into a new nation after the Franco-Prussian War of 1870. To a growing landless class, the perpetual threat of military service contrasted greatly to the reports of free homesteads to immigrants in a neutral land across the ocean. In 1866 over 100,000 Germans emigrated and the number increased to an average of 130,000 annually until 1873. A fourth wave began in 1880 and continued for five years which was followed by a shorter rise from 1891-92, when a total of 244,000 Germans immigrated to the United States.

Bertha Williams, whose father led a group of German immigrants to the Palouse in 1886, visited her father's birthplace in Schleswig-

Holstein in 1908 and remarked that she still found the same conditions there that had compelled George Engelland to leave a quarter of a century earlier. "Farm land and opportunity were in short supply," she recalled, "and again the storm clouds of war on the continent were gathering." Like thousands of others, Engelland had chosen to participate in what a 1901 editorial in Chicago's *Record-Herald* called America's "era of land speculation, town-building, and westward movement. These conditions were made known in Germany. Cheap lands, light taxes, the need of laborers, and the opportunity to gain a competence in a short time by toil—these were the conditions that attracted the Germans."

Origins of the Colton-Uniontown Catholic Germans

The first Germans to settle in large numbers in the Palouse were from a colony of Catholic families that passed through the area on the Kentuck Trail in 1867 enroute to the Willamette Valley. Many would later return, however, to resettle in the Palouse Country. One of the leaders of the original colony, Michael Schultheis, was the son of German emigrants who lived near Jefferson City, Missouri, in 1840 but had relocated to Stearns County, Minnesota in 1857. They were drawn to the upper Midwest by reports of newly opened lands for homesteaders. Bishop Magloire Blanchet, a French-Canadian priest who was bishop of Washington Territory's Nisqually Diocese, visited with the Stearns County Catholic families in the fall of 1866 after they had spent nearly a decade "grubbing brush." The bishop intended to raise support for his mission work and recruit in order to populate his sparsely settled diocese which extended from Fort Colville to Walla Walla (J. Kleinz, 1960).

Father Blanchet's tales of the Northwest generated considerable enthusiasm among the disgruntled German farmers who were not sat-

Needs Paint

South of Union Town, Washington

isfied with the climate and soil conditions on the Minnesota frontier. After weeks of consideration a group decided to head westward and reached Fort Abercrombie on the Dakota border the last week of June, 1867. There, these eighteen families learned that a larger train under the leadership of "Captain" P. D. Davey was expected shortly and was to travel the same route they intended to take. A decision was made to remain and travel with the Davey train although it did not arrive until two weeks later.

Davey's plan called for departing St. Cloud, Minnesota on May 15th so that they would have enough time to travel safely over the Northern Plains route to Helena City, Montana. He announced through the Minneapolis newspapers that spring that he was forming a train and also circulated a number of handbills. According to the terms of the travel contract, "every passenger paid $125.00 and received therefore free transportation, care and 50 pounds of luggage free. The teams were to be hitched with oxen. To every wagon were assigned 4 passengers, a driver and one cook." Rumors were circulating about the hazards of travel through Indian country and for this reason all were expected to arm themselves.

The various parties assembled on June 25th and departed for Fort Abercrombie where the German Catholic families had been waiting to join the main group. The full column was now composed of three groups: Davey's train of Americans, Swedes, Norwegians and others who were heading for the Montana gold fields; the German train of twenty-six wagons enroute for Oregon; and a United States Army supply train of sixteen wagons under the command of a government contractor, H. Hager, who was taking a herd of about 100 beef oxen to the forts along the Missouri River. A company of infantry escorting this latter group provided protection for the entire column. The civilians were organized into specific companies each electing officers and establishing night watches and guards.

The German train departed Fort Abercrombie on July 12th and was followed the next day by the other groups. The slow but steady speed of the wagon train paced by the oxen continued over hundreds of miles of Dakota and Montana grasslands. The various perils associated with overland wagon routes were meticulously recorded in the journal of Henry Lueg, a Prussian-born emigrant of 1861 who accom-

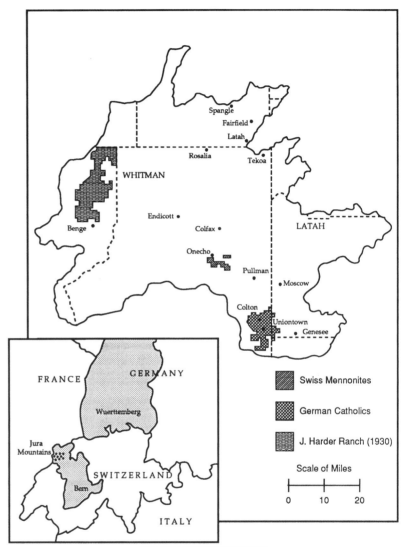

THE JURA MOUNTAIN REGION, SWITZERLAND AND ONECHO, WASHINGTON, c. 1890

panied the Davey train to Montana and then joined the German Catholics on the final portion of the trip to Oregon. After two weeks, according to Lueg, Davey showed himself to be "a drunken and care-

157

less person," and he demanded payment from the German train for his services as guide. The Germans, however, traveling ahead in a separate group, felt under no obligation to him.

After three months of burdensome travel plagued by hordes of mosquitoes, harassed by drunken soldiers, troubled by Indians attempting to stampede their livestock and slowed by enormous buffalo herds blocking their route, the column finally reached Helena City, Montana where Davey brought suit against the Germans for failing to pay his fee of $612. The argument was settled in a court in which the cause of the Germans was championed by Lueg. The judge ruled in their favor, but they had been delayed four extra weeks and the winter snows were rapidly approaching in the mountains. Meanwhile, as Lueg noted, "several others came into the camp, among them a Catholic priest from Helena, who baptized a child that had been born at Fort Ransom. The priest also arranged to celebrate Mass because the entire membership of the German train belonged to the Roman Catholic Church". Several German families decided to remain in Helena City, but on October 11th the remainder of the German train, sixteen families in twenty-one wagons, left for Oregon with Frank Niebler serving as guide. Three other wagons continued on with them. German members of the train included Niebler's other brothers, Michael and George, Michael Schultheis, J.B. Wittman, P. Jacobs, and J. Schoffen.

The train lumbered on alone over the Rocky Mountains following the distance markers to Walla Walla which had been carved in trees along the Mullan Road by the grading crews a decade earlier. Lueg noted that "the trip through the mountains is exceptionally hard on man and beast." On the Hell Gate they encountered the jagged cliffs of the river, and by the end of the month several of the children were ill with mountain fever, one of whom died shortly thereafter. By early November the group was running dangerously low on food. They remained briefly at the Coeur d'Alene Mission to celebrate Mass and repair the wagons. On November 14th they reached Spokane Bridge where those in need were able to purchase provisions from two local suppliers.

They decided to travel the Kentuck Trail to Walla Walla journeying through the heart of the Palouse Country. The group first camped at the "California Ranch," one of the earliest farms in that area, located about twelve miles southwest of Spokane Bridge. On November 17th, they continued on and Lueg noticed a gradual change in the local topography: "Crossed a number of soft hills with open woods. The soil is very rich and not in the slightest rocky." The road led through present Freeman and the men cut wood for campfires on Hangman Creek since none was available on the treeless prairie, much of which had been burnt due to the carelessness of previous travelers. The travelers continued southwesterly and passed near the present sites of Rosalia and Thornton and on the 20th they descended into the Palouse River canyon at a point near Joseph DeLong's farmstead. Lueg's journal mentions the presence of a ranch there, and he recorded, "the valley here looks very romantic. On the other side of the river are high, steep rock cliffs. As there are no bridges at hand, we must drive through the river." On the following morning the river was forded and they traveled under threatening skies to a point near present Dusty where they camped for the night.

The pathfinders reached the Snake River on the afternoon of the 22nd, and the group ferried across three and four wagons at a time on a crudely built barge which slowly moved across the wide river. The train had traveled over seventy-five miles through the Palouse Country and many of the German farmers probably observed with Lueg that, "the soil all around here is very rich and fertile." Several days later the weary pioneers finally arrived in Walla Walla. There the train dispersed with some families, including the Schultheises, Wittmans, and Nieblers continuing on to St. Louis, Oregon, a small farming community on the Willamette Valley's French Prairie. The group had covered nearly 1900 miles in five months and ten days in an epic journey undertaken by some of the region's earliest pioneers. Tales of hardships and highlights during the trek would be recounted in some Palouse families for generations.

After five difficult years on the French Prairie, many of the German Catholic families were dissatisfied with the climate and farming conditions in the rain shadow of the Cascades. About 1873 the Michael Schultheis family moved to Walla Walla where he found temporary employment while exploring possibilities for settlement in the region. Schultheis learned that the best lands in the Walla Walla

Valley had already been claimed, but the local parish priest, Father Thomas Duffy, told him that vast areas in the fertile Palouse Hills were still available and worthy of his consideration. Schultheis was not unfamiliar with the Palouse since his journey eight years earlier had taken him directly through the region. In the spring of 1875, the family again loaded up a wagon and traveled northeast from Walla Walla and forded the river at Lewiston. They continued up the steep grade and on to Union Flat where they arrived in April. Schultheis vowed that if it would snow that first night on the isolated prairie, they would return immediately to Walla Walla. A grandson later recalled the story of how his grandmother "never prayed for snow so hard as she did that night...." But no snowfall came, and the family decided to remain, squatting on unsurveyed land near present Uniontown, Washington (A. Bauer, 1971).

They moved into an abandoned cabin nearby and planted a large garden, the seeds for which had been thoughtfully purchased in Walla Walla. They raised potatoes, green and yellow beans, wedge peas, carrots, onion, rutabagas, cabbage, and corn and found that everything would grow well in the fertile lowland soil but was susceptible to frost damage. For preserves, the women and children gathered wild gooseberries, elderberries, and serviceberries. The bunchgrass was broken up slowly into small fields which were sown to flax for several years producing a beautiful panorama of blue blossoms every summer. At first flax commanded a higher price than wheat, but its value soon declined.

To build his own cabin, Schultheis cut timber in the forested areas to the east and hauled them to his homesite. The family was heartened to learn that other German families had settled nearby in the vicinity of present Genesee, which began as a small townsite in 1875. About 1876 a number of German Catholic families, following Schultheis's example, began settling along upper Union Flat Creek. Among these were the Schoffen, Wittman, and Jacobs families who also had come through the Palouse on the 1867 trek. Other German families, both Catholic and Protestant, who had settled in that vicinity by the spring of 1878 included John Jacob Schlee, John Hoefer, Conrad Tuschoff, Joseph Greif, and over a dozen others as settlement expanded along Union Flat, Thorn, and Cow Creeks. Most were natives of Westphalia,

Nassau, Bavaria, Baden, and the Rhineland.

The Germans both raised livestock and farmed. The first crops raised on the flats were flax, wheat, oats, and barley. The Germans fertilized their fields with manure which was not then a universal practice in the area. Grain was hauled to Lapwai and Lewiston where wheat sold for 35¢ to 50¢ a bushel in the mid-1870s. Most of the German settlers planted small orchards of apples, cherries, pears, prunes, and other fruit. Garden produce was stored through winter in large underground cellars. Old World methods such as mortise and tenon construction were sometimes used in framing large barns with hand trimmed, heavy beams. The site of Uniontown was surveyed in 1879 and a quarry was later dug nearby. A large brick kiln in town provided an economical building material. Early businesses owned by Germans included Peter Jacobs's Brewery, Wieber Blacksmithing, and the Greif Distillery. The neighboring community of Colton was also platted in 1879 as heavy German settlement was also taking place in that vicinity. A flour mill was constructed there in 1880 and in 1884 a cheese factory was built by C.M. Wolfard although it only operated for a short time (F. Yoder, n.d., and G. Druffel, 1977).

The German Catholics continued to be a devout people in their new home, building permanent structures for worship whenever possible. In 1875, the year that German Catholic settlement began in the

UNIONTOWN CATHOLIC SISTERS, c. 1915 (MASC, WSU LIBRARIES)

Rolling Palouse Fall

North of Genesee, Idaho

region, Bishop Blanchet of Nisqually assigned the Palouse Country to the Walla Walla Parish, under the jurisdiction of Father Thomas Duffy. Duffy's assistant, Father John B. Brondel, convinced his superior to allow the families in the Uniontown area to construct a church and by March, 1878 thirty-eight men had pledged their support "towards building a Catholic Church at Upper Union Flat." The structure was completed in the spring of 1879 and was named for the great English missionary to Germany, Saint Boniface. In April, 1882 the parish received its first permanent pastor, Father D. M. Cesari, and on a Sunday in October the resounding echoes of anvils announced the dedication of the new church. In 1885 St. Andrew's Convent and Parochial School opened in Uniontown under German-speaking Benedictine Sisters from Switzerland who remained there until 1894 when they moved into a new motherhouse in Colton where one year earlier, Saint Gall's Catholic Church had been built.

The Latah County German Community

Although the German settlers along upper Union Flat Creek during the 1870s were predominantly Catholic, large numbers of German Protestants were settling in the Genesee area as early as 1874. Among the first to settle near Genesee was the family of Christian and Fredericka Scharnhorst. Both were natives of Germany but had immigrated as children to America. Scharnhorst lived in Keokuk County, Iowa, and later relocated to Kansas where in 1872 he decided to cross the Plains with his family. They traveled in a train of sixteen wagons to the Willamette Valley but two years later settled on land about six miles west of Genesee near the present Washington-Idaho line. He acquired considerable property in the vicinity by homesteading, preempting, and establishing a timber culture all on adjoining lands. The Scharnhorsts had eight children, characteristic

of the large family size common to many pioneer families who settled in the Palouse.

Other pioneer German families in the Genesee vicinity included those of Theodore Kluss (1877), Charles Ebel (1878), Christ Burger (1879), and Christian Wahl (1880). Most of these people were Lutheran and in the following decade (1888) they established St. John's German Lutheran Church in Genesee. In the same year Emmanuel German Lutheran Church was organized in Cameron. German Protestant settlement expanded during the 1880s eastward into the Juliaetta and Kendrick districts and to the northwest in the vicinities of Uniontown, Moscow, Palouse, and Endicott. All four of these communities became preaching points for German Lutheran missionaries in the late 1880s.

German Settlement in Spokane County and the Rosalia Area

The other area in the Palouse that experienced heavy settlement by Empire German Protestants was the southeastern corner of present Spokane County. In this vicinity were located the tiny hamlets of Spangle, Fairfield, Waverly, Latah, and in northeastern Whitman County, Rosalia. In 1887 two separate groups of German settlers arrived in this area to begin a major influx of German farmers. The Frederick Kienbaums, August Sassenhagens, and Ferdinand Pagels were all German immigrant families who had settled in Nebraska in the 1870s. Sassenhagen and Kienbaum had first located in Illinois in 1864 and 1866, respectively, while Pagel had immigrated from Germany to Wisconsin in 1869. Eventually they all moved to the same vicinity of northern Dodge County, Nebraska, until repeated crop failures led them, like thousands of other frustrated farmers, to migrate to the Pacific Northwest. In 1877 they traveled together over the Union Pacific transcontinental line to California

Genesee Luthern   *North of Genesee, Idaho*

and then journeyed to Walla Walla. The men found employment at a local ranch but met a fellow whose brother-in-law, John Kelso, had just settled on Hangman Creek near present Waverly. He had reported good land available in the area for prospective settlers. Anxious to find land of their own, this word-of-mouth news induced the trio to explore the territory, and each of the men secured preemptions on adjacent quarter sections near Hangman Creek between present Fairfield and Latah. They returned to Walla Walla and transported their families by wagon to their new homes along with a small herd of cattle. There were very few settlers in the area at that time and the pioneers began at once to break the heavy sod. They fashioned crude harrows out of bunches of thorn bushes which were fastened to long poles and dragged them over the fields after hand broadcast seeding. The Germans procured seed oats from Major R.N. Wimpy, a pioneer of 1872 who had settled on Hangman Creek (G. Adams, 1960).

Another group of Germans that settled in the upper Palouse Country in 1877 included the families of John Schloatz and George Horlacher and Horlacher's sister, Barbara. After coming from Germany, they also had first settled in the Midwest, but adverse conditions induced them to relocate to Astoria, Oregon. They moved again and temporarily lived in a dugout about four miles south of present Rosalia until they obtained lumber to build houses on homesteaded land nearby. The Horlachers also procured a timber culture and planted about twenty acres of box elder, dogwood, and locust trees which remain today as one of the last timber cultures extant in the central Palouse. The western Oregon press reported immigration news frequently in the 1870s, especially as the

ANDREW AND ALMA RICHTER, c. 1915
(MASC, WSU LIBRARIES)

flow increased in the latter part of the decade. In 1877 an article in the *Corvallis Gazette* stated that, "A steady tide of immigration is pouring into the Palouse Country" and predicted that within "a few years more," grain producing there would greatly increase.

Other German families continued coming to the Palouse in the late 1870s as many who settled in the upper Palouse in 1877 corresponded with friends and relatives in the Midwest and Europe and induced some to join them. Most were natives of Wuertenburg, Pomerania, and Schleswig-Holstein. Some of the German pioneers were bachelors who preferred to marry German women but found it necessary to advertise in newspapers in Germany to find them. Albert Mestermann, a native of Mecklenberg who had settled near present Tekoa about 1879, found his bride in this manner as did at least other Germans. Early German settlers who followed to the Rosalia-Tekoa area included Hans Mumm, Jacob Blank, Christian Imhoff, and Frederich Widman. In 1888 members of this group organized the first German Methodist Church in the Palouse Country under Presiding Elder George Hartung. Their first church building was constructed in 1899 under the leadership of Reverend George Bucholz (B. Williams, 1987; J. Blank, 1987).

German settlement continued to spread throughout southeastern Spokane County in the late 1870s and early 1880s along a wide band from Spangle to Tekoa. Among the earliest German settlers were Claus Jurgens, John Steen, Gottfried Hein, Neil Kahlke, and Charles Asmus in the Waverly area in 1874; Theodore Schneider to Plaza in 1879; Peter Desgranges to the Rockford area in 1880, Frederich Suksdorf of Spangle, and George Engelland to Tekoa in 1883. In 1887 many of the German farmers in this part of the Palouse joined together to form the *Gegenzeitige Deutsche Feuerversicherung* (Mutual German Fire Insurance Company), later the German Mutual Assistance Association of Spokane and Whitman Counties. The organization also had many subscribers in Idaho and did much to protect the investments of the German-American homesteaders.

As enclaves of German settlement expanded, the immigrants often joined together to establish churches with services conducted in the native tongue. As early as 1885, the Reverend Henry Schuknecht, a circuit-riding preacher in the German Evangelical Church began ministering to a group of families in the small community of Latah, which he described in 1885 as containing "a school house, store, grist mill, photographer's tent and saloon." The congregation continued to expand and in 1902 they organized German Zion Evangelical Church. Another influx of Germans occurred between 1903 and 1904 when the Wolf, Janson, Bippes, Haxmon, and Rahm families settled in the Latah vicinity. Christ Lutheran Church was founded by Germans in Fairfield in 1890 (W. Steveke, 1957).

The German Stockmen of the Western Palouse

Germans also settled around the turn of the century in the drier and sparsely populated western Palouse where the families of Andrew Richter, William Weidrich, Harm Schlommer, Alexander Siegel, and Jacob Harder applied a cultural propensity for hard work to establish an enduring presence. Perhaps the first German family to settle in this area was Phillip Fuchs and his widowed sister Elizabeth Gastrich, natives of Bochum, Germany who settled on lower Union Flat in 1879. Gastrich's ten-year-old daughter, Susanna, accompanied her mother and uncle on the long journey across the Atlantic and Isthmus of Panama where they boarded another vessel bound for San Francisco. The tiny party of intrepid foreigners eventually reached Washington Territory where they heard fertile lands were available for homesteading and selected property on the stream north of present LaCrosse. In 1882 brothers Albert and Charles Guske came to America from Stettin, Germany as stowaways aboard a ship destined for New York. They then journeyed to the home an older brother in Iowa but the newcomers decided to push west after hearing about opportunities for employment and acquiring land through the Northern Pacific Railroad. They arrived in the Palouse in 1883 and worked at grading railroad beds for the growing network of the N. P.'s Oregon Railway & Navigation Company lines in the area. In 1890 Albert Guske married Susanna Gastrich, whose mother had died four years earlier. Albert farmed with Susanna's Uncle Phillip and the family gradually expanded their holdings along Union Flat Creek (V. Guske, 1989).

The earliest pioneers in the area west of the lower Palouse in Franklin, Whitman, and Adams counties faced two formidable challenges to securing a viable livelihood. Since most of this district received less than 12 inches of annual precipitation, homesteaders usually confined their work to stockraising in the coulees and broad prairies of scattered sagebrush and bunchgrass. Large tear-shaped islands of fertile loessial soil rose among the seas of lichen-covered glacial boulders and desiccated alkali playa. Successful farming of these places would require decades of trial, error, and research in appropriate tillage methods and in the development of grain varieties suited to the harsh environment. Many of the earliest settlers also found it impossible to adequately provide for more than a small herd of cattle on the quarter-section allowed under the Homestead Act. Even individuals able to purchase pre-emptions or railroad land soon realized that rangelands of several sections were needed to provide the same forage afforded on a fraction of that space in the dense virgin grasslands native to the central Palouse.

Protection from overgrazing on the fragile land, innovative irrigation practices, hard work, and thrift characterized a ranching philosophy held by many of the Germans who settled in the western Palouse. An astute application of these principles combined with no little risk enabled Jacob Harder of Adams County to acquire the largest contiguous ranch in the Pacific Northwest. The youngest of five brothers in his native Schleswig-Holstein, Harder immigrated to the United States in 1884 to join brothers Max and Hans who had settled near present Kahlotus. The three Harders were nearly forced out when virtually all the cattle they had been raising on the open range froze to death in the notorious winter of 1889. Following that disaster they became among the first in the area to irrigate pastureland when they diverted water from Washtucna Lake springs to a hundred acre alfalfa field. The enterprise flourished and enough hay was stored annually to prevent a similar tragedy from happening again.

The brothers began purchasing property from the Northern Pacific Railroad around 1900 and formed the Hardersburg Townsite and Improvement Company to boost local development. A town was platted next to the lake in 1901 giving birth to Kahlotus which boasted a depot, grain warehouse, hotel and two general stores within a year. The influx of settlers to the area at that time and resulting closure of the open range prompted Jacob Harder to begin looking for "land that couldn't be plowed." In 1906 he bought a 3,500 acre ranch on Cow Creek about a dozen miles east of Ritzville. Moving with his wife, Annine, and two small children to the place the following June, Harder began with a herd of 250 herefords and applied the same pioneering principles he had learned by experience in the lower country. Diligence and perseverance enabled the Harders to acquire adjacent holdings from Benge to Sprague over the next three decades covering 110,000 acres (A. Harder, 1960; M. Phillippay, 1973).

Demographics and Cultural Contributions

Although German-born residents of Whitman and Latah Counties numbered only 229 individuals in 1880, by the end of the decade the total was 716. They constituted the largest foreign-born group (21%) in the Palouse in 1890, a position they also held in 1900 when they totalled 864 individuals in Whitman and Latah Counties (19.6% of the total foreign-born). The population of first generation German immigrants in the Palouse had declined by 1910. The First World War in Europe led to further reversals and by 1920 there were 715 German-born residents in the two counties (14.8% of the foreign-born). The Germans, however, had more children than other immigrant groups; in 1920 members of the first and second generation constituted 20.8% of all foreign groups in Whitman and Latah Counties.

The significance of the German presence in the Palouse goes beyond a mere recitation of their numbers in the region. Through skills as agriculturalists, they made great contributions to area economic development. During the first decade of settlement, most pioneers entering the Palouse Hills engaged in stock raising or subsistence farming on the flats. The early settlers were conditioned to Eastern methods and those practiced in the Willamette Valley, which involved clearing low woodland areas as these were deemed best for crop production. In the Palouse, the grassy hills were actually superior to the bottomlands both in terms of soil fertility and temperature conditions. The bunchgrass culture of the prairies had developed an extensive root system through the ages that provided a high organic content and protection from erosion. The soil particles demonstrated a remarkable capacity to absorb and retain moisture and the hillsides and tops were much less susceptible to frosts and less difficult to work

than the wetter lowlands. Not long after the German Catholics began settling in the Palouse, they learned to grow their wheat on the higher ground, just as other pioneers had begun to do (D. Meinig, 1950).

The Germans love of music led to the formation of many community groups like "The Uniontown Brass Band." Historian John A. Platt recalled that a group of Genesee musicians included John and Henry Meyer, Charles and Carl Egbel, and Theodore Lorang, Jr. among others who probably were not German. Germans also were reported to make excellent sausage and wine. Platt wrote that in the 1890s bicycling became very popular in Genesee and several riding clubs were formed for weekend excursions on countryside dirt roads. On one trip, ten cyclists stopped for a rest at the home of a German bachelor who tended a fine vineyard and had a cellar filled with wine casks. He insisted that his guests sample each cask, which led to a party lasting the weekend. Platt said that several members of the club did not return to town until the following Monday, and that they arrived pushing their bicycles (J. Platt, 1975).

One German prominent in the area, John P. Vollmer, was a businessman whose tactics were known to make enemies. In his day he owned banks at Lewiston, Grangeville, and Genesee, and was dominant in establishing Kendrick and Genesee as well as his own Vollmer, all in Latah County. As Idaho agent for the Northern Pacific Railroad, he decided where the rails would be laid and subsequently opened businesses at key locations. He was reputed to be Idaho's first millionaire, and was called the "shrewdest" and "most aggressive" man in the state. After opening his own store at Huff's Gulch in 1891, he renamed the bustling trade center Vollmer and soon had amassed more than 32,000 acres of land—much of it by foreclosing on loans made to small farmers. By 1897 the citizens of the town, including many of Vollmer's financial victims, decided by a vote of 29-109, to rename the community, and "Troy" was the popular choice (A. Driscoll, 1970).

Vollmer's influence over Genesee was so great that he was able to move the town. In 1888 the Spokane and Palouse Railway planned to extend its line to Genesee; Vollmer, as a partner in the railroad, decided to bypass the established townsite because much of it was owned by Jacob Rosenstein, a Jewish merchant, who wanted more for right-of-way than Vollmer cared to pay. So Vollmer bought 40 acres of land hearby and established "New Genesee." He terminated the railroad there, and soon many businesses moved from "Old Genesee" to Vollmer's site. Eventually even Rosenstein followed, physically moving his store closer to the railroad depot, a process that required three months. When Vollmer died in 1917, the *Genesee News* reported that the inventory of his estate was in excess of two million dollars (K. Peterson, 1979).

Perhaps in an effort to disassociate themselves from the Fatherland during World War I, Palouse Country German Americans enlisted for military service in large numbers. Approximately 2,500 men and several dozen women undertook military training and assistance at W. S. C. in Pullman from 1917-18, and some 2,000 from the region were actually deployed as soldiers, pilots, radio operators, mechanics, nurses, and in other rolls. Conscripts came from virtually every community in the Palouse with the highest numbers from Pullman, Moscow, and Colfax. However, the highest percentage of servicemen relative to population registered from Colton, Uniontown, and Rosalia, where large numbers of German lived. The 114 young men who served from Colton constituted the highest percentage of those eligible from any community in the entire state. Five recruits from these towns did not return home—Elmer Ogle, John McRae, Que Sanders (Rosalia), George Weiber (Uniontown), and Charles Maynard (Colton).

Lt. Maynard was the Palouse Country's first casualty of the war and fell on June 8, 1918 at Belleau Woods where he and a thousand men turned back five German divisions in a pivotal battle of the campaign. Marshal Petain awarded the young marine the French *Croix de Guerre* posthumously. Others who did survive, like Rosalia's Edward Rickard, were present in France at the war's end and fought against poison gas, wire entanglements, and "Big Berthas" in the decisive battles at St. Mihiel (September, 1918) and Argonne Forest (November, 1918). On the home front Palouse area residents led the nation in per capita contributions of flour sent to the troops in Europe and raised approximately $10,000,000 in the five Liberty Bond Drives which substantially exceeded their goals in Rosalia, Tekoa, LaCrosse, and Garfield (L. Wenham, 1920)

Palouse Jewish Families and Regional Economic Development

Some of the Palouse Country's earliest and most successful businessmen were German Jews who came to the Northwest in the 1850s with the mining advance to supply clothing, tools, and other articles to the fortune seekers. Among the earliest of these entrepreneurs in the region were Martin, Adolf, and Sigmund Schwabacher, brothers from Germany, who first opened a general merchandise store in the boomtown of Walla Walla about 1860. With the completion of the Mullan Road across the Northern Rockies in 1862, Walla Walla became linked with Ft. Benton, Montana to facilitate traffic from the Missouri River to the Columbia River and Pacific Coast. This route skirted the western Palouse and had a significant impact on population growth in Eastern Washington. According to a territorial memorial, the road directed "a constant stream of population into the region" as immigrants arrived to mine, farm, and engage in other enterprises.

The Schwabachers expanded their operations to Dayton and Colfax in the 1870s and put their brother-in-law, Bailey Gatzert, into business at Wallula. Gatzert, a native of Worms, Germany, soon demonstrated a remarkable talent in merchandising and moved to Seattle in 1869 to find opportunities that would make him and his in-laws one of the territory's wealthiest families. Spokane's first Jewish businessman was likely Simon Berg who established a general merchandise store there in 1879. He was followed in the next several years by a number of Jewish families who succeeded in various enterprises including Solomon and Simon Oppenheimer. The latter was responsible for attracting Dutch investment to the region and was a prime mover in the establishment of the Holland Bank of Spokane. The bank acquired extensive holdings of agricultural lands in the Palouse and undertook efforts to colonize the properties.

Reflecting the diversity of economic interests characteristic of many early Jewish immigrants to the region, Julius Galland moved to Farmington from Oregon in 1883 to operate a general mercantile store, and in association with two brothers opened a second store in Palouse in 1888. In the spring of 1891 they relocated to Spokane and founded the Galland Burke Brewing Company. After ten years of prosperous operation the company was sold and in 1906 the Galland brothers organized the Northwest Loan and Trust Company.

One of the region's Jewish businessmen whose efforts significantly contributed to agricultural development in the Palouse was Aaron Kuhn. A native of Germany, Kuhn had emigrated to the United States in 1873 at the age of sixteen and operated stationery and cigar stores in Nevada, California, and Idaho before coming to Colfax in 1883. His general mercantile business prospered with the region's development and Kuhn carefully invested his profits in local real estate. By the 1890s he had become a major grain merchant, shipping as much as 1,500,000 bushels annually through his network of sixteen warehouses in Whitman and Latah counties. In 1902 he sold most of his Palouse grain operation to Portland's Interior Warehouse Company and purchased controlling interest in the Traders National Bank of Spokane. Like many prominent Spokane businessmen of the early 1900s, Kuhn's career was forged through his entrepreneurial experience in the Palouse. Other Jews remained in the Palouse to operate small businesses in the rural communities. Henry Dernham and William and Emmanual Kaufmann opened a general mercantile in Moscow in 1889 and were followed by Moses Vandevantner who came to farm near Cornwall in northern Latah County but opened a general store in the town shortly afterward (N. Durham, 1912).

Prior to 1900, the vast majority of Jews in eastern Washington were Ashkenazim from Germany who, like Vandevantner, had come as single men. During Washington's territorial and early statehood period they were rapidly acculturated into the dynamic life of emergent Northwest cities and rural communities. Through hard work and mutual support they attained middle class income levels in a relatively short period and became prime movers in the development of area political and educational institutions. Although not a populous group in the Palouse, the Jews retained cultural traditions and their numbers increased with career opportunities associated with the region's three state universities.

One whose contributions became internationally significant was Frank Golder, a native of Odessa, Russia who was hired in 1910 to teach history at W.S.C. Golder never lost a fascination with his native land and had developed a special interest in Russian exploration and trade in the Pacific. The Harvard University graduate continued his research in these areas while teaching in Pullman and his classes

attracted a wide following. Golder was probably instrumental in arranging a performance at Pullman by the Imperial Russian Symphony in 1911. His book *Russian Expansion in the Pacific* (1914) was the first of many notable publications he authored on the subject. In 1913 he obtained a grant from the Carniege Foundation to study first hand the cataclysmic events happening in Europe on the eve of the First World War. Golder delved deeply into the Russian State Archives until the 1917 Communist Revolution. He was an eyewitness to the Bolshevik uprising in St. Petersburg and Moscow and continued to work assiduously gathering diaries, broadsides, newspapers, and government publications during this historic period. Golder eventually acquired a collection so massive that two railroad boxcars were needed to transport the contents under extremely difficult circumstances to safety in the West. Golder was forced to flee eastward on the Trans-Siberian Railway and return to the Palouse via Vladivostok and by ship to Seattle.

The collection eventually reached the United States where it formed the nucleus of Stanford University's Hoover Institution on War, Revolution, and Peace. Golder continued to teach in Pullman until 1920 when he moved to Stanford to head the Hoover Library. Golder also served as a principal inspector for the American Relief Administration's efforts under President Warren Harding to deliver humanitarian aid to Russia during the years of famine that followed the Russian Civil War. Golder's scholarly efforts at W.S.C. launched an entirely new academic field as he is considered "the father of Russian studies" at the university level in America and his contributions significantly influenced the nation's foreign policymakers for Eastern Europe and the Soviet Union (H. Chevigny, 1965).

The Onecho Swiss Mennonite Community

As the Palouse Country provided many European immigrants with the economic prosperity for which they had emigrated, it also became a haven for those who fled for religious reasons. To the German-speaking Swiss Mennonites who began arriving in the Almota and Onecho areas of the Palouse in the 1880s, settlement here marked the end of a long and often troubled history which their people had endured for centuries in central Europe. The Anabaptist movement was born during the Reformation in Zurich, Switzerland, in 1525 when several theologians met to discuss a variety of issues which were already considered heretical by both the state Reformed Church and Roman Catholic Church. Such doctrines included separation of church and state, freedom of religion, adult baptism, and pacifism. The Zurich meeting gave new direction to the movement. Adherents came to be called Mennonites, named after Menno Simons who led the parallel Dutch movement. Persecution by state officials followed them, but the majority tenaciously clung to their faith.

In the 1600s some Swiss Anabaptists migrated to Moravia where they became known as Hutterites while others fled in the following century to the German Palatinate and eventually to Pennsylvania where they were called Amish. Those remaining in Canton Bern, Switzerland, became known as Bernese Mennonites, but most of them moved in the 1700s to the rugged Jura Mountains along the French border. Here they settled in northeast Canton Bern in the vicinity of such villages as LeLocle, La Chaux-de-Fonds, and Sonnenberg. Although French was the language of the native inhabitants, many of the Mennonites relocating there continued to speak German.

Although the more violent forms of persecution were no longer used against them by the late eighteenth century, severe social restrictions remained in force. A Mennonite's children were not considered legal heirs of what little property he might possess since their baptisms were not conducted by state church clergymen and therefore invalid. Furthermore, Mennonites could not own land so they were compelled to pay rents and till only the high plateaus of slopes away from the village markets. The mountainous terrain was stony and dry but suitable in some areas for raising such subsistence crops as spelt (a variety of wheat), oats, barley, peas, potatoes, and flax, and their talent in cheesemaking later gave the Swiss an international reputation.

Each family usually had a few

goats and a cow which was often hitched to a horse for the arduous task of plowing the steep slopes. Their method of plowing was explained by the son of an early nineteenth-century immigrant to the United States:

Two men were always necessary, one to plow and the other to drive. From four to six persons followed the plow to hoe the furrow. Their plows looked like the old prairie plows of our own country. They had two wheels under the beam to regulate the depth of plowing. One drove continuously back and forth along the side of the hill and all the furrows were made toward the bottom of the hill and then the ground from the last furrow was transported to the top of the hill in order to fill the last furrow (D. Gratz, 1953).

The eminent nineteenth-century Swiss author, Henrich Zschokke, once traveled through the Jura Mountains and was deeply impressed by the life of these Anabaptists whom he found very hospitable and "so content, so pious and without hypocrisy." He also noted their plain dress and that the married men always wore beards.

The problem of high rents in the area was complicated in the early 1800s by overcrowding resulting from the high Mennonite birth rate. At the same time, the Napoleonic Wars raged in Europe adding to the unsettled conditions among the pacifistic Mennonites. The worst disaster to strike the region, however, was the famine that gripped the entire country in 1816, caused when inclement weather ruined the harvest. Food supplies remained limited for several years and resulting death and disease reached every district of Switzerland. The combined effect of all these events led to the first group of Bernese Mennonites to migrate to America. The first was Jacob Schrag of Wyningen who immigrated to Pennsylvania in 1816. In the next year his father, Benedict Schrag, and several Bernese families followed but later relocated with others to establish Sonnenberg, the first Swiss Mennonite colony in the Midwest, located in Wayne County, Ohio.

FALL PLOWING, c. 1910 (MASC, WSU LIBRARIES)

Letters streamed back to the Jura about the fertile soil and abundance of land available for homesteading. Furthermore, it was reported that the Mennonites could freely practice their religion and procure exemptions from military service. In 1830 Bernese Mennonite emigration reached its highest point and the members began to disperse throughout Ohio into such places as Putnam County with the arrival there of Michael Neuenschwander in 1833, and into the Pandora, Bluffton, and Findlay districts. Neuenschwander's son, John, subsequently moved to Polk County, Iowa, in 1849 to begin Bernese Mennonite settlement in that state. Periods of particularly heavy Mennonite migration to the United States were in the 1850s and 1870s when efforts were made to implement compulsory military service in Switzerland (J. Lehman, 1969).

The Swiss colony that was transplanted to the Palouse Country was also Bernese Mennonite and the man directly responsible for its location here was an ordained minister from Switzerland, Reverend Phillip Roulet. He led a group of fourteen families to Butler County, Ohio, in 1867 which then relocated to Iowa two years later. In 1873 they settled near Pulaski in Davis County where there was an Amish settlement. Like most Bernese Mennonite families, Reverend Roulet had many relatives still living in Switzerland who read his letters about life in America. His sister, Julia, remained in the Jura and married a widower with two sons, Christian Aeschlimann, who lived near LeLocle. To this union was born ten more children, six of whom would pioneer Swiss Mennonite settlement in the Palouse Country: Frederick, Samuel, Paul, Rosina (Rubin), Sophia (Schlunegar), and Ernest (S. Aeschliman, n.d.).

In 1880 Reverend Roulet's nephew, nineteen-year-old Sam Aeschliman, decided to join his uncle in Iowa and was followed within another year by his brother and sister, Paul and Rosina. Other members of their family, Sophia and Frederich, with his new bride Marie Rosine (Rubin), followed in 1885, but found that virtually all the homestead land had already been claimed. An adventurous friend of the Aeschlimanns, fellow Iowan Mennonite Joseph Stevick, decided after a cyclone demolished his farm buildings in the spring of 1885 that he would travel to Washington Territory to investigate settlement opportunities. This was frequently the kind of motivating factor that led many to settle in the Palouse. Cheney's *Northwest Tribune* had already reported that, "A curious fact in connection with the receipt of letters at the Land bureau requesting information about the country is that large numbers are always received from regions affected with cyclones, violent showers and blizzards. These letters invariably make their appearance in great quantities from a district just recovering from one of these disastrous visitations."

In the fall of 1885 the Stevick family reached Almota which was then a bustling young community on the Snake River. Stevick selected a homestead in the sheltered canyon about one mile west of town and chose a homesite in an area protected from strong winds by ridges on three sides. He later acquired an adjacent timber culture claim as well as a half-section of lieu land. Several years later Stevick acquired additional holdings near the home of J.C. Wicks, whose back porch served as the Onecho post office, and the family moved there (E. Gay, 1974).

Sam and Paul Aeschliman immigrated to Almota late in the fall of 1886 and rented farmland near the town. One year later their oldest brother, Fred, came out with his family and that of his brother-in-law, Chris Schlunegar. Schlunegar, a native of La Chaux-de-Fonds, had married Sophia Aeschliman a year earlier in Iowa. This group traveled over the Union Pacific Railroad to San Francisco and then by steamer up the coast and Columbia and Snake Rivers to Almota. Another brother-in-law, William Rubin (husband of Rosina Aeschliman), and Paul Mauer arrived about 1887 from Ohio. They were followed in 1889 by Lewis J. Allenbach who had spent two disappointing years in Kansas after he emigrated from Switzerland.

One of Almota's founding fathers, the venerable Henry Hart Spalding, befriended the Swiss immigrants and provided housing for them and advised them on how to obtain farmland. He encouraged them to settle around Almota which at that time was the principal Snake River shipping point for Palouse grain. Sheltered beneath the bluffs on the river's northernmost bend, Almota became a crossroads for pioneer stage traffic, a junction of Snake River navigation, and Palouse Country freighting. By 1882 the town boasted a store, Spalding's hotel, saloon, express office, flour mill, other businesses, and numerous residences. With the arrival of the railroads Almota gradually lost its importance as a trade center but was still in its prime when the first Swiss immigrants arrived. Fred Aeschliman, trained as a cooper in his native Switzerland, soon found work as a wheelwright and blacksmith in Almota. The town echoed daily with steamboat whistles, rolling grain wagons, clanging hammers at the blacksmith's forge, and the myriad sound associated with a frontier river town.

The custom in Mennonite villages in the Jura Mountains dictated that men were taught a trade in order to provide a source of income during the long winter months. The chief desire of these colonists in the Palouse was not to continue the old part-time trades, but to obtain their own farms. By 1890 most of them had purchased or were renting farmland in the Onecho area. They continued to exhibit a great deal of cooperation among themselves during harvest, however, and also maintained cordial relations with the earlier homesteaders in whose midst they settled. This cooperation is best illustrated through the history of their church. The first church services conducted in the Onecho area were begun in 1876 by a Methodist circuit-rider, Reverend M.S. Anderson. Although a congregation was never formally organized, a number of families continued gathering regularly for worship for years in a country school. Without a church of their own, the Swiss in the area were welcomed to these services when they moved into the area. In 1891, Paul Aeschliman went to Kansas to study for the ministry and at the completion of his program in 1893, the Onecho community asked him to be their regular pastor.

On July 1, 1893 the first Mennonite church in the state was organized and named "The First Mennonite Church of Colfax, Washington." Reverend Aeschliman was elected pastor and an arrangement was made with the Methodists to continue cooperative services; Reverend Aeschliman would preach three Sundays each month while a Methodist pastor would conduct services at least once each month. Though Aeschliman preached in German his sermons were translated into English. The fellowships decided in 1895 to construct a church building and when questions arose regarding its ownership, both memberships again cordially resolved the problem. The land was donated by a Methodist, the Mennonites supervised the construction and everyone joined together to raise the money and to build it. Both pastors participated in its dedication and it was simply called "The Onecho Church."

The Fred Rohrbach family came directly to Colfax from Bern at the urging of Godfrey Horn who was the owner of a meat market in Colfax. Horn was able to persuade more of his Bernese relatives to travel over with Rohrbach in 1874. A few years after he came, in 1877, land sold for $1.25 an acre for homestead or the railroad land could be purchased for $2.60. Farmers like Rohrbach could sell their grain at Sprague or Cheney, Washington, and sometimes as far away as Spokane. The Rohrbachs raised a large family on the farm outside of Colfax where Mr. Rohrbach was known for his milk cows and cattle. His son Fred later raised and bred Brown Swiss cattle. Other Mennonite families continued to come to the Onecho community from the Midwest and by 1890 there were 119 Swiss-born residents of Whitman County (4.8% of the total foreign-born population). This movement continued after the turn of the century and in 1901 another group arrived from the Pandora settlement in Ohio. In this group were Adam Hilty and A.A. Gerber (V. Hilty, 1987). By 1920 the number of their European-born in Whitman County had declined slightly to 108 while the scattered native-born Swiss living in Latah County totalled forty-nine individuals (P. Rubin, 1973).

Though never a populous group on the Palouse, the Swiss Mennonites exemplified an important aspect of the immigrant experience in the region. They were welcomed and even assisted by Henry Spalding and other Americans who preceded their settlement and were allowed to worship with those in whose midst they settled. It was a welcomed contrast to the rugged life and discrimination they had faced among the native populace in the mountains of northwest Switzerland. They had come to America seeking freedom of religion and land to farm. In the Midwest they could practice their faith but many later arrivals were unable to find available farmland. In the Palouse, however, they had opportunity for both religious freedom and prosperity.

Bertha Engelland Williams
Tekoa, Washington

High spirited and affable Bertha Williams spent much of her life-time in the Palouse on the farm of her German immigrant father near Tekoa and as a pioneer schoolteacher in area schools. With a lifetime rich in experiences on the Palouse frontier, Bertha was a great story-teller and historian in later years and shared the reminiscences that follow with David and Gladys E. Guilbert while in a retirement home near Lacy in 1975.

Often as a girl, I wondered what dreams must have danced through the heads of the young Stender sisters; Frauke, who became my mother, and Lisa, which led them to leave home. They must have been enticing visions for these girls joined four German emigrants from Hamdorf, Germany, for the long, uncomfortable journey to America and the pioneer hardships of the Pacific Northwest. Leading this little band to eastern Washington was young George Engelland, my father, who had but recently taken up a homestead near what is now Tekoa. He had returned to Hamdorf to attend the funeral of his mother. As steerage passengers, these young people sailed from Bremen in June, 1886. Steerage was the migrants' way to get here in those days as it was the cheapest form of transportation.

Most of those who left European shores then did not possess a surplus of money. They came to the U.S. with hopes of bettering their economic status, as well as enjoying more freedom and leaving behind the severe class distinctions that existed in Germany and other countries. After three or four weeks at sea, George Engelland's band landed in Baltimore. There an immigrant train for the West was waiting on the dock. Mother often spoke of the weari-ness of that long trip by ship and slow moving train. Along the way, her curiosity was aroused by the "white buttons" as she called them, on the doors of the houses in the small towns they passed through. She discovered they were used to open the doors. In Germany only latches, called "klinks," did this job. So one of her first impressions of America was that of a land of round, white door knobs.

On reaching Cheney, it was necessary for all the group to spend the night in a rooming house there. The Stender sisters were both severely bitten by bed bugs so aside from being weary from the long train ride and the weather being sultry and warm, it was also a very itchy, lumber wagon trip from Cheney to North Pine, where another of the Stender sisters lived. During the many days of tiresome trav-el, George Engelland evidently came to the conclusion that his homestead cabin was going to seem very lonely away from the com-panionship of the attractive girls in the immigrant group. Along the way he had proposed and, on July 7, 1886, Frauke Stender and George Engelland were married by a judge at the Watson school-house in the neighborhood of North Pine, the post office for all that country.

Father moved onto the 160 acre homestead in an April snow-storm in 1884. He often told me of his impressions of the beauty of the open prairies. While bunchgrass predominated, wild roses, ser-viceberry shrubs, and sunflowers grew with here and there a pine tree. Through the seasons carpets of buttercups, pink phlox, grass widows, yellow bells, and pasque flowers bloomed. There were the blues of lupine, wild hyacinth, camas, and larkspur. Later came wild geraniums. In the low places, huge beds of wild iris flourished. Flowers now extinct in that area were beds of tiny, pale blue violets, lavender mariposa lilies, and on damp shrubby north hillsides, dain-ty, pale purple wild orchids, known as lady slippers. This, then, was the place father brought mother after they were married at North Pine.

Fortunately Mother had brought stout homespun clothes and a feather bed or two from Germany so that, despite the drafty cabin, they did not suffer excessively from the cold. She feared the Indians, the coyotes, the treelessness (at that time she would not even admit that pines were trees), the horses and cattle roaming the wide open, unfenced country—in fact, everything about the new life was terrifying to mother and it took some time for her to adjust to these strange conditions. Complicating her life, she knew no English. But fortunately her nearest neighbors, two families of Mestermans, were both German so she could talk with them.

However, this further delayed her learning the language of her new home. One of the decorations in the new shack was on a board on which Father had printed "I DO NOT SPEAK ENGLISH." When a stranger came to the door when mother was home alone, she would point to the sign. Soon she was asked to help with the meals for the crew at harvest time on the S. L. Jamison place. The chief cook, Mary Blue, knew no German, so they communicated more or less in sign language and here Mother learned her first English words. Later, when she had acquired a little more English, Mother helped Mrs. John Schau cook for the harvesters. Mrs. Schau was a rapid talker and mother was unable to understand all she said. Every once in a while, Mrs. Schau would say, "Don't you think so, Frauke?" Mother would invariably say, "Yes," Mrs. Shau laughed and replied, "This time, you should have said, 'No.'"

Prairie chickens, now extinct in that area, were very numerous then. Father told of taking his shotgun down to Hangman Creek and returning with a gunny sack full of birds. These were dressed out and salted down to become an important source of meat. They also butchered a pig or two and made sausage and other pork products which they smoked and which were therefore edible year round. They seldom killed a beef as it was impossible to keep beef from spoiling unless it was brined, and even it did not keep well for any length of time. Dried prunes and dried apples were the chief fruits eaten. These were bought at Farmington or Connell's. Potatoes and other vegetables were grown on the homestead and some chickens and a cow were added so the family had fresh eggs, milk and butter. Mother said that even in those first years they never suffered from lack of food. It took five years to prove up on a homestead and then a deed was given by the United States government. All this time there was no Tekoa so all trading was done at Farmington or Colfax which were on a wagon freight route connecting with the boats running up the Snake River. Some earliest homesteaders made annual trips to Walla Walla for trading purposes.

It's hard to recognize now that when my father brought his bride to his homestead in 1886, less than 100 years ago, there were more people living on farms in the Palouse Country than there are now and that most of the towns were stage or freight stations with hardly any population at all. In my lifetime, the Palouse changed from the vast sea of grass with unbroken sod and families on each 160 acres to fewer families on large acreages. It has gone from horse-powered threshing outfits to self-propelled combines. Tekoa became a roaring, wide-open town and then subsided into today's pretty, tree-shaded, quiet rural community.

Palouse Rainbow

East of Colfax, Washington

Chapter VII:

THE NORWEGIANS AND SWEDES

"The first year it was pretty hard for us.... We had a few chickens that laid awfully good, so we lived almost entirely on bread and eggs. I believe it was thirty years before I would eat an egg after that!"

—Aurthur Bjerke, 1973

The Nordic peoples of Norway, Sweden, Finland, Denmark, and Iceland also immigrated in unprecedented numbers during the nineteenth century due to regional economic and social pressures. As was the case with German-speaking immigrants to America, many Nordics first clustered to form ethnic communities across the upper Midwest. Some adventurous souls from these states journeyed to the Washington coast as early as the 1850s to inaugurate one of the largest European migrations to the Pacific Northwest. A significant number of Norwegians and Swedes came to make their home in the Palouse where the western slopes of the Bitterroot and Clearwater Mountains were fondly reminiscent of their picturesque European homeland.

Nineteenth Century Nordic Emigration

In terms of the comparative size of population in the Nordic countries, Norway contributed the largest percentage of immigrants to the United States and was second only to Ireland on this basis for all European nations. Although the number of Norwegian immigrants who entered the United States in the nineteenth century was not great when compared to the total immigration from Europe, they did constitute major foreign-born elements in areas of the upper Midwest and Pacific Northwest. The first significant Norwegian immigration to North America began in 1825 with the voyage of the tiny sloop Restauration which transported fifty-three passengers and crew to New York. A steady stream of Norwegian immigration to all parts of this country, however, did not begin until 1836. Census figures reveal that it continued at a highly variable rate until 1866 when the first period of mass emigration began which continued until 1874. A second and larger mass immigration began in 1879 and lasted a dozen years. During the 1880s, Norwegian immigrants to the United States totalled 186,290. A third major wave began in 1899 and continued through the next decade.

Lack of farm land was a principal factor in people's decision to emigrate from Norway since three-fourths of the land there could not be cultivated. In a nation characterized by a mountainous terrain, farming districts were located only in the rolling southeastern meadowland and in the scenic valleys of the southern interior, but most of the remaining quarter of the land was forested. Industrialization came late to Norway due to the lack of large iron and coal deposits. Many Norwegians in the nineteenth century, therefore, were engaged in fishing, trade, professional work, or in the case with half, farming. From this latter group most of the emigrants came. As was the case in Ireland, the rural populace was rigidly divided into several classes. The freeholders, economically the most powerful of the agricultural classes, were the independent owners of both small and large estates. However, the traditional *odel* system provided the eldest son with the inheritance of the family farm. The cotters were also freemen but had little chance of advancing in the socially rigid system and were required to render occasional service to the Ubondeu in return for the privilege of tilling a few acres of his land. The lowest but most populous classes of renters, the farm workers and servants, had even less opportunity in a land where their burdensome labor resulted only in perpetual poverty (C. Qualey, 1938).

Guidebooks were distributed throughout Norway, much to the dismay of the local officials and clergy, explaining the conditions of settlement in America. Most letters from Norwegians in the Northeast (*America-breve*) depicted a life of prosperity and adventure further encouraging emigration. Norwegian settlement gradually spread across the country from New York to Wisconsin and Minnesota and beyond to the Dakotas. A pioneer Norwegian minister in North Dakota reported that, "Those who live in the older settlements learn that great reaches of fertile and free lands are to be had to the west-

*Morning Squall**

South of Moscow, Idaho

ward, and so they again turn toward the new and unseen." As the frontier pushed westward, Norwegian immigrants moved with it in search of land and its riches. Several Norwegians and Swedes followed the rush of gold seekers to California in 1849 and created a sensation in their homelands when they returned shortly afterward with stories of great wealth to be found on the Pacific Slope (T. Blegen, 1931). Recorded from those leaving in 1850 from Trondheim for the West Coast was a song of future expectation which ended sadly with the following verse:

> To thee, beloved land, I bid farewell. Soon I no longer shall view
>   thy beauty nor hear the music of thy waterfalls.
> The snow-capped mountains will fade from sight and slowly thy coast
>   will sink away in the mists like a mother being lowered in the grave.
> No glimpse then of thy tallest peaks; only a lonely sail
>   on the boundless deep.

Origins of the Idaho Palouse Norwegian Settlement

In the 1860s Norwegian miners penetrated Idaho in their continuing quest for gold, and by 1870 several Scandinavian miners and mule packers were working in Nez Perce County including a Norwegian, Charles Nelson. Another early Norwegian immigrant, Peter Abrahamson, was farming on Union Flat Creek in 1871, but most who came early in the decade favored the Genesee area in present Latah and Nez Perce Counties. In the Palouse the wanderers found fertile plains and valleys girded by "snow-capped mountains and waterfalls" that reminded them of their native land. The first Norwegian to permanently settle in northern Idaho was Tonnes Moller, a native of Sogndal, Stavanger, who settled in the Genesee Valley in 1876. It had been named for New York's Genesee Valley after a native of that state named Stone travelled through the valley in 1870. The first settler in the area was an Hungarian immigrant, Jacob Kambitch, who began raising stock on Cow Creek in 1871. Other settlers came to the area in 1872 and three years later a tiny hamlet developed about a mile east of the present town. Moller soon acquired ownership of a boardinghouse in the valley and put up a large sign with the name "Genesee Hotel" painted on it. The settlement was soon identified with the name and developed into a bustling pioneer community as additional Norwegian,

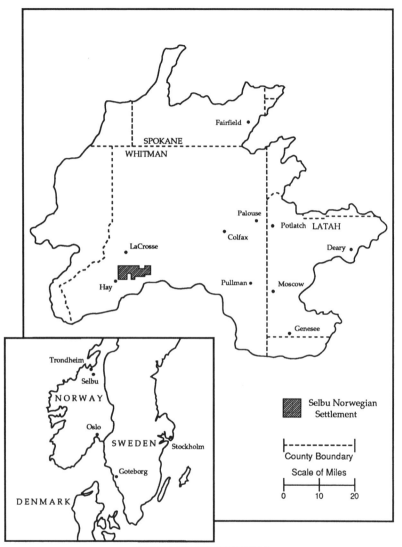

THE SCANDINAVIAN PENINSULA
AND PALOUSE REGION NORDIC SETTLEMENTS, c. 1890

German, and American immigrants settled near there and along Cow Creek (M. Ulvestad, 1907).

Following Moller's arrival in 1876, the following Norwegians also

175

came: John Tetln, Hans Smith, Knud Bergquam, Hans Tvedt, Casper Johnson, Andrew Christiensen, Iver Christensen, Carl Christensen, James Jacobsen, Charles Fering, Ole O. Hensen, Martin Anderson, and Eric Peterson. These pioneers first lived in either sod houses or log cabins. Their nearest supply center was Lewiston, located twenty miles away at the confluence of the Snake and Clearwater Rivers and the trip necessitated a grueling journey down and up the long, steep grades to the river. In 1877 they erected barricades for defense in the Nez Perce Indian War.

In the summer of 1877, John C. Saether immigrated to Latah County and told of his journey in a letter to Scandinaven. Through such correspondence, regularly published in the Norwegian-America press, many Norwegian immigrants in the East learned about the Palouse Country. Like other early Norwegian settlers in the Palouse, Saether had first lived in Wisconsin but in July, 1877 traveled by railroad to San Francisco, then by steamer to Portland and eventually reached Thorn Creek where he found abundant water, timber, and fertile rolling hills. He reported that there were only two other Norwegian families in this part of Latah County at the time of his arrival, as well as a Danish and a Swedish family. Settlement increased rapidly and by 1878 between twenty and thirty families resided in the immediate vicinity.

Scandinavian settlement was also growing in Paradise Valley around Moscow. The first Norwegian immigrant arrived there in 1877, Samuel Johnson, a native of Telemark who had traveled extensively in the United States. He cautioned those coming from the Midwest to expect hilly land not considered tillable by their standards, but he liked the area better than any he had seen in the nation. In 1878 Canud Madison settled on a timber claim about seven miles west of Moscow in the vicinity of Blaine where many Norwegian and Danish immigrants later settled. Madison had emigrated from the Bergen district to Illinois and served in the Union Army during the Civil War. Another Norwegian pioneer, Iver Burke, also settled in the area in 1878, establishing a large farm and orchard in the Fallon district of Whitman County (Lever, 1901).

In the early 1880s considerable Scandinavian immigration continued into southern Latah County. Members of one group inspected lands in the Moscow and Genesee areas in the summer of 1880. They were a party of a dozen Norwegians who had left Jewell County, Kansas on July 5. This group traveled by emigrant train to San Francisco and by steamer to Portland where they boarded a river boat operated by the Oregon Railway and Navigation Company. This company offered reduced rates to prospective settlers and cooperated with the Union Pacific Railroad and Oregon Steamship Company in arranging for special immigrant fares from the Midwest to the Pacific Northwest. The O.R.&N.Co. operated several portage railroads where their steamers could not navigate up the Columbia River rapids, and the Norwegians had to make six transfers before they finally reached Lewiston. The group then set out for the Genesee Valley and one of the members, John Toskey, described this final phase of their trip:

On the morning of the 27th [July] we set out in a northerly direction toward the large Norwegian settlement, where we have both relatives and friends. We had now come to Norway; the region cannot be compared with any of the plains in the East. Here we saw large and small mountains rising in the distance, immense tracts of timber, hills and valleys, and prairie land; and far to east we could make out snow-clad peaks of the Bitter Root Mountains proudly raising their heads to the sky. Nature is grand in the fullest sense of the word; nothing is lacking to make the picture impressive. The poet and artist will find here in their proper proportions subjects to record for others. Toskey also offered practical information on farming in the area:

...In the Northern part of the territory the climate is very favorable for rich [crop] production. Late in the fall we have sufficient rain and in the winter snow and at times rain. Late in the spring and in early summer we have showers that give the crops a good start and healthy development. In July and August no rain falls; and harvest begins generally in the month of August. The soil is deep and rich. Wheat yielded last year [1880] from 35 to 50 bushels per acre, and other crops were equally good.

Toskey reported that two sawmills and a flour mill were operated in the vicinity, and the grain market would soon expand with the completion of the Northern Pacific transcontinental line. The Norwegian noted that plenty of government land was still available in the Blaine district between Genesee and Moscow and that many American farmers in these areas were willing to sell their claims. He estimated the number of northern Idaho Norwegian families at about 200. There were also many young Norwegian bachelors in the area who Toskey thought would be most receptive to an influx of Norwegian women. Although he did not consider the lifestyle of the Norwegian immigrants "opulent," he did predict that "with effort and industry they will attain a comfortable status within a few years." In the summer of 1882 Engvald Halvorsen left Minnesota in the company of other Norwegians bound for the Pacific Northwest. Halvorsen had lived in a part of Minnesota where no trees grew and he disliked the severe winters of the upper Midwest. In contrast, the group found good soil and timber in the southeastern Palouse where the winters were milder and the summers free of pestering mosquitoes.

During these same years, Norwegian settlement began to spread eastward into present south-central Latah County. In 1879 Nicholas and John Olson, natives of Bergen, homesteaded in Driscoll Ridge about eight miles northwest of Kendrick, Idaho. John and George Driscoll, father and son, had come to the ridge from Canada the year before with Patrick Cunningham and all filed the first homesteads there. The Olson brothers, skilled woodsmen after twenty years of experience in the Minnesota and Wisconsin forests, hand hewed the timbers used in the framework of their cabin and did the same for many of their neighbors' homes and barns. Scandinavian settlement expanded during the following decade to neighboring American and Burnt Ridges (A. Driscoll, n.d.).

Scandinavians also penetrated the more heavily timbered areas to the east. Henry B. Jorgensen, a native of Flettefjord, Norway, was prospecting with a Swede in scenic Park Valley when they decided that it would be an ideal place to homestead and became the first to locate in the valley. Soren Nelson, a native of Balders, was the first Norwegian immigrant to settle in the vicinity of Anderson. By 1891, several others had joined Jorgensen and Ole Goldstrom, his Swedish companion, in Park Valley. They were all Norwegian and included the Hellerud, Jelleberg, Dahl, and Swenson families and two bachelors—Ole Torgeson and Peter Enger (O. Slind, 1980). In 1891 Edward Swenson's family traveled from Minnesota to Park Valley where his older brother had settled a year earlier. He later described the difficulty of the last part of their three day journey from Moscow to the valley:

When we got down to the river the horses had to ford the river. There was no bridge...and the water was high, and they had a foot log there for us to walk across. When they got across the river they had to take the wagon apart and use just the hind part of the wagon to carry what few things they could load on there, to get up the hill on the east side:...[The road] wasn't graded much, so they had to lock the hind wheels. They had chains along. They cut down a little fir tree and tied [it] behind the wagon to hold back.

Since the pioneers were only able to bring the most necessary household wares and provisions, neighbors would join together to welcome new arrivals and help to complete the first project in the new land—building a dwelling. Whenever possible, a location was found close to fresh water and trees and ground where the cabin was to be built was carefully smoothed out. A log foundation was laid so that the cabin floor was higher than the ground level. Edward Swenson noted "they cut down green trees and peeled the logs and notched them together. And they found cedar there...to split for shakes...for the roof. It didn't cost much to build in those days, except a lot of hard work." Next a log barn was erected, then a chicken house, root cellar, and woodshed. The Swensons lived in their cabin for eight years until a new one was built out of hewn logs. Unable to pay the $20.00 charged by a neighbor to hew the logs, Swenson made 2,000 twelve-foot cedar fence rails and delivered them to the man. Many of the Park Valley settlers regularly worked in the Genesee area harvests until they had cleared enough land to support themselves (E. Swenson, 1976).

The nearest trade centers were the tiny communities of Kendrick and Troy, founded in 1889 and 1890 respectively. Deary was not established as a townsite until 1904 when it was reached by the railroad. The pioneers in the valley were largely self-sufficient, subsisting to a great extent on venison, grouse, partridge and, in the spring and summer, salmon and mountain trout. Occasionally bear were taken. After the ground was cleared and broken, they planted a few fruit trees and established small farms. Eventually better roads were built into

Paradise Ridge Blizzard

Paradise Valley, Idaho

the valley which facilitated travel to the neighboring communities to the east where more Scandinavians were settling in the better farming districts. Edward Dahl, one of the original Park Valley homesteaders, relocated with his family to North Bear Ridge in 1896. He co-authored a number of articles with Eric Lian inviting Norwegian immigrants to settle in that vicinity which were published in the Minneapolis Tidende in the late 1890s. Nearly a dozen families responded by moving from Minnesota to the Bear Ridge area.

In 1880 there were 136 Norwegians and Swedes living in Nez Perce County while only 20 were recorded in Whitman County. In Nez Perce County, this amounted to 17.4% of the total foreign-born and this proportion sharply increased during the following decade since in 1890 the Norwegians alone constituted 22.8% (325 individuals) of the foreign-born element living in Latah County, newly created out of Nez Perce County, Idaho. This rise was due in part to the continued favorable reports from the Genesee Valley which were being published in upper Midwest Norwegian newspapers. Some articles, however, were written with qualifications. One published in 1885 related that while harvest had been good, the price of staples in the area were nearly double what they were in Wisconsin. Flax yields averaged 25 bushels per acre and sold for $1.00 while one could expect 30 to 35 bushels with wheat but it sold for only 50 cents. Although the better farmlands had already been homesteaded in southwestern Latah County by the end of the decade, railroad land was still available and in 1889 heavy immigration took place along Paradise Valley between Moscow and Genesee. At the same time other Norwegians found land to the northeast in the vicinities of Cornwall, Troy, and Nora (Bjork, 1958).

Emil G. A. Christiansen, Pastor and Doctor

The American synods of European churches did more than minister to the spiritual needs of the immigrant pioneers. Their churches aided in the adjustment to life in the New World while facilitating contact with both the homeland and other ethnic enclaves on the Western frontier. Soon after their arrival in the Palouse, the Norwegian immigrants sought pastors of their own kind. The Rev. Emil G.A. Christensen has been called the Northwest's first Norwegian minister

and his Genesee church, founded in 1878, the first Norwegian congregation in the Inland Pacific Northwest. Born in 1838 in Christiania, Norway, Christensen came to America as a young boy and later pioneered mission work in Dakota Territory for the Norwegian Synod. In 1876 he and his family journeyed to Portland to serve former parishners who had settled on the Northwest coast, but two years later accepted the call from Genesee. He built a house on land which he homesteaded and helped erect the congregation's log church in 1880. One member, Jacob Tonning, described the simple but historic beginning of Our Savior's Lutheran Church:

Last winter trees were cut to be used in the spring to build a church, and this plan was carried out. As soon as the roads to the forest were passable the timber was hauled. Everything moved with the greatest of speed. From this one can see that our church was built of logs, and it is nicely fashioned. In size it is 19 by 25 feet and 12 feet high.... It can seat a hundred people, has an altar, a communion rail, a pulpit, and a baptismal font.... The latter is covered with a white linen cloth trimmed with lace...and as we live near the woods, there is no dearth of attractive cedar wreaths with which to beautify our church. Work began on July 28 and August 14 the building was ready.

Rev. Christensen had received medical training for missionary work and was pressed into service as a doctor on occasion during his ministry at Genesee. Historian John A. Platt of Genesee recalled:

I can remember mother was ailing with what she thought was rheumatism. We drove over to Dr. Christensen's house in the bobsleigh. Dad and we kids went into the office and stayed while mother was examined by the doctor in his office. While we journeyed home, father asked mother what the doctor had said. Mother said, "He gave me some pills to take and told me to get some red flannel underwear.

The scattered nature of Norwegian settlement forced Pastor Christensen to travel extensively throughout the Pacific Northwest but he suffered from health problems, so he argued for more assistance from the synod. By 1884, however, doctrinal conflicts surfaced, and a split in the Genesee church led to organization of a second, Norwegian-Danish Augustana Lutheran Church, and several years later a Scandinavian Methodist Church was also functioning in the town. Such religious diversity was typical of Norwegian-American life. In the Idaho Palouse, congregations of the Norwegian-Danish Methodist Church were organized by pioneer missionary C. J. Larsen in the 1880s. These included Moscow in 1885, Blaine in the following year, and Rockford in 1889. Preaching stations were established in 1902 at Wilmer, Troy, and Bear Creek. Norwegian Lutherans later established churches, often with other Scandinavians, in Deary, Avon, Park and Bear Ridge, all in present Latah County, and near Lacrosse in Whitman County, Washington.

Spokane County Norwegian Settlement

Norwegian immigration also flowed into southern Spokane County. One Norwegian family was farming on Rock Creek near present Rockford according to the 1878 territorial census. The H. Fuisons were living on the edge of the Palouse prairie and his family included one married son and several children while a Finlander, Charles Neuman, was farming nearby as were several Swedes. About the same time other Norwegians, mostly young men, had settled near Cheney before the town was platted by the Northern Pacific Railroad in 1880. R. Holt, writing later from Cheney, stated that the Norwegians there seemed to be doing well for themselves because of good local crops and the availability of work in sawmills and on the railroad.

A man who had major impact on Norwegian immigration to Spokane County in the 1880s was Olaf Windingstad, a Norwegian land agent in Cheney who worked for the Northern Pacific Railroad. According to a contemporary, in response to many questions from Scandinavians, he described Washington Territory in greatest detail, especially the rolling country of the Great Plateau of the Columbia, only half of which was settled in 1884. There was room, he said, for thousands of people, and the soil was a rich black loam with a clay subsoil. This country was penetrated by the Northern Pacific Railway, which had forest, grazing and farmland for sale at one fifth down and the balance in five payments at 7 percent interest. The climate, he said, was milk in winter, thanks to a warm southwest chinook [wind]; wheat production was 20 to 40 bushels per acre and it sold for 60¢ to 75¢.

Such information campaigns, launched among many immigrant groups by the Northern Pacific induced great numbers of Norwegians to settle in the northern Palouse during the 1880s, particularly in the Washington communities of Spokane Falls, Rockford, Fairfield, Cheney, and Medical Lake. Norwegian immigrant Anders Peterson purchased a quarter-section of bunchgrass and rocky pastureland from the Northern Pacific twenty miles south of Cheney in 1888. He was joined by his teenage cousin, Albert Owes, in the following year and the two aggressively worked together to build the livestock operation and acquire additional farm and rangeland to total 7,000 acres over the next four decades. The men were later joined by Owes' nephew, Osborne Belsby, who eventually took over the enterprise and expanded the livestock operation into one of the largest in the region (L. Belsby, 1996).

A number of Norwegians gravitated in 1886 to the Rockford area where H.M. Tostenson deemed the local terrain the "best farm land one could wish for." John Hanson, another immigrant of 1886, found that while the homestead land around Rockford had already been taken, land was available from the railroad or speculators at $5.00 to $10.00 per acre. He also warned that markets were distant and prices were low. However, the "dark clayey loam was a wonderful soil, even on the hills" and though it received little rainfall, crops yielded well. He anticipated the opening of the adjacent Coeur d'Alene Indian Reservation to settlement which could provide new homes for thousands of immigrants and noted that already "about Rockford are quite a few Swedish and Norwegian families, and some are well off." In 1888, Lars Gunderson of Rockford reported that twenty sections of land in the area owned by Marshall Field and Company of Chicago were for sale at $12 to $50 per acre. That year the railroad arrived and the population boomed. Gunderson noted that prairie chickens, geese, and fish were abundant

MR. AND MRS. OLE SLIND, LACROSSE (MASC, WSU LIBRARIES)

and he estimated that with about $2,500, one could establish a farming operation and shortly double the value of his investment.

The Palouse Selbu Norwegians

Norwegian immigrants had settled thinly in Whitman County along the Idaho border since the 1880s in the vicinities of Farmington, Palouse, and Pullman but the Selbu congregation near Lacrosse marked the only area of heavy Norwegian settlement in the county. It was begun in 1901 by Peder I. Wigen, a native of the Trondheim district in Norway, who had immigrated with his parents to Minnesota in 1872. Through the years a large enclave of emigrants from the village of Selbu near Trondheim was established in southeastern Minnesota. By the turn of the century, however, the bitter winters and repeated crop failures led Wigen and others to consider moving west, so he read with interest a letter published in Scandinaven by Elias Molee, a teacher and traveling lecturer originally from Tinn, Telemark, who had settled at Lacrosse in 1900. Molee described that area which, while located in the drier southwest portion of the Palouse, still had fertile lands available for settlement.

Peder Wigen and his brother, Joergen (George), both moved permanently to Washington in 1901 after inspecting it carefully. They purchased about 1,000 acres of land located six miles south of Lacrosse, Washington, on Mud Flat Creek and in the fall of that year Joergen returned to Minnesota to bring out his family. In the winter they were joined by another brother, Jens, who settled near Penawawa, and John Carlson who also bought farmland in the vicinity. Their families journeyed west in the spring of 1902 and were followed in the same year by John Aune, Peter, John, Torsten and Henry Bacon, Halvor Bacon, Halvor Garberg, Peder Hagen, Ole Krogstadt, Arnt Nervig, and Dan Stokke. Most settled on unbroken ground southeast of Lacrosse (I. Sather, 1987).

In January, 1903 Selbu Evangelical Lutheran Church was formally organ-

ized, but the congregation continued to meet in the Mud Flat Schoolhouse, as it had since May, 1902 until the new church was completed in 1904. Pastor Ivar Andreassen of Deary, Idaho, first served the congregation which was strongly influenced by the pietistic theology of Norwegian theologians Hans Nielson Hauge and Nicholai Gruntvig and remained more conservative in outlook than most other Lutheran synods. The Norwegian exodus to the southwest Palouse increased substantially in the spring of 1907 when twenty-five people immigrated directly from the Selbu area in Norway. Reporting on their appearance, the Colfax Gazette observed that "the Norwegians of that vicinity are progressive farmers and became good citizens." Among this group were the families of Ole, John, and Haldo Kjosness, Henrik and Halvar Nervig, Ole G. Slind, John Walli, and from neighboring Rissa, Norway, Ole F. Christoferson and Lars Danielson. Still others joined the group in 1908 from Minnesota including Henry Kyllo, Louis Emberson, and Mikkel Aftret. With the increase of Norwegian farmers, their area of settlement gradually expanded into the Hay and Penawawa areas near the Snake River where they transformed the dry, unbroken prairies into productive fields of grain. Subsequent arrivals included the Aune, Garberg, Myklebust, Sather, and Stephenson families (M. Slind and F. Bohm, 1990).

The native-born Norwegian population of Whitman County jumped from 56 in 1900 to 136 by 1910. During the same period their numbers in Latah County rose from 379 to 612. The national figures for Norwegian immigration were rising as well since many Scandinavians fled Europe during the first decade of the twentieth century for economic reasons and to escape growing militarism on the continent. After 1910 the number of Norwegian immigrants in the Palouse steadily declined as most open lands had been claimed.

Emigration From Sweden

"They live like pioneers on the frontier." With these words the famed missionary Eric Norelius described the

SELBU LUTHERAN CHURCH NEAR HAY, c. 1929 (MASC, WSU LIBRARIES)

Golden Mist

North of Waukon, Washington

Swedish colonists at Cordelia, Idaho (near Moscow), in 1885. One of the founders of America's largest Swedish denomination, the Augustana Lutheran Church, Reverend Norelius was on a Pacific Coast missionary tour and was surprised to see how primitive conditions were in the Palouse Country. He was, however, heartily welcomed by his fellow churchmen and predicted that "with patience and diligent labor they will undoubtedly succeed eventually." This group and other Swedish immigrants did prosper in the area where by 1890 they were the largest European ethnic group in Latah County—a distinction they maintained for several decades.

The vast majority of Swedish emigrants came from rural areas where, as in neighboring Norway, society was stratified into the land owners (gentry and peasants) and the various classes of rural landless (crofters, cotters, farm laborers and servants). Although the total area of agricultural lands more than tripled from 1750 to 1850, the increase in population of the lower class during that time was even greater. The economic problems of the rural landless, and particularly the laborers and servants, became acute by the middle of the nineteenth century as many could not maintain an adequate standard of living. In the 1850s, the country entered the market as a grain exporter as grain prices in Europe rose. This led landholders to begin consolidating their holdings to increase production. Businessmen engaged in land speculation while farmers mortgaged their properties in order to accumulate more land. A financial depression ensued after grain prices fell in the 1860s which combined with the effects over-speculation in farm lands to force many in Sweden into bankruptcy. These conditions caused high unemployment in both the countryside and southern industrial districts. Simultaneous crop failures complicated the situation and led to the Great Famine in Sweden which began in 1866 and lasted through the decade. During those four years 80,491 Swedes emigrated to the United States and some eventually came to the Palouse (F. Janson, 1931).

Contemporaneous with events in Norway, three separate waves of emi-

grants arrived on American shores between 1850 and 1920 when approximately 2,100,000 Swedes came to this country; the first group arrived in 1866, the same year that the American Emigrant Company began advertising widely in the rural Swedish press through its agent in Gothenburg. This first wave continued for about a decade, peaking in 1869 when six steamship companies carried on an active business by transporting roughly 32,000 Swedes to America. The exodus grew to its greatest proportions in the second wave between 1879 and 1893 when more than a half-million Swedes immigrated to the United States. The third wave lasted through the first decade of the twentieth century when about 220,000 journeyed to America.

Swedish Settlement in the Eastern Palouse

Swedes were first drawn in appreciable numbers to the inland Pacific Northwest by the gold strikes of the 1860s in the Colville and Clearwater districts. Although no Swedish farmers were located in the Palouse at the time of the 1870 federal census, several Swedes were involved in mining activity in the Clearwater River area. They included mule packers August Benson and Francis Skinner and a gold miner, Stephen Baker. Edward Patterson, also a native of Sweden, was operating one of the several saloons in the frontier settlement of Lewiston. In 1872 Martin Anderson arrived in Paradise Valley and preempted land some six miles north of present Moscow. Possibly the first Swedish immigrant farmer to settle in the area, Anderson decided in 1873 to homestead a parcel of land located nine miles northwest of Genesee. He had come to the United States in 1865 and lived in New England until moving to Portland, Oregon in 1871. Another Swedish immigrant, Eli M. Johnson, homesteaded near Anderson in 1874. Johnson was originally from the fertile southern coast country of Blekinge in Sweden but had immigrated in 1863 to Chicago and later to Port Townsend, Washington, before settling in the Palouse. In 1877 Peter Pauls homestead-

O. R. & N. Co. DEPOT, LACROSSE, c 1910 (MASC, WSU LIBRARIES)

ed land three miles northeast of Genesee and by the end of the decade a considerable number of Swedes had settled in the area between Moscow and Genesee. About the same time, Swedish settlement began expanding eastward into the Potlatch River, Bear Creek, and Park Valley areas.

Considerable immigration by Americans, Swedes, and other groups continued to the Moscow area in the late 1870s as prospective farmers eagerly sought the fertile bottomlands of the valley and the small town rapidly grew. In the spring of 1877 the Stewart and Beach sawmill was completed northeast of the town and in the same year Moscow was platted. Another sawmill opened near town shortly afterward which allowed for the construction of a number of new businesses that were established in the bustling community which soon became the chief trade center for the county. The town boasted a population of 300 in 1880 when the C. Moore and Company flour mill was built. In the following year businesses within the city included three general merchandise stores, two hotels, butcher shops, saloons, blacksmith shops and farm implement stores, one hardware store, and various professional offices. The Nez Perce News described the town in 1881 as "a lively thriving, enterprising, progressive place, and will take a boom this summer. The people are never tired of talking of the Palouse Country and they are right, for if there is a better country in the world, we have never seen it." Having traveled half-way around the globe in search of a new homeland, many of the Swedes likely agreed (L. Harker, 1941).

Swedish emigrant Oliver S. Peterson opened the first butcher shop in the town a year after his arrival in 1879. Soon other businesses were operated by Swedes which were patronized by the growing numbers of Nordic families settling in the area. Immigration surged with the arrival of the Columbia and Palouse Railroad in 1885. The Northern Pacific's Spokane and Palouse line reached Moscow in 1890. Construction on this section had begun in 1886 and it led from Marshall Junction through Spangle, Rosalia, Oakesdale, Belmont, Garfield, Palouse, Albion, Pullman, and Uniontown, Washington to Genesee, Idaho. A branch was then built from Pullman to Moscow and the grain district in southwestern Latah County was finally encircled when the line was extended through Joel, Troy, and Kendrick to

Juliaetta, Idaho in 1891. Lewiston was finally reached in 1898.

The contract for grading the Spokane and Palouse from Marshall was awarded to Nils A. Nelson, a Swedish immigrant. Originally from the Swedish island of Oland, Nelson emigrated in the late 1870s and spent several years in Chicago and in the Cripple Creek and Leadville mines of Colorado. His older brother, Andrew, joined him in Colorado and they came together to the Pacific Northwest about 1884 to try farming near the railroad town of Ainsworth at the confluence of the Snake and Columbia Rivers. Upon arriving there they found a land of sand and sagebrush described by an army surveyor as "a bleak, dreary waste." For the two former Baltic islanders, the desolation was too much to endure after the first crop failed. "We buried our boots and machinery in a sand pit, saddled our horses...and started for greener pastures," Nils later recalled.

The brothers rode to the Spokane country where they heard of railroad construction work for the Northern Pacific and found there a terrain and soil much like their native land. Nils became acquainted with the grading contractor for the Spokane and Palouse line who had commenced work, but when he had to suddenly forfeit the contract for personal reasons, Nils was appointed to succeed him. The railroads had traditionally turned to immigrant labor in building their lines across the West and many Swedes and Irish worked together on the Northern Pacific crews. Nelson was well liked by the workers and construction progressed through the "center of the great wheat belt" southeast from Marshall toward their destination at Genesee. Large camps of tents appeared regularly along the route and many workers learned that farmland in the area was still available through the railroad or individuals wanting to sell their claims. About 1889 a number of Swedish laborers homesteaded on the pine covered hills at Dry Ridge about five miles west of present Troy (E. Nelson, 1972).

In the 1880s Swedish settlement in Whitman County, Washington, was scattered along the eastern border in the vicinities of Palouse, Albion, and Pullman. In 1880, however, only twenty Scandinavians were living in Whitman County although the number of Swedes there had increased to 101 ten years later. In Spokane County Swedish brothers Andrew and Edward Patterson were farming near Pine Grove (Spangle) as early as 1878 and several other Swedish emigrants were farming nearby in the Latah and Rock Creek Valleys. By 1880 there were 43 Swedes and Norwegians living in Spokane County, and by 1886 a considerable Swedish community had developed around Rockford, which one Scandinavian gleefully described as "rolling prairies" of the "best farm land one could wish for" with forests where "the trees are so far apart you can plow around them."

The vast majority of Swedes in the Palouse, however, settled in Latah County where by 1890 the Swedish-born population numbered 355. While most Swedes located on farmland or worked in the forests, others pursued trades and lived in Moscow. A number of immigrants working on the railroad were quartered in the city during the winters and in one such example, Nils Nelson boarded at the home of a newly arrived Swedish family, the Andrew Linds. About 1889 Nelson and his brother purchased land near the south outskirts for six dollars an acre. Nils then married the daughter of the Linds. Over time many Swedish families congregated on the hill in the southeast part of Moscow which became known as "Swede Town."

Such ethnic neighborhoods were a characteristic of many pioneer communities in the American West. They allowed the emigrant to feel secure and maintain identity in America's highly competitive and pluralistic society since most foreigners arrived in their somewhat bewildering surroundings with slim financial resources. The development of national communities was a mixed blessing as it also encouraged the immigrant's suspicion of the larger society by fostering isolation from mainstream America. Furthermore, when political circumstances were involved, as in the classic case with Germans during World War I, antagonisms could also form within the group. These often developed along generational lines and resulted in the suppression of the native tongue and the alteration of surnames. Among the Swedes in the Palouse, however, affirmation of their cultural heritage was maintained through both language and religion for many years.

Swedish Missionaries and the Rural Lutheran Church

Sweden was predominantly a Lutheran country, and in the Palouse the majority of Swedish churches were Lutheran although several Swedish Methodist congregations were also organized.

Palouse Pastoral*   *South of Viola, Idaho*

185

Missionaries from both denominations were active in the region during the 1880s and Peter Carlson, the minister who pioneered Lutheranism among the Swedes in the Northwest, also had a deep interest in populating the Palouse with Swedish settlers. He was born in 1822 in the province of Smaland, Sweden. By his own accounts the family lived in poverty but he eventually attained a level of relative comfort by 1854 although he decided to immigrate to Boston and eventually settled in Illinois. In 1856 he became a colporteur for the American Tract Society and traveled extensively through Illinois, Iowa, Wisconsin, and Minnesota. Three years later he was ordained by the Swedish Lutheran United Conference and in 1879, in association with the Augustana Synod, became the church's first missionary on the West Coast.

Reverend Carlson established Portland as the base of operations for this immense charge. In February, 1880, he noted that "boatloads of people are going inland from Portland to take up land, and if the people from Minnesota are at all interested, they better hurry." He arranged for an inspection tour of the area east of the Cascades by two men in April, then wrote letters to the synod urging Swedes to colonize the region. Preferring the drier, inland climate himself, Carlson made a personal exploration trip by steamer in late April to Lewiston on a free pass. He also visited several families in Colfax who had taken up land near Moscow. He returned to the Palouse again in the fall and visited a large Swedish settlement about seven miles southeast of Moscow where his sons John and Andrew lived in rather primitive conditions. In November, 1880 Reverend Carlson organized the Cordelia congregation among the Swedish settlers, the first Swedish Lutheran church in the Inland Northwest. In the early 1880s he conducted services in Cheney, Spokane Falls, Palouse, and Pullman and as he traveled through the area he composed letters to friends in the Midwest describing its scenic beauty (R. Norling, 1939).

In 1883 three Swedish families gathered at the home of Gustaf Johnson in Moscow to celebrate Christmas with a traditional Jul Otta or early morning worship service. Another Swedish custom that endured was the Christmas Eve feast while a festive holiday meal for most Americans usually was held on Christmas Day. With the arrival of other Swedish families in Moscow the spring of 1884, Carlson was able to organize a congregation of fourteen members that organized annual celebrations around these events. That spring Westdala Swedes arrived in Troy from Ashtabula, Ohio, and Carlson began to hold services among them in the fall. He organized a congregation there, Westdala Lutheran Church, in 1886. Dr. Eric Norelius, newly appointed in 1885 as Superintendent of the West Coast Mission, visited the Swedish colonists in the Palouse during April of that year and described the pioneer conditions at Cordelia:

As I trudge to and fro among these Swedish settlers and see how poor many of them are, how simple and down-right uncomfortable many of the homes are, and under what primitive conditions pioneers must exist, I am reminded of the rugged times I spent in Minnesota just a few years ago. I know that the Rev. Peter Carlson has endured incredible deprivations since coming out here to carry on the mission of church.... It is nearly impossible to interpret for people in the East what life on the western frontier is like.

The next day Dr. Norelius traveled to Moscow where he stayed at the home of one of the town's first Swedish immigrants, Gustav Johnson, a skilled carpenter. He recorded a markedly different feeling for his new surroundings:

It seems to me that this would be a good place for Swedish people to settle. The worst criticism I have heard is that the land is somewhat hilly and hard to cultivate, although the soil is rich and productive. The average yield of wheat is about thirty to forty bushels to the acre; flax seed, about twenty bushels per acre; potatoes, from one hundred to one hundred and fifty bushels per acre; and corn, from fifty to sixty bushels per acre.

Dr. Norelius journeyed on to conduct mission work in Oregon but soon returned to the East. Pastor Carlson, however, remained in the Palouse and ministered to area Swedes from 1886 until 1892 when he entered an active retirement. Other Lutheran churches with considerable Swedish membership were later established in Deary and Troy. Swedish Methodism had a brief history in the Palouse with the first church organized in the Bear Creek area of Latah County in 1891 though it disbanded in 1900. Other Swedish Methodist congregations functioned between 1902 and 1906 at Nora and Albion.

By 1900 the number of native-born Swedes in Latah County had climbed to 541 and they constituted 27.9% of the total foreign-born element. The Swedes continued to be the largest foreign-born group in the county in 1910 (771 individuals) and in 1920 they represented 31.2% (668 individuals) of the foreign-born population. During this period in Whitman County their immigration involved fewer numbers, ranging from 119 in 1900 (5.1% of the foreign-born) to 132 individuals in 1920 (4.9%). The surge in Swedish immigration to the eastern Palouse after 1900 corresponded to the national experience as the third major wave of Swedish immigrants entered the United States. The fact that so many were entering Latah County even though most of the best farmland had been taken was due to the settlement of Swedes already in the area, many of whom were related to the new arrivals, and the opportunity for employment in the flourishing lumber industry.

Swedish Labor in the Palouse Forests

Employment in the timber industry in the Palouse broadened considerably in 1903 with the opening of the Potlatch Lumber Company's mill in Potlatch, Idaho. It was termed the largest and most modern facility of its kind in the world and was financed by Weyerhaeuser interests who realized the great potential of the industry in the region. The importance of these lumber resources was described in a June, 1900 issue of the *Spokesman-Review*:

Few people realize the vastness and richness of the country lying east of Palouse along the Palouse River in Latah county, Idaho, extending from this town [Palouse] 35 miles up the river and culminating in the Hoodoo mining district, which is now being thoroughly developed, with every respect of becoming a producer of great wealth in gold, silver and copper. Few districts of the same size contain so many varied but important resources and natural advantages as this. The country abounds in timber, from which millions of feet have been cut annually for the past 25 years and floated down the river to saw mills or converted into lumber by the saw mills located in the timber. This district has furnished most of the lumber used in buildings in the Palouse Country since its first settlement, yet the supply has not been noticeably diminished. There are apparently, almost inexhaustible supplies of splendid "saw" timber still standing and in viewing the

district from one of the small mountains by which it is surrounded, one can see nothing but timber in all directions, the places from which the timber has been cut during the past 25 years appearing like garden patches or small fields compared to the vast forests surrounding.

Before 1900 most men working in the woods were not professional loggers but small farmers or farm workers who logged in the winter. The Olson brothers on Dry Ridge near Troy provide an example of how many immigrants could profit by both farming and logging, work to which most had been accustomed in Scandinavia and the Midwest. The Olsons began work on a contract with the Sexton and Codd Mill of Palouse and in the winter season beginning in November, 1899 cut 500,000 feet of lumber. Several mills were operating on the North Palouse River in 1900 with Palouse and Colfax being the principal centers of activity. Nearly all the timber came from the great forests of pine and tamarack in northeast Latah County where the tiny hamlet of Princeton was established as a trade center for the scattered logging camps (R. Swanson, 1958).

The immense log drives down the North Palouse River took place annually in the spring and involved many workers. An eyewitness recalled the operation:

Logs were cut in the winter and the skid started early in the spring when the mountain snows swelled the Palouse. A million feet (of logs) down to the Palouse mills and on to Colfax was a gigantic task of 40 to 60 men working three weeks to get the logs to the mill here (in Palouse) and about 45 or 60 days to get them to Colfax.
During the drives around 400 men, many of them locals, were on the job. Most loggers were huge, husky men although strength was not the main requisite of a prime logger after the tree was felled. To get the logs down the river required men with brains and nimble legs. The logs were rolled into the river and floated down until they formed a jam. The loggers then had the hazardous task of climbing across the mass of logs and breaking the jam until the logs were once again on their way downstream.

Prior to Weyerhaeuser's entrance into Palouse area lumbering, most local ventures operated on a relatively small scale and frequently changed hands. The forerunner of the Potlatch Company was the Palouse River Lumber Company which was organized in 1895 by several Palouse businessmen. In 1903 it was purchased by the Potlatch Lumber Company which then arranged to build the Washington, Oregon and Montana Railroad into its newly acquired timber belt of 100,000 acres along the North Palouse River and its tributaries. One reporter correctly observed that construction of the line would also affect the agricultural development of the area.

People conversant with the country through which this railroad is to pass say that it will prove a paying proposition from an agricultural standpoint as well as from lumbering. Most of the land near the railroad for the first 25 miles out of Palouse is a rich agricultural sections. The country has been kept back as a farming community chiefly because of the lack of railroad facilities. It is the belief that the building of the road will bring scores of settlers into the country....so far the only town of any importance along the proposed right of way is Princeton, Idaho, a small village about 15 miles from Palouse, as the road will run.

With the completion of the new mill at Potlatch in 1906, the smaller lumber companies in the eastern Palouse began to cease operations. Having provided for local needs for a quarter-century, corporate lumbering now opened world-wide markets to timber products from the region. Employment opportunities for immigrants grew with the company and this ushered in a new period of immigration to the sparsely populated areas of the North Palouse River in the first decade of the nineteenth century. Many Swedes were given work at the mill while others established prosperous farms in one of the last areas to be settled in the Palouse Country. The difficulty of clearing land combined with the uncertainty of crop yields in the far eastern Palouse forced many homesteaders to work at other jobs. "My mother had to do most of the work—the hayin' and everything—because he [father] had to be out working because there was no income from the farm for the family," explained Philip Asplund. The cleared timber itself was a major source of income. From Troy, Idaho, cordwood was shipped to Moscow, Genesee, and other Palouse towns where it sold from $2 to $3 per cord (E. Kincaid, 1934; F. Bohm, 1980).

As Troy grew it provided secondary employment. The Troy Lumber and Manufacturing Company was organized in 1904 and was the largest lumber operation in the area until the Potlatch mill was built

in 1906. Other industries included the Troy Roller Mills and the Troy Fire Brick Company. Chartered in 1905, the First Bank of Troy gained a national reputation for its easy loan policies and its independent ownership which lasted into the 1970s. Troy at the turn of the century with its three saloons and thriving business district served the needs of loggers and transient railroad workers. Its wide main street was said to have been designed so that traders who had been drinking would be able to turn their four-horse teams around without too much trouble.

Located five miles northeast of Troy, the small sawmill town and trading center of Nora was established about 1892 as a predominantly Scandinavian community with a reputation for outstanding food served at Ole Edwardson's boarding house. It was an overnight stop for travelers between the Bovill-Park areas and Moscow, and they used two rooms upstairs and a folding davenport downstairs for lodging. The Edwardsons charged $3.50 per week for meals and lodging. Some Nora residents also enjoyed drinking. Ruthford Erickson recalled that when he was about thirteen a neighbor woman would send him to fetch a bucket of beer for her at the Nora saloon. She would drink the beer from a long-handled dipper while rocking in her chair and smoking a pipe (A. Driscoll, 1970).

Deary was also a timberman's town. It was settled in the 1880s and '90s mainly by Scandinavians who had first lived in the upper Midwest. William Burkland remembered that his parents had been in Minnesota for six years. "Then they heard about this country and the homesteads and the timber. And my dad, he was a timber man. He was in timber all his life....He could hit the same place twice with an axe." Among the early settlers around Deary were L.O. Byers, John Drury, George Clark, Ben Dennis, Dave Peterson, Arthur Bjerke, A.M. Johnson, Jack Sturman, and John Anderson (W. Burkland, 1976).

The Scandinavian population in the Genesee area was concentrated to the north along Cow Creek and in the Blaine district. Early settlers had the family names of Johnson, Halverson, Hanson, Olson, Christensen, Knutson, Peterson, Swenson, Martinson, Tonning, Danielson, Isaaksen, Bergen, Borgan, and Jacobson. The Nordics who chose to settle in the area did not find Palouse bunchgrass to turn but heavy timber standing in the way of cultivation. "If you like to work in the woods, go to Troy," was the message that Oscar Thomason received in Sweden from his brother-in-law, and Thomason decided to accept the invitation. When one early homesteader wrote to people in Minnesota that it took twelve horses to pull Troy carrots out of the ground, he may have been preoccupied with clearing stumps. And when questioned about the steep land around Troy, he gave another answer worthy of Paul Bunyan: "That's nothing, it all leans downhill!" A majority of the first settlers in the forested area around Troy, Idaho, were Swedes but there were also many Norwegians. The similarities in their customs, accent, and family names came to blur the original distinctions in ethnic origin and they became known to outsiders as Scandinavians. Further east in Deary, Joe Wells, a lumberman who won respect for his hard work and good citizenship, is reputed to have joked that he was the only "Whiteman" in those parts, the rest were Swedes and Norwegians. What made the story funny was that Wells was a Black (Driscoll, 1970; K. Peterson and R. Waldbauer, 1974)!

Cautious Looks

Arthur Bjerke
Deary, Idaho

Arthur Bjerke was born in Norway in 1886 and moved with his family to the vicinity of Deary, Idaho in 1891. He resided on the original family homestead until his recent passing. These recollections are from on interviews conducted in 1973 by Sam Schrager for the Latah County Historical Society Oral History Project. Used by permission

I was born in Norway in the same house that my father, grandfather, and great-grandmother were born. Times were pretty hard in Norway, so we came to Dakota. I remember when we lived in Dakota in a sod shanty that was no more than a cellar. I was four when we came west to Idaho. When we got to Spokane the railroad depot was just a rough lumber shack, because the whole town had been burnt down in the big fire. We moved to our Brush Creek homestead on the seventeenth day of March 1891 and I have been here ever since.

The first year it was pretty hard for us to get groceries or anything. We had a few chickens that laid awfully good, so we lived almost entirely on bread and eggs. I believe it was thirty years before I would eat an egg after that! And I don't care for an egg now. You could buy all the butter you wanted for five cents a pound, eggs for five cents a dozen, a sack of flour forty-nine pounds for fifty-cents— but you didn't have the money to buy it with. That was when Cleveland was president, along about 1893, and its was hard times for everyone. 1893 was a wet year, and the grain sprouted in the field. It wasn't good for much except to feed the hogs or cattle. About the best a man could earn in the harvestfield was seventy-five cents a day. I knew a man named Anderson who worked all summer, and by the fall he only had fifty cents. He and his wife hid it away real good—so good that they never did find that fifty cents to start the winter out. But they got through. They had a cow or two and a little flour, and they raised a few spuds. That was just about all they had to eat—milk, butter, bread, and potatoes.

The homesteaders couldn't file on their places without money so they were just squatting. If they moved away from the place for thirty days to get a job and earn money, somebody else would have moved into their cabin. There were quite a few that lost their farms because they just didn't have the money to file. They couldn't borrow because there was no one around with cash to lend. My sister had been working at McConnell's Store in Moscow, and she let Dad have a few dollars so that he could file. The country was heavily timbered with black pine when we came. There wasn't much underbrush because the Indians kept it burnt off. My parents started clearing and breaking up the land to seed to timothy for hay. We had to harvest by hand until Dad got the biggest part of the stumps cleared. Then we were able to use a horse-drawn mower.

We had one neighbor at first. Martin Olson moved onto his homestead the day after we did. He lived with us until he got his cabin built. Some of the first families around here were Louis Halseth, M.S. Perry, the Lawrences, Andrew Berg, and the Ericksons. Then Ed Magnuson came, and so did Eric Larson and Ben Lee. The homesteaders visited quite a lot together. They were sociable, and if they met on the road they would drive the horse and wagon to a shady spot and sit and visit for an hour or so. There were lots of dances on Saturday nights, and there was always someone who could play music. They would have a real good time.

I started herding cattle when I was sixteen years old. I took care of some of four hundred head. Part of them belonged to Ivar Bjerke, and part to two men named Hooker and Andy. They had meadows leased by Cherry Butte, Horse Ranch, and Elk River. We would move the cattle up in the spring and let them graze, first one place and then the next. I lived in a tent and was with the cattle all the time. I had a little black dog with me, and he was a dandy! He was a good cattle dog and a good hunting dog. I would leave him to guard the camp when I went into the woods. He would keep bears out and nothing could get past him. I got to know all of the land between Avon and Elk River while I was herding cattle those three years. I'd go around the cattle a couple a times a day to keep them from getting too far spread out.

In the early days people used to keep big bulls called oxen for the heavy work. At first all the skidding of logs was done with oxen, instead of horses. The oxen had a yoke over their necks with a chain that could be hooked to pull a wagon or logs. You could go into the brushiest patch with them and they could bend over trees as big as your arm. The driver had no line or reins. He used a stick and would call "Gee!" and "Haw!" to guide them. "Gee" was for right and "Haw" was for left. Those bulls would understand that pretty well. Maybe if there was a big log, they would put on four or six bulls to pull it out. Almost all of the sawmills around here used bulls in the early days. The logging was done in the winter. The bulls skidded out the logs as far as the skid road and then horses were used to haul the logs to the mill.

The very first settlers in around Deary were seven Germans, but they left pretty quick. People called it the "Seven Devils Country" on account of those seven Germans. One was named Mike Tebor and another was Albert Riggs. A lot of people from North Carolina settled around the same area, including Negro Joe Wells and his family. Joe had been born a slave and was freed after the Civil War. Frank and Crom Wells treated him just like a brother. Joe's wife Lou was a good cook, and people who traveled through the country used to stop a their cabin to eat and rest. They had three children, and we were all the first ones to go to school here, along with my sister, the four Halseth boys, and Hawkin Peterson. Joe and his family were well liked here, and there was never a party where they weren't included.

The men who homesteaded on the site of Deary before it was a town were Bert Crooks, Joe Bailock and Roundtree. The schoolhouse sits on land that belonged to Bert Crooks. Along about 1905 the Potlatch Lumber Company came into the country. First they built a mill over at Potlatch, and then they built the railroad in here so they could log this part of the country. They decided to start a town at Deary, so they bought the land and named it after their logging boss, Bill Deary. Two of their men, McGowen and Henry, divided the site into lots for the town and sold them. The town grew pretty fast. I remember quite a few stores when it first got started. There was a saloon, a drugstore, and some great general stores.

I visited with Mox Mox a few times. He was tall and a good Indian. He used to come up to Bovill every year with his family and some other Indians, until they put that railroad in. Hugh Bovill, the man that started the town there, was his friend. Mox Mox didn't like to see the people sell their timber to the lumber company, because then it would be cut. He told Bovill, "They're spoiling the country now." And they did! After that the Indians didn't go up to Bovill any more. I don't blame them at all, because the white men just took the country away from them. It was really their country to begin with.

*Evening Glow Palouse River**

South of St. John, Washington

Chapter VIII:

THE VOLGA AND BLACK SEA GERMANS

*"Just like any new country you come into, it's the people that have to develop it. The thing was...
to have the ambition, roll up your sleeves and go to work."*

—Conrad Schmick, 1983

Preparing their children for the arduous journey that lay beyond the broad Russian steppe, Peter and Mary Schmick reminded their children of ancient Israel's exodus to the Promised Land. Throughout the spring of 1900 the couple had made plans with several other families in the Volga German colony of Yagodnaya Polyana (Berry Meadow), Russia to join relatives in America. Their son Conrad recalled from the distance of nearly a century the German chant they learned by candlelight:

> *We are going to America,*
> *The land where milk and honey flow,*
> *Where cows comes home with sweetbread*
> *Resting upon their horns.*

Weeks later when temporarily residing with other immigrant families at the Russian German "Palouse Colony" near Endicott, Washington, Conrad would join his young friends to raid wild honey combs in hollow trees along the Palouse River and herd milk cows home with their udders spurting milk after a day's grazing on the luxuriant pasturage. "Look and see," the elders reminded them, "You have the milk flowing from the cows and the honey flowing from the trees—just as we said in Russia that it would be!"

The Germans from Russia were the first European colonist group with which the Northern Pacific Railroad attempted to populate its vast lands in the Palouse through its subsidiary, the Oregon Improvement Company. No Russian Germans lived in the Palouse prior to the construction of the Northern Pacific's Palouse and Columbia line in 1882, but by the end of the century the Russian Germans were the second largest European group in Whitman County (327 individuals). They never settled in large numbers in either Latah or Spokane counties, preferring the hilly prairies of Whitman County where by 1920 they had become the largest for-

eign-born group (798 Russian-born or 29.8% of the total foreign-born population).

The German Colonial Enclaves in Russia

The Russian Germans who settled in the Palouse Country were from two German colonial enclaves in Russia, one on the lower Volga River and the other on the northwest coast of the Black Sea. The vast majority of those immigrating to the Palouse came from the Volga region although a group of Black Sea Germans settled in the Palouse in 1905. Germans first established colonies on the lower Volga in the 1760s during the reign of the Russian Empress, Catherine the Great. Catherine, herself an ethnic German, was determined to develop the untamed southwest portion of her empire, but having little success with national relocation efforts, turned to her native Germany where the independent states, principalities, and free cities of the late eighteenth century numbered in the hundreds. After a century of continental warfare many of the entities were bankrupt and poverty and famine were widespread. After the outbreak of the Seven Years War in 1756 many Germans sought to flee the chaos. The area comprising present Hessen was the scene of repeated disasters during the war, and while many Germans died in the strife or fled to America, others looked in the opposite direction to Russia.

Amid the despair and destruction in Hessen, many peasants learned of an unusual proposal, Catherine the Great's Manifesto of 1763, in which she invited colonists to populate the fertile areas of the lower Volga region under liberal terms including immunity from all taxes, draft exemption, and land possession "for external time." In an overwhelming response, approximately 27,000 Germans made the long trek to Russia between 1765 and 1767. They established 104 colonies along the lower Volga River in the region surrounding

Saratov. Among those emigrating from Hessen during the summer of 1766 was a group of eighty families who had come from thirty-seven villages in the hilly Vogelsberg and adjacent districts. From this group the majority of Volga Germans in the Palouse descended.

After a year-long journey to the Volga, they founded the village of Yagodnaya Polyana on the hilly, western side of the Volga River. Stories of the epic trek have been passed down through generations of Volga Germans whose families subsequently relocated over a century later to the Palouse. Family patriarch Conrad "C. G." Schmick of Colfax, for example, related that his ancestor Peter Schmick arrived at his destination in the fall of 1767 only to find that "nothing on the vast uninhabited steppe had been prepared for their arrival. They were forced to dig earth homes (*zemlyankii*) in the ground; these were covered with wood from their wagons. The new settlers lived in these earth dwellings until the village could be planned and built." Following a difficult period of adjustment, the colonists prospered and expanded their domain to the drier districts east of the river where a number of "daughter colonies," like New Yagodnaya, were founded in the late 1850s (R. Scheuerman and C. Trafzer, 1980, Conrad G. Schmick, 1979).

Following the example of Catherine, Tsar Alexander I inaugurated a campaign to colonize the northern Black Sea region which he had wrested from Turkish control early in the nineteenth century. Promises similar to Catherine's were made to induce settlers to emigrate from Germany and thousands responded between 1803 and 1857, establishing 153 colonies in the Black Sea region. Among these were the villages of Guldendorf, Neuburg, and Gross-Liebental, founded between 1804 and 1806 mainly by Germans from Wuertenburg. From these Black Sea colonies other Germans also immigrated to the Palouse. As did the Volga Germans, the Black Sea Germans constructed small, well planned villages surrounded by large communally-owned fields.

Plots of land were regularly distributed among the males through a local democratic assembly, the village *mir*. However, by 1860 there were over 200,000 Volga and Black Sea Germans and the individual family acreages of the prolific colonists had been severely reduced despite the opening of new districts to their settlement. In addition to this problem was a dispute among the Protestant clergy in the

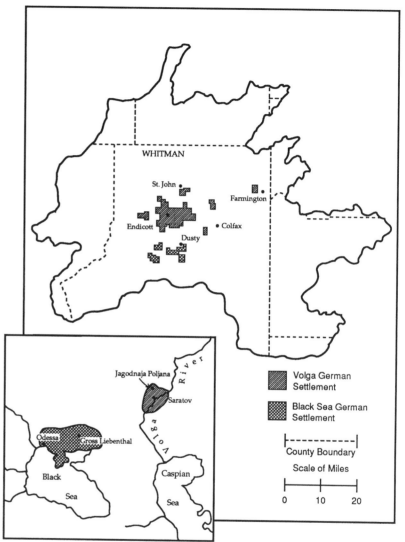

THE VOLGA AND BLACK SEA GERMAN COLONIES
IN RUSSIA AND THE CENTRAL PALOUSE, c. 1890

colonies. The growth of a pietistic movement known as the Brotherhood (*Bruederschaft*) led to antagonisms between the official Lutheran clergy in Russia and Brotherhood members who emphasized

194

Palouse Evening Storm*

Looking Northeast From Steptoe Butte

a personal faith based on piety and prayer. Although this division never led to the formation of a new denomination among the German colonists in Russia, the dispute was carried to America where German Congregationalism was born.

Conrad Schmick remembered being present at a Bruederschaft meeting in his home and hearing the elders speak of impending danger in Russia because of both religious and political conditions. In contrast a handful of letters from America was held up as the bearer said, "Our brothers in America write telling of much land, free churches, and fair laws." The reference to law may have been related to the growing antagonism in this particular village, Jagodnaja Poljana, over mandatory Russian language instruction for boys. In retrospect, the main reason for Russian German emigration to America proved to be another Tsarist decree—this one by Alexander II. In 1871 Alexander abrogated all of Catherine's privileges of settlement given to the German colonists.

Particularly troublesome to the tsar was the fact that they had maintained their German identity through the many decades of life in Russia. When a temporary grace period extending exemption from military service was annulled in 1874, thousands of Russian Germans reacted by emigrating to the North and South America. They left Russia in three major waves. The first began in the 1870s, followed by others between 1887 and 1893, and 1903 to 1914. By 1920 there were some 116,535 persons in the United States who had been born in Russia and who considered German their mother tongue. Most had settled in the Dakotas, Kansas, Nebraska, and Colorado where they engaged in farming. Others, however, continued to move westward (R. Sallet, 1974).

Volga German Immigration to the Palouse and Railroad Colonization Strategy

The first Russian-Germans in the American West, about seventeen families, arrived in Portland in 1881 after spending several years on the dry, grasshopper-infested Kansas plains. Members of this vanguard included Conrad Appel, Phillip Fuchs, George Green, Henry Repp, and several Klewenos, Ochses, and Schiermans. They had first immigrated to Rush and Barton Counties in Kansas

between 1875 and 1878. Most were natives of the villages New Yagodnaya, Schoental, and Schoenfeld which were daughter colonies of Yagodnaya Polyana and neighboring Pobotschnoye. The group obtained special emigrant fares through the Union Pacific Railroad and Oregon Steam Navigation Company to travel to Portland where they had heard good farmland was available.

After their arrival in Oregon, however, they were disappointed to find that the best lands had already been taken and what ground was available

GENERAL THOMAS R. TANNATT, c. 1885 (MASC, WSU LIBRARIES)

was unfit for cultivation. The frustrated immigrants turned to work at a local lumber mill and for the railroad which was then grading the huge Albina fill in present Portland. They learned the railroad was offering to sell 150,000 acres of "the finest agricultural lands in the northwest," which would be accessible by rail in 1882. When approached by the Volga Germans about settlement opportunities east of the Cascades, railroad officials saw a chance to implement their new plans for colonization in the Palouse. Northern Pacific Railroad magnate Henry Villard had acquired vast acreage in the Palouse Hills and he placed retired Civil War general Thomas R. Tannatt in charge of its development.

The Volga German "Kansas Colony" families in Portland inquired about the company's new lands in the Palouse in the spring of 1881 and an inspection tour was arranged for several representatives of the group—Phillip Green, Peter Ochs and three Schierman brothers; Conrad, Henry, and John. The *Walla Walla Weekly Statesman* printed a letter received by R. W. Mitchell, a Colfax agent for the company's land department:

Five locating agents of the Kansas colony, composed of about

70 families, passed through here Thursday on their way to inspect lands of the O.I. Co. Col. Tustin is in charge of the party. They look like solid, progressive farmers, such as we are willing to welcome to our broad acres. One of them remarked, "If the land is anything like what we've seen around Dayton, I guess we can be suited. We are surprised and delighted at what we have seen." Mr. Mitchell of the O.I. Co. will meet this party in the Palouse Country next week.

Writing from Dayton to Villard's office, Tannatt relayed his intentions for dealing with the group in a note on May 10. "I want to sell them a township and will on Mr. Oakes' return if there is any trade with them." Indeed, the vanguard returned favorably impressed with the land's fertility and the hilly topography reminded them of the Volga Bergseite. Tannatt planned to meet with them in Portland to arrange the sale but he found them reluctant to enter into such a massive deal on behalf of the others in Kansas. The village mir system in Russia had conditioned them to farm communally small fields, not entire townships. After considering the possibilities, several families decided to move to the Palouse the following year when the men could secure employment on Villard's Palouse line which was to be built through the Palouse. They would have time then to select company lands on which to establish a small colony.

Some members of the immigrant vanguard came by wagon while Tannatt arranged for others to travel over the lines of the Oregon Railway and Navigation Company to its terminus at Texas Ferry on the Snake River. They arrived there in October, 1882 and some of the men walked twenty miles to Endicott to procure wagons to transport their families and belongings to Endicott the following day. One of the spokesmen for the colony, Phillip Green, stated that he "had written home setting forth the fact that the land, climate and general outlook of this [Palouse] country, was all that could be desired." He also communicated to Tannatt that, "Three other Kansas colonies have sent inspectors or agents with the present party, who are to locate land for other coming immigrants. There is to be an exodus from Kansas this fall."

Some of the families lived in tents and company houses in Endicott while others who first settled on lands in the country fashioned crude earth pits similar to the *zemlyankii* dug by their ancestors on the Volga. In the following spring lumber was obtained from Colfax to build wooden houses. Many of the Volga Germans went to work extending the Columbia and Palouse line to Colfax which was reached the following year. In October, 1882 a local paper reported on the progress of the colony:

Delegation for the Palouse Country—Calling at the office of O.I. Co. on Monday to introduce gentlemen for the East we found quite a delegation to whom Gen. Tannatt was explaining the Palouse Country and arranging for settlement. Some weeks since a portion of the Kansas Colony now here, with their own teams will be met by additional teams at Texas Ferry, to carry out household goods sent by train. Gen. Tannatt will meet them in Endicott, to complete contracts and outer houses built for their use. This organized method of handling immigrants is doing much for the Palouse Country, directly and indirectly for all of eastern Washington. The ample capital of O.I Co. and their simple method of dealing promptly with new comers, upon an easily understood plan, is most proper—Mr. Greene who is with those who left on Saturday says twenty-four families are on the way hither and those now at Endicott are much pleased with the country and their reception.

Adding new impetus to regional development was the long awaited completion of the Northern Pacific Railroad on September 8, 1883 when the final gap was closed on the transcontinental line at Gold Creek, Montana. More Volga Germans streamed into the area with other immigrant groups as the months long, grueling wagon journeys were shortened to ten days by relatively inexpensive rail transit. Some members of the original group expressed doubts about their decision to leave Kansas for the Palouse frontier. Returning to the Midwest was a frequent topic of discussion during the winter of 1883-84 but the hardy pioneers resolved to stay in the new land.

The Volga German "Palouse Colony"

The tumbled landscape of the Palouse reminded the Volga

Germans of their homeland on the Russian steppes. They collectively purchased a quarter section of land five miles north of Endicott which was divided equally, reflecting the mir method of land tenure to which they had been accustomed in Russia. The colony consisted of the families of Peter and Henry Ochs and those of Conrad, Henry, George, and John Schierman. They were joined by the John Schreiber and Phillip Aschenbrenner families and all worked together in the building of the first eight homes which were simple three-room structures. A small herd of livestock was maintained and they planted large gardens of potatoes, melons, corn, and sunflowers. They found that wheat and barley grew particularly well on the chestnut brown soil, given the Russian name chernozem by area agronomists, as well as oats which were planted on the higher areas bordering the bluffs. In the Palouse they learned by experience with other farmers that contour farming was a necessity. The immigrants soon realized that with the abundance of prime farmland and mechanized methods of cultivation and harvest, an individual could acquire and manage larger estates in relative self-sufficiency unlike the small plots they had tended on the slopes in Russia. This led other early Volga Germans like Conrad and Christina Kammerzell, Phillip and Anna Green, Henry and Mary Repp, and Henry and Anna Litzenberger to settle in neighboring areas where they purchased their own farms. The river colony served for years, however, as a clearing house lodging newly arrived immigrant families from Russia until they could make more permanent arrangements (C. Schmick, 1979).

Other families chose to pursue business ventures in neighboring towns that served the needs of the agrarian populace. Early Volga German businesses in Endicott included H.P. Kleweno's general store, Youngman and Langlitz's harness shop, and a saloon operated by Henry Litzenberger. By 1885 approximately a dozen Volga German families were in the Palouse and all had come through Kansas. About 1890 the first large groups began arriving in the Palouse direct from the mother colony of Yagodnaya Polyana with lesser numbers from other villages. In that year first-generation Volga Germans in Whitman County numbered about 100 and this grew to 327 in 1900. In 1892 their settlement expanded to Farmington with the arrival there by train of the Peter Fischer and John Koch families Among the first to settle in the Lancaster district were Henry Repp, Adam Kleweno, Conrad S. Schierman, and Henry Schneidmiller. The latter's two sons, Manuel and Elmer Schneidmiller, relocated to the Post Falls area following World War II where they were instrumental in establishing the Rathdrum Prairie grass seed industry..

Volga Germans in the Farmington area are credited with introducing lentils and other legumes to the Palouse Country. J. J. Wagner, a native of Kolb, Russia who settled south of Farmington, obtained lentil seed from a fellow Seventh-Day Adventist named Martin. Wagner was interested in marketing a high protein, vegetarian food source and harvested a small plot which provided enough seed to plant about an acre in 1917. The crop yielded well and Wagner sold the lentils to wholesaler B.C. Gordon in Spokane. Wagner's production steadily expanded as did the range of other legume varieties he and others planted which came to include Chilean lentils, China or wedge peas, and garbanzos (P. Wagner, 1988).

VOLGA GERMAN PALOUSE COLONY NEAR ENDICOTT, c. 1895 (MASC, WSU LIBRARIES)

LUTHERAN PALOUSE CONFERENCE OF THE OHIO SYNOD, ENDICOTT, c. 1915 (MASC, WSU LIBRARIES)

Many immigrants like C. G. Schmick's father found employment in various community business and heavy labor occupations as Colfax and surrounding towns were enjoying an unprecedented period of prosperity. The major trade center for Whitman County, Colfax's population had risen from 1,649 in 1890 to 2,783 in 1910. By the same time the population of the county reached its highest point in any census—33,280. The Volga Germans in Colfax congregated in the city's northeast section along First Street in what became known as "Russian Town" although they hated being labeled as "Russians." Here one could daily see women clad in brown woolen shawls and head scarfs, talking in their Hessian accent while their children played Kneeps, a simplified form of Karoom, and other Old Country games. By 1910 the number of Russian-born residents of the county reached 557 and this increased to 798 in 1920. This number also reflected a group of Black Sea Germans who came to the Palouse in 1905.

Whitman County's Black Sea German Enclave

The only settlement of Black Sea Germans in the Palouse began in 1904 when the Volga Germans of the Endicott Congregational Church extended a call to the Reverend Henry Vogler of Eureka, South Dakota. Reverend Vogler was serving the German Congregational parish in Eureka which was composed of Black Sea Germans who had settled heavily in that region. He married one of the daughters of Peter Uhl, a Black Sea German who had immigrated to Eureka in 1887 from Gross Liebental, Russia. Uhl's three other daughters had married Black Sea Germans who had also settled in the Eureka area. Barbara and

Rosina married two brothers, Jacob and John Stueckle, respectively (both natives of Guldendorf, Russia), while Magdalena had married Philip Broeckel.

Following Rev. Vogler's arrival in Endicott early in 1904, he and his wife settled on a farm about two miles east of present Dusty though he continued his ministry. In the fall of the year they were joined by his wife's parents, the Peter Uhls. The Voglers and Uhls enjoyed their new life in the Palouse while the rest of their relatives in South Dakota disliked the cold climate and disappointing crop yields. After reading favorable reports on the land and climate in the Northwest, the three brothers-in-law and John's son-in-law, Fred Steiger, decided in 1905 to journey over the Northern Pacific line to Washington. In preparation for their new farming venture, a freight car was chartered to transport the group's seven draft horses, hack, and twelve-foot Hodge header. They later found the header to be too light for the hillsides and purchased a heavier fourteen-foot McCormick. Steiger and Broeckel were selected to accompany the freight car and were followed a few days later by the other nine adults and their twenty-six children for whom an entire passenger coach was chartered. The group arrived in Endicott on Sunday morning, March 5, 1905.

The families lived through the spring near Dusty while the men worked and scouted in eastern Washington and Oregon for suitable farms. In July the group purchased nine quarter-sections (1,440 acres) of land about two miles east of present Dusty on Alkali Flat Creek from the Burrell Land Company in Colfax for $30 per acre. Lots were cast to fairly divide the land among the heads of the families who then turned to the task of building homes and barns.

Though each farm was privately owned, they cooperated in many farming operations and later joined together to establish St. John's German Congregational Church in 1926. A few Black Sea German families like that of Michael Pfaff settled elsewhere in the Palouse in 1920s when depressed grain prices and low yields forced some landowners to sell their property to immigrants like Pfaff who had saved enough working elsewhere in America to make a downpayment on a new life in the Palouse. The Pfaff family had originally settled among relatives in South Dakota before moving on to Washington and eventually acquired property near Garfield (J. Stueckle, 1962 and 1980).

The German Department of the Congregational Churches in America began in 1846 among German immigrants who had settled along the Iowa frontier and by the 1860s had grown into a leading German Protestant denomination in the United States. Its origins on the West Coast can be traced to the arrival of the Volga Germans in the Palouse Country in 1882 since the Endicott Congregational Church was organized by some of these immigrants in 1883. Reverend Thomas W. Walters, resident pastor of Plymouth Congregational Church in Colfax, first ministered to this group in 1883 until a traveling German from Ritzville, Reverend Fruicht, learned of their need. In a meeting held in Endicott in 1888, this congregation and others in Ritzville and Walla Walla were the first West Coast congregations formally accepted into the German Congregational Church.

Other Russian German churches of this denomination were later established near Lacrosse (1895) and in Colfax (1897). Volga German Lutherans in the Palouse Country were without a minister until 1887 when pioneer missionary Reverend Henry Rieke of the Ohio Synod found their colony on the Palouse River. He organized Trinity Lutheran Church in Endicott among some of these families in 1890, and the founding of other Volga German churches followed in Farmington (Christ Lutheran, 1896) and Colfax (Peace Lutheran, 1902). The split within the Russian German religious community into Congregational and Lutheran denominations was an outgrowth of the earlier dispute in Russia between the pietistic Brotherhood and more liturgically-oriented Lutherans.

With the outbreak of the First World War in 1914, Russian German emigration from Russia was severely curtailed and after the 1917 Bolshevik Revolution in Russia it virtually ended. Unfortunately for those who had immigrated to the Palouse, the Russian-Germans found themselves identified with two European countries not popular in America. The introduction of church services in English became widespread during World War I although German services did continue among many first-generation Russian-Germans in the Palouse until the 1960s. While the number of native-born Russian Germans in the Palouse declined after 1920, these colonist farmers had come at a critical time in the history of the region and contributed to its transformation into one of the world's most productive dryland farming regions.

CONRAD G. SCHIMICK
ENDICOTT, WASHINGTON

"C.G.," as he was popularly known to his many friends, was a man who readily express his deep gratitude to God and his adopted country for the blessings of family and farm life he knew in the Palouse Country. The patriarch of five generations, he retired from his Endicott farm to live in Colfax where he was interviewed by Don Kackman in April, 1981 and by Richard Hamm in June, 1983 for the Whitman County Historical Society Oral History Project. The following narrative was compiled from these interviews. Used by permission.

I was born in the village of Yagodnaya Polyana in Russia. The town was just an ordinary large village of German people. It increased up to about 15,000 to 16,000 inhabitants; ninety percent or better were poor people, poor peasants. We kids didn't get to go very far. Oh, we went with our parents into Saratov, the big city about the size of Spokane, and there we seen the trains and the different things we didn't see in the village. Most of the people didn't get out very much.

Every year, usually it was a custom in the spring of the year and the fall of the year, to migrate from there to whatever country they went. When my folks left there, in 1900, I was in lack of two or three months of being eight years old. Well, it was a big experience for a kid like me. I can remember when we hit the high seas and a storm overtook us and just swept over the main deck. They give out the alarm that everybody's supposed to duck down on second deck, you know. There was a storm coming up. There happened to be an Austrian fellow just coming back from the kitchen, who had a big bunch of boiled potatoes. A wind come along and blew his hat off and he dropped his pan of boiled potatoes, and they rolled all over. This shipmate, he got after him: Why didn't he get off the deck? So, he went and got him and took him by the neck and downed him on the second [deck]—just give him kind of a rough deal there. He come back to see that everybody's off the deck. There was three or four of

us boys there, watching the rudder that drove the boat. Boy, we got quite a tongue lashing! We was innocent, but nevertheless, the law was the law with them fellows. After that, we never showed up above while the storm was on.

This storm and some of those lasted for days, you know. The folks were on there about thirty days, riding around on the high seas. Pretty near everybody got sick. That was terrible! They were "feeding the fish." I never got sick a bit. Us youngsters done pretty good, so we got up to the kitchen and get the cook to have mercy on us kids, and we took a lot of those eats down to our folks. That was our chore. This boat was supposed to be a passenger boat, though it was mixed: livestock and passengers. The livestock was down, right in the same place. We could see them hollering and moving and all this. In place of having a first class ticket, you know, you got a second or third, whatever you could get. Us youngsters could sneak around and look at what was going on. The top deck was mostly for first class passengers. They had their class of music, and they had some dancing to keep people up with their spirits and great exercise where you couldn't walk very far, just on the deck there.

From New York to Kansas, I think it took two or three days. The locomotives were just like it was back in the old passenger ship: it was very slow. Our destination was to come to Endicott. We made it to Kansas, and the folks run out of money. They had some friends that came there several years before, and that's where they stayed for a week or two. My folks wrote to some of their friends at Endicott, and they sent them enough money whereby they could get there. And that's the way they helped one another. They went into the land of milk and honey, where the milk flowed and the honey flowed. It was a new land. The things we seen, we didn't see out in the Old Country. We seen horses and teams with wagons. But, here, it was different. It was a little further advanced—nicer wagons and hacks, or democratic wagons. The kids were the same, but they were dressed better. You could tell we were immigrants because the way we were dressed.

As young kids, we were called "Russians," and would fight one another just like kids do, you know. We were not truly named or called right, because we weren't Russian-blooded people. We were just *from* Russia. But that was what we were called, where we lived,

"Russian Town," in Colfax. They nicknamed each part of the town. Down over in the flat was a section they called "Poverty Flat," a poor man's district. And ours was "Russian." The younger fellows thought it was kind of a disgrace to talk the German language; many of them neglected their mother tongue. I adopted the American language, but there was some of them that didn't. Sort of a disgrace to talk German if the rest of the kids couldn't understand. Now, everybody, they've intermarried, and we're just like one big family.

Our people were very religious. When they left Russia, they had faith, and their Bible, and what they called a *Wolgagesangbuch*. And that faith today is still with our people. Most of them have clinged to what they've been taught by their parents. My parents were very strict, and we were disciplined. I don't say they were any better, but we knew what it was all about. When I got to be about nineteen years of age, I left the folks down there at the old homestead. Being a young man, I looked for a mate. I happened to be fortunate to run into my first wife, and we got married. We then went and leased a ranch out of Endicott about a mile. We farmed there for about two years, and then we were fortunate to get our present ranch, a section of "school land." I leased it from the state and there's where I spent all my younger days until retirement.

I broke up most of that sod; it was very hard work. The plows, what they called in those days the modern "Flying Dutchman" plow, was not a very husky plow. So I tried to work that ground into sod and couldn't do it. John Deere came out with a brand new plow, which I bought, and I broke this sod. That was two kinds of sod. One was called "bunchgrass" sod; it wasn't too hard to break. The other was what they called "buffalo grass." But it was curly and black and tough. I had plowed that with the new plow, and it took eight horses. It was good humus in that it didn't work up until maybe twenty-thirty years afterwards, no longer. It would plow so hard that it would just roll over. It was hard to develop—it took time and years.

Just like any new country you come into, it's the people that have to develop it. The thing was....to have the ambition, roll up your sleeves and go to work. If you did, and watched yourself, you had an opportunity to get somewheres.

CONCLUSION

"The story of mankind is written with grass and grain."
—Emerson

The first people of the Palouse Country maintained an intimate relationship with the land and ranged extensively through a complex seasonal round planned to utilize the region's natural bounty. The earth provided them with every necessity of life including nutritious roots, berries, fish, and game. The domains of four Plateau Indian tribes stretched across portions of the Palouse and all of these people shared a common heritage to a great extent. The Palouses, Coeur d'Alenes, Nez Perces, and Spokanes lived, worked, and married each other in a fluid social world. Each was distinct with its own enclave of winter villages, dialect, and tribal identity, but they moved freely across the region in a seasonal cycle requiring a sophisticated understanding of the natural world.

Numerous geographic features were given spiritual significance as remnants of legendary beings and events. Native religion emphasized nature as more than an expression of the Creator's work since the ground, plants, and wildlife shared with humans a life force. The Indians of the Palouse believed that they had been given their ancestral lands to live upon and honor, and these ideas formed the basis of their religion. They considered themselves guardians of the vast Palouse Country, not possessors, and for them to surrender their lands was literally against their religion. Neither the land nor they had dominion over the other; their existence and preservation was deemed one of mutual significance.

Yet this symbiotic relationship was a major limiting factor in the proliferation of the Plateau tribes. With an economic base determined by ancestral hunting and gathering patterns, the Indians of the region maintained stable populations until recurrent epidemics brought by European-American explorers and traders in the late eighteenth century significantly reduced their numbers. Not even the impact of the horse's introduction a generation earlier and resulting benefits to travel could compensate for the slaughter by the invisible enemy. Because

they lacked natural immunities, Indians of the region perished in large numbers from smallpox, measles, and dysentery after 1780 and some Palouse area tribal populations were likely reduced by as much as half over the next forty years. At the time of systematic European-American settlement in the Palouse, the native peoples were contending with the debilitating effects of recurrent epidemics that left some villages entirely abandoned. Their reduced numbers coupled with a cultural belief that could not conceive of private land ownership protected by force of law virtually disarmed the Palouse area tribes before the Interior Wars of the 1850s.

The outcome of the Walla Walla Treaty Council of 1855 also significantly altered the status of Indians who were native to the Palouse region. They were forced to cede their vast domain south and west of the Palouse River and were ordered to relocate to the Yakama, Umatilla, or Nez Perce Reservations. A few members of the Palouse tribe clung to footholds along the Snake River through the remarkable service of an army officer, Major J. W. MacMurray, who prepared their applications under the terms of the Indian Homestead Act. The vast majority, however, were removed to area reservations. The tribes living north of the Palouse River eventually also surrendered title to their ancestral lands. Through the dedicated persistence of the Jesuit missionaries at the Coeur d'Alene's Sacred Heart Mission, negotiations for a reservation under that tribe's jurisdiction were begun in 1866. Fearing that problems would arise with the burgeoning immigrant traffic over the Mullan Road which passed near the mission, the Jesuits and tribal leaders induced most members of the tribe to relocate to the southern corner of the reservation beginning in 1870 to establish an enduring presence in the fertile North Palouse River valley.

The Progression of Settlement

As a result of government policies designed to dispossess area

*Quilted Hills**

East of Colfax, Washington

tribes of most of their ancestral domain in the region and their dramatic population decline from recurrent epidemics, the Palouse Country was virtually unoccupied when European-Americans first entered the region in significant numbers. Although a handful of American-born settlers began moving into the Palouse in the 1860s, the first immigrant surge took place between 1870 and 1871 when clusters of settlement emerged where the Palouse River forks at present Colfax, and along Union and Rebel Flat Creeks. As the names of these two streams indicate, the majority of pioneer families originally settling there were from the East. Twenty-two different states were represented among the Palouse's adult inhabitants in 1870 when the region's total population amounted to only 170. Of the foreign-born, fourteen were from Ireland—more than any single American state had contributed. Most of the newcomers to the central Palouse area were young families who had journeyed west on the Oregon Trail searching for good land in the Willamette Valley only to find that they were not well suited to the climate or the best areas there had already been claimed.

They sought settlement possibilities east of the Cascades once the tribes of the Columbia Plateau had been defeated in war and forced to sign away their rights to lands that the territorial governments and speculators were proclaiming to be the most fertile in the world. For many frontier families who had not yet exercised their Homestead Act rights, the prospect invited investigation, and in many instances men first traveled to the Palouse alone or in small groups to inspect the land. Frequently the response was positive despite the substantial obstacles of rural isolation. An associated surge of interest promoted by coastal papers, however, bolstered populations in the region's nascent trading centers at Walla Walla and Lewiston. Without the rapid development of marketing and supply outlets at these two places in the 1870s, settlement of the Palouse would have been significantly delayed.

An ethnic profile of Palouse settlers indicates that the overwhelming majority beginning with the first surge of immigration in 1871 were native-born Americans. By 1880 they comprised 81% of the total population and their relative proportion grew to 90% by 1920. Their access to the region was facilitated by political, linguistic, and cultural identities that enabled them to better contend with problems of

transportation, legal requirements for public land entry, and aspects of commodity marketing in a rural economy. Their most significant advantage in contrast to the European immigrants was simply the proximity of their original homes to the Palouse Country. While travel to the region could be an arduous undertaking from the Willamette Valley or the East prior to the advent of the railroads in the 1880s, the challenge of relocation to another part of one's own country was not nearly as formidable as emigration from a foreign country. This demanded expense and stamina for the trans-oceanic crossing, a modicum of fluency in a new language, and a distinctive attitude of self-reliance since return to the homeland would not be feasible.

European immigrants to the Palouse were members of the lower and middle agricultural classes with little chance of inheriting land. They often chose to immigrate during times of economic adversity on the continent. In many cases they were young and healthy, determined to build a more prosperous life in the "Promised Land" of opportunity. Another aspect of their selection began after their initial migration since many first settled in Midwestern states where they engaged in farm work until various conditions compelled some to reconsider their situation. Crop failures as well as climactic and social adjustments left the beleaguered Midwestern immigrants with three alternatives. They could return to the homeland, resign themselves to the local circumstances, or risk a new quest for security in a land rumored to be as fertile and pleasant as any on earth—the Pacific Northwest. The latter course was chosen by the first European immigrants who settled in the Palouse.

Many came expecting to find land in Oregon or Washington and soon learned of the great potential for newcomers in the Palouse. After their arrival there another stage in the selection process continued to sift out the immigrant dedicated to building a permanent and productive life. Unlike American-born settlers, the Europeans were more keenly aware of their isolation and were less likely to relinquish their homestead rights. They had endured the struggles of a journey stretching half-way around the globe that had often consumed many years of their lives. In the Palouse they were determined to finally demonstrate to themselves and to others that they were capable of achieving the success which they had so long sought. The environmental conditions of the Palouse were conducive to supporting an industrious, law-abiding agrarian populace. Crop failures were virtually unknown and the transportation problems which inhibited widespread settlement during the first ten years of immigration during the 1870s were overcome by the railroads in the next decade.

In the earliest stage of resettlement, the pioneer immigrant often journeyed alone or in a small group to explore the new setting. If prospects were good the pioneer may have corresponded with family and friends back home and persuaded them to follow. In this way Michael Schultheis acquainted the German Catholic colony from Minnesota in the 1870s with opportunities in the Colton-Uniontown area just as Archie and Peter McGregor contacted their kinsmen in Ontario a decade later about life in southwestern Whitman County. At that time the Volga German farmer Phillip Green who had recently settled near Endicott, was describing the area to relatives in the Midwest and Russia. Sounding Green out on the possibilities of a move from Kansas, his brother-in-law replied that, "...if life yielded as little as the last years it would be better we moved to you." The second stage of migration began as a small stream of migrants followed to the new place. Similar circumstances were repeated with the Swiss Mennonite Joseph Stevick who landed at Almota in 1885, the Norwegian Lutheran Peder Wigen and his kinsmen who pioneered settlement southeast of Lacrosse in 1901, and dozens of others like them. So enticing were the prospects for prosperity in the Palouse that the population leaped to over 52,000 by 1910 when the rural Palouse became the most densely settled rural area of the Inland Northwest.

Reflecting the final phase of resettlement patterns similar elsewhere in the American West, large numbers of villagers from specific areas in the East and Europe joined in the movement as the extended family network grew substantially with each passing year. The nucleus of the Colton-Uniontown German Catholic colony became other families from the 1867 wagon train that followed Schultheis. Walla Walla press accounts from the 1870s and 1880s contain frequent reference to these movements. A typical entry from 1878 reads, "Another wagon train of immigrants passed through the city today destined for the Palouse Country." Most groups at this time were native-born American and the articles often mentioned areas of origin and specific destination: Iowans to Oakesdale, Ohioans east of Colfax; families from Tennessee to Steptoe and from Illinois to Spangle. Waves of newcomers were entering from the north and south onto the rolling unclaimed Palouse prairies, called "the Mecca of immigrants" by the *Walla Walla Union*. That significant numbers from entire European villages joined in the pilgrimage is evident in the experiences of Palouse's Russian German, Swiss Mennonite, and Norwegian Lutheran communities. The schoolmaster in the Volga German colony of Yagodnaya Polyana, Russia, for example, estimated in 1910 that nearly one fourth of the villages 2,500 inhabitants had left for the United States or Canada during the previous two decades. The number of Whitman County Russian-born that year was 589 and the overwhelming majority were from that very village. In the southwestern Palouse the McGregor sheep operation recruited experienced French herders from the eastern province of Haute-Alpes early in the nineteenth century. Many of these men, like brothers Emile and Maurice Morod, Ernest Biques, and Maurice Vasher, remained with the company to make their homes in the Palouse.

Palouse Country Italians and Greeks

The formation of the Potlatch Lumber Company in 1903 ushered in a new phase of employment opportunity in the Palouse for immigrants from southern Europe who were recruited by the Spokane offices of the All Nations Employment Agency and Northwestern Employment Agency. Though company officials preferred northern European workers, Italians and Greeks were directed to Potlatch as early as 1908 to meet the demands of a burgeoning business that employed hundreds of men to cut down and process the massive white pine forests of the eastern Palouse. Ethnic enclaves soon emerged in Potlatch as the company followed a policy requiring employees to live in the town. Accordingly, Greek, Italian, Japanese, and Scandinavian neighborhoods developed on the north side of town where the sounds of weekend bocciball matches and smells of barbecued yachnee and other Mediterranean delicacies revealed Potlatch's cultural diversity. The community also hosted a inter-faith "Union Church," a Catholic Church, and evening English classes offered to those intent upon naturalization. Some Italians later relocated to the neighboring communi-

*Kamiak Butte Spring**   *North of Pullman, Washington*

ties of Onaway and Princeton after the company relaxed its hiring policy while other Italians and Yugoslavs were employed at the company's Elk River sawmill (K. Peterson, 1987).

Among workers recruited in 1902 for construction of the Camas Prairie Railroad along the north bank of the Snake River was a young Greek immigrant, Gust Delegianes, from the small farming village Kandila in the mountainous Pelopenessian Peninsula. The railroad to Lewiston was opened in late 1909 and upon completion of his work along the line near Penawawa, Delegianes decided to seek employment in the bustling port community because the climate and small farms on the bottomland and adjacent slopes reminded him of his native land. His brother Christ had immigrated in 1904 and eventually found work first as a bootblack and then as a railroad shop mechanic in Seattle. Gust encouraged his brother to join him in Penawawa where local orchardists eagerly sought dependable laborers for summer work and fall harvest. Gust found work on the Silas Smith ranch where he learned how to prune, irrigate, and tend the countless other chores requisite for successful orcharding. Christ joined his brother in Penawawa about 1912 and the two formed a partnership to lease the Smith ranch. About the same time two of their cousins, brothers Mike and George Delegianes, also arrived in the area.

The Delegianes family partnership prospered on the land leased from Smith and after a couple years the three men decided to buy about three hundred acres of their own four miles upriver from Penawawa. In 1914 they planted seventy acres to Moorpars apricots, Alberta and Hale peaches, Mount Morincy cherries, and other fruit and also raised vegetables and melons, all of which at first were ardously watered from barrels carried on wagons. Within several years the orchards and gardens were in full production while the men also maintained over two hundred adjacent acres in pasture. A small Greek colony emerged in the vicinity as other Greeks including John, Louie, and Nick Delegianes worked in area orchards for extended times. Several members of the Delegianes (Delegans) family were married and raised their children in the community teaching them to observe traditional Greek Orthodox festivals and name days while maintaining other distinctive cultural traditions (S. Deleganes, 1977; J. Deleganes, 1989).

The Asian and Black Experiences

Barriers to inclusion of certain ethnic groups prevented widespread settlement in the region by Asian and African Americans. As historian Gail Nomura has observed, Asian Americans "were instrumental in the economic growth of Washington yet they were from the start subject to exclusion and discrimination." Chinese were denied voting rights in 1853 by the newly created Washington Territorial Legislature in the first of a series of laws clearly racial in sentiment. The federal Chinese Exclusion Act of 1882 stunted the growth of Asian American settlement by distorting their population composition and creating among the Chinese an aging, "bachelor" society. Registering a decline exceeding the national trend, the Palouse Chinese population declined by 75% during the 1880s. They had begun the decade as the largest foreign-born group in the region but by 1890 numbered less than 200. A district court decision that year in North Idaho held that Chinese had "no rights whatever on mining lands" and this ruling coupled with Congressional restrictions on their citizenship effectively prevented Chinese from acquiring land although many remained in the region to supply goods and services in rural communities.

The African American experience in the Palouse during the settlement period involves a similar history of intolerance and frequent discriminatory treatment by the European American majority. African Americans were attracted to the Pacific Northwest in the late 1800s seeking a place with less prejudice and more opportunity than was known in the South. Although African Americans in Washington Territory could not vote until Congress enacted the Fourteenth Amendment to the Constitution in 1866, they were permitted here, unlike Oregon, to legally purchase and own property. Relatively few risked breaking away from their scattered enclaves of settlement west of the Cascades to move eastward. Only nine Blacks were registered in the 1880 census for Whitman and Nez Perce Counties and they were employed as manual laborers. Among the earliest African Americans in the Palouse were the Wells brothers—Joseph, Louis, Grant, and Crom. The four North Carolina natives settled in Latah County in 1889 where they worked at logging and blacksmithing. Perhaps the first African American to homestead in the region was

William King, a native of Wake County, North Carolina who immigrated to Spokane in 1902 before bringing his family West a year later. After working as stonemason in the city for many years he joined others in entering a homestead lottery in 1910 for thirty-six quarter sections adjacent to the southern boundary of the Coeur d'Alene Indian Reservation. King's number was drawn and he relocated to his claim, later known as King Valley, near present Tensed. At the time of his death in 1927, the family had purchased nearly 500 acres in the vicinity and they eventually acquired some two and one-half sections covering virtually the entire valley (F. King, 1973). The experience of most African Americans in the Palouse, however, was characterized by manual labor for area farmers during the work year with winters spent in Spokane or Lewiston.

The New Social Order

The period of large-scale immigration to the Palouse came to a close by 1920. World War I had interrupted European emigration during the second decade of the twentieth century and the first of the three increasingly restrictive United States immigrant quota laws of the Twenties was enacted in 1921. The effects of these events coupled with the fact that Palouse lands were virtually all claimed and settled by 1915 effectively curbed further immigration to the region. Since the late 1870s the majority of Palouse area residents have been American-born though by 1920 the total number of foreign-born in Whitman and Latah Counties (2,862) represented 8.6% of the total population (31,323). However, due to the large birth rates among the foreign-born, their first, second, and third generations constituted approximately one-third of the total population in the Palouse. The four largest European groups each constituted over 10% of the total foreign-born in 1920, these being the Russian Germans (17.0%), Swedes (16.6%), Germans (14.8%) and Norwegians (10.6%). Smaller European elements were the Irish, Swiss, English, Scots, Greeks, and Italians.

The new social order in the Palouse, as elsewhere in the American West, also contributed to assimilation. No longer was one confined to a level of society on the basis of birth as had been the case in many nineteenth century European nations. The Homestead Act rendered all eligible citizens potential economic equals on the unclaimed frontier. Learning English and engaging in American politics were not seen as threatening the individual and national identity of the immigrant. Rather, free public education and the democratic process were viewed as blessings generously offered which enabled the newcomers to capitalize on the opportunities of life in a free land. Still, the immigrant could maintain elements of personal identity through the institution of the church. It was more than sanctuary of religious faith although this was of preeminent value to devout immigrant pioneers. The church also protected the native language and the many cultural traditions associated with the Old World. Catholic, Lutheran, Methodist, and Mennonite immigrants in the Palouse often reached accommodation in their areas of settlement with American-born members of their respective denominations through cooperative services or shared premises.

Likewise, the diverse rural populace generally came together to establish local farm cooperatives for marketing crops and although several parochial schools were established in the Palouse, in most areas public schools received broad local support.

Many newcomers to the Palouse found more than just opportunities for employment. They found a new homeland. Though typically characterized by a

ROCK LAKE, c. 1920

rolling terrain of fertile land, the Palouse landscape varied from a vast expanse of rangeland in the west to the undulating hills of the central Palouse and eastern forested mountains of Idaho. The snow-capped peaks of the Bitterroots gave Norwegian farmers in the eastern Palouse the impression of a "New Norway" just as the timbered slopes of the same area seemed familiar to the immigrants from Sweden's southern highlands.

In the same manner the Volga Germans, whose people had labored for over a century on the steep slopes of the Volga *Bergseite*, eagerly sought the unbroken hills of the central Palouse as did many of their fellow Teutons from Prussia, Saxony, Hesse, and Baden. The settler's plows also changed the landscape as cultivation exposed the fertile but fragile Palouse slopes to the destructive forces of wind and rain. The same toil that replaced the native grasses with the world's highest yielding dryland grains and legumes has caused serious environmental problems through erosion and sedimentation of the soft, mellow earth. Crop and livestock production also brought biotic change through the introduction of foreign plant species unknowingly transported here with seed grain by immigrants and in transcontinental boxcars.

The cultural backgrounds of families in the Inland Pacific Northwest remain as varied as the region's landscapes to which many immigrants formed mystical attachments because of geographic similarities to their homelands. Motives for coming to the region have been as complex as the individuals who harbored them with hopes for prosperity and eagerness to flee adversity both playing important roles. In other instances adventurous souls responded to wanderlust that had worked for generations to weave the colorful fabric of American, European, and Asian culture. This spirit, combined with idealistic visions of life in the Far West, lured many foreigners and Easterners to find new homes in the Palouse during the period 1860 to 1920. The resiliency of their cultures is reflected by the fact that in 2000, nearly one-third of the area's residents still claim a single ethnic ancestry. To be sure, historical and geographical factors in the region have led to cultural change; yet ethnic groups in the Palouse remain characterized by distinctive social, religious, and occupational patterns of Eastern American and foreign origin. From the Swiss Mennonites and Russian Germans of Whitman County to the Swedes and Norwegians of Latah and Spokane Counties, cultural identities forged in the region's colorful era of settlement are retained and celebrated throughout the rural Palouse.

"Feeding a Dream: The Palouse Pitches In"

The headline on an April, 1992 special supplement to the *Spokesman-Review* captured the spirit of a remarkable regional effort that cast the Palouse Country in a more recent role of international significance. Although taking place long after the era of immigrant settlement, the Northwest campaign to "feed the dream" was rooted in the Palouse Country's pioneer past and would not likely have grown to such magnitude had it not been for the hundreds of families from Eastern Europe and Russia who had been living in the area since the 1880s. The chaotic conditions of life under the beleaguered communist regimes in Eastern Europe and the Soviet Union during the 1980s produced a stream of Slavic immigrants seeking a new life in America just as others had sought escape tsarist oppression a century earlier. Washington Senator Henry Jackson had placed principle above popularity in the 1970s by spearheading legislation linking emigration from the U.S.S.R. to American grain sales. Choosing pragmatism over precept, the Soviets eventually relented and allowed a steady if limited flow of Jews, Germans, and others to leave the country.

The international aid organization World Relief sought to find churches in the Northwest, through Connell's Linda Unseth, to help resettle the newcomers who made it to the United States and especially congregations with a Russian heritage. Several denominations were contacted in the Palouse Country which led to an influx of families like Yuri and Alla Derevenchuk, natives of Zhdanov, Ukraine, who found sanctuary in area communities including Endicott, St. John, Pullman, and Moscow. At a 1992 New Year's Day gathering, some of the Soviet émigrés suggested sending a fifty-pound parcel of food to a relative's family in the U.S.S.R that was facing deprivation during the harsh winter. Word of the wider need circulated among several Palouse area churches where concerned members had read of the Soviet government's unprecedented public appeal for relief supplies to care for tens of thousands of children in state-run orphanages.

The nation was experiencing significant economic dislocations in the wake of a controversial campaign launched under Mikhail Gorbachev to implement limited market-oriented policies and deal openly with issues regarding the countries troubled past. Neither his administration nor the Soviet Union itself would survive the changes. On January 5, 1992 Kurt Campbell of Harvard University's Kennedy School of Government reported on Pullman's KWSU radio, "…the assumption that the nuclear weapons control structure will remain intact when starvation is rampant is extremely naïve." That same month, U. S. Secretary of State James Baker and C.I.A. Director Robert Gates publicly voiced similar grave concerns about an impending Soviet famine and the prospect of arms control problems. Cold War suspicions still ran high between both nations and the United States was reluctant to qualify the U.S.S.R. under the Department of Agriculture's PL-480 guidelines for eligibility to receive foreign aid.

Radio listeners and émigré sponsors throughout the Palouse were quick to respond under the leadership of several individuals who met in February to organize a project named "Operation KareLift" to render food and medical assistance to Soviet orphanages and children's hospitals. The volunteer group was directed by Pastor Stan Jacobson of Endicott's Trinity Lutheran Church, local parishioners Marilyn Bafus and Margaret Schmick, Lee McGuire of Thornton, and William Schmick of Pullman. McGuire and Schmick had experience with the Washington Association of Wheat Growers, headquartered in Ritzville, the Idaho-Washington Pea & Lentil Producers Associations of Moscow, and the Idaho Bean Commission.

Following presentations to these organizations, the appeal was widely publicized in area grower publications. Alex McGregor of

the McGregor Company offered a fleet of heavy-duty trucks to carry any donated commodities to West Coast ports while St. John Grange Supply offered fuel for cross-state transportation needs. Washington State Secretary of State Ralph Munro and Assistant Secretary Michelle Burkheimer pledged to arrange free trans-Pacific shipment to the principal Soviet Far East port cities of Vladivostok and Yuzhno-Sakhalinsk on Russian trade vessels returning from Washington and Oregon. In the event that approach failed due to bureaucratic roadblocks, Munro ventured to promise, "We'll get everything you can raise over there even if I have to carry it on my back!" Having just returned from a trip to the Soviet Union, Munro had disturbing knowledge of the crisis and the will to confront any barriers to the KareLift effort.

Aid poured into storage facilities across the Palouse Country throughout the late winter months of 1992 with major donations of bulk dry foods made at B.N.P. Lentils and Wanooka Farms of Farmington, Fairfield Grain Growers, Genesee Union Warehouse, St. John Grain Growers, and Wheat Growers of Endicott. To the organizers' great relief, manager Joe Hulett at Wallace Grain & Pea Company of Palouse, another substantial corporate donor, volunteered to handle all accounting for KareLift farm commodity gifts. Semi-truck transportation within the Palouse and to processing facilities in Spokane was contributed by Alexander Trucking and Inland Empire Distributing of Spokane where Buckeye Beans combined legumes, purled barley, pasta, and spices, provided by McCormick-Schilling, into a nutritious soup blend with recipes translated into Russian by the Derevenchuks.

In March other significant donations were made by Moscow's Dumas Corporation, George F. Brocke & Sons, Inland Empire Pea and Grain Association, Moscow Seed, Spokane Seed, Northwest Pea and Bean,

PALOUSE COUNTRY KARELIFT COMMODITIES; KHABAROVSK, RUSSIA, 1992

Oakesdale Grain Growers, Pottratz Processing of Latah, Stegner Grain of Pullman, and the Garfield Union Warehouse. These combined efforts yielded over fifty tons of processed dry peas and lentils, twenty tons of dried beans, eighteen tons of garden seed, twelve tons of all-purpose flour, seven tons of dehydrated foods, forty tons of clothing, and two tons of medical supplies. Many Palouse residents made cash donations which were used to purchase bulk flour and pasta at wholesale prices. An additional twelve tons of family care packages were assembled by Washington and Alaska Rotarians.

Secretary Munro's office succeeded in procuring Russian ships to carry much of the stockpile to the Soviet Far East while Senator Slade Gorton and aid Dan Kirschener arranged White House authorization for Spokane Air Force Base Commander Arne Weinman to fly supplies from Spokane directly to an inland distribution site at Khabarovsk, Russia. With memory of the KAL 007 flight disaster still fresh in the public mind, some MAC C-141 crewmembers were dubious at the prospect of penetrating Soviet air space, heavily outlined in a red border on their maps, with an Air Force jet. Such a mission would be the first flight of a U. S. military aircraft to a Soviet city since World War II. Not included on the international bill of lading was a contraband load of donated basketballs and Russian Bibles.

As Major Jeffrey Zink, Fairchild's cargo coordinator, watched the massive Starlifter being loaded, he poignantly shared with a news reporter, "I'd rather our first planes in there carried food than what we were trained to deliver." By late spring, 1992 all shipments were successfully made by sea and sky to orphanages and children's hospitals under the supervision of Western observers including Pastor Jacobson through Russia's Merciful Samaritan Mission and Peter and Anita Deyneka of Russian Ministries. After working for hours to help unload the KareLift vessel *Pestova* at the port of Vladivostok, a burly Russian stevedore who headed the operation sat for a moment on a pallet of sacked lentils from the Palouse. He studied an American who had worked alongside him without exchanging words all morning. Finally, the Russian broke the uneasy silence. He pointed to an enormous brown bird that cir-

cled high above the ship and said without expression, "It is a rare omen of good fortune for us to see this bird." He then smiled and sighed, "You know, we should have been friends all these years."

In September, 1994 the first democratically elected president of Russia, Boris Yeltsin, made his inaugural visit to Washington, D. C. where he and President George Bush signed the historic treaty of friendship signaling an official end to the Cold War era. In spite of earlier speculation in the national press that Yeltsin would also make a major foreign policy speech in New York or Chicago, the Russian president's press secretary announced that his only other destination would be the Pacific Northwest. On September 29, President Yeltsin was introduced to a capacity crowd in Seattle's Westin Hotel Grand Ballroom by Washington's governor, Palouse Country native Mike Lowry. Yeltsin then spoke of the prospects for a new future without our nations existing any longer under the specter of nuclear holocaust.

From Yeltsin's standpoint, the unexpected monumental and substantially peaceful changes had not taken place because of military threats or social unrest. Rather, he had come to the Northwest to thank the region's farmers and other citizens whose efforts two years earlier "to render assistance in Russia's hour of need," represented "a key factor in my decision to normalize relations between our two countries." He and Russian Foreign Minister Vladimir Lukin then met privately with relief organizers to personally express their appreciation on behalf of the Russian citizenry. Palouse Country volunteers had toiled anonymously for months to unload grain bins, transport tons of legumes and flour, translate soup recipes, collect containers of aspirin and vitamins, and gather shoes and coats for children they would never meet. At the same time they had also been making an enduring contribution to world peace (*Spokesman-Review*, April 26, 1992; B. Yeltsin, 1994).

Reconcile, Friendly, Token of Peace
On Friday, October 13, 2000, thirty young people stood near the confluence of the Palouse and Snake rivers at nearly the same hour and day Lewis and Clark had noted a stockpile of Indian fishing gear there nearly two centuries earlier. The morning had begun

with scattered rain just as the captains had noted in their journals on that date. Enroute to Lyon's Ferry we had seen Louis Gaiser on his Palouse River ranch driving his favorite Percheron team of Bandy and Shadow with a wagonload of hay to feed his cattle. Had it been five years since the school flag stood at half-mast in honor of our former guide Ray Reich's passing? Something like that I supposed. He would have liked seeing such a fine stand of fall wheat already starting to grace the Palouse slopes we passed. We drove by tiny Winona where I remembered stepping down with my brother from our first and only Palouse Country passenger train ride, the region's last, as a boy of six.

Copies of Clark's diary for this day in 1805 were with each student and I reread his line about Sacajawea reconciling "all the Indians as to our friendly intentions." She was, he had written, "a token of peace." Clad in buckskin at our destination was Ranger Gary Lentz of Dayton's Lewis and Clark State Park who was also armed with a .54 caliber rifle nearly identical to those from the Harper's Ferry Arsenal issued to Corps of Discovery members. Before introducing Gary, I pulled from my wallet a small tattered note with hastily scribbled lines I read from time to time and shared with students. The words were from extemporaneous remarks made by historian Stephen Ambrose the previous summer when he and filmmaker Ken Burns attended the premier of the Burns's masterful documentary *Lewis and Clark: The Journey of the Corps of Discovery*. The film was appropriately shown outdoors on an enormous screen beneath the stars on a sandy Snake River bank near Lewiston and Clarkston where the Corps had camped in the fall of 1805. (By some pleasant coincidence Mr. Yenney's widow, Helen, and I found ourselves sitting next to each other in the crowd that evening.)

To Professor Ambrose, the story of Lewis and Clark was one of commitment and friendship. "Theirs is a saga of people coming together for noble reasons," I read to the students, "setting high goals and working hard to meet them, of demonstrating respect for people who look and speak differently. The expedition of Lewis and Clark, spoken almost as a single name, is the story of uncommon friendship and selfless dedication to each other and to those for whom they were responsible. Friendship is ultimately about giving; it is the founding principle of any civil society, and is the basis of our humanity." A peculiar silence hung in the air that most parents and teachers can recognize. The students seemed to be taking to heart these magnificent words and I was mindful of Joshua Heschel's observation about moral education, that values are not formally taught. They are learned by example at home, in the community, and through stories of individuals who exemplified these ideals despite all their flaws and did not succumb to course of least resistance to meet their objectives. Moral values are, Heschel had written, "caught, not taught."

Mountain man Gary Lentz told our young people about the Jefferson Peace Medallion that had been found a short distance from where we now stood when the graveyard at Palus was relocated in 1964 because of flooding by the Lower Monumental Dam reservoir. He passed around a weighty bronze replica of the object for us to inspect. Elberton's John Elwood, a popular Palouse Country folk musician, played Jeffersonian era dulcimer and pipe music that may well have been familiar to expedition fiddler Pierre Cruzatte who had often entertained Corps members and Indians around evening campfires. John had earlier mentioned to me how muddy the Palouse looked for a fall day and I remembered the grim statistics on upstream soil erosion. Yet progress was being made on some fronts. Soil loss in the Palouse, the highest in the nation for decades, had fallen during the 1990s to less than two tons per acre—the lowest since measurements had been kept in the region, but still not enough for sustainability.

JEFFERSON PEACE MEDALLION (REVERSE SIDE)

Government records of the annual Columbia Plateau watershed salmon catch often exceeding 20,000 tons between 1870 and 1920, were now scarcely one-tenth of that number even in good years. The runs were in precarious decline despite an occasional bump up in the numbers brought about by conditions at sea and artificial hatches rather any improvement in river habitat. I had recently been reading Nez Perce elder Horace Axtell's winsome *Little Bit of Wisdom*, an open-hearted memoir filled with wry self-deprecating humor published that very October. Appearing on the cover like a ghost from an Edward Curtis sepia-tone print, Horace first describes a personal journey to war where he happens upon the crater at Nagasaki shortly after the cataclysmic blast. The upheaval brings to mind long suppressed images of the carnage at the Big Hole Battle where his warrior ancestor Timlpusmin fought alongside the Palouse Huishuis Kute before being killed at Bear Paw. My class had just been discussing the public remarks of an area government official advising Horace's tribe to accept greater outside authority in jurisdictional issues or "there could be bloodshed."

I thought about the challenges facing this next generation whose hopeful representatives were gathered before us along the shores of the Palouse River that morning and how these seemed even more formidable than the grizzly bears and Rocky Mountains encountered by Lewis and Clark. We are obliged to understand and share with young people exemplars of contemporary progressive change living in our midst like the Horace Axtell and Carrie Jim Schuster elders, Mary Jane Butters and Read Smith conservationists, and humanitarians Alla Derevenchuk and Joe Hulitt who all persist like the spring Chinook that battle against hooks and nets, dams and murky depths. The personal search of the prairie past in quest of one's self and responsibilities in the landscape is an uncertain but vital endeavor. Without informed whilom perspectives we cannot wisely seek fulfilled futures. Society's complacent reliance upon agricultural bounty from places like the Palouse Country is illusory, based on false assumptions of plenteous and perpetual production.

So much had changed in the Palouse just in my generation. I had boyhood memories of crossing the Snake River here on the very ferry now moored in retirement a few hundred feet from our fieldtrip gathering. I remembered reading about the discovery of Lewis and Clark's Jefferson Peace Medallion and subsequent flooding of the canyon when I was their age. Farms covering a single section of 640 acres provided well for the needs of a large family in 1965. Thirty-five years later the average Palouse farm was nearly four times that size, displacing hundreds of rural families, and putting economic strain on many rural communities. At the most fundamental and enduring level, we move in surroundings as fluid, sensitive, and precious as the Salmon People. Outlooks focused on the immediate present cast shallow answers to the complex issues of security and fulfillment for posterity in a world of changing markets, climate, and environments. I had given the students a copy of Clark's journal for this autumn day because I wanted each one to consider the value of those words Clark had chosen in another time of unprecedented change throughout the West—reconcile, friendly, token of peace. Later in the day I would ask them what medallions and lives might have in common.

Weathered and Worn

South of Potlatch, Idaho

BIBLIOGRAPHY

Unpublished Manuscripts

Aeschliman, Stella. *"The Genealogy and History of Sam Aeschliman."* Typescript. In possession of the author, n.d.

Bauer, Albert. *"An Account of Early Days in Colton."* Typescript. WSU Archives, Pullman, Washington, 1971.

Cameron, Mable. *"The Farmington Settlement."* Typescript. WSU Archives, Pullman, Washington, n.d.

Hickman, W.F. Letter. Union Flat, W.T., December 4, 1872. Cage 1640, WSU Archives, Pullman, Washington.

Kyllo, David. *"Selbu Lutheran Church History."* Typescript. In possession of the author, 1974.

Leeper, Lonnie. *"Memoirs and Reminiscences of Pioneers in Southeastern Washington."* MSS. WSU Archives, Pullman, Washington, 1941.

Lueg, Henry. *"Journal of a Trip from St. Paul, Minnesota to Portland, Oregon (1867)."* Typescript. WSU Archives, Pullman, Washington.

Moses, Mary Owhi. *"The Mary Moses Statement, 1918."* W. C. Brown Collection. Manuscripts, Archives, and Special Collections, Holland Library, Pullman, Washington.

Nomura, Gail. *"Washington's Asian-Pacific Communities."* MSS. Pullman, Washington, 1988.

Oliphant, J. Orin. *"Articles on the Early History of the Palouse Country, No. 2."* Typescript. WSU Archives, Pullman, Washington, n.d.

Seltice, Andrew and Joseph Seltice. *"Narrative."* MSS. Oregon Province Archives, Gonzaga University, Spokane, Washington, n.d.

Swannack, Jervis. *"Jervis and Wallula Swannack: My Parents."* Typescript. In possession of Walter Swannack, Endicott, Washington, n.d.

"They Did Not Live in Vain." Typescript. Rosalia Battle Days Museum, Rosalia, Washington, 1945.

Wagner, Paul. *"Birthplace of the Lentil, USA."* Typescript. In possession of Dennis and Terrill Wagner, Farmington, Washington.

Williams, Bertha. *"A History of the Fraternal Benefit Association."* Typescript. EWU Archives, Cheney, Washington, n.d.

Yoder, Fred. *"Stories of Early Pioneers in Whitman County, Washington."* MSS. WSU Archives, Pullman, Washington, 1937.

Books, Pamphlets, and Congressional Records

Allen, John E., Marjorie Burns and Sam C. Sargent. *Cataclysms on the Columbia.* Portland: Timber Press, 1986.

Archer, Sellers G. and Clarence E. Bunch. *The American Grass Book.* Norman: University of Oklahoma Press, 1953.

An Illustrated History of North Idaho embracing Nez Perces, Idaho, Latah, Kootenai and Shoshone Counties. Western Historical Publishing Company, 1901.

Axtell, Horace and Margo Aragon. *A Little Bit of Wisdom: Conversations With a Nez Perce Elder.* Lewiston, Idaho: Confluence Press, 1997.

Bancroft, Hubert Howe. *The History of Washington, Idaho, and Montana, 1845-1889.* San Francisco: The History Company, 1890.

Bjork, Kenneth O. *West of the Great Divide: Norwegian Immigration to the Pacific Coast, 1847-1893.* Northfield, Minnesota: The Norwegian-American Historical Association, 1958.

Blegen, Theodore C. *Norwegian Migration to America, 1825-1860.* Northfield, Minnesota: Norwegian American Historical Association, 1931.

Brown, William C. *The Indian Side of the Story.* Spokane: C. W. Hill Printing Company, 1961.

Bryan, Enoch H. *Orient Meets Occident: The Advent of the Railways to the Pacific Northwest.* Pullman, Washington: The Student Book Corporation, 1936.

Burns, Robert I. *The Jesuits and the Indian Wars of the Northwest.* New Haven: Yale University Press, 1966.

Busacca, Alan J. *Loess Deposits and Soils of the Palouse and Vicinity. Quaternary Nonglacial Geology—Conterminous U.S.* Geological Society of America, 1991.

Camp, Oscar A. and Paul C. McGrew. *History of Washington's Soil and Water Conservation Districts.* Pullman: Washington Association of Soil and Water Conservation Districts, 1969.

Chevigny, Hector. *Russian America: The Great Alaskan Venture.* London: The Cresset Press, 1965.

Clark, Ella E. *Indian Legends of the Pacific Northwest.* Los Angeles: University of California Press, 1953.

Cox, Ross. *Adventures of the First Settlers on the Oregon or Columbia River, 1810-1813.* London, 1849.

Creighton, J. J. *Indian Summers: Washington State College and the Nespelem Art Colony, 1937-1941.* Pullman: Washington State University Press, 2000.

Crithfield, June. *Of Yesterday and the River.* Pullman, Washington: WSU General Extension Services, 1973.

Curtis, Mrs. Dale and Mrs. Edgar Kerns, compilers. *Early Pioneers of the Thornton Area,* n.p., n.d.

d'Angelo, Pasquele. *Pascal d'Angelo: Son of Italy.* New York, 1924.

Douglas, David. *Journal Kept by David Douglas During His Travels in North America, 1823-1827.* London: Royal Horticultural Society, 1914.

Douglas, William O. *Go East, Young Man: The Autobiography of William O. Douglas.* New York: Random House, 1974.

Drake, Oliver, and Yakima Canutt. *Stunt Man: The Autobiography of Yakima Canutt*. Norman: University of Oklahoma Press, 1997.

Driscoll, Ann Nilsson. *They Came to a Ridge*. Moscow, Idaho: LCHS, 1970.

Drury, Clifford M. *Marcus Whitman, M. D., Pioneeer and Martyr*. Caldwell, Idaho: The Caxton Printers, 1937.

Durham, N.W. *History of the City of Spokane and Spokane Country*. Spokane: S.J. Clark, 1912.

Durham, Nelson W. *Spokane and the Inland Empire*. Spokane: N.p., 1912.

Elkins, Grace and others. *Oakesdale Memories*. Alpha Study Club, n.d.

Erickson, Edith E. Colfax 100 Plus. Colfax, Washington: by the author, 1981.

Erickson, Edith E. and Eddy Ng. *From Sojourner to Citizen: Chinese of the Inland Empire*. Colfax, Washington: University Printing, 1989.

Fahey, John. *The Inland Empire: Unfolding Years, 1879-1929*. Seattle: University of Washington Press, 1986.

Faust, Albert B. *The German Element in the United States*. Cambridge: The Riverside Press, 1909.

Fronek, Millie E. *Pioneering in the Lower Palouse and the LaCrosse Country*. By the author, 1973.

Gay, Elliott. *Yesterday and the Day Before*. N.p., 1974.

Gibbs, Rafe. *Beacon for Mountain and Plain: Story of the University of Idaho*. Caxton, Idaho: The Caxton Printers, 1962.

Gibson, James R. *Farming the Frontier: The Agricultural Opening of the Oregon Country, 1786-1846*. Seattle: University of Washington Press, 1985.

Gilbert, Frank T. *Historical Sketches - Walla Walla, Whitman, Columbia and Garfield Counties, Washington Territory, and Umatilla County, Oregon*. Portland: Printing and Lithographing House of A.G. Walling, 1882.

Gratz, Delbert L. *Bernese Anabaptists and their American Descendants*. Scottsdale, Pennsylvania: Herald Press, 1953.

Guske, Veva. *"The Guske Centennial Farm."* Unpublished manuscript, 1989.

Haines, Francis. *Appaloosa: The Spotted Horse in Art and History*. Austin: University of Texas Press, 1963.

Hansen, Marcus. *The Atlantic Migration, 1607-1860: A History of the Continuing Settlement of the United States*. Cambridge, Massachusetts, 1940.

Harder, Alana, Gladys Engles, and others. *Sprague, Lamont, Edwall, Washington: Stories of our People, Land and Times*. Fairfield, Washington: Ye Galleon Press, 1982.

Harder, Annine. *Opportunities of the Golden West*. Spokane: Ross, 1960.

Hatley, George B. *Pioneer: The Life & Times of Riley B. Hatley*. Moscow: By the author, 1998.

Hedges, James B. *Henry Villard and the Railways of the Northwest*. New Haven: Yale University Press, 1930.

Hildebrand, Lorraine Barker. *Straw Hats, Sandals and Steel: The Chinese in Washington State*. Tacoma: Washington State Historical Society, 1977.

Hitchman, Robert. *Place Names of Washington*. Tacoma: Washington State Historical Society, 1985.

Hunn, Eugene and James Selam. *Nch'i-Wána, "The Big River:" Mid Columbia Indians and Their Land*. Seattle: University of Washington Press, 1990.

Johnson, Randall A. *Cashup Davis and his Hotel on Steptoe Butte*. N.p., n.d.

Kane, Paul. *Wanderings of an Artist among the Indians of North America*. London, 1859.

Keith, Thomas B. *The Horse Interlude*. Moscow: University of Idaho Press, 1976.

Keyser, James D. *Indian Art on the Columbia Plateau*. Seattle: University of Washington, 1992.

Kincaid, Garret D. *Palouse in the Making*. Palouse: The Palouse Republic, 1934.

Kincaid, Garrett D. and A.H. Harris. *Palouse in the Making*. N.p., n.d.

Kingston, Ceylon S. *The Inland Empire in the Pacific Northwest: The Historical Essays and Sketches of Ceylon S. Kingston*. Ye Galleon Press, 1981.

Kirk, Ruth and Carmela Alexander. *Exploring Washington's Past: A Road Guide to History*. Seattle: University of Washington Press, 1990.

Kleinz, Msgr. John P. *A Short History of St. Boniface Parish, Uniontown, Washington*. Moscow, Idaho: The Idahonian, 1960.

Kowrach, Edward J. and Thomas E. Connolly. *Saga of the Coeur d'Alene Indians: An Account of Chief Joseph Seltice*. Fairfield, Washington: Ye Galleon Press, 1990.

Kung, Shien-woo. *Chinese in American Life*. Seattle: University of Washington Press, 1962.

Lehman, James O. *Sonnenberg: A Haven and an Heritage*. Kidron, Ohio: Kidron Community Council, Inc., 1969.

Lever, W.H. *An Illustrated History of Whitman County*. By the author, 1901.

Lindberg, John. *Background of Swedish Emigration*. Minneapolis: University of Minnesota Press, 1930.

Manring, Benjamin F. *Conquest of the Coeur d'Alenes, Spokanes, and Palouses*. Fairfield, Washington: Ye Galleon Press, 1975.

McDermott, Paul D. and Ronald E. Grim. *Gustavus Shohon's Cartographic and Artisitic Works*: An Annotated Bibliography. Washington, D. C.: Library of Congress Geography and Map Division, 2002.

McGregor, Alexander Campbell. *Counting Sheep: From Open Range to Agribusiness on the Columbia Plateau*. Seattle: University of Washington Press, 1982.

McWhorter, L. V. *Hear Me My Chiefs!* Caldwell, Idaho: The Caxton Printers, 1953.

Meinig, Don. *The Great Columbia Plain: A Historical Geography*. Seattle: University of Washington Press, 1968.

Miller, Thelma. *A History and Genealogy of the Miller and Allied Families*. Middleboro: Chedwato Service, 1973.

Mills, Randall V. *Sternwheelers Up Columbia: A Century of Steamboating in the Oregon Country*. Palo Alto, California: Pacific Books, 1947.

Monroe, Julie R. *Moscow: Living and Learning on the Palouse*. Charleston, South Carolina: Arcadia Publishing, 2003

Moorwood, William. *Traveler in a Vanished Landscape: The Life & Times of David Douglas, Botanical Explorer*. New York: Clarkson N. Potter, 1973.

Moulton, Gary E. *The Journals of Lewis and Clark. Vol. V*. Lincoln: University of Nebraska Press, 1988.

Mullan, John. *Report of Lieutenant Mullan, in Charge of the Construction of the Military Road from Fort Benton to Fort Walla Walla (36th Cong., 2nd sess., H.E.D. 44)*. Washington, D.C., 1860.

Nicandri, David L. *Italians in Washington State: Emigration, 1853-1924*. Tacoma: Washington State American Revolution Commission, 1978.

Norwood, Gus. *Washington Grangers Celebrate a Century*. Seattle, Washington: Washington State Grange, 1988.

Palouse Cooperative River Basin Study. Washington, D.C.: U.S. Department of Agriculure, 1978.

Peltier, Jerome. *A Brief History of the Coeur d'Alene Indians, 1806-1909* Fairfield, Washington: Ye Galleon Press, 1982.

Peterson, Keith C. *Company Town: Potlatch, Idaho and the Potlatch Lumber Company*. Pullman: Washington State University Press, 1987.

Petersen, Keith. *This Crested Hill: An Illustrated History of the University of Idaho*. Moscow: University of Idaho Press, 1988.

Peterson, Keith. *Troy, Deary and Genesee: A Photographic History*. Moscow, Idaho, 1979.

Piper, Charles V. and R. Kent Beattie. *Flora of the Palouse Region*. Pullman: Washington State Agricultural College, 1901.

Piper, Charles V. and R. Kent Beattie. *Flora of Southeastern Washington and Adjacent Idaho*. Lancaster, Pennsylvania: New Era Printing Company, 1914.

Platt, John A. *Whispers from Old Genesee and Echoes of the Salmon River*. Fairfield, Washington: Ye Galleon Press, 1975.

Pomfret, John E. *The Struggle for Land in Ireland, 1800-1923*. Princeton, 1930.

Qualey, Carlton C. *Norwegian Settlement in the United States*. Northfield, Minnesota: Norwegian-American Historical Association, 1938.

Reed, Mary E. and Keith Petersen. *Virgil T. McCroskey: Giver of Mountains*. Pullman: WSU Department of History, 1983.

Relander, Click. *Drummers and Dreamers*. Caldwell, Idaho: Caxton Printers, 1956.

Richards, Kent D. *Isaac I. Stevens: Young Man in a Hurry*. Provo: Brigham Young University Press, 1979.

Roe, Frank G. *The Indian and the Horse*. Norman: University of Oklahoma Press, 1955.

Sacred Heart Mission Baptismal Register. Desmet, Idaho. Hovember, 1861.

Sager, Matilda J. *A Survivor's Recollections of the Whitman Massacre*. Spokane: Daughters of the American Revolution, 1920.

Sallet, Richard. *Russian-German Settlements in the United States*. Fargo, North Dakota: Institute for Regional Studies, 1974.

Salutos, Theodore and John D. Hicks. *Agricultural Discontent in the Middle West, 1900-1939*. Madison: University of Wisconsin Press, 1951.

Scheuerman, Richard D. and Clifford E. Trafzer. *The Volga Germans: Pioneers of the Pacific Northwest*. Moscow: University of Idaho Press, 1980.

Schrier, Arnold. I*reland and the American Emigration, 1850-1900*. Minneapolis: University of Minnesota Press, 1958.

Sieveke, William C. and others. *History of Latah Zion Church*. Latah, Washington, 1957.

Slind, Marvin G. and Fred C. Bohm. *Norse to the Palouse: Sagas of the Selbu Norwegians*. Pullman: Norlys Press, 1990.

Smith, Roy. *Smith Brothers: Shor-iz*. By the author, 1960.

Spalding, Eliza Warren. *Memoirs of the West*. 1916.

Splawn, Andrew J. *Ka-Mi-Akin: The Last Hero of the Yakimas*. Caldwell, Idaho: The Caxton Printers, 1944.

St. John, Harold. *Flora of Southeastern Washington and Adjacent Idaho*. Pullman: Students Book Corporation, 1937.

Stern, Theodore. *Chiefs and Traders: Indian Relations at Fort Nez Perces, 1818-1855*. Corvallis: Oregon State University Press, 1993.

Stevens, Isaac I. *Report of Explorations for a Route for the Pacific Railroad*. 33th Congress, 2nd session, SED 78; Washington, D. C., 1860.

Stratton, David H., ed. *Spokane and the Inland Empire: An Interior Pacific Northwest Anthology*. Pullman: Washington State University Press, 1991.

Sung, Betty Lee. *The Story of the Chinese in America*. New York: Collier Books, 1971.

Swift, Kay. *Who Could Ask For Anything More?* New York: Simon and Schuster, 1943.

Trafzer, Clifford and Richard Scheuerman. *The Northwest Tribes in Exile*. Sacramento: Sierra Oakes Press, 1987.

Trafzer, Clifford E. and Richard D. Scheuerman. *Renegade Tribe: The Palouse Indians and the Invasion of the Inland Pacific Northwest*. Pullman: Washington State University Press, 1986.

Trimble, William J. *The Mining Advance into the Inland Empire*. Madison: The University of Wisconsin, 1919.

Trunkey, Miriam. *We Got Here From There*. St. John, Washington: St. John Women's Club, 1976.

Tyrrell, J. B., ed. *David Thompson's Narrative of His Explorations in Western America, 1784-1812*. Toronto: The Champlain Society, 1914.

Ulvestad, Martin. *Nordmaendene i Amerika, deres Historie og Rekord*. Minneapolis, Minnesota: History Book Company, 1907.

Villard, Henry. *The Early History of Transportation in Oregon*. Eugene:

University of Oregon Press, 1944.

Wagner, Palmer. *The American Appaloosa Anthology*. Colbert, Washington: By the author, 1999.

Waldbauer, Richard C. *Grubstaking the Palouse: Gold Mining in the Hoodoo Mountains of North Idaho, 1860-1950*. Pullman: Washington State University Press, 1986.

Warre, Henry J. *Sketches in North America and the Oregon Territory*. London, n.d.

Wenham, Lou E. *With the Colors: An Honor Roll*. Lewiston, Idaho: By the author, 1920.

West, Leoti L. *The Wide Northwest*. Spokane: Shaw and Borden, 1927.

White, Sid and S. E. Solberg, eds. *Peoples of Washington: Perspectives on Cultural Diversity*. Pullman: Washington State University Press, 1989.

Winther, Oscar O. *The Old Oregon Country: A History of Frontier Trade, Transportation, and Travel*. Bloomington, Indiana: Indiana University Publications, 1950.

Winthrop, Theodore. *The Canoe and the Saddle*. Boston: Ticknor and Fields, 1863.

Articles

Buechner, Helmut K. "Some Biotic Changes in the Statue of Washington, Particularly During the Century 1853-1953." *Research Studies of the State College of Washington*, XXI: 2 (June, 1953).

Chadwick, Kent. "Waiting for the Black Robes." *Palouse Journal, 36* (Winter 1988).

Douglas, Jesse S. "The Origin of Population in Oregon in 1850." *Pacific Northwest Quarterly*, XLI (April 1950).

Druffel, Gerald. "Profile of a Pioneer." *Bunchgrass Historian*, 5:1 (Spring 1977).

Elliott, T. C. "Journal of David Thompson." *Oregon Historical Quarterly*, XV: 4 (1917).

Gaines, E. F. and E. G. Schafer, "Wheat Varieties in Washington in 1939." *WAES Bulletin* 398 (April, 1941).

Haines, Francis. "Horses for Western Indians." *The American West*, 3 (Spring 1966).

Hatley, George. "Appaloosa Sires of the Palouse Country and the Men Who Rode Them. *The Western Horseman* (March, 1954).

Himes, George H., ed. "Letters Written by Mrs. Whitman from Oregon to her Relations in New York." *Transactions of the Oregon Pioneer Association, 1891*.

Joseph, Young Chief. "An Indian's View of Indian Affairs." *North American Review*, 128 (1879): 412-33.

Kaiser, Verle G. "Straight as an Arrow—The Kentuck Trail." *The Pacific Northwesterner*, 23:2 (Spring 1979).

Kammerzell, Miriam. "The History of the Wilcox Community." *Bunchgrass Historian*, 5:1 (Spring 1977).

Kingston, C. S.. "Ferries Over the Snake River and the Texas Road." The *Spokesman-Review* (August 12, 1951).

Leibo, Steven A. "From Whence They Came: The Chinese Departure from East Asia." *Bunchgrass Historian*, 10:1 (Spring 1982).

Nisbet, Jack. "The Palouse Mammoths." *The Inlander* (August 5, 2001).

Repp, Alisa. "Palouse Empire Horseracing." *Palouse Country Magazine*. Spring, 1989 (1:1).

Roth, Jean. "The Whitman Massacre, November 1847." *Seattle Genealogical Bulletin* (47:2), Winter, 1998.

Rubin, Pearl. "History of the Onecho Bible Church." *Bunchgrass Historian*, 1:1 (Spring 1973).

Thompson, Albert W. "The Early History of the Palouse River and Its Name." *Pacific Northwest Quarterly*, 62 (April 1971).

Todd, C. C. "Origin and Meaning of the Geographic Name Palouse," *Washington Historical Quarterly*, XXVI (July, 1933).

Wegars, Pricilla. "The Chinese Work Force in Moscow, Idaho, and Vicinity, 1880-1910." *Latah Legacy*, 15:4 (Winter 1986).

West, J.B. "The Development of Railroading in Whitman County." *Bunchgrass Historian*, 2:2 (Summer 1974).

Yoder, Fred. "Pioneer Adaptation in the Palouse Country of Eastern Washington, 1870-90. *Research Studies of the State College of Washington*. VI: 4 (December, 1938).

Yoder, Fred R. "Social Processes in Pioneering." *Research Studies of the State College of Washington*, 10 (1942).

Theses and Dissertations

Meinig, Donald W. "Environment and Settlement in the Palouse, 1869-1910." Master's thesis, University of Washington, Seattle, 1950.

Norling, Reuben E. "Peter Carlson, Pioneer Pastor, of the Evangelical Lutheran Augustana Synod of North America." Master's thesis, University of Idaho, Moscow, 1939.

Swanson, Robert W. "A History of Logging and Lumbering on the Palouse River, 1870-1905." Master's thesis, State College of Washington, Pullman, 1958.

Yeager, Walter M. "The Pioneer's Problems of Land Acquisition under the Public Land Laws in Southeastern Washington: 1850-1883." Master's thesis, Washington State University, 1961.

Oral Histories

Adler, Jacob. Tekoa, Washington, January 2; 1973.

Aeschliman, Rupert. Colfax, Washington; August 2, 1980.

Axtell, Horace and Andrea. Lewiston, Idaho; May 17, 2003.

Bacca, James. Potlatch, Idaho; September 24, 1976. LCHS.

Belsby, Louise. St. John, Washington; November 5, 1996.

Bezdicek, David. Pullman, Washington; June 4, 2003.

Bjerke, Arthur. Deary, Idaho; March 5, 1973.

Blank, Julia. Rosalia, Washington; July 30, 1980.
Blumenschein, Conrad. St. John, Washington; May 6, 1980.
Burkland, William. Bear Creek, Deary, Idaho; April 20, 1976.
Delegans, Jim. Spokane, Washington; August 5, 1989.
Delegans, Sophie. Colfax, Washington; July 10, 1977. WCHS.
DeLong, Ray. St. John, Washington; July 19, 1980.
Demos, Gus. Potlatch, Idaho; August 7, 1975. LCHS.
Devlin, Leonard. Dusty, Washington; July 16, 1980.
Emberson, Joseph. Colfax, Washington; July 28, 1980.
Eng, Owen. Colfax, Washington; July 25, 1989.
Garrett, Forest. Spokane, Washington; March 25, 1979.
George, Andrew. Toppenish, Washington; November 15, 1980.
Harder, Herman and Henry. Aspen Creek Ranch, Washington; May 3, 2003.
Hastings, Eula. Pomeroy, Washington; May 8, 2003.
Henry, John. Colfax, Washington; April 22, 2003.
Hilty, Vern. Colfax, Washington; July 24, 1987.
Howard, Robert. St. John, Washington; August 20, 1996.
Howell, Jim Sr., St. John, Washington; April 9, 1991.
Huntley, Ramon. Endicott, Washington; February 8, 2003.
Jim, Mary. Parker, Washington; April 2, November 10 and 11, 1979.
Johns, Willis M. Spokane, Washington; June 26, 1983.
Kamiakin, Arthur Tomeo. Nespelem, Washington; June 16, 1972.
Kissler, Loretta. Colfax, Washington; July 31, 1980.
Knittel, Kathleen. St. John, Washington; September 27, 1993.
Kromm, Ben and Bernice. Colfax, Washington; May 4, 2003.
Kromm, John and Kay. Dusty, Washington; April 11, 2003.
Lally, Joyce. Endicott, Washington; March 28, 2003.
Lautensleger, Mildred. Vancouver, Washington; April 6, 2003.
Leitz, Glen. Fairfield, Washington; February 24, 1994.
Leonard, Jim. Spokane, Washington; April 23, 2003.
Lockhart, B.E. St. John, Washington; July 22, 1980.
Mayo, Leslee Lockhart. Los Angeles, California; May 19, 1997.
McGregor, Sherman. Mockonema, Washington; October 15, 1972.
McNeilly, Bill and Polly. Colfax, Washington; August 9, 1980.
Metzker, Ethel. Spokane, Washington; March 11, 2003.
Miller, Glen and Buelah. Diamond, Washington; August 5, 1993.
Miller, Gordon and Clinton. Ewan, Washington; April 20, 2003.
Ochs, Marlo. Endicott, Washington; October 8, 1991.
Parrish, Dick. Benge, Washington; May 10, 1993.
Patrick, Isaac. Mission, Oregon; May 8, 1981.
Patterson, Faye. Ewan, Washington; January 16, 1996.
Peone, Emily. Nespelem, Washington; April 4, 1981.
Philleo, Jack. Cheney, Washington; November 5, 1979.
Reich, Evelyn. Colfax, Washington; May 7, 2003.
Rice, Peter. Colfax, Washington; March 3, 2001.
Riehle, Rich. Colfax, Washington; May 16, 2003.
Roe, Dennis. Colfax, Washington; June 12, 2003.

Sather, Ida. Tacoma, Washington; April 30, 1980.
Schierman, Dave. College Place, Washington; July 9, 1972.
Schmick, Conrad G. Colfax, Washington; April 14, 1979. WCHS.
Schnaible, Rev. Fred. Moscow, Idaho; July 25, 1980.
Sharbono, Tom. Coeur d'Alene, Idaho; September 20, 1995.
Slind, Oscar and Ruth. Kendrick, Idaho; August 5, 1980.
Smith, Read. St. John, Washington; March 25, 2003.
Stueckle, J.A. Lacrosse, Washington; July 17, 1980.
Stueckle, Rosa and Louisa. Lacrosse, Washington; July 17, 1980.
Terrell, May. Cashmere, Washington; March 6, 2003.
Vogel, Oroville. Pullman, Washington; October 5, 1973.
Whealen, Richard. Colfax, Washington; July 31, 1980.
Williams, Bertha. Tekoa, Washington; July 30, 1980.

Newspapers
Cheney Free Press
Cheney Enterprise
Colton News-Letter
Colfax Gazette
Colfax Commoner
Elberton Wheatbelt
Endicott Index
Fairfield Standard
Garfield Enterprise
Genesee News
Kendrick Gazette
LaCrosse Clipper
Lewiston Teller
Moscow Mirror
North Idaho Star (Moscow)
Oakesdale Tribune
Palouse Gazette (Colfax)
Palouse City Boomerang
Palouse Republic
Pullman Herald
Rosalia Citizen-Journal
St. John Journal
Spokesman-Review
Sprague Advocate
Tekoa Standard-Register
Walla Walla Statesman
Washtucna Enterprise

INDEX OF NAMES AND PLACES

Abe, Kenji 151
Abrahamson, Peter 175
Adler, Jacob 91
Aeschliman, Christian & Julia 168
Aeschliman, Frederick & Marie 168-69
Aeschliman, Sam & Paul 168
Aftret, Mikkel 181
Albion, Washington 22, 84, 102, 123, 186
Alden, John 43
Alkali Flat (Whitman County, WA) 85, 133, 199
Allenbach, Lewis 168
Almota Creek (Whitman County, WA)
Almota, Washington 23, 33, 34, 45, 55, 57-58, 59-60, 68, 76, 83, 94, 143, 150, 168-69
Alpowa, Washington 47, 72
American Ridge (Latah County, ID) 177
Anderson (Latah County, ID) 177, 183
Anderson, John 188
Anderson, Martin 176, 183
Anderson, Nils & Vendla 97
Anderson, Rev. M. S. 169
Andreassen, Rev. Ivar 181
Angell Ferry, Washington (see Blackfoot Ferry)
Appel, Conrad 196
Archer, Sara 105
Armstrong, Ed 132
Armstrong, Joshua 132
Arrasmith, Joseph & Susanna 59
Aschenbrenner, Phillip 198
Asmus, Charles 162
Asplund, Philip 188
Atkinson, Rev. George 83, 92
Aune, John 181
Avon (Latah County, ID) 180, 190
Axtell, Horace 213-14

Babbitt, Sec. Bruce 28
Babcock, Frank 63
Babcock, Georgia Donner 63
Bacon, Halvor 181
Bacon, Peter, John Torsten & Henry 181
Bacon, Russell 55
Bafus, Marilyn 211
Baker, Marion & Louisa 82

Baker, Stephan 183
Ballaine, Link 66
Barbee, O. E. 111
Barron, Joseph 68
Beach, L P. 68
Bear Creek (Latah County, ID) 184, 186
Bear Ridge (Latah County, ID) 179, 180
Beattie, R. Kent 22
Beavert, Virginia 51
Belsby, Osborne 180
Benge, Washington 50, 55, 164
Benson, August 183
Berg, Andrew 190
Berg, Simon 165
Bergquam, Knud 176
Biques, Ernest 206
Birdsell, Dan 12
Bjerke, Arthur 188, 190
Bjerke, Ivor 190
Blackfoot Ferry, Washington 6, 56
Blailock, Joe 191
Blaine (Latah County, ID) 176-77, 180, 188
Blank, Jacob 162
Blue, Mary 171
Bohler, J. Fred 102
Bones, Pete (Palouse-Cayuse) 52
Boone, Daniel & Amelia 64-66
Borah, Sen. William & Mary 97
Bovill, Hugh 191
Bovill, Idaho 188, 191
Braun, Louise 12
Breeding, W. P. 143
Brink, Carol Ryrie 96
Brislawn, Matthew & Mary 97
Broeckel, Philip & Magdalena 199
Brondel, Fr. John 161
Brush Creek (Latah County, ID) 190
Bryan, Dr. Enoch 98, 105
Buchanan, John 63
Bucholz, George 162
Buffalo Eddy (Nez Perce County, ID), 20
Burger, Christ 161
Burke, Iver 176
Burkheimer, Michelle 211
Burkland, William 188
Burnt Ridge (Latah County, ID) 177
Butters, Mary Jane 214

Burrow, William 55
Byers, L. O. 188

Caldwell, Samuel 56
Canfield, Homer 92
Canutt, Joseph 87
Calhoun, A. J. 83
California Flat (Whitman County, WA) 81
California Gulch (Latah County, ID) 140
California Ranch (Spokane County, WA) 55, 158
Calkins, Claude 118
Cameron, Idaho 161
Camp Grizzle (Latah County, ID) 143
Camp, Herb 77
Canutt, Alexander & Sallie 58
Canutt, Enos "Yakima" 77-78
Canutt, Joseph 87
Carlon, Peter & Annie 71
Carlson, John 181
Carlson, John & Andrew 186
Carlson, Rev. Peter 186
Carrico, Adam 143
Carroll, Harry 109
Caruna, Joseph, S. J. 70
Cataldo, Joseph, S.J. 41, 50
Cataldo Mission 48
Central Ferry (Whitman County, WA) 23, 57, 78, 91
Cesari, Fr. D. M. 161
Chambers Flat (Whitman County, WA) 120
Channeled Scablands 26-27
Charbonneau, Jean Baptiste 35-36
Charbonneau, Toussaint 35
Cheney Normal School; Cheney, Washington 109
Cheney Normal School Heritage Center (E.W.U.); Cheney, Washington 109
Cheney, Washington 26, 31, 47, 51, 73, 91, 94-96, 110, 144, 180
Chester, Washington 3
Chimineme, See-moo 51
Chirouse, Eugene M., O.M.I. 41
Christensen, Andrew 176
Christensen, Rev. Emil G.A. 179
Christiensen, Iver & Carl 176
Christoferson, Ole 181

Cisney, Joseph 120
Clark, David 68
Clark, George 188
Clarke, John 38-39
Clearwater Mountains 18
Clearwater Post 38
Clearwater River (Idaho) 34, 38, 42, 140
Clough, Orville 92
Codd, Patrick & Margaret 134
Codd, William & Brigett 134
Coe, L. W. 57
Coeur d'Alene Indian Reservation, Idaho 50-51
Coffee, John 130
Colestah (Klickitat Indian) 47-48, 70
Colfax, Washington 30, 51, 52, 58, 59, 63-64, 67, 68, 73-74, 82, 85, 86, 89, 92, 94, 96, 97, 102, 104, 118, 126, 133, 135, 144, 148, 149, 150, 154, 165, 166, 169, 198-99, 200, 202, 205, 206
Collins, Orville 62
Colter, John 39
Colton, Washington 30, 51, 92, 115, 165, 206
Columbia Plateau Trail (W.S.P.) 96
Colville Indian Reservation 13-14, 75
Colville Lake (see Sprague Lake)
Colville Trail 38, 49, 55
Comegys, George & Margaret 82
Conner Museum of Natural History (W.S.U.); Pullman, Washington 20
Coon, Dick 2
Coplen, Henry 20
Cordelia (Latah County, ID) 183, 186
Cornelius, Cpt. Thomas 117
Cornwall (Latah County, ID) 166, 179
Cossitt, Gertrude 62
Costello, John & Anna 98
Cow Creek (Latah County, ID) 23, 175, 188
Cow Creek (Adams County, ID) 37-38, 55, 164
Cox, Anderson 68
Cox, Phillip 77
Cox, Ross 38
Cram, C.C. 58
Crawford, John 78
Crooks, Bert 191
Cummings, W.T. 58

Cunningham, Patrick 177
Cutler, Steve 66

Dahl, Edward 178
Danielson, Lars 181
Daubert, Adam 85
Daughtery, Dr. Richard 28
Davenport, John 60, 110
Davenport, Joseph 68
Davey, P.D. 157-58
Davidson, Thomas 56
Davis, A.E. 71
Davis, Ben 66
Davis, H.L. 117
Davis, James "Cashup" &
    Mary Ann 94, 127-29
Davis, Nathaniel & Harriet 97
Davis, William & A. E. 71
Davison, B.W. 82
Day, Henry L. 98, 117
Day, Jerome 97
Dayton, Washington 58, 59, 165
DeHaven, James 130
De Smet, Pierre, S.J. 41
Deary, Bill 191
Deary, Idaho 177, 180, 186, 188, 189,
    190, 191
Deep Creek (Latah County, ID) 68
Delaney, Matilda Sager 43-45
Delegianes (Delegans), Gust &
    Christ 208
Delegianes (Delegans) John, Louie &
    Nick 208
Delegianes (Delegans), Mike &
    George 208
DeLong, Joseph 57, 66, 158
DeMoy, Victor 47, 51
Dennis, Ben 188
Derevenchuk, Yuri & Alla 210, 211,
    214
Dernham, Henry 166
Desgranges, Peter 162
Desmet, Idaho 51
DeSmet, Pierre, S.J. 41
Devlin, John 133
Devlin, Leonard 133
Devlin, Patrick & Catherine 133-34
Deyneka, Rev. Peter & Anita 212
Diamond, Washington 59, 127
Diomedi, Alexander, S.J. 51
Disney, Mrs. Walt 77
Donahoe, Thomas
Doty, William & Susan 73
Douglas, David 38-39
Douglas, William O. 116, 118
Drouillard, George 35

Dowling, Frank & Annie 127
Dowling, Owen 127
Downing Creek (Whitman County,
    WA) 70
Driscoll Ridge (Latah County, ID) 132,
    177
Driscoll, Ann N. 132
Driscoll, George 177
Driscoll, John 132, 177
Drouillard, George 35
Drury, John 188
Dry Fork Creek (Whitman County,
    WA) 86
Dry Ridge (Latah County, ID) 184,
    187
Duffy, Fr. Thomas 159, 161
Dunning, Chap C. 77
Dusty, Washington 85, 92, 105, 127,
    133, 198, 199

Eastern Washington University
    (see Cheney Normal School)
Eaton, John 68, 70
Ebel, Charles 161
Edwards, Anderson 71
Edwardson, Ole 188
Eells, Rev. Cushing 92-94
Eells, Rev. Myron & Myra 42, 92
Egbel, Charles & Carl 164
Elberton, Washington 68, 98, 100
Eldorado Gulch (Latah County,
    WA) 140
Elposen (see Tekoa, Washington) 74
Elk River, Idaho 190, 208
Elwood, John 213
Emberson, Louis 181
Endicott, Washington 1-13, 161, 193,
    197-99, 200-02, 210, 211
Eng, Owen 135, 151, 154
Eng, Pete 154
Engelland, George & Frauke 155, 162,
    170
Enger, Peter 177
Erickson, Ruthford 188
Escure, John & Marcus 98
Esquatzel Coulee (Franklin County,
    WA) 26
Evans, Willis & Emma 94
Ewan, Washington 85, 100, 103
Ewart, James & Jennie 62
Ewartsville (Whitman County,
    WA) 62, 105
Ewing, William 64

Fairfield, Washington 91, 95, 99, 148,
    161, 162, 163, 180, 211

Fallon (Whitman County, WA) 176
Farmington, Washington 15, 45, 64,
    68, 73-74, 85, 88, 91, 96, 97, 143,
    165, 171, 198, 200, 211
Faultz, Matthew & Matilda 45
Feenan, Peter 127
Fering, Charles 176
Fincher, Catherine 133
Fincher, Emsley & Mary 58
Finlay, Jacques 37
Fischer (Fisher), Peter, John &
    Adam 198
Fisher, Sam & Helen 76-78
Fishook Jim (Palouse headman) 52
Fleweree, D. A. 85
Florel, V. H. 111
Ft. Astoria 39
Ft. Colvile 40
Ft. Colville 40
Ft. Lapwai 55, 72, 132
Ft. Okanogan 38
Ft. Russell Historic District; Moscow,
    Idaho 97
Ft. Spokane 38-39
Ft. Vancouver 30-40
Ft. Walla Walla 40, 44, 47
Four Lakes, Battle of 47, 49
Four Mile (see Viola)
Four Mile Creek (Latah County, ID) 64
Franseen, Robert & Andrina 97
Fredin, Adeline 51
Freeman, Washington 158
Freeze, John 68
Freeze (Latah County, ID) 68-69
Friel, Jack 102
Fryxell, Dr. Roald 12, 28
Fuchs (Fox), Phillip 196
Fuchs, Phillip 163
Fusion, H. 180

Gaines, E. F. 111
Gaiser, Lewis 1-3, 212
Galland, Julius 165
Garberg, Halvor 181
Garfield, Washington 92, 96, 100, 102,
    119, 148, 165, 200, 211
Gastrich, Elizabeth 163
Gatzert, Bailey 165
Gault, Dr. Franklin 99
Genesee, Idaho 64, 91, 112, 130, 159,
    161, 164-65, 175, 177, 179, 184,
    211
George, Andrew 76-79
George, Annie 13
Gerber, A.A. 169
Gin Sing 137, 141-43, 149, 154

Giorda, Joseph, S.J. 51
Glenwood (Whitman County,
    WA) 107
Git Wing 150
Glover, Chuck 1
Gold Creek (Latah County, ID) 140
Gold Hill (Latah County, ID) 143
Golder, Dr. Frank 166
Goldstrom, Ole & Jorgensen 177
Gordon, B. C. 198
Gordon, Emery 77
Gordon, James & Mary 71
Gordon, Worden
Gorton, Sen. Slade 212
Gould, John 59
Granite Butte (Whitman County,
    WA) 18
Granite Point (Whitman County,
    WA) 60
Gray, William 57-58
Green, Phillip & Anna 196-98, 206
Grey, Zane 118
Grief, Joseph 159
Griffin, Worth 75
Griswold, John 143
Gunderson, Lars 180
Guske, Albert & Susanna 163
Guske, Charles 163
Gustafson, Dr. Carl 28

Hagen, Peter 181
Hahtalekin (Palouse chief) 72-74
Hall, James 62
Halseth, Louis 190
Halsey, Henry 70
Halvorsen, Engvald 177
Hanford, Edwin. H. 82, 96
Hangman Creek (see Latah Creek)
Hanson, John 180
Hanson, R. A. 119
Harder, Anne Maybelle 76
Harder, Hans 76, 163
Harder, Jacob & Annine 76, 163
Harder, Max 163
Harding, John 56
Hardy, Dr. John 13
Harrington, Washington 95, 118
Harris, Ed 85-86
Hartung, George 162
Harvard, Idaho 92
Hastings, Alvin & Alfred 91
Hatley, George & Iola 78
Hatley, Riley & Rachel 73
Hatwai Creek (Whitman County,
    WA) 62
Hay, Washington 77, 92, 102, 181

Haynes, Abraham & Virginia 73
Hein, Gottfried 162
Henderson, Louis 100
Henderson, William & Minnie 110
Hengen, Dr. Nona 49, 114
Henry, Byron 100
Henry, Dr. Margaret 10
Hensen, Ole 176
Hergert, Conrad 119
Hickman, Cuthbert 113
Hickman, Floyd 78
Hickman, W. F. 126
Hilty, Adam 169
Hodgins, H. B. 130
Hoefer, John 159
Hole-in-the-Ground (Whitman County, WA) 26, 27
Hollingsworth, Hezekiah 68, 126, 134
Holt, Alfred 62
Hoodoo (Latah County, ID), see Woodfell
Hoodoo Mountains, Idaho 18, 120-21, 140, 143, 187
Hooper, A. J. 70, 91
Hooper, Albert 70, 91
Hooper, Ernest 70
Hooper, Washington 76, 85, 94, 96, 108-09, 119
Hopkins, C. B. 99
Horlacher, George & Barbara 162
Horn, Godfrey 169
Howard, R. J. 96
Howard, Gen. Oliver 72
Howard, George & Emma 70
Huckleberry Creek (Latah County, ID) 83
Hubbard, Faye 78
Hubbard, Goalman & Nancy 78
Huff's Gulch (Latah County, ID)
Hulitt, Joe 211, 214
Hume, Horace 119
Hunter, George 76
Huntley, Elmer 66, 82
Huntley, George 82
Huntley, Hugh 100
Huntley, Phoebe 82
Huntley, William 82
Husishusis Kute (Palouse shaman) 72-73
Husishusis Moxmox (Palouse chief) 76, 191
Husishusis Poween (Palouse headman) 76

Iddings, Edward J. 113
Imhoff, Christian 162

Jackson, Sen. Henry 210
Jacobs, Peter 158, 159
Jacobson, James 176
Jacobson, Rev. Stan 210
Jamison, S. L. 170
Jaso Bridge (Franklin County, WA) 91
Jaussaud, Leon 91
Jerome Creek (Latah County, ID) 143
Jim, Fishook (Palouse headman)
Jim, Mary 14, 29-30, 51, 52-53, 76
Jim, Thomas & Harry (Palouse Indians) 52
Johns, Edward & Emily 3
Johns, Willis 10
Johnson, A. M. 188
Johnson, Arden 2
Johnson, Casper 176
Johnson, Edward 58
Johnson, Eli 183-84
Johnson, Gustav 186
Johnson, Samuel 176
Johnson, Washington 102, 131
Jones (Devlin), Edward & Katherine 126, 133
Jones, Nard 117
Jorgensen, Henry 177
Joseph (Nez Perce chief) 72-74
Joset, Joseph S.J. 41, 49, 50-51
Juliaetta, Idaho 91, 94, 100, 161
Juniper Dunes Wilderness Area (Franklin County, WA) 20
Jurgens, Claus 162

Kahlke, Neil 162
Kahlotus, Washington 7, 20, 26, 90, 91, 163
Kaiser, Veryl 109
Kambitch, Jacob 64, 175
Kamiak Butte (Whitman County, WA) 18, 19, 22, 42, 43, 44, 93, 122, 141, 149, 207
Kamiakin, Arthur Tomeo 13-14
Kamiakin, Cleveland & Alalumti 75, 76, 79
Kamiakin, Khaiyous (Palouse Indian) 52
Kamiakin (Yakama-Palouse chief) 29, 38, 41-42, 46-49, 76
Kamiakin's Crossing (Whitman County, WA) 49
Kammerzell, Conrad & Christina 198
Kamoshnite (Yakama Indian) 41
Kanawyer, John 60
Kane, Paul 43
Kaufman, William & Emmanual 166
Kebla, John & Francis 94

Kellogg, Isaac 56
Kellogg, L. E. 99
Kelly, John 97
Kelso, John 162
Ken Hock 135, 137, 154
Kendrick, Idaho 59, 97, 161, 164, 177
Kennedy, Will 132
Kennewick Man 28
Kenny, Jenny 75
Kentuck Ferry, Washington 68
Kentuck Trail 56, 127, 155
Ke Pow Han (Palouse chief) 35
Ketchum, C. E. 98
Khalotas the Elder (Palouse chief) 36, 39, 46
Kienbaum, Frederick 162
Kile, Adam & Marinda 71
Kincaid, A. A. 143
King, Ervin 109
King, Frank
King, Mildred
King, William 209
King Valley (Benewah County, ID) 209
Kinnear, Patrick 130, 132
Kinear, Percy 132
Kinney, Gen. John 10
Kintchi, Christian & Louisa 98
Kirschener, Dan 212
Kjosness, Ole, John & Haldo 181
Kleweno, Henry & Adam 198
Kleweno, Pat 1
Kluss, Theodore 161
Knight, Riley 62
Krogstadt, Ole 181
Kuhn, Aaron 60, 166
Kyllo, Henry 181

LaCrosse, Washington 30, 56, 77, 91, 163, 165, 180, 181, 183, 200, 206
LaFollette, William & Mary 60
Lake Lewis 19
Lakin, George 71
Lakin, Tom 71
Lamb, Chet 78
Lamont, Daniel 91
Lamont, Washington 50, 91, 94, 96, 97, 99, 129
Lancaster, Washington 103
Lapwai, Idaho 72, 73, 77
Lapwai Trail 38, 49
Larson, C.J. 180
Larson, Eric 190
Latah County Fairgrounds; Moscow, Idaho 100
Latah County Historical Museum; Moscow, Idaho 100

Latah Creek (Spokane County, WA) 30, 51, 48, 63, 158, 185
Latah, Washington 161, 162, 211
Latah County, Idaho
Lawrence, Claude 111
Lee, Ben 190
Lee Doon 150
Lee, Daniel
Lee, Joseph & Mary Ann 63
Lee, M. D. 66
Leitch, Michael 64
Leitchville (Whitman County, WA) 64
Lentz, Gary 213
Lenville, Idaho 130
Leonard, Jim 10
Leonard, T. A. 85
Lewis & Clark Expedition 34-36, 212-13
Lewiston, Idaho 20, 38, 51, 55, 57, 59, 61, 63, 78, 95, 124, 141-42, 144, 148, 150, 154, 205, 209
Lian, Eric 179
Lieuallen, Almon & Noah 64, 92
Lincoln County, Washington 95
Linehan, Art 132
Linehan, Tom 130, 132
Lind, Andrew 185
Little Palouse Falls (Whitman County, WA) 26, 43
Litzenberger, Carl 10
Litzenberger, Clara 8
Litzenberger, Henry & Anna 198
Litzenberger, Phillip & Sophie 4
Lloyd, A. J. 76
Lockhart, John 14
Longwell, Vera 9
Looking Glass (Nez Perce chief) 71-74
Lorang, Theodore 164
Love, James 119
Love, Lewis & Mary 59
Lowry, Gov. Mike 212
Lucas, George (see Pahala Washeschit)
Lueg, Henry 157-58
Luft, August & Willene 55
Luft, Dan 71
Lyons Ferry (Whitman County, WA) 27, 58, 212
Lyons, Daniel & Anna 58, 76
Lyons, Perry

Mackay, J. A. "Brooks" 86, 149
MacMurray, Maj. J. W. 203
Madison, Canud 176
Magnuson, Ed 190
Mah Young 141

Malden, Washington 71, 91, 92, 96, 100
Manchester, Benjamin 85
Manning-Rye (Whitman County, WA) 145
Marmes Man 28
Marmes, Roland & Joanne 28
Martin, Gov. Clarence 110
Martin, F. M. 110
Morod, Emile & Maurice 206
Marshall, Washington 184
Mary Minerva State Park (Latah County, ID) 83
Massey, Edward 49, 55
Masterson, William 85-86
Matheny, Isaiah 60
Matlock Bridge (Whitman County, WA) 70-71
Matlock, Preston & Kerlista 71
Mau, Rev. Carl 10
Mauer, Paul 168
May, Thomas 68
Maynard, Charles 165
McAuliff, James 56
McConnell, Gov. William & Louisa 95, 96, 97
McCroskey, J. P. T. & Mary Minerva 82-83
McCroskey, R. C. 96
McCroskey, Virgil 83
McDonald, Andrew 40
McDonald, Finan 37
McElroy, Jack 55, 70
McGregor, Dr. Alexander 211
McGregor, Alexander, Archie & John 85, 206
McGregor, Maurice 108
McGregor, Peter & Maude 75, 85, 108, 206
McGregor, Sherman 119
McGrew, Paul 109
McGuire, Lee 211
McKenzie, Daniel 66
McKenzie, Donald 37, 38
McLoughlin, Dr. John 39
McNeilly, Andrew, Robert & William 62, 124
McRae, John 165
McSweeney, Charles & Annie 100
McWhirt, Cyrus & William 56
Meatu Kinma (Palouse-Cayuse) 77
Medical Lake, Washington 180
Meldrum, Henry 68
Mestermann, Albert 162
Meyer, John & Henry 164
Mica, Washington 55

Michels, C. A. 111
Miles, Gen. Nelson 74
Miller, Charley 86
Miller, Francis 113
Miller, Glen & Beulah 103
Miller, Mark 97
Milwaukee Road Trail Corridor (B.L.M.) 96
Mineral Creek (Latah County, ID) 83
Minnesota Flat (Whitman County, WA) 81
Minnesota Ridge (Latah County, ID) 179
Missouri Flat (Whitman County, WA) 66
Mitchell, R. W. 196
Mockonema (Whitman County, WA) 90, 100
Moctelme Valley (Benewah County, ID) 51
Molee, Elias 181
Moller, Tonnes 175
Morod, Emile & Maurice 206
Monteith, John 72
Moore, Charles 95
Morrision, E. H. 95
Moscow Mountain (Latah County, ID) 18, 19, 91, 142-43
Moscow, Idaho 30, 46, 63, 64, 68, 73, 78, 85, 91, 92, 94-97, 99, 100, 102, 105, 110, 118, 119, 143, 144, 148, 150, 161, 166, 176, 179, 180, 184, 185, 186, 190, 210, 211
Moses, Mary Owhi 29
Mraz, Wilson & Anna 73
Mud Flat Creek (Whitman County, WA) 181
Mullaley, Mike 132
Mullan Road 46, 49-50, 56, 158, 203
Mullan, John 46, 49-50
Mulouin, Maxim 55
Mumm, Hans 162
Munro, Ralph 211, 212
Murphy, Robert & Thomas 129

National Appaloosa Museum & Heritage Center; Moscow, Idaho 78
Neff, Samuel 91, 92
Nelson, Charles 175
Nelson, Lars 109
Nelson, Nils & Andrew 184
Nelson, Soren 177
Nervig, Arnt 181
Nervig, Henrik & Halvar 181
Neshnepark Keeook (Nez Perce chief) 34

Nespelem Art Colony (W.S.C.) 75
Neuman, Charles 180
Neuman, William 55
Newberry, A. A. 89
Newlon, Thomas 56
New York Bar (Snake River) 81
Nez Perce National Historic Park; Spalding, Idaho Site 34, 77
Nez Perce Indian Reservation, Idaho 46, 72-75
Nez Perces Mission 42
Nichols, Len 130
Nickodemus, Krato 51
Nickodemus, Lawrence 51
Niebler, Frank, George & Michael 158
Nigualko (see Tensed, Idaho)
Nomura, Gail 208
Nora (Latah County, ID) 179, 186, 188
Norelius, Rev. Eric 183, 186
North Pine (Whitman County, WA) 170
Northwest Museum of Art & Culture; Spokane, Washington 76
Norton, Thomas 129
Notman, David 68

Oakesdale, Washington 129-30, 206, 211
Ochs, Henry 198
Ochs, Peter 196-97, 198
Ochs, Phillip 5
Ogle, Elmer 165
Old Mission State Park; Cataldo, Idaho 77
Oliphant, Mrs. S. B. 98
Oliphant, Winchester 95
Olson, Martin 190
Olson, Nicholas & John 177
Onaway, Idaho 208
Onecho (Whitman County, WA) 168-69
Oppenheimer, Simon & Solomon 165
Owes, Albert 180
Owhi (Yakama chief) 41, 46, 48-49

Page (Franklin County, WA) 51, 76
Pagel, Ferdinand 161
Pahala Washeschit (Star Doctor) 74
Pahka Pahtahank (Palouse warrior) 74
Palouse Boomerang Print Museum; Palouse, Washington 100
Palouse (Big) Cove (Whitman County, WA) 85
Palouse Empire Fairgrounds; Mockonema, Washington 100
Palouse Falls 232, 24-25, 27, 43-44

Palouse (Lyons) Ferry, Washington 55
Palouse Hills 19-20, 23, 43, 55, 79, 106-08
Palouse Junction (Connell, Washington) 90
Palouse Landing (Perry, Franklin County, WA) 55
Palouse Rapids 57
Palouse River 18-20, 23, 26, 27, 30, 35, 43, 66, 212-14
Palouse, Washington 64, 68, 73, 92, 97, 99, 102, 119, 120, 143, 144, 148, 161, 165, 211
Palus (Palouse village) 37, 38, 46, 49, 50, 52, 60, 70, 76, 77, 79
Pambrum, Pierre 40
Pampa (Whitman County, WA) 77
Pandosy, Charles, O.M.I. 41, 42
Pangburn, George 55
Paradise Valley (Latah County, ID) 63, 64, 91, 92, 176, 178-79, 183
Park Valley (Latah County, ID) 177, 180
Parrish, Dick 2-3
Parvin, Roy & Zaidee 78
Pasco Basin 19
Pasco, Washington 96
Patterson, Andrew 184
Patterson, Edward 183
Pauls, Peter 184
Penawawa, Washington 42, 55, 58, 72, 73, 76, 133, 143, 148, 181, 208
Penawawa Creek (Whitman County, WA) 49, 126
Penawawa Ferry, Washington 58
Penrose Library (Whitman College); Walla Walla, Washington
Peone, Emily 14, 29, 48, 76
Peone Prairie (Spokane County, WA) 50
Pereia, Anthony & George 98
Perkins, James & Minnie 42, 63, 96, 100, 126
Perkins House Museum; Colfax, Washington 99
Perry (Franklin County, WA)
Perry, M. S. 190
Person, Anna 120
Peterson, Anders 180
Peterson, Dave 188
Peterson, Eric 176
Peterson, Hawkin 191
Petersen, Olaf 97
Peterson, Oliver 184
Pettyjohn, Jack 76
Pfaff, Michael 199-200

Philleo, T. A. E. 62
Pine City, Washington 68, 71, 102, 105
Pine Creek (*Tohotonimme, Hngwsuum*), Battle of 47
Pine Creek (Whitman County, WA) 23, 47, 64, 85, 86
Pine Grove (see Spangle, Washington)
Piper, Charles 22
Plainville (Whitman County, WA) 62, 90
Plante, Antoine 158
Platt, John 164, 179
Plaza, Washington 47, 162
Pleasant Hills (Whitman County, WA)
Pleasant Valley (Whitman County, WA) 70
Plummer, Idaho 51
Point, Nicholas, S.J. 41
Points, Frank 63
Polatkin (Spokane chief) 47
Pomeroy, Washington 59
Poorman Creek (Latah County, ID) 140
Potlatch Creek (Latah County, ID) 34
Potlatch River (Latah County, ID) 81, 184
Potlatch, Idaho 18, 51, 59, 68, 78, 92, 153, 187-88, 191, 206
Potts, Robert & Emily 55, 98
Poween, Tom (Palouse headman) 13
Powers, J. G. 143
Powers, William 63
Poyakin (Palouse headman) 76
Prince, Nathaniel 82
Prince, Reuben 82
Princeton, Idaho 92, 187, 208
Privett, Cyrus & Andrew 94
Pullman, Washington 22, 30, 63, 66, 73, 86, 91, 92, 94-97, 99, 100, 102, 105, 108, 110, 165, 210, 211
Pun Loi 141
Purdue, Idaho 92
Pyramid Peak (see Steptoe Butte)

Qualchan (Yakima warrior) 29, 47, 48
Quinn, John 132

Ragsdale, William 92
Rathdrum Prairie (Kootenai County, ID) 198
Rawls, Luke 86
Rebel Flat Creek (Whitman County, WA) 22, 62, 205
Reich, Ray 1-3, 212
Repp, Henry & Mary 196, 198
Repp, Mildred 10

Revere (Whitman County, WA)
Richter, Andrew & Alma 162, 163
Rickard, Edward
Rieke, Rev. Henry 200
Riggs, Albert 191
Riley, Lester 78
Ringer, L. M. & Sophia 58
Riparia, Washington 34, 56, 57, 91
Ritchie, John 74
Ritzville, Washington 144, 164, 200, 211
Rock Creek (Spokane County, WA) 30, 185
Rock Creek (Whitman County, WA) 23, 26, 37, 56, 68-70, 94
Rock Creek (B.L.M.) Area (Whitman County, WA) 98
Rock Lake (Whitman County, WA) 22, 26-27, 37, 42, 66, 209
Rock Lake City, Washington 22, 63, 94, 97
Rockford, Washington 31, 68, 92, 162, 180
Rockie, Dr. William 109
Rohrbach, Fred 169
Roosevelt, Pres. Franklin 108
Roosevelt, Pres. Theodore 105, 108
Root, James 59
Rosalia, Washington 20, 47, 51, 64, 88, 96, 148, 161, 162, 165
Rose Creek Preserve (Whitman County, WA) 39
Rosenstein, Jacob 164
Ross, Scott 130
Rothrock, F. M. 97, 98
Roulet, Rev. Phillip 168
Ruark, Joseph 55
Rubin, William & Rosina 168
Ruddy, Michael & Elizabeth 62
Russell, John 64

Sacagawea 35, 36, 213
Sacred Heart Mission; Cataldo, Idaho 41
Sacred Heart Mission; Desmet, Idaho 50-51
Saether, John 176
Sager, Matilda (see Delaney, Matilda)
St. John, Edward 91
St. John, Washington 1, 64, 70, 82, 91, 92, 102, 198, 210, 211
St. Joseph's Mission 41
St. Michael's Mission 56
Sam Lee 150
Sanborn, William & Flossie 97
Sanders, Que 165

Sassenhagen, August 161
Sauer, Les 78
Scharnhorst, Christian & Fredericka 161
Schau, Mrs. John
Scheuerman, Donovan & Mary 5
Scheuerman, Henry & Mary 3-4
Scheuerman, Karl & Mary 4-5, 59
Schierman, Conrad, George, Henry & John 196, 198
Schlee, John 159
Schloatz, John 162
Schlommer, Harm 163
Schlunegar, Chris & Sophia 168
Schmick, Conrad 194, 196, 201
Schmick, Margaret 211
Schmick, Peter & Mary 193
Schmick, Dr. William 211
Schnaible, Rev. Fred 13
Schneidmiller, Henry 198
Schoffen, Jacob 158, 159
Schreiber, John 198
Schuknecht, Rev. Henry 162
Schultheis, Michael 155, 158, 206
Schuster, Carrie Jim 51, 76, 214
Schwabacher, Adolph, Martin & Sigmund 165
Selam, James 76
Silcott's Ferry, Washington 58
Simas, Joseph & Manuel 98
Sissom, Ben 66
Seltice, Andrew (Coeur d'Alene chief) 51, 74
Sharbono, Tom 35-36
Shattuck, Dr. Charles 113
Sheahan, Patrick 130
Silva, Frank & Manuel 98
Siegel, Alexander 163
Silcott, John 56, 58
Slind, Ole 180-81
Slocum, T. M. 56
Slowiarchy the Elder (Palouse chief) 50
Slowiarch the Younger (Palouse chief) 85
Smick, Jim & Maxine 7
Smith, Andrew 71
Smith, Andrew J. & Melvina 70
Smith, Frank 66
Smith, George & Nancy 58
Smith, Hans 176
Smith, Lillis 85, 117
Smith, Lucius 85
Smith, John & Sarah 63, 70-71, 176
Smith, Ray 12
Smith, Read 109, 214

Smith, Silas 208
Smith, Virgil 70
Smith, William 105
Smohalla (Wanapam shaman) 52
Smoot Hill Ecological Preserve (Whitman County, WA) 39
Snake River 27-28, 30, 31, 37, 52, 83, 143, 212-14
Snyder, Ralph 118
Sohon, Gustavus 43, 50
Spalding, Rev. Henry Harmon & Eliza 42-43, 77
Spalding, Henry Hart & Mary 42, 45, 58, 59, 83, 168
Spangle, Washington 22, 31, 62, 64, 73, 94, 102, 105, 148, 161, 162, 185, 206
Spenser, W. R. 109
Spillman, W. J. 110-111
Spokan Garry (Spokane chief) 42, 46
Spokane County, Washington 95
Spokane House 40
Spokane Plains, Battle of 48
Spokane River 37
Spokane Trail 49
Spokane, Washington 50, 95, 105, 165, 209, 211
Sprague, Roderick 12
Sprague Lake (Adams County, WA) 22, 41, 55, 94, 98
Sprague, Washington 51, 85, 91, 92, 94, 96, 97-98, 99, 102, 144, 164
Spring Valley (Whitman County, WA) 83
Stanford, Idaho 92
Stanford, Inman 92
Stanley, John Mix 43
Starbuck, Washington 76
Steen, John 162
Steiger, Fred 199
Steinke, Max 85
Steptoe Butte (Whitman County, WA) 17-18, 19, 21, 22, 26, 30, 32, 42, 49, 50, 54, 79, 83, 94, 129
Steptoe, Col. Edward 47
Steptoe, Washington 87, 206
Stevens, Gov. Isaac 41, 45-46, 49, 55
Stevick, Joseph 168, 206
Stewart, Orville 66
Stokke, Dan 181
Stratton Butte (Whitman County, WA) 18
Stoughton, J. A. 45
Stromberger, Jacob & Anna 98
Strychine Creek (Latah County, ID) 143, 148

Stueckle, Jacob & Barbara 199
Stueckle, John & Rosina 199
Sturman, Jack 188
Suksdorf, Frederich 162
Sundown, Jackson 74
Sunset, Washington 102, 103
Sunwold, Andrew & Gertrude 3
Sunwold, Arthur 9
Swannack, William & Hannah 129
Sweet, Willis 95
Swenson, Edward 177
Swier, G. B. 109
Swift, Kay 78
Swift, Levinius & Cornelia 88

Tannatt, Gen. Thomas 88-89, 91,
    196-97
Tebor, Mike 191
Tekoa, Washington 73, 91, 92, 96, 100,
    148, 150, 162, 165, 170, 171, 148, 150,
    162, 165, 170, 171
Tekoa Mountain (Spokane County,
    WA) 18
Teksaspa (Palouse village) 56
Tenessee Flat (Whitman County,
    WA) 81, 83
Tensed, Idaho 31, 51, 209
Territorial Road 58, 59
Tetln, John 176
Tewa Teenaset (Chief Bones) 77
Texas City (Whitman County, WA) 94
Texas (Teksas) Ferry, Washington 56,
    197
Texas Lake (Whitman County, WA) 56
Texas Rapids 35, 60
Texas Ridge (Latah County, WA) 81
Texas Road 56
Thatuna Range 18, 22, 38
Thomash (Palouse shaman) 52
Thomason, Oscar 189
Thompson, David 37
Thorn Creek (Latah County, ID) 62,
    82, 176
Thornton, Washington 82, 100, 102,
    211
Three Forks (see Pullman, Washington)
Tibbs, Harold
Tierney, Thomas 64
Tilcoax the Elder (Palouse chief) 47
Tilma, Idaho 51
Timothy (Nez Perce chief) 58
Timothy, Ignace 51
Tomer, George 64
Tomilson, Alexander 129
Tonning, Jacob 179
Toohoolhoolzote (Nez Perce shaman)

72
Torgenson, Ole 177
Tormey, Michael 56
Toskey, John 176
Tostenson, H. M. 180
Troy, Idaho 97, 132, 164, 177, 179,
    180, 186, 187-88, 189
Truax, Daniel 91
Truax, Sewell 60
Trimble, Joseph 140
Tshimikain (Spokane) Mission 42
Tsiyiyak (Palouse Indian) 41
Tucannon River (Columbia County,
    WA) 35, 56
Turnbull, Cyrus 62
Turnbull National Wildlife Refuge;
    Cheney, Washington 62
Turner, Nye & Ruth 50
Turner, Thomas & Martha 70
Tuschoff, Conrad 159
Tvedt, Hans 176
Tyler, Washington 17

Uhl, Peter 199
Umatilla Indian Reservation, Oregon
    74
Union Center (Whitman County,
    WA) 30, 123, 127, 134, 161, 175,
    205
Union Flat Creek (Whitman County,
    WA) 30, 49, 50, 55, 62, 66, 125
Uniontown, Washington 51, 99, 102,
    156, 159, 161, 164, 165, 206
University of Idaho; Moscow, Idaho
    96, 99, 102, 109, 110, 113
Unseth, Linda 210

Valleyford, Washington 100
Vandevantner, Moses 166
Vasher, Maurice 206
Vassar, Idaho 92
Vassar, James 92
Villard, Henry 86, 90, 196-97
Vincent (Coeur d'Alene chief) 47
Viola, Idaho 64, 102
Vogel, Dr. Oroville 111-12
Vogler, Rev. Henry 199
Vollmer, Idaho (see Troy)
Vollmer, John 164

Wagner, J. J. 198
Wagner, Palmer 78
Wah Lee 150
Wahl, Christian 161
Waiilatpu (Cayuse) Mission 42, 43
Walker, Rev. Elkanah & Mary 42

Walla Walla River 40
Walla Walla, Washington 40, 59, 88,
    205
Walli, John 181
Wallula, Washington 40, 57, 75, 124,
    165
Walters, Rev. Walter 200
Warre, Henry 35, 43
Warren, Felix 50, 59, 75
Warren, Hugh 59
Warren, James & Eliza Spalding 45
Wascopam (Dalles) Mission 42
Washington State University (W.A.C.,
    W.S.C.); Pullman, Washington 98,
    99, 102, 109, 113, 166
Washtucna Coulee (Franklin County,
    WA) 72
Washtucna Lake (Franklin County,
    WA) 72
Washtucna, Washington 20, 90, 91, 96,
    118
Waverly, Washington 3, 63, 91, 94, 95
    96, 161, 162
Wawawai, Washington 23, 41, 55, 59,
    60, 72, 150
Wawawai Creek (Whitman County,
    WA) 60
Weeatkwal Tsiken (Palouse headman)
    70, 76
Weinman, Lt. Col. Arne 212
Weippe Prairie (Clearwater County,
    ID) 74
Wellesley, Idaho 92
Wellpinnit, Washington 79
Wells, Joe & Louis 189, 191, 208-09
Wells, Grant & Crom 208-09
West, Leoti 102
Whelan, Nicholas & Catherine 123-26
Whelan (Whitman County, WA) 105
Whistalks (Spokane Indian) 48
Whipple, Cpt. Stephen 74
White Bird (Nez Perce chief) 72-74
White Bluffs (Franklin County,
    WA) 19
White Bluffs Road 55
Whitman County Historical Society
    Museum (see Perkins House)
Whitman, Dr. Marcus & Narcissa
    42-43, 44
Wicks, J. C. 168
Widman, Frederich 172
Wieber, George 165
Wiedrich, William 163
Wigen, Peder, Jens & Joergen 181
Wilcox (Whitman County, WA) 30,
    123

Wildshoe, Peter 51
Willada, Washington (see Lancaster)
Willard, A. B. 96
Williams, Bertha 155, 170
Williams, Charlie 75
Willow Creek (Whitman County,
    WA) 48
Willow Springs, Washington
    (see Cheney)
Wilmer (Latah County, ID) 180
Wimpy, R. N. 63, 162
Wind, Henry 55
Windingstad, Olaf 180
Winona, Washington 85, 91, 100, 105
Winter, William 59
Winthrop, Theodore 42
Witimyhoyshe (Palouse chief) 46
Wittman, J. B. 158, 159
Woerman, Elray 119
Wolfard, C. M. 159
Woodfell (Latah County, ID) 92
Woods, Charles 129
Woody, J. M. 68
Work, John 38, 40
Workman, Cliff 13
Worley, Idaho 51
Wright, Col. George 47
Wright, Layfayette 85

Yakama Indian Reservation, 74
Yale, Idaho 92
Yelleppit (Walla Walla chief) 35
Yenney, Mr. 10-12, 213
Youmas, Andrew 51
Young, Robert 91
Yuen Kam 154
Yusyus Tulekasen (Palouse headman)
    76

Zanzibar 70
Zink, Maj. Jeffrey 212
Zinner, Russ 109

Richard Scheuerman lives with his wife, Lois, in their hometown of Endicott, Washington and teaches at Whitworth College in Spokane. He holds degrees in history, Russian, and education and has written several books and articles on regional themes including *Renegade Tribe*, a history of the Palouse Indians co-authored with Clifford Trafzer, which received the 1987 Governor's Writers Award. He is also the recipient of the Washington State Historical Society's Robert Gray Medal for contributions to history education and the 2000 Governor's Award for Excellence in Education.

John Clement is a landscape photographer who resides in Kennewick, Washington with his wife, Sharon, and their four children. A graduate of Central Washington State College, he majored in cultural geography and geology. He has received over fifty regional, national, and international photographic awards including induction of his work into the National Photographers Hall of Fame in 1988. Among his audio-visual productions is the critically acclaimed program, *Four Seasons of the Drylands*, which features the sublime scenery of the Inland Pacific Northwest.

JEFFERSON PEACE MEDALLION (OBVERSE SIDE)